From
Privileged
to
Dispossessed

James W. Long

From

Privileged

to

Dispossessed

The Volga Germans,
1860–1917

University of Nebraska Press
Lincoln & London

Library of Congress Cataloging-
in-Publication Data
Long, James W., 1942–
From privileged to dispossessed.
Bibliography: p.
Includes index
1. Germans—Russian S.F.S.R.—
Volga River Region—
History. I. Title.
D K 34.G3L66 1988
947'.800431   88-1144
I S B N 0-8032-2881-3

Acknowledgements for the use of
previously published
material appear on page x.

To Pat, Marc, and David

Contents

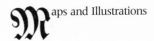 aps and Illustrations

𝔄cknowledgments

This study is an offspring of the Germans in Colorado Study Project, which originated in 1975 under the direction of Sidney Heitman. Under the agreed-upon scholarly division of labor, the charge devolved upon me to investigate the Volga Germans within the context of prerevolutionary (1917) Russian history. The following work is but one result of that commission. In order to fulfill my scholarly obligations, I first conducted extensive bibliographical research, resulting in publication of *The German-Russians: A Bibliography* by ABC-CLIO Press (Santa Barbara, 1978), an annotated bibliography of Russian-language materials pertaining to the diverse groups of Germanic settlers who had immigrated and settled at various times in the Russian Empire.

The present work owes much to the support of several sources. I am particularly indebted to the International Research and Exchanges Board, which sponsored a six-month research trip to the Soviet Union; without such an opportunity this work would not have been possible. Financial assistance from the Germans from Russia in Colorado Study Project, Colorado State University, and a professional development grant from the dean's office are also gratefully acknowledged.

My work has also benefited from the suggestions and support of colleagues. I owe a personal debt to Sidney Heitman for his constant encouragement and interest in this study, and for information about the Volga Germans under Soviet rule. Kenneth Rock enlightened me about the history of Volga German immigrants and descendants in America. Roger Bartlett also shared his encyclopedic knowledge of sources. My own knowledge of the history of the

Lower Volga region has been considerably broadened by participation in stimulating discussions of the project exploring the history of Saratov Province, headed by Rex Wade and Scott Seregny. The participants' camaraderie and generosity have convinced me of the incalculable worth of such collaborative efforts. Special thanks go to project members Scott Seregny, Donald Raleigh, and Timothy Mixter, who provided valuable documentation.

The professional assistance and advice of many people greatly facilitated my research and writing. I wish to express my appreciation to the library staffs of the University of Illinois, the Library of Congress, the New York Public Library, and the Hoover Institution. My thanks also go to the staffs of the Saltykov-Shchedrin Library and the Library of the Academy of Sciences in Leningrad, and the Lenin Library in Moscow. Deborah Clifford deserves special thanks for reading and editing the manuscript. I wish to recognize Joyce Patterson's meticulously skillful preparation of the maps. Finally, I am deeply grateful to Leila Charbonneau for her excellent copyediting and indexing.

I am grateful for permission to use, in revised form, material from my articles already published elsewhere: "The Volga Germans and the Zemstvos, 1865–1917," *Jahrbücher für Geschichte Osteuropas* (Franz Steiner Verlag, Wiesbaden and Stuttgart) 30 (1982): 336–61; and "Agricultural Conditions in the German Colonies of Novouzensk District, Samara Province, 1861–1914," *Slavonic and East European Review* 57 (October 1979): 531–51. Permission from the *Institut für Auslandsbeziehungen* in Stuttgart, the *Bundesarchiv* in Koblenz and from Brock Gammel to use photographs is also appreciatively acknowledged.

I would add a note on technical matters as well. Transliteration from Russian is based on the Library of Congress system, except for a few Anglicized terms in common usage. Dates follow the Julian calendar (in use in Russia until 1918), which was twelve days behind the Gregorian calendar (used in the West) in the nineteenth century and thirteen days behind in the twentieth. Most, but not all, colonies had a Russian and German designation; in the text, the Russian name is given first followed by the German name in parentheses.

I am deeply grateful for my family's encouragement, particularly for the forbearance of my wife Pat, who good-naturedly fulfilled the numerous roles and burdens of a single parent while I conducted research in the Soviet Union. To my two sons, Marc and David, thanks for being my staunchest supporters, never questioning if "the book" would be published, but only wondering when.

Introduction

This is a study of the Volga Germans spanning the years 1860 to 1917, a period of rapid change in European history that formed a historical watershed in the modernization of Russia. The combined impact of a multiplicity of reforms and phenomenal economic activity, and subsequent restructuring of the state and society, profoundly transformed the Volga Germans. Contrary to the stereotypical depiction of the Volga Germans as living in a time warp, allegedly frozen in time—undisturbed, untouched, and isolated from the beginning of their eighteenth-century settlement until Stalin's deportation in 1941—the truth is that they adapted remarkably to ever-changing circumstances.[1] This study shatters most widely held historical views about the Volga Germans, but it also adds a vital chapter in the history of the multinational Russian Empire, illustrating well the striking continuity of Russian-Soviet nationality policies.

While much attention has been devoted to the history of Volga German immigration, this is the first in-depth study examining the Volga Germans within the context of Russian history.[2] Unlike the few general works on the Volga Germans, which present them as innovators and agents of change acting upon the environment within their parochial borders, this book depicts them as traditional peasantry reacting to the Russian milieu. How did the foreign settlers who immigrated to the Lower Volga region of the Russian Empire in the eighteenth century adapt to the physical conditions of their new homeland? For example, the book addresses how the Russian steppe frontier shaped the Volga Germans, disputing the popularly held myth of the Volga Germans as model farmers invited to tame and transform the Russian frontier. How did these outsiders appear to the government and people of Russia, and, particularly, how did the bureaucracy treat these frontier settlers? This study focuses on these peoples as victims of forces beyond their control: natural elements, which made earning a living unpredictable and precarious; tsarist policies, which originally protected them, then neglected them, later discriminated against them, and ultimately alienated them; and virulent political nationalism, which made them pawns in the nationalist European rivalries, leading to their persecution and exploitation as scapegoats. In fact, the Volga Germans were loyal, productive Russian subjects who became deeply attached to their new homes and chosen motherland.

More specifically, this study examines the political, economic, and social history of the Volga colonies. The political aspects cover the loss of special government protection, increased bureaucratic interference, participation in the zemstvos, and the rise of political consciousness. The economic history explores the transformation of agriculture from peasant subsistence to commercial farming, with considerable attention devoted to agricultural history, but also to economic diversification of the colonies into commercial and industrial centers. Finally, the social history looks at social stratification, structures, and relationships among the colonists, with particular emphasis on how economic change, government policies, and education affected society.

The Volga German experience was but a part of a truly revolutionary phenomenon sweeping Europe. Between 1860 and 1917, Europe changed beyond recognition as people generally became better fed, housed, educated, and governed. Material prosperity advanced as goods and trade became internationalized; after 1860, the amount of grain reaching Europe increased dramatically and food prices fell rapidly. This economic expansion was aided by the world's stock of gold doubling between 1889 and 1904. A revolution in technology occurred; villages became towns; and literacy and universal education became the norms. It was also a time of great movement: millions of European emigrants departed their countries, with a small Volga German minority joining the exodus, but their history has been treated repeatedly. Of course, not all Europeans benefited equally, but few remained unaffected by this socioeconomic revolution. Not the least of these were the Volga Germans.

Up to the time of the great reforms and modernization drives of the second half of the nineteenth century, the Russian Empire could be characterized as politically undergoverned and economically underdeveloped. The bureaucratic centralism, political and socioeconomic integration, and industrialization of modern state building were all chiefly post-1850 manifestations. Yet out of these changes rose the storm that grew to hurricane force in 1917. As Marc Raeff stated, "We sense that Russian society and culture underwent earth-shattering changes."[3] These changes profoundly influenced the lives of the Volga Germans.

The Russian government's specific policies toward the Volga Germans altered course during this period, becoming inept and counterproductive, and thus replaced a relatively enlightened century's tutelage of the colonies; but its policies toward all peoples of the empire, except the privileged landed gentry, had similarly deteriorated. The specific policies toward the Volga Germans were in keeping with the overall nationality policy of the late tsarist period, which arose in the 1860s, as one scholar has described it, as the "coincidence of internal crisis in the Russian center [the appearance of a Russian revolutionary intelligentsia] and Polish borderlands of the empire that brought to power in St. Petersburg a new generation of officials who profoundly distrusted all autonomous social and political forces in Russia and who believed that her salvation could come only from firm authority and resolute action from above by the government."[4] The coincidence of German nationalism and rise of a united German state on Russia's western border would make the Volga settlers especially suspect.

Rarely has so much historical misinterpretation and misinformation surrounded a people as that concerning the Volga Germans. The history of the Volga Germans, like all history, is the product of a people's response to specific conditions and circumstances. The Volga Germans experienced a particular combination of land conditions and tenure, climate and geography, and government administration and policy, which greatly influenced their history and made them such an interesting people in the vast ethnic sea of the Russian Empire. Much of the confusion arose out of a misunderstanding of the processes at work in the colonization of the Russian Empire, particularly the failure to distinguish the numerous waves of foreign colonists and the diverse origins and destinations of the foreign settlers. A recent popular history widely read in the United States mistakenly described the migration and settlement of German-Russians: "The German-Russians came from the Ukraine and Crimea; they were Germans who had migrated to Russia in the *early 1800s*, settling at first along the Volga, *north of the Black Sea*[5] (my italics). Even George Rudé, the eminent social historian, confused the origins of the Volga Germans by suggesting that many of them were Prussians.[6]

The significant expansion of the territorial limits of the Russian state in the seventeenth and eighteenth centuries opened up vast tracts of frontier lands which, because of the immobility of Russian serfs, the government decided to populate by foreign colonization. The manifestos of Catherine II and Alexander I, examples of the active encouragement of immigration by most European states at that time, laid the foundations for considerable foreign emigration to Russia, a significant part of which consisted of peoples from various German principalities, who risked arrest to escape military devastation, and religious and political oppression. Roger Bartlett recently laid to rest the widely held belief that the Russian government specifically sought German settlers: "Although Russian diplomats occasionally showed prejudice against particular nationalities, the predominance of Germans among the early colonists was overwhelmingly the result of conditions and circumstances in Europe, rather than of the predilections or policies of Catherine and her ministers."[7]

The approximately 100,000 immigrants with some Germanic heritage gradually became collectively and indiscriminately identified simply as German colonists, imputing a homogeneity and uniformity that never existed, considering the diverse backgrounds of the immigrants, their varied arrival times, and their settlement in widely separated areas of Russia. The appellation "German-Russian" confounded the problem even more, because the German colonists became confused with the large number of Germans who lived on lands annexed to the empire, or who had traveled alone to Russia.

The German-speaking colonists arrived in three waves. The initial wave of approximately 25,000 moved quickly into Russia between 1764 and 1769, and settled in 104 colonies in the Lower Volga River Valley in the southeastern part of European Russia. A half century elapsed before the second wave of approximately 50,000 to 60,000 flowed intermittently into Russia between 1803 and 1823, forming 209 colonies over 600 miles west of the first wave in the most southern part of the Russian Empire, not far from the Black Sea. Because of their proximity to well-known bodies of water, the two groups have often been labeled Volga Germans and Black Sea Germans respectively. The third and final wave—more a steady trickle—extended from 1830 to 1870, when the government permitted about 25,000 to 30,000 colonists to settle in the western

Ukraine and Volynia. By World War I, the descendants of all these colonists still residing within the Russian Empire numbered 1.7 million.[8]

The Germanic ethnocentric historical approach, which has dominated research of the Volga colonists, depicted the Volga Germans as an indistinct element within the larger German-Russian historical context, characterized as a forced Babylonian captivity in an alien land from which they withheld their loyalty and allegiance, clinging instead to their ancestral homeland in Western Europe.[9] The most recent example of this type of historical literature is Ingeborg Fleischhauer's *Die Deutschen im Zarenreich* (1986). Even though the author distinguishes three major German constituencies—Baltic Germans, urban residents, and colonists—the actual situation was more complex than presented. While such research has contributed in innumerable ways to uncovering the Volga German past, it has also contributed to considerable misinformation and distortion. Few ties linked the Volga Germans with other German-Russians, their socioeconomic conditions varied significantly, they originated in no common homeland, and the Russian government adopted no uniform policy toward them.

The Volga foreign settlers were not captives, but eager and willing immigrants who abandoned the turbulent conditions of the West for a more prosperous and promising life in the East. They departed for a permanent, new homeland, expectantly anticipating a fresh, unfettered, and ample life for themselves and their offspring. Although the early years were a time of great hardship and misery, the Russian steppe frontier eventually provided them with a satisfactory standard of living, and they adapted quickly as subjects of their new motherland. During the first century of their frontier existence, they lived quite isolated, little known except as footnotes of history. Few ever returned to Bismarckian Germany, and those who departed to the New World were by no means peculiar, forming only a minuscule fraction of the forty million European emigrants who quit the Old World during the second half of the nineteenth century. The overwhelming mass of them stayed, buffeted and tormented by the whims of nature, the modernization and reform of the Russian state, and the economic revolution sweeping the Western world.

The Volga Valley

St. Petersburg

Moscow

Volga River

Nizhnii
Novgorod

Kazan

Samara

Atkarsk

Saratov

Ekaterninenstadt

Golyi Karamysh

Medveditsa R.

Rovnoe

Kamyshin

Don R.

Tsaritsyn

Volga R.

Don River

Sea
of Azov

Astrakhan

CASPIAN SEA

BLACK SEA

Volga German Settlements

NORTH SEA

Oslo

Helsinki

St. Petersburg

Volga R.

Kazan

Dublin

Stockholm

Moscow

Samara

London

Berlin

Warsaw

Elbe R.

Dnieper R.

Saratov

Volga R.

Brussels

Bonn

Prague

Kiev

Tsaritsyn

Paris

Rhine R.

Danube R.

Vienna

Vistula R.

Bern

Budapest

Astrakhan

CASPIAN SEA

Loire R.

Milan

Belgrade

Danube R.

BLACK SEA

Madrid

Rome

Ankara

MEDITERRANEAN SEA

Athens

Chapter One

Geography, Demography, and Settlement of the Colonies

The foreign colonists did not move to a steppe paradise in the 1760s, despite the exaggerated claims made by government and private recruiters about the riches and lushness of the Lower Volga. The original settlers found a wild, unprotected, and uninhabited frontier awaiting them. Although Kalmyk and Kirghiz forays had abated by the beginning of the nineteenth century, the Lower Volga remained a remote, rugged frontier well into the century. Compared with the central provinces of Russia, it was an area where few large, noble landowners settled; of those who did, most refused to live on their estates, preferring to remain in their comfortable residences near Moscow or St. Petersburg, over 500 miles and a week's journey away. As late as 1844, the governor of Saratov Province, Andrei M. Fadeev, on one of his inspections, expressed surprise upon finding estates where respectable people lived comfortably.[1] Much more typical of the provincial gentry in this region would be the Aksakov family as depicted in *A Country Gentleman*.

The foreign settlers entered a region of remarkable cultural diversity, with Orthodox, Catholic, Protestant, and Muslim well represented. Muslim nomads and, later, traders and artisans roamed the land; as late as the 1840s the Kalmyks still lived a nomadic life in the trans-Volga steppe in what eventually became Novouzensk District. The tsarist government long regarded the Lower Volga as a safety valve zone where undesirables could be exiled and where dissidents fled. Fugitive serfs and peasants fled there in large numbers in the seventeenth and eighteenth centuries; various schismatics had moved into the region, making it for a time a religious haven. In 1841 the tsar's troops leveled three schismatic monasteries and forced their followers to accept the Orthodox faith and ritual. Emperor Nicholas I exiled many Polish insurgents there after the crushing of the 1831 rebellion; more followed after the 1863 Polish uprising. Beginning in the 1830s, the tsarist government had also designated the Lower Volga as a place to resettle state and Crown peasants. Within a day's journey, one could visit Muslim, Catholic, Orthodox, Old Believer, Lutheran, Reformed, and Mennonite communities. Thus the Volga Germans lived in an ethnically mixed but predominantly peasant-populated region.

Another feature of the Lower Volga region—the domination of climate over the agricultural economy—is an unattractive characteristic shared by the American Great Plains. The unstable climate caused violent extremes in economic prosperity for all its inhabitants. The Volga settlers lived peaceably alongside their peasant neighbors, but engaged in a relentless and constant struggle with nature. Nature provided the elements of the soil, and the moisture, heat, and light essential for crops to grow. Yet the land and climate of their new homes in no way resembled what the emigrants had left behind in Western Europe; in fact, the first colony elders acknowledged that the dissimilar physical conditions contributed significantly to the early extreme distress of the colonists.[2] The Lower Volga lacked a good natural endowment, placing enormous physical constraints on all who decided to settle there. These constraints limited and affected the development of the colonies, because the backward state of farming there made it impossible for the people of the region to overcome such natural impediments. Throughout their history, the Volga colonists unequivocally recognized that the physical environment, over which they had no control, remained their constant and implacable foe.

The area of settlement of the Volga colonies lay in a semiarid zone frequently afflicted with drought. Acclimation to the temperature extremes was not easy. The harsh continental climate could be generalized as one of short, hot, often broiling summers (74° F) and comparatively dry, but long and bitterly cold winters (20° F). Without the stabilizing effect of a large body of water, temperatures rose and fell dramatically, both from day to day and from season to season. The insufficient, highly variable rainfall—twelve to sixteen inches annually—along with high summer temperatures made agriculture a high stakes gamble, the settlers nervously, if unconsciously, counting the days between rains. The minimum precipitation needed for crops raised by ordinary methods is about twenty inches annually, and the greater part should fall in the growing season. Yet almost half of the sparse Lower Volga rainfall fell during the dead agricultural period from October to April, thereby missing the critical early growth period of spring wheat in May and early June. Strong, dry southeasterly winds from the Central Asian deserts remained a scourge of agriculture, burning up crops and causing considerable harvest fluctuations and disastrous dust storms. These dry winds prevailed during March, April, and May, making spring short and spring planting critical, for the winds quickly dried out the soil. The winds abated somewhat during the summer, only to be followed by a thick, oppressive haze with a yellowish hue, often so thick it completely blocked out the sun; and the air became dry and hot, causing crops to wither. It remained stifling hot day and night with temperatures in the eighties, provoking people to call it "hell's oven."

In the winter, but especially in February, steppe blizzards stormed into the Lower Volga. Sometimes these severe ice storms blasted the colonies in April, after the completion of spring planting and the release of livestock to open fields. The colonists called this late spring storm a "deathmaker," or *Totmacher*, because heavy crop losses resulted in famine, and thousands of the livestock froze to death in the storm.[3] Inadequate snow cover, late spring frosts, and early autumn frosts frequently combined to damage crops extensively. The frost danger was very serious; 170 frost-free days are desirable for farming, but the Lower Volga averaged only 106. Winter thawing and rains formed an ice crust on the fields almost annually, harming winter crops. The long, harsh winters also required that livestock be sheltered six months of the year (October through March), limiting the size of livestock herds because of the scarcity of meadows and pastures, and the unsuitability of the region for fodder crops.

Another characteristic of the weather of the Lower Volga, also reminiscent of that of the American Great Plains, remains its variations or fluctuations in rainfall. Searing the landscape, protracted drought afflicted the region like a painfully slow, insidiously dreadful disease. Over an extended period of five or six years, the annual precipitation might be fairly good and agriculture would flourish. Then a cycle of five or six years of drought conditions would follow, worse even than normal, which reestablished the low rainfall averages. As American historian Frederick Merk remarked about the Great Plains, such rainfall fluctuations often deceived frontier farmers: "These cyclical variations have been traps to settlers. In times of more than average rainfall, pioneers were lured out beyond the safety on the Plains. In drought periods, they had to abandon farms that had been built up at great pains."[4]

Although weather conditions were fairly uniform among the colonies, considerable diversity existed in their natural resources, but particularly in regard to the soil, water, and forests. While generalizations are difficult and sometimes distorted, it can be stated that the original colonies were better endowed with natural resources than the daughter colonies founded after 1840, and that the mountain-side settlements in Saratov Province were blessed with better physical conditions than the meadow-side colonies in Samara Province. The earliest settlers naturally chose the best lands, leaving only marginal lands for the latecomers. For security against the nomads, the settlers who crossed the Volga to live on its eastern bank huddled tightly together along the river, thereby permitting other peasants to homestead around them and to cut off these colonies from choice lands. So compact were they that it was frequently said that from the church steeple of one colony a person could see all the other meadow colonies.[5] The original colonies on the eastern or left bank lay generally between the Irgiz River in the north and the Eruslan River in the south, with most of them being adjacent to the Volga River or tributaries of the Volga, such as the Karaman and Eruslan rivers.

The original right or western bank colonies generally lay much more scattered, fifteen to twenty miles usually separating villages, and a considerable distance from the Volga River. Most of the settlements were situated between two towns, south of Saratov and north of Kamyshin, and two rivers, west of the Volga and east of the Medveditsa; thus they lacked the contiguity and compactness so characteristic of the trans-Volga settlements. Three isolated colonies founded northwest of the town of Saratov lay over sixty miles from the next closest colonies. Also very unlike the eastern bank colonies, all except two western side colonies were far from the Volga. Most of these colonists never viewed the Volga, living anywhere from twenty to forty miles from it, because the government had earlier granted the west-bank lands of the Volga to Crown peasants. Many of these colonies in Saratov Province were on or near the nonnavigable (except for shallow flatboats) Medveditsa and Karamysh rivers, tributaries of the Don.

A striking physical contrast in the settlement areas of the colonists existed, perhaps comparable to the diverse geography and climate of Kansas and

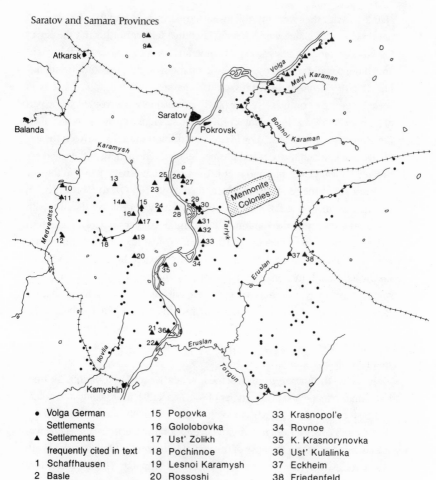

Saratov and Samara Provinces

- • Volga German
  Settlements
- ▲ Settlements
  frequently cited in text
- 1 Schaffhausen
- 2 Basle
- 3 Tsug
- 4 Orlovskaia
- 5 Obermonzhu
- 6 Ekaterinenstadt
- 7 Tonkoshurovka
- 8 Iagodnaia Poliana
- 9 Pobochnoe
- 10 Grechinaia Luka
- 11 Med. Krest. Buerak
- 12 Linevo Ozero
- 13 Norka
- 14 Splavnukha
- 15 Popovka
- 16 Gololobovka
- 17 Ust' Zolikh
- 18 Pochinnoe
- 19 Lesnoi Karamysh
- 20 Rossoshi
- 21 V. Dobrinka
- 22 N. Dobrinka
- 23 Talovka
- 24 Golyi Karamysh
- 25 Sosnovka
- 26 Kazitskaia
- 27 Berezovka
- 28 Sevastianovka
- 29 Iablonovka
- 30 Tarlyk
- 31 Skatovka
- 32 Privalnaia
- 33 Krasnopol'e
- 34 Rovnoe
- 35 K. Krasnorynovka
- 36 Ust' Kulalinka
- 37 Eckheim
- 38 Friedenfeld
- 39 Alt Weimar
- ◆ Russian Cities
- ☁ Russian Villages

Nebraska with their verdant, rolling eastern farmlands and flat, arid western prairie (although Saratov and Samara lay much farther north, with the city of Saratov the same latitude as Calgary, Alberta). The Volga River effectively separated the colonists into those who lived on the west side, the so-called mountain side (*die Bergseite*) in what would be Saratov Province, and those who settled on the east or meadow side (*die Wiesenseite*) in what would later be part of Samara Province. The mountain-side colonists enjoyed better soils than their meadow-side compatriots. They lived in a transition soil zone between the fertile Don steppe and the semiarid Caspian steppe.[6] The quality of the soil deteriorated basically from north to south. The richest lands were found in the few colonies along the Medveditsa River, such as Linevo Ozero (Hussenbach), Grechinaia Luka (Walter), and Medveditskoi Krestovoi Buerak (Frank), with good lands also near the Karamysh River in the colonies of Golyi Karamysh (Balzer), Norka, and Gololobovka (Donnhof). (Most colonies had two names; here the Russian is given first and the German in parentheses. Refer to Map 2 for the location of those cited in this chapter.) The best soil found in these colonies was a light type of chernozem, a fertile soil but with relatively little humus to retain moisture. Colonies situated farther south or not near a river had sandy, clayey, and rocky soil with little chernozem, but even this soil produced good harvests if there was adequate precipitation. A dry summer, however, burned up plants in such soil.

Formerly the grazing grounds of the nomadic Kalmyk and Kirghiz, the treeless Samara steppe had diverse types of soil, less fertile, more sandy and saline, and better suited for pasture than lands of the mountain side. As late as 1855, the Ministry of State Domains foresaw livestock raising as the major element of the colonies' economy because of the very thin layer of topsoil underlaid with clayey soils which made the region marginal for cropping. The soil was richest in the original colonies along the Volga, becoming progressively poorer in the southern parts of the province. Easy to plow, these sparsely grassed soils quickly became depleted if repeatedly cultivated. As early as 1853, Andrei Leopol'dov, an astute observer of the region, noted that only five years' harvests completely exhausted the soil, and that manuring was impossible because the settlers used manure for fuel.[7] The lands in the southern part of Novouzensk District generally became too sandy and saline for cultivation. Thus the soil conditions of the Samara steppe were not well suited to support dense population and extensive cultivation.

The inhabitants of the trans-Volga steppe also suffered from a shortage of surface water, which became critical during the hot summers. The Eruslan, Karaman, and Tarlyk rivers—nonnavigable tributaries of the Volga—flowed near several colonies but carried little water. In the summer the rivers dried up, and what water remained was brackish and unfit for drinking. In many places the rivers and streams virtually had no banks. The waters of the Volga could be used by only a few colonies because the steppe rises very gradually from the Volga to the east, making it impossible to channelize some of the Volga waters (except during spring flooding) for use during the dry summer. A low water table necessitated the digging of deep wells, a difficult feat without advanced technology. Therefore, during spring planting and summer harvesting in distant fields, the meadow-side colonists usually had to cart water for the animals and field workers.

The mountain-side colony area, despite its name, was generally flat to hilly unforested, rolling terrain with rich ground cover, bisected by several rivers which provided adequate water. The colonists' unrestricted cutting had depleted most of the forests, leaving the area barren. Writing in 1866, a colonist stated, "Today Lesnoi [Forested or Wooded] Karamysh could more properly be called Pustoi [Empty or Barren] Karamysh."[8] In Iagodnaia Poliana, inhabitants said the only place wood could be found was in the church steeple! The major exception to this description was the range of higher, broken hills paralleling the Volga River, which extended all the way from Kazan to present-day Volgograd. This hilly and rocky terrain cut by ravines and valleys became the home for several colonies, such as Sosnovka (Schilling), Talovka (Beideck), and Ust' Kulalinka (Galka). Here some oak, elm, and maple still stood. This terrain made travel and field work difficult, and also served to isolate the colonies. The two major rivers of the region were the Medveditsa and Ilovlia, both tributaries of the Don, but several smaller rivers, streams, and lakes also provided the colonists with water for lush meadows and power for water mills.

Even though the tsarist government directed the establishment of foreign colonies on the Lower Volga, their actual pattern of settlement lacked any order and looked like a patchwork quilt, with the new western emigrants' settlements interspersed among state peasant and Crown peasant settlements inhabited by Russians and Ukrainians. The government's efforts to arrange an orderly and uniform settlement, chiefly the idea of Catherine II's favorite, Count Orlov, had failed as a result of illegal seizures of colonists' lands by state peasants and nobility, existing settlements located on choice lands (forcing the scattering of colonies), and the whims of the original colonists themselves, who sometimes refused to homestead in their designated areas. The colonists soon learned that imperial bequests to royal favorites, such as various members of the Naryshkin, Sheremetev, Razumovskii, and Vorontsov families, took precedence over colonist claims; several areas originally designated for colonist settlement later became part of the estates of these great families. The government's inability to collect *obrok*, or land rent, from those who illegally seized and used state lands indicates the limitations of government authority on the Lower Volga frontier. Land disputes, illegal seizures, and belatedly and poorly drawn land surveys (some colonies waited fifty years for their land surveys) long engaged colony officials in the dispatch of endless petitions and delegations to the appropriate government agencies. The official surveying of Saratov Province lasted from 1798 until 1835, while that of Samara Province extended from 1798 until 1842.[9]

A visitor to the Volga colonies in the 1860s would have been surprised at the remarkable changes that had occurred in the century since their founding, most notably the significant proliferation in the number of colonies and colonists. The years between 1765 and 1800 had been harsh and lean ones for the settlers, but general prosperity ensued as a result of a series of bountiful harvests and the cessation of disruptive nomadic attacks, all of which contributed to a decrease in the rate of mortality. In less than a century, population had increased almost tenfold from 25,000 to 240,000. In the 1760s, most of the colonists had lived west of the Volga River on the rolling and rock-strewn terrain between the towns of Saratov and Kamyshin; in the post-1860 period, the majority of the colonists lived east of the Volga on the steppe lands of Samara Province. The number of colonies had reached 165, compared with the 104 original settlements.

The 1860s witnessed the last phase of the government-sanctioned colonist resettlement program, instituted in 1840 by the minister of state domains, Count Paul Kiselev, to fulfill government land promises made in 1797 and to alleviate tight land conditions within the colonies.[10] By the 1830s, the colonists, especially *die Bergseiter*, experienced serious land shortages and repeatedly petitioned the government for additional land grants. A very high birthrate and illegal seizures of lands, earlier designated for the colonies to accommodate such population increase, led to the promulgation of the law of March 12, 1840, which assigned additional lands to the colonists. Because so few unoccupied state lands remained in Saratov Province, the result of thousands of state peasants being resettled in the province between 1790 and 1840, most of the new allotment lands lay within the less hospitable trans-Volga steppe of Novouzensk District of Samara Province along the Karaman, Eruslan, and Torgun rivers. Lands were to be distributed on the basis of fifteen dessiatinas per male colonist, with the cost of resettlement to be borne by the colonies, not the government. By 1870, sixty-six new settlements had been founded; the meadow side had fifty-three new or daughter colonies, whereas thirteen new colonies appeared in the southern part of Kamyshin District (formed into Ilovlinskaia and Ust' Kulalinskaia townships) in Saratov Province.

The resettlement program posed no serious obstacles to the overpopulated meadow-side colonies, because vacant state lands could still be found near the original settlements along the Karaman River, although not adjacent to the Volga. The resettlement was quick and fairly smooth because the terrain was familiar and the moving distances short. Such was not the case for the resettlement of the mountain siders, for they were quite reluctant to cross the Volga to begin a new life on the Samara steppe. Most of them preferred not to resettle, and there was no way the colony government could force them to do so. On state lands along the Eruslan and Torgun rivers, the tsarist government had planned to relocate 16,853 male colonists and their families; by 1866 only 11,860 had actually resettled, therein indicating their unwillingness to live on the treeless, flat, semiarid prairie. Generous enticements that failed included equipment, grain, loans, and cash payments as much as 100 rubles per man, offered by the mother colonies to drain off excess population. Perhaps the colonists' experience was not unlike that of the American settlers' push past the 98th meridian into the High Plains of the Dakotas; western Kansas, Nebraska, and Texas; eastern Colorado; and Wyoming and Montana, also popularly and disdainfully known as the "Great American Desert." Walter Prescott Webb has recounted the peculiarly appalling effects the High Plains had on women.[11] At least the trans-Volga steppe women, settled in villages rather than on individual homesteads, were spared some of the isolation and loneliness of the High Plains' frontier women.

Naturally, the settlers went reluctantly to the steppe. The colonists still envisioned the steppe as the lawless domain of the nomads, the Kalmyks and Kirghiz, who would steal horses and plunder crops. Colonist mistrust and ill will lingered from the confused and disastrous founding of the original settlements, which was marred by bureaucratic delays in preparing surveys and assigning lands, corrupt administrators, illegal land seizures, and broken government promises. The colonists' preconceived notions were not altogether unfounded. In fact, the bureaucratic arm of the tsarist government barely extended to Novouzensk District, offering little in the way of security for the settlers. Only in 1838 did the government begin to survey lands in Novouzensk District; shortages of personnel, the inexperience of the surveyors, and all sorts of chicanery and bribery resulted in poor surveys. Bribery of surveyors was commonplace, and all knew that "He who gave most got most." Ministerial disputes long delayed the implementation of the resettlement program and aroused the colonists' suspicion of government good will. In 1835, Count Egor Kankrin, minister of finance, urged that no more state lands in the trans-Volga steppe be granted the colonists, reserving them instead for land-short state peasants living in the central provinces.[12] Kankrin evidently became irritated with the colonists upon hearing reports that some of them had illegally seized vacant state lands. However, Count Paul Kiselev, minister of state domains, visited the colonists and found them to be just as much in need of land as the state peasants. Thus the land decree of March 12, 1840, represented a Kiselev victory over Kankrin.

Homesteaders on the eastern steppe confronted major obstacles. Moving livestock, household goods, and farm equipment hundreds of miles required numerous carts, wagons, and money for travel provisions and construction of homesteads. According to a colonist and authority on the resettlement, A. A. Klaus, only the generous concessions offered by the older colonies in the form of grain, loans, cash payments, and wagons made it possible for poorer families to resettle. Once at their designated place, settlers planted crops and constructed sod houses, there being a notable absence of wood and stone on the steppe. In 1869 Wilhelm Stärkel, one of the first pastors to the new steppe colonies, admitted his initial dislike of the area, but tried to present the steppe in its best light while also indicating the colonists' disdain for their new home:

Consequently, it is considerably more desirable on the mountain side of the Volga where one can enjoy all these things [greater contrasts in scenery and vegetation]. And yet I can also love the steppes . . . . And while it is disliked by mankind, I feel myself the more closely drawn to it, knowing that in God's eyes, what man considers unlovely, belongs to the best and the most noteworthy. And I believe the great expanses of earth, despite their ugliness, are more valuable than we would deem them to be . . . . Even though many primitive mud huts still exist there, I will often find myself going in to these people who themselves were called together in this everlasting Palestine.[13]

The Volga German age of colonization finally ended a century after the first immigrants appeared in Russia, their settlement in the Lower Volga region only becoming fixed and defined during the decade of the 1860s. One of their major future problems would be living within these fixed and narrow limits. Many decided to emigrate and others to migrate out of the region to other parts of the empire; however, all of this would be done by individual colonists and at their own expense with no aid from the government or colonies.

One of the chief problems confronting the Volga settlers in the post-1850 period remained how to accommodate a rapidly growing population on a fixed land base. The government-assigned lands provided only a short-term solution to the colonists' land needs. While post-1860 land conditions within the colonies remained fixed and static, population did not. Tremendous population pressures confronted the colonists during the last decades of tsarist rule. Once the immigration to Russia had ended by 1768, the great growth in the population of the colonies resulted from natural increase. Although accurate data are not available for all periods, generally speaking in the nineteenth century the colonist population doubled about every twenty-five to thirty years, with births exceeding deaths about two to one. Observers of this phenomenon marveled at the colonists' fecundity. By the mid-nineteenth century official reports expressed surprise at the number of colonists:

> Such a rapid, and also such a regular, increase of the population is all the more remarkable, because settlers from abroad or from other foreign colonies, played a very insignificant role in the population increase; it came about through natural increase, through births, as can be seen by the fact that in only sixteen years [between 1838 and 1854] the natural increase of colonist population, that is, more births than deaths, amounted to 33,957 male souls and 31,811 female souls, or 65,768 of both sexes. Consequently, this amounts to an annual average increase of 2,122 male souls and 1,988 female souls, or 4,110 of both sexes.[14]

The same report attributed this increase to the colonists' general well-being (*blagosostoianie*) and concluded that the Volga Germans loved to live in large

Table 1: Population Trends

Year	Saratov Province	Samara Province	Total
1798	23,193	16,000	39,193
1816	35,088	25,658	60,746
1834	62,409	45,843	108,252
1850	94,345	70,682	165,027
1854	98,976	76,201	175,177
1857	112,842	85,758	198,600
1865	114,063	123,836	237,899
1868	119,282	131,863	251,145
1871	n.a.	n.a.	270,589
1886	134,194	173,519	307,713
1897	162,887	215,180	378,067
1912	215,380	265,209	480,589

families. As a result, "A very noticeable rapid population increase is represented in these people." An 1870s observer enthusiastically admired the vigor of the colonists: "They are a very fecund race with great vitality [*ves'ma zhivuchuiu i plodovituiu rasu*]."[15] After 1850, in numerical terms alone this meant that about 100,000 new Volga Germans were added to the population every twenty years. The German population in Novouzensk District soared by almost quadrupling between 1859 and 1908. The German birthrate even exceeded the often-cited nineteenth-century population explosion of the Russian peasantry. Table 1 gives a representation, if not entirely accurate, of the post-1850 growth patterns of the colonists.[16]

The 1897 total includes only those German-speaking persons living outside towns and cities. Another listing, which includes German-speaking urban dwellers, gives a total population of 498,110. The 1897 census also reported 32,409 German-speaking residents living in the Don Forces Oblast adjacent to Saratov Province, some of whom were probably former Volga colonists, but it is not possible to determine how many. Thus a more realistic 1897 population figure for the Volga Germans is half a million.

The implications of rapid population growth were numerous, serious, and quite complex. Where would land be found for the young colonists to till, particularly those born after 1840 and the last government land resettlement program? Would Samara Province, where the majority of the colonists lived after 1860, be able to supply the needed land? By 1897, over 40 percent of the colonists lived on the trans-Volga steppe lands of Novouzensk District, a remarkable shift of population from the more humid west bank to the semiarid east bank. In Kamyshin District, population densities doubled from 15.4 per dessiatina in 1852 to 33.8 in 1890. Population changes brought alterations in the ratio of colonists to noncolonists in the Lower Volga. By 1897, colonists were only 7 percent of the population of Saratov Province (a decline from the high of 10 percent), but had increased to 8 percent of the population of Samara Province.

The physiognomy as well as the population of the colony settlements also profoundly changed during the nineteenth century. The early settlement was a small, linear village or *Dorf* with two rows of houses stretching along its broad dusty main street and shorter side streets running perpendicularly. The largest had a few thousand inhabitants, while smaller ones had only a few hundred. As population increased and new households formed, the settlement broadened with streets constructed parallel to the main street and lined with new rows of homes. As the settlement gradually expanded, one side of the main street became popularly known as the better, upper part of town or the *Oberdorf*, while the less desirable, so to speak "wrong side of the tracks" section was labeled the *Unterdorf*. Although few public buildings graced the first settlements, typically the location of the church, school, and village well determined the demarcation of upper *Dorf*. Thus the earliest small, unheated log or stuccoed church normally stood on the *Unterdorf* side in the very center of the colony. Adjacent, if the colony was prosperous enough, stood the parish school, which, being heated, doubled as the place of worship in winter; otherwise the church served as the classroom.

The construction and modification of religious edifices graphically illustrated not only the spiritual commitment of the inhabitants but the material progress of each settlement. As the precarious early years waned and the harvests became more plentiful, almost ritualistically every spring even the smallest of sanctuaries and prayer houses were whitewashed. Brick and stone churches, although many were quite modest, appeared in the colonies increasingly after the mid-nineteenth century; for example, the prosperous and large Balzer community completed its brick sanctuary only in 1851. Imposingly beautiful, if not symmetrical, houses of worship ornamented a few settlements; the wooden, classic-columned Norka church, famous for its finely decorated interior and pipe organ, was not completed until the 1880s. Only the largest villages had a belfry.

The earthen dugouts of the original settlers were quickly replaced by sturdy though not roomy thatched-roof structures, usually small, rambling log or wattled sod houses, the latter being most common in the treeless meadow-side villages. The typical sod-brick, straw-thatched, and steep-roofed eastern steppe house was practically a square structure, about seventeen feet wide and twenty-two feet long, with a seven-foot ceiling and a partition separating the kitchen from the living area.[17] The floors and walls were plastered with a thick clay and later whitewashed. These sod homes contrasted sharply with the larger, more durable wood structures on the west bank, and stood as testimonials to the spartan life of the steppe. Similarly, the carefully placed rye straw bundles attached by rows to a center beam distinguished the Volga Germans' sod home from that of their Russian neighbors, which had straw thrown on the roof and trampled down. The haphazard addition of wings, rooms, and floors transmogrified household dwellings as inhabitants tacked on space to meet family needs. Fences soon appeared, demarcating the yard of each dwelling, which also included a summer kitchen (so great was the fear of the fire danger) and a root cellar. Behind the fenced courtyard, but still on the household's personal allotment, sprouted the family's outbuildings: livestock pens and sheds, outhouse, granaries, and workshop or toolshed. Meadows and pastures were usually near the village, often adjacent to the lower *Dorf*, with the fields laying a considerable distance from the settlement.

By the mid-nineteenth century, the upper *Dorf* in the more affluent settlements had clearly gained the distinction as the choice neighborhood of greatest social prestige, being nearest to the heart of the community and the vital source of water. The well site was particularly critical on the meadow side, where well water was hard to tap and yard wells uncommon. The more prosperous families built finer wooden, brick, or limestone houses to display their greater fortunes, a real sign of exceptional wealth being a large brick house with outbuildings also of brick or cement block, all roofed with sheet metal. The absence of rock and brick on the meadow side necessitated importation at considerable added cost.

New secular buildings also transformed the bucolic exterior of settlements and physically symbolized the subtle changes transpiring within the economy and society. The number and variety of such structures were directly proportional to the size of settlement. General stores, which the settlers usually called by their Russian name *lavki,* craft shops, water- or wind-powered mills, and state-owned liquor stores exhibited an expanding and more diversified economy. A jail, post office, public school, and public hall, where the village assembly convened, signified the maturing government sector and resultant extension of administrative functions. Orphanages and rest homes for the aged and infirm manifested community welfare services to the less fortunate. By the eve of World War I, the few very largest urban centers, particularly the Volga port colonies and ones like Norka on heavily traveled roads, could boast of a hospital, hotel, restaurant, several taverns, brickworks, sawmills, large flour mills, and grain elevators.

By the end of the century, most colonists noted that the villages had gotten quite crowded, leading to a notable rise in property and personal disputes. Yet the populations of most settlements remained small and immobile enough for everyone to know all, and for the majority to be known most of their lives only by nickname. The physical diversity of the Volga German settlements, however, was always the norm, not the exception. Each had unique features and characteristics. At one extreme were a few large settlements which had grown into clean and thriving towns, though none could match the stone-paved streets of Saratov; at the other end remained the numerous poor and very backward villages, little altered by and frostily indifferent to the revolutionary socioeconomic changes sweeping Russia and Europe, whose only dignity was the lonely steeple visible on the distant horizon.

hapter Two

From Paternalism to Bureaucratism

After the debacle of the Crimean War, the Russian government embarked on a broad set of reforms which would significantly alter the status of all residents of the Russian Empire and transform the nature of the state itself. Although the reforms were particularly intended to address the alarming conditions of the Russian peasantry and the socioeconomic backwardness of the Russian state, they were to have a tremendous impact on the foreign colonists on the Lower Volga. As the hoped-for rural self-administration failed to realize the needs of the state, the St. Petersburg government issued numerous controls and directives to ensure that the peasantry met its obligations to the state, even though many of these enactments violated local autonomy. In 1867, following on the heels of the emancipation of serfs and state peasants, the government charged the Ministry of State Domains with the drafting of regulations to implement land and administrative reforms for all colonies in Russia, with the ultimate goal of "complete amalgamation of the colonists with the peasantry in all areas: social position, administration and government."[1] After review and approval by the State Council and Alexander II, the regulations proposed by the ministry became law on June 4, 1871.

   Although not noted for their swift or vigorous implementation, the government's original paternalistic policies generally treated the settlers quite favorably, or at least benignly, and conferred upon them considerable autonomy and privileges. These tutelary policies slowly gave way in the post-1860 period to administrative changes that revoked all forms of special treatment and accorded the colonists the same status as the peasantry. In its relations with the colonists, the government changed radically: formerly a special guardian or protector of the settlers, it now became an unresponsive and insensitive bureaucracy, often hostile to and jealous of what it perceived to be an unintegrated and ungrateful pampered foreign element. The inclusion of the foreign settlers in the separate class or estate of the peasantry, many of whom had been little more than slaves of their landlords, obviously was regarded by many colonists as degrading. This is an important distinction often overlooked in the study of the Volga colonists. The colonists had never suffered the servile status of Russian serfs; they had no nobleman interfering in their lives. Their status was much closer to that of the state peasants, yet the state was generally a less harsh master than the private landlord. However, by the turn of the century, colonists often felt that government policies had become decidedly discriminatory.

Although peasants and colonists enjoyed extensive authority to address local needs through communal institutions of self-government, during their first century of settlement the Volga Germans remained segregated in Russia under a special administrative system that reported directly to the Ministry of the Interior (later to the Ministry of State Domains) in St. Petersburg. The colonists usually referred to this ubiquitous administrative system as the *Kontora*, officially known as the Saratov Office for the Guardianship of Foreign Settlers. Its offices were in the town of Saratov, and its sole responsibility was the administration, or trusteeship, of the Volga colonies. By the 1860s, the Kontora had a staff of twenty-four, headed by a director who was ably assisted in the execution of policy by four highly paid inspectors (700 rubles annual salaries), whose frequent and regular colony visits were intended to assist in the improvement of the well-being of the colonists, to maintain order in the colonies at all times, and to ensure that the settlers adhered to government directives.[2] Under the Kontora's watchful eyes, the colonies experienced much closer government supervision and scrutiny than did the state and Crown peasants, whose numerous settlements were quite remote from provincial and district capitals. The Kontora survived until 1871, when the government decreed that the Volga Germans would be subject to the same paternalistic and increasingly bureaucratic provincial administration imposed on all peasants.

One of the most valuable services of the Kontora, especially beneficial for the colonists, was its function as a ready channel of communication to higher authorities. In a state as enormous as the Russian Empire, with an administration known neither for efficiency nor rationality, a small, foreign-speaking group on the distant fringe of the Russian frontier could never have expressed its collective voice in remote St. Petersburg. Manned by German speakers and some former colonists, the Kontora was always much more sympathetic and responsive to the colonists than the Russian provincial officials who governed them after 1871, many of whom did not contain their animus toward the colonists as xenophobia spread. Although not always responsive, the Kontora, as required by law, had at least received the colonists' petitions and presented them to the appropriate central authorities in St. Petersburg. The Kontora's vigorous representation in St. Petersburg of the critical land shortage in the colonies deserves much of the credit for the realization of supplemental land allocations in 1841. With the abolition of the Kontora, the colonists' grievances were muted and their appeals became mired in provincial bureaucracies. The best example of the Kontora's effectiveness would be to compare its representation of the colonists' land needs in the 1830s and 1840s with the dilatory and unsupportive action of the Saratov and Samara provincial governors in 1906 when the colonists unsuccessfully sought access to the Peasant Land Bank. Since the provincial authorities had generally regarded the colonists as privileged and even spoiled by the government, the colonists found few sympathetic supporters after 1871. It took fifteen years, for example, for the colonists to learn from provincial bureaucrats why they still paid an individual annual assessment of twenty-two kopecks to support the long defunct Saratov Kontora. In 1886, Samara provincial authorities arbitrarily replied without explanation that the assessment had simply become another "obligatory state revenue."[3]

The record of the Kontora will not be fully revealed until archival access is granted, but available materials clearly show it to be one of the more effective and progressive institutions within the imperial bureaucracy. The Kontora's success apparently was chiefly due to capable leadership, close attention to the implementation of policies, and periodic follow-up supervision. Whereas state peasants rarely or irregularly encountered imperial bureaucrats, the Volga Germans looked upon the visits of the inspectors with some awe, if not dread. A colonist left this account of an 1860s inspection:

In the summer the Director [of the Saratov Kontora] himself traveled around the colonies to inspect township administration. His arrival was a great event. They lodged him in the home of the village elder, which meant, of course, that the whole family had to vacate the house. They fed him holiday dishes. A few persons from the township guarded the house. In order not to miss his arrival, although it would have been difficult since he traveled only in the daytime and the day of his arrival was precisely set, curious observers manned the bell-tower and did not take their eyes off the road on which the Director would travel. As soon as his carriage was observed, the village bell sounded and from that moment no one had the right to use the street along which the Director's cortege would proceed. Of course, before his arrival the street had been harrowed, rolled smooth, swept and partly covered with sand. His cortege was majestic. All around the carriage pranced the best 10–12 horses of the colonists ridden by village officials, who had journeyed to the village boundaries during the morning to escort the Director's carriage from the neighboring township. Along the streets of the settlement stood the colonists, each in front of his house, who removed their hats and made low bows several feet in advance of the approaching carriage. During the day, anyone passing the elder's house had to doff his hat no matter if anyone was standing at the window or not.[4]

There is abundant evidence that the Kontora was staffed by very able men, several of whom completed distinguished careers in the higher echelons of the Russian imperial bureaucracy.[5] As early as the 1770s, the Kontora staff was praised for its honesty and ability, and noted to be strikingly better than the rapacious Saratov Province bureaucracy. In the 1840s, Konstantin Popov, a lifelong servitor in Saratov Province government, acknowledged the pervasiveness of corruption and incompetence within the provincial administration, but he also singled out for commendation the superior leadership and administration of the Saratov Kontora: "Here served the best bureaucrats, and everything was kept clean and neat, and the bureaucrats, for that time received good salaries and incomes."[6] Since the salaries were paid by the colonists, it could be said that they received their money's worth. Similarly, one of the most astute observers of the colonies, the colonist and historian Gerhard Bonwetsch, singled out the Kontora for its "proper and beneficial supervision and control" of the colonies, which he attributed to a fortuitous succession of honest and efficient directors.[7] It must also be noted that this agency which directed the destinies of the colonies was largely staffed with colonists. Thus the Kontora understood the colonists, probably sympathized with them at least in their grievances against the government, and looked after their best interests, albeit in a sometimes heavy-handed, paternalistic fashion, notably in its strict supervision of morality. The Kontora reported with some alarm that during the 1845–52 period, over half the adjudicated cases involved seduction, lechery, and fornication, indicating that the sanctity of the marriage union and maidenhood were frequently violated in the colonies. To combat illicit sexual relations, it ordered village authorities to report every illegitimate birth, so that the perpetrators of such vile acts would not escape proper legal punishment.[8]

Although it is impossible to catalogue all of the Kontora's achievements, mention of a few will at least indicate some fruitful initiatives. With foresight and perseverance, administrators established two teacher training schools in 1833, long before education became a concern in the colonies. Fire posed a terrible hazard to the largely wooden settlements, prompting the Kontora to enact fire protection and insurance and to punish severely all violators, a policy approved by the Ministry of State Domains and later imposed on the communes of state peasants. In 1870, to combat drunkenness and heavy drinking, it restricted the sale of hard liquor to only one tavern in each colony. It established a system of grain reserves and granaries to protect the colonists from the unpredictable rigors of nature. Careful monitoring of the full capacity of the granaries provided the colonists with a kind of social insurance that their neighbors did not enjoy. Thus, in 1871, as the doors were about to be shut at the Kontora, it could report that colony granaries contained almost 150,000 chetvert of winter grain and 107,000 chetvert of spring grain. Reports also indicated that eighty-two colonies had followed its advice and implemented a communal tillage, whose harvests were used for seed or sold to help pay off colony debts. In 1870, the colonies had earned 60,760 rubles from their sales.[9] It also created savings and loan banks.

One last, qualifying comment must be made about the role and influence of the Saratov Kontora. A consequence of the Kontora's administration of the colonies from Saratov until 1871 was a lack of government integration and cooperation among the various colonies. There was no horizontal integration among the colonies: they communicated vertically with the Saratov Kontora and rarely horizontally with each other. With the Kontora located in a foreign Russian city, no "capital" emerged as a political or cultural center for the Volga Germans. Had the Kontora operated out of a major colony, such as Ekaterinenstadt or Golyi Karamysh, perhaps it would have eventually emerged as the political administrative center of the Volga Germans. This particularism is evident in the close identification each settler felt with the colony—often to the point of not even knowing the names of other colonies—and the constant references to a person as either a "mountain sider" or "meadow sider."

Likewise, the small German element living in Saratov, some quite wealthy and culturally sophisticated, were not administratively part of the colonies, inasmuch as they were registered urban residents who devoted their political energies chiefly to municipal affairs of a Russian town. Consequently, the growing urban Volga German middle class, which could have provided political leadership, found itself socially and economically distanced from the rural settlers.

The 1871 disbandment of the Kontora and delegation of its functions to two provincial capitals served to perpetuate and increase political particularism among the Volga Germans. The trans-Volga settlements found themselves subordinated to Samara officials whose offices were 300 miles upriver. In 1866, Novouzensk District authorities had petitioned that the district be made part of Saratov Province because of its close proximity and economic ties with its capital, Saratov. A former Kontora official predicted "very serious inconveniences, not only economic but even administrative" if the colonies were administered by two separate provincial authorities.[10] A good example of the dual treatment meted out to the colonists was the more rigorous Russification pursued by Samara provincial authorities; in 1915, they swiftly and strictly enforced the use of Russian names for the colonies and refused colonist requests for resettlement. The Saratov authorities never rigorously or consistently enforced such unpopular policies.

Until the enactment of the 1871 legislation, village government was vested in the colony assembly, meeting at least monthly but sometimes more frequently, to which every household sent a member and whose elected officials were charged with upholding state laws. The assembly's jurisdiction was considerable, if limited only to village matters, chief of which was the periodic redistribution of the common lands, but which also included the allocation and collection of all taxes, the expulsion of unfit households, the construction and repair of village buildings, including the church and school, and the adoption and supervision of the village budget. Administrative authority was vested in the assembly-elected colony elder, originally called the *Schulze* but later the *Vorsteher*, the counterpart of the Russian village elder, or *starosta*. The elder and his two or more assistants (*Beisitzern*) were elected for a two-year term. The chief duties of the elder were to maintain order, collect taxes, and act as the justice of the peace, which meant presiding over the village court to adjudicate minor disputes. Because of the size of the colonies, the nature of village politics, and the diverse responsibilities of the village elders, they could not rule as

Volga German Settlements

Saratov Province

Samara Province

Districts		Cities	
①	Novouzensk	1	Saratov
②	Nikolaevsk	2	Kamyshin
③	Kamyshin	3	Atkarsk
④	Atkarsk	4	Samara
⑤	Saratov	5	Nikolaevsk
		6	Novouzensk
		7	Sarepta
		8	Simbirsk

potentates, but rather usually managed colony business in tandem with local oligarchies, groups of prominent village figures who dominated village life for years at a time. Colony records were kept by a permanent clerk, *der Schreiber*, a paid official who was selected by the assembly and served at its pleasure.[11]

The highest level of colony government was the township (*Bezirk* or volost) assembly, which joined village elders and other elected representatives from several colonies; the largest township contained thirteen settlements while the smallest had only three. Political unity or cohesiveness thus never developed among the colonies, because there was never a convocation in which representatives from all colonies assembled. This meant that the colonists not only were segregated from the Russian and Ukrainian peasantry but remained divided internally. The township assembly, in turn, elected its officials: the township elder served a three-year term, two to four assistants had two-year terms, and the township clerk enjoyed a permanent but powerful post.

The 1871 legislation changed, but did not radically transform, the structure of village and township government in the Volga colonies. Except for three isolated colonies in northern Saratov Province, each colony remained segregated within its own township, not amalgamated with peasant settlements. Internal government changed. It already had become nearly impossible to get enough heads of households to convene village and township assemblies; now these two institutions were made representative organs rather than directly participatory ones. Henceforth, colonists could elect one household head per ten households to represent them in the village commune and one per twenty-five households to represent them in the township assembly. The collective power of the communal assembly, however, remained and continued to discharge the colony's fiscal, land, and communal obligations.

As the agricultural crisis worsened and peasant obligations could not be met, the government took steps to strengthen the commune, which was seen as a way to protect the interests of both the state and the poverty-stricken peasantry. In 1893, the government seriously impeded withdrawal from the commune by requiring individuals to pay all redemption payments or to find some other community member to assume them. The law also prevented individual peasants and colonists from redeeming their entitled land shares without a two-thirds vote of the communal assembly, and also prohibited the sale of community lands to anyone but persons of the peasant class. The chief consequence of this action was to limit greatly the mobility of the rural classes.

It is difficult to determine whether the 1871 legislation markedly changed the nature and functioning of the Volga German township and village assemblies. The preexisting communal assemblies never were democratic and egalitarian, because not all colonists were equal. Only heads of households voted, and influential individuals—such as the more prosperous colonists, the pastor, the village elder, and the clerk—could exert influence in subtle ways. Some have argued, although weakly, that the smaller, representative post-1871 assemblies could be more easily manipulated.[12] Most of the meetings of the commune remained peaceful, except those infrequent ones discussing land repartitions, which often became stormy sessions sometimes leading to violent outbursts.

The 1871 law also stipulated that all decisions and official correspondence of the village and township assemblies, as well as the township courts, had to be written in Russian. The original 1768 instructions issued to the Saratov Kontora had directed that officials communicate with the new colonists in their native dialect; colony officials therefore had little incentive to learn Russian. The 1871 legislation abrogated this and ordered the colonists henceforth to communicate in the language of the Russian provincial bureaucrats. Facility in Russian became a prerequisite for holding a village office. This fostered a new type of local functionary who was bilingual in Russian and the Volga German dialect, and for some time these officials carried both Russian and German titles. At the township level, there was the *starshina* (or *Obervorsteher*), while at the village level could be found the *starosta* (or *Obervorsteher*) and the *pisar'* (or *Schreiber*).

The 1871 legislation also adversely affected the system of justice within the colonies, which had gained a popular reputation for fairness, if not swiftness, primarily owing to the Saratov Kontora's careful review of judicial matters. The judicial section of the Saratov Kontora handled all serious legal matters within the colonies, such as crimes and major financial claims, and also acted as the appeals court for the colonies; however, as time passed, the court became jammed with cases, many of them less than serious. Although the post-1871 village and township courts were still conducted by judges initially elected by the proper local assembly (after 1889, selection was done by the land captains), the disappearance of the salutary functions of the Saratov Kontora opened wide the door to the corrupt machinations of local authorities, and later the land captains, to punish opponents, line their own pockets, or gain personal advantage.

Therefore, the Volga Germans reaped no benefits from the much-lauded judicial reform of November 1864, which established an independent judiciary with well-trained jurists, trial by jury, and a legal code based on Roman concepts of property rights. The legal code of the colonists came to be based on the double system: a special statutory peasant law (*krest'ianskoe pravo*) and an unwritten customary law, which was interpreted in peasant courts defined by special regulations. Until 1906 and the Stolypin reforms, such legal concepts as private property and individual rights of ownership did not exist within the legal and social environment of the rural masses of the Russian state.[13] Although scholars heatedly debated whether such a thing as unwritten customary law existed in Russia, what was cited as examples could only be described as barbaric travesties of justice. Illiterate, corrupt peasant judges—who greedily accepted bribes—swiftly meted out harsh physical punishments, including the lynching of thieves, to those not able to pay the piper. Under the new regimen, one common complaint heard among the colonists was that corporal punishment was used excessively and inflicted too harshly. Although the role of the land captain in peasant life (explained below) was considerably reduced in 1906, and a 1912 law ordered the reform of peasant courts, until 1917 the Volga Germans as peasants remained set apart as members of a large rural society whose customs, values, and institutions were considered distinctly different from and inferior to smaller but more influential groups within Russian society.

The statute of June 4, 1871, contained a noteworthy clause not found in the serf and state peasant emancipation acts. Article 9 explicitly granted the colonists a ten-year grace period to decide whether they wished to abandon their holdings and leave Russia. Those renouncing Russian citizenship and emigrating were not held responsible for any of the capital loaned to the original colonists; however, all private and public debts had to be paid. Although the land arbitrators informed the colonists of the right to emigrate, the colonists did not respond immediately. By the end of 1872, provincial authorities reported that none of the colonists had availed themselves of the privilege to emigrate; however, they did report that many communes were encouraging families to resettle instead in Samara Province by granting eighty rubles to every resettled male.[14] Only after 1874, and the introduction of military conscription, would a few colonists find emigration an attractive alternative.

The state's extension of administrative control over the Volga Germans was neither rapid nor effective. In fact, between 1871 and 1889, the bureaucratic authority of the state was weakly felt within the colonies. Since the land arbitrators, who implemented the new land reform and supervised the colonies between 1871 and 1874, were chosen from the ranks of former Saratov Kontora bureaucrats, a smooth transition was facilitated. However, between 1874 and 1889, supervision of colonist and peasant affairs was undertaken by an understaffed and alien three-member district committee (*uezdnoe po krest'ianskim delam prisutstvie*), consisting of the district police chief, the district marshal of the nobility, and a member selected by the provincial zemstvo assembly. With a small staff and too many rural settlements to supervise, these committees simply could not satisfactorily enforce the administration of justice, maintain law and order, and collect taxes in the colonies. The result was a notable decline in law and order; an upsurge in horse stealing between 1875 and 1882 was but one manifestation of the problem.[15]

In an effort to reform rural affairs, particularly peasant officials' mismanagement and abuse of power, the government in 1889 abolished the district committees and introduced the land captains, or *Landhauptleute*.[16] Despite the government's good intentions, many Volga Germans came to resent deeply the intrusion of land captains in their affairs. While many of their actions probably were well meaning and directed mainly toward the largest colonies, particularly the township seats, the land captains' interference in village and township matters alienated and disaffected the colonists. Virtually nothing pertaining to local affairs escaped the purview of this new official. The land captain, in effect, became the chief judge and magistrate of a rural area, exercising broad powers over the colonists and their elected village and township elders, including the right to suspend them from office and to impose disciplinary punishments. Even decisions of the township and village assemblies could be vetoed by this new local potentate. As an official of the central government, he remained completely independent of the Volga Germans; he was confirmed in office by the minister of the interior and subordinated to the provincial governor, although the latter provided little supervision. Moreover, some were indifferent or blind to what happened in the colonies; being Russian, they could more easily comprehend the workings of the Russian settlements under their jurisdiction. In the early 1890s, several Volga German township elders "fled" or "escaped" (*sbezhali*) the arbitrary actions of the meddlesome land captains by resigning their administrative offices and seeking elective positions in the zemstvos, where they could more effectively influence rural life.[17] The revolutionary events of 1905–6, which resulted in the paralysis of government authority, emboldened colonists to make public denunciations of the land captains. One colonist harshly attacked them in the press:

> They [land captains] transformed elected village and township elders into policemen, who, upon the orders of the land captain, arrested their own voters and put them in jail, where they themselves also were put upon the order of the land captain.
>
> They made pastors and priests into bureaucrats, who, being rewarded with decorations and awards, had to betray the confidences and beliefs of their parishioners.
>
> They made teachers purveyors of their Russification ideas and inculcated in pupils the ideas of meekness and submissiveness.[18]

The fact remains that the powerful land captains had almost limitless opportunities to interfere in the judicial, administrative, and internal affairs of the Volga German settlements. This contrasted sharply with the political vacuum of the 1870s and 1880s.

The colonists had markedly varied experiences with land captains, because they formed parts of several land captain constituencies. The southern colonies of Kamyshin District apparently received the most beneficent direction. Their first land captain was a jurist, particularly well liked by the colonists for his fair enforcement of tax assessments and collections; he was given credit for largely eliminating the illegal pocketing of surplus tax monies by the village elders and clerks. He also preserved badly exploited colony forests by curbing overcutting and requiring reforestation. In 1910, another land captain received commendation for his efforts to promote better farming methods and land use in the colonies.[19]

The colonists of northern Kamyshin District endured over twenty years of the vindictive, corrupt rule of Mikhail Khristoforovich Gotovitskii, who maintained his office and residence in the colony of Lesnoi Karamysh (Grimm) until April 1917, when the colonists expelled and publicly denounced him. His "crimes" against the colonists included tampering with the township assemblies by refusing to confirm the elected candidates, and by fining and even jailing township assembly members for refusing to pass his resolutions; pocketing fines of village and township officials—in one case alone, over 500 rubles which should have gone in the township treasury; appointing unauthorized persons to the local school examination commissions (which examined students and awarded graduation certificates); and imposing his decisions on township courts and inequitably assessing fiscal and military obligations on the colonies.[20] Under Gotovitskii, village and township self-government became a sham, because the officials of these units had become totally dependent on him. As a result, few colonists wished to occupy these posts or even bothered to participate in the village assembly unless threatened, knowing its decisions could and most likely would be overruled. The three colonies of Iagodnaia Poliana township in Saratov District also labored under arbitrary and offensive land captains. In 1904, the colony assemblies were stripped of control of the leasehold enterprises located on communal lands; the land captain, in connivance with the township elder, usurped the right to determine the lease terms and lessees, particularly of the lucrative water-powered mills, which in the past had been strictly controlled by the village assemblies.[21] In 1906, the colonists complained of the callousness of the land captain who, despite two consecutive crop failures which caused acute destitution in many Volga German households, ruthlessly exacted payment of all taxes including arrears; instead of showing leniency and compassion, the land captain seized the livestock and personal property of defaulted colonists and auctioned off the goods in Petrovsk, the nearest town.[22]

There is no evidence to indicate that the Samara Province settlers fared any better under land captains. Because of the dearth of nobility in Nikolaevsk and Novouzensk districts, several years elapsed before a full complement of land captains could be arranged and considerable disgruntlement was expressed over the fact that two-thirds of them were self-seeking, unqualified outsiders "sent from Petersburg," with only four coming from Samara Province. The most common complaints leveled against the land captains here were their manipulation of township election, to ensure that the favorite of the authorities was chosen, and their flagrant interjection into legal disputes.[23]

The intrusion of the land captains and other bureaucrats concerned and frustrated the Volga Germans, not so much because of their tyrannical behavior, but primarily because of their great numbers and prerogatives, which made local government much more cumbersome, complex, and time consuming. What is often described as the autonomy and self-government of the pre-1860s colonies could be more accurately described as an absence of government because of the inability of the tsarist government to extend its influence down to the local level. But by the 1890s, many more appointed officials, often Russians and outsiders, had appeared on the local scene, including the land and police captains and the school and tax inspectors, all playing a pivotal role in the affairs of the colonists. These officials also reported to three different ministries and sometimes feuded over jurisdictional rights. Even the vigorous Peter Stolypin was stymied in his efforts to eliminate provincial administrative weaknesses when he was governor of Saratov Province and local representatives of the central ministries jealously resisted his attempts to curb their jurisdictional prerogatives.[24] Increasingly, village decisions and functions required the consent, review, or supervision of the ubiquitous bureaucrat. Gradually the role and function of village and township elders transmuted from one of representing and administering the local affairs and concerns of the colonists to one of executing bureaucratic requirements for which the Russian higher authorities held them strictly accountable. Most of the time, they disseminated and implemented governmental decrees; prepared the necessary government reports; kept the village tax, court, and business records; and enforced payment of taxes.

The colonists frequently complained of the paralysis of colony government, caused by the unwillingness or inability of colony officials to do anything without the approval of the appropriate state-appointed official. In 1905, the press reported considerable discontent among the trans-Volga colonies over the immobilization of village government; formerly, village elders had promptly executed the decisions of the village assembly but now could do nothing without the permission of the *nachal'niki* (authorities), who invariably never agreed on anything.[25] What the police chief approved or ordered, the land captain often overruled; the absence of clear lines of authority and the unwillingness of village leaders to initiate action resulted in the torpidity of colony government. In 1906, the colonist Jacob Dietz publicly expressed this frustration with bureaucratic officiousness: "The fate of our German colonists serves as a graphic example of how our all-encompassing bureaucratic system can lead to such poverty, ignorance, and intellectual decay . . . ."[26]

The imperial government had been particularly generous in its original financial concessions to foreign settlers, granting exemption from all taxes for thirty years. In fact, because of the difficulties of settlement, the government granted tax deferments so that only in 1809, forty-four years after their arrival, did the colonists begin to pay taxes at the same rate as the Saratov Province peasantry! The new tax rate of 6 rubles 28 kopecks per male soul (consisting of a 1 ruble poll tax, a 5 ruble 10 kopeck land tax, and an 18 kopeck general state tax) was based on the number of colonist "souls" listed in the 1798 census, but the colonists were instructed to assess the rate on each colonist on the basis of land tilled. This last instruction was based on no egalitarian principle; rather, because of illegal seizures and the disarray of surveying, the government acknowledged it could not determine the precise amount of land in the possession of the colonists. There were indications that the colonists impeded the survey to avoid payment of taxes. The Ministry of the Interior reported: "It has even been noted in the reports of the Guardianship Office in Saratov that the colonists themselves hamper land surveying and intentionally prevent its speedy execution in order to remain in their present tax-free condition."[27]

Until the reforms of the 1860s, the main direct taxes paid by the rural population were the poll or head tax, which averaged one to two rubles until its abolition in 1886; the land tax, or *obrok*, which varied over time and by region according to land fertility, and remained until 1886 when it was converted into redemption payments; and a general assessment usually used for road maintenance and transportation, paid sometimes in kind or services. In addition, obligatory labor service was a nonmonetary tax required from peasants and colonists alike, although colonists were not subject to the harshest form of labor—military service. Exemption from military conscription meant that the colonists always had more working taxpayers, so that proportionally they paid less taxes than the peasants. The peasants, on the other hand, had to absorb the taxes of the village conscripts, who were listed on the tax rolls but unable and unavailable to pay their share of taxes. Until the land shortages of the second half of the century, the colonists also had larger landholdings than most peasants. The foreign settlers did pay a "colony" tax amounting to twenty-two kopecks in 1870, which chiefly covered the expenditures of the Saratov Kontora and the salaries of the Protestant and Catholic clergy.

After the 1870s, the direct taxes paid by rural classes generally were classified as state (the poll and land taxes), zemstvo, township, and village. In 1872, the government introduced the *pozemel'nyi nalog*, commonly called the zemstvo tax because it financed this new institution; it was assessed on land and amounted to eight kopecks per dessiatina in the 1880s in the Lower Volga region.[28] State and zemstvo taxes were assessed on the amount of arable land; tax officials assessed each district so much in taxes on the amount of arable land in the district. The district tax officials, in turn, assessed the villages and settlements, also on the basis of the amount of arable land held by each. Finally, the village assembly levied the taxes on each household on the basis of its land allotment.

The colonists and peasants also had to pay taxes to support local government, particularly the costs of maintenance of township and village functions. The greater part of these taxes went to pay the salaries of the numerous local functionaries—including not only officials such as elders and clerks but also the clergy, drivers, watchmen, shepherds, teachers, and factotums—as well as to cover any local construction. Although these taxes varied considerably depending on place and time, it is interesting to note that the share of taxes going to local government increased while those to the state decreased. In 1870, 63 percent of colony taxes went into state coffers, 11 percent was earmarked for the zemstvo, and 26 percent was locally expended; by 1900, the respective figures were 46 percent, 16 percent, and 38 percent. This may also partly account for the increased incidence of local officials' fraudulent appropriation and even outright theft of colony funds.[29]

The Volga Germans had a unique and more equitable method of assessing township and village taxes, which Russian officials noted differed from the method used in the neighboring peasant settlements. Usually the Russian settlements lumped together all the monetary assessments owed by them, and then divided them equally among all those individuals holding a land allotment. The Volga Germans assessed only some payments equally among all landholders. In the case of township and village tax assessments, they paid part of them from other communal revenues, such as fees for livestock grazing and tree cutting, and lease rents from mills and public property; this resulted in the better-off colony households indirectly paying more in taxes. In a few colonies with a significant number of members in emigration, the lease rents from their unclaimed allotment shares, called the "Amerikanerland," generated almost 40 percent of village revenues.[30]

Even though direct taxes weighed most heavily on the peasant class and rose by about 10 percent between 1883 and 1901, the colonists never regarded them burdensome, inasmuch as direct taxation never emerged as a public issue or source of conflict among the Volga Germans. Speaking about the period just before World War I a former colonist admitted, "Still [direct] taxes were not prohibitive. I remember my father usually paid about seven rubles a year which didn't seem excessive."[31] While taxes may not have seemed particularly heavy, the government's discriminatory scheduling of peasant tax payments to coincide with the end of the harvest season (October 1) surely worked to the peasants' disadvantage, because they were forced to market a larger part of their harvests at a time when prices were lowest; had they been able to hold on to their grain and sell it in the spring, the price would have been 11 percent higher.[32] Only following years of bad harvests did colony tax arrears accumulate, such as in the periods 1871–80 and 1885–86, although the good harvests of 1882–83 enabled the settlers to pay off the arrears of the preceding decade, indicating that taxes were not oppressive. Colonist arrears need not be accepted as proof of Volga German impoverishment, as there is considerable evidence to support the contrary, that peasant arrears attested to the central government's limited ability to extract state taxes from the local communes, which displayed great skill in fending off government claims to their resources by concealing the true state of communal finances, thereby letting arrears accumulate year after year without fear of government retaliation.[33]

Indirect taxes were another matter entirely, because by the turn of the century they were 87 percent of total state revenues. Since proposals for a broader based income tax were constantly shelved, the government met its mounting expenditures, associated with the ambitious economic policies of Minister of Finance Sergei Witte, primarily by indirect taxation. The pronounced shift to protectionism in the late 1870s and the upward revision of tariffs in the 1880s (intended chiefly to maximize government revenues) affected the lower classes most, because the highest rates were on goods of general consumption, such as tea, textiles, fish, iron, and coal. Although the indirect tax on spirits was the most productive, other important revenues were the taxes on sugar, kerosene, matches, tobacco, and tea, all of which had risen sharply in the 1890s. The tax on sugar had risen 350 percent between 1881 and 1894.[34] The plethora of excise taxes and duties levied on almost every conceivable product and service became onerous and irksome. As the colonists increasingly frequented the marketplace, they felt a growing irritation over the ever-rising excises on goods that had become an essential part of their daily life.

Of all the administrative and fiscal measures the Russian government instituted, none caused more initial concern and alarm than the announcement of the military draft. For this reason, the year 1874 was a significant historical watershed for the Volga Germans, because in that year the Russian government abrogated the Volga Germans' century-old exemption from military service. General Dmitrii Miliutin's introduction of universal military conscription removed the burden of military service from the lower classes and extended it to every able-bodied male irrespective of class. Catherine II's Manifesto of July 22, 1763, had exempted the colonists from military service, a privilege also retained by the nobility and merchantry. The 1874 law established a six-year term of active service and a nine-year term in the reserves, and it also excluded draft-age colonists from the ten-year right to emigrate provision of 1871; in 1888, the government reduced active duty to five years, but extended the reserve obligation to eighteen years. After the Russo-Japanese War, the term of active service was reduced to three years and reserve duty to fifteen.

The colonists' military exemption had come under government scrutiny and public criticism as early as the 1850s. In 1852, when granting Prussian Mennonites permission to settle in Samara Province, the imperial government had declared that new foreign settlers would receive only a twenty-year exemption from military service. In 1860, the first public expression attacking the Volga Germans' freedom from military service appeared in a St. Petersburg newspaper article by Aleksandr Leopol'dov, who concluded that the Volga colonists should be conscripted or, barring that, made to pay for their continued military exemption to aid Russia in rebuilding its defeated army. A writer sympathetic to the colonists challenged many of Leopol'dov's allegations, but agreed that subjects of a state should bear public duties equally without exemptions.[35]

The universal conscription law of 1874 was based on peacetime conditions and, in fact, did not enroll many recruits. The number of men conscripted each year depended on the contingent required by the military: in 1874 it was 150,000; it rose in 1900 to 320,000, in 1906 to 450,000, and in 1914 to 585,000, but never representing much more than a third of the annual total contingent.[36] However, the law's shorter term of service and maintenance of a large reserve component had tremendous implications, in that many more individuals served in the armed forces. Because the prosperity of peasant families, and therefore the state, depended primarily on the number of workers, the 1874 conscription law drafted men only from families with several workers. Also, the costs of equipping and training every draft-age youth would have been prohibitive. Therefore, each year approximately 54 percent of the draft-age young men were exempted from active duty in the military service. Most exemptions (48 percent) were granted on the basis of domestic or family reasons; 6 percent were based on failure to meet physical standards. Sole surviving sons, married men, or sons and grandsons who were the only workers in their households were unconditionally exempted from military service. Others, such as sons who were the second workers in their households, next eldest sons with brothers on active duty, and sons whose elder brothers had died while on active duty, received conditional exemption. They would be drafted only if the number of nonexempted recruits was inadequate to meet the military's annual contingent. While sole surviving sons were never liable for military service, the conditional exemptees could be called up in time of war. Similarly, even though the Volga Germans became liable for military service, many nationality groups remained exempt, such as the Finns and Muslims.[37]

The annual conscription levy took place in the fall after the harvest. Any young man having his twenty-first birthday before October 1 of that year was subject to the draft. On November 12, 1874, the first Volga German draft lottery occurred in the colony of Linevo Ozero in the presence of the provincial governor, M. N. Galkin-Vraskii, and an observer for the emperor, Major-General V. A. Rodionov. The colonies had ten draft centers, all except one including both Russian and German settlements. After the Orthodox clergy blessed the Russian peasants in the public square, the draft-age colonists retired to the Lutheran Church for religious services. The pastor's sermon, based on the twelfth chapter of Romans, stressed the theme of obedience, duty, and service, and exhorted all those present to fulfill their duties if conscripted. After the service, the young men gathered in the schoolhouse for the lottery. The first order of business was reading and verifying the eligibility list; given the opportunity to raise questions and challenge eligibility, the Germans raised none, while three Russians appealed. The authorities declared 275 eligible: 115 Russians and 160 Germans, with the draft center responsible for supplying 58 recruits. After a fifteen-minute break, the lottery began, with each young man drawing his lottery number out of a drum placed in front of a mirror and a picture of Emperor Alexander II. The drawing did not conclude until nine that evening. The following morning the draft authorities announced the names of the draftees, which included 37 Germans and 21 Russians, who were instructed to report for active duty December 20 at Kamyshin. Draft authorities reported that the lotteries at the other centers had proceeded as quickly and efficiently as the first one at Linevo Ozero.[38]

Despite their initial fears and concerns, the Volga Germans obediently but resignedly accepted military conscription. Unlike the Mennonites, the Volga Germans never objected to the draft on religious grounds. Visitors to the colonies noted strong antipathy to conscription, but instead of protest and resistance encountered public acquiescence.[39] Although the departure of the first recruits was a sad and emotional occasion, the Volga Germans gave them up without resistance. The loss of labor concerned the father of the household, the removal of a son to a distant foreign place alarmed the mother, while both parents fretted about Catholic and Protestant kin serving in an army of another faith. Although the government reassured them that their sons were not going to war and would serve a short term, during which they would be well fed and clothed, it seemed incomprehensible to the colonists why some unknown emperor out of necessity had to dispatch their sons and brothers to some godforsaken parts of the empire where they would face unknown trials and tasks.

On the day the recruits were mustered, great commotion occurred in the colonies, particularly the smaller ones where everyone personally knew the young men. Weeping and wailing women, the mothers, sisters, girl friends, and other relatives of the conscripts, came to say farewell, see them for the last time, and give the recruit one last embrace or gift. Although there was frequently singing and shouting, the embarrassed and often drowsy recruits went to their service without uproar and without commotion, as they had been carousing with their male friends since the evening before. When the first letters and photographs began to arrive in the Volga German settlements, the loss of the absent recruits became more tolerable. With each call-up, there was less weeping and agitation. Military service became grudgingly accepted as one of life's burdensome duties that one endured.

The 1874 conscription act unexpectedly fostered the Russification of the young male colonists, serving as the most powerful stimulus for them to learn Russian. Military service promoted Russification because of the "mixed unit" policy of the Russian army, which dispersed minority recruits among units often far from their homes. The large multinational element within the Russian Empire—over one-third of the people were non-Slavic—and the suspected unreliability of the numerous minorities were the chief reasons the Russian general staff created mixed ethnic military units. The military sought to have all units three-quarters Russian and one-fourth from the minorities, yet the quarter could not be composed of just one minority group. Thus the Volga Germans now recognized the necessity of learning Russian, because their sons were destined to serve in Russian units. As one colonist acknowledged, "Especially it [learning Russian] began to penetrate with the introduction of military service upon them."[40] The first non-Russian-speaking Volga German recruits had such difficult military service that some colonists sent younger sons to live in good Russian homes in neighboring settlements, where they learned Russian. A better solution was found in the establishment of Russian language schools—private cooperative and zemstvo—in the colonies. Invariably those colonists who had become fluent in Russian were the ex-soldiers, who had had to function in a completely Russian environment. As one Volga German readily admitted about the "Russianized" Volga German soldiers: "But those boys served in the army and they took a lot of Russian. They were good in the Russian."[41] Likewise, the former soldiers became strong advocates for Russian language instruction in the schools, arguing convincingly how much more difficult military service was for the non-Russian speaker. Often, it would be the ex-soldier who convinced his father to train his younger brothers in Russian.[42]

Undoubtedly, military service promoted literacy among the Volga German recruits as it did among the Russian peasants. Recent research by two scholars has considerably strengthened the long-held view that the years in the army greatly aided the spread of peasant literacy. John Bushnell asserted that "the Tsarist army became the single most important source of literacy for Russian peasants." Ben Eklof, on the other hand, discovered that the chief contribution of the army "may, in fact, have been its encouragement of schooling in the country, of literacy gained *before* induction" (italics in the original).[43] Recruits possessing the examination certificate, earned upon successful completion of three years of primary education, served only a four-year term.

The clean, close-cropped Volga German soldier returned to his settlement transformed, a "real" man with enhanced social stature. The discharged soldier symbolized strength and courage because he had endured the harsh military regimen. He also represented independence and self-sufficiency, having lived alone in an alien and unknown world. Although sometimes the brunt of jokes, the veterans enjoyed the respect and admiration of the villagers, who clustered around them as they told exciting tales of army life and fascinating events in the outside world. One veteran, who served in 1907–10, saw his first automobile, airplane, and telephone while stationed near Kiev. The years of military discipline and cleanliness marked off the soldier physically from the unkempt, nonmilitary village youth. Veterans assumed increasing leadership and authority in the community. As one colonist said, "At the community meetings they [former soldiers] shoved the elders and those who had not served into the background."[44]

Yet to be explained is the common refrain that the Volga Germans fled Russia to escape military conscription. In fact, there was little emigration from the Volga colonies in the 1870s. During the ten-year grace period, the government closely monitored Volga German emigration, but concluded it was too insignificant to be of any government concern or to cause any economic disruption in the region. The Saratov provincial zemstvo reported that only a few families, between 450 and 500, or about 2 percent of the Volga German population, had emigrated between 1874 and 1881.[45] While true that the 1874 law initiated the first, limited emigration, conscription soon ceased to be the primary motive for emigration. An author familiar with this early emigration stated, "With the lapse of years the colonists on the Wolga [*sic*] had come to look upon conscription as a matter of course, and letters relating the hardships in the New World had given military service the appearance of a lesser evil."[46] In 1877, an avowed critic of the Volga Germans admitted that only a few colonists had emigrated or planned to emigrate, and that their acceptance of the draft was commendable: "But the indifference and undisguised tranquility of the Germans, who appeared for the drawing of the first draft lottery numbers at the end of 1874 . . . forces us to repudiate our conjecture which was so unfavorable to the Germans."[47]

Data from Saratov and Samara provinces indicate that between 1874 and 1914 the Volga Germans annually supplied 800 to 1,500 recruits to the Russian military, depending on the annual levy set by military authorities. Thus, every year about one of every five draft-eligible, twenty-one-year-old male colonists entered the Russian army. Of all the conscripts from Saratov and Samara provinces, about one in twelve was a Volga German. By 1914, then, conservatively speaking, 50,000 Volga Germans had spent time in the ranks.[48]

Mobilization of reservists, not conscription, drove more Volga Germans from Russia, and until 1904—three decades after the introduction of the draft—their reservists had never been activated. This is the reason the Russo-Japanese War of 1904–5 generated such consternation and dismay among the Volga

Germans, because it represented the first encounter with mobilization; at the time of the Russo-Turkish War of 1877–78 no Volga German reservists existed, for none had yet completed the six-year term of active duty. The call-up of reservists during the Russo-Japanese War triggered an exodus of Volga Germans, which has been confusedly and erroneously described as an attempt to avoid conscription. The Russo-Japanese War suddenly and drastically interrupted the tranquil life of the colonists, who had never experienced the implications and ramifications of modern warfare, for being in the reserves during peacetime was no great burden. Although liable for training, but not more than twice and for periods not longer than six weeks, in fact because of reasons of economy, reservists usually were called up only once and for just two weeks. The 1904–5 mobilization weighed heavily on the colonists, causing many of them to fear and suspect future mobilizations, and may even help explain the recurring rumors of war which swept the colonies between 1906 and 1914.

Beginning in 1904, many Volga German reservists—men between the ages of twenty-five and forty-three, some of whom had been discharged as far back as 1886—decided to emigrate illegally rather than face being reactivated to fight in some distant war of no concern to them. These emigrants were not the single, twenty-one-year-old conscripts, but older men, now married, many with families, and some acting as the sole head of the household. Even a father could be mobilized, while his healthy nondrafted sons had no obligations. Thus the mobilization of reservists for the Russo-Japanese War involved thousands of colonists (about 20 to 25 percent of male villagers), while the annual conscription only affected about 500 young men with no family obligations. Consequently, most of those Volga Germans who fled Russia for military reasons were veterans who feared being recalled to active duty.[49]

During the Russo-Japanese War, the government ordered no general mobilization of the Russian army, calling up instead only selective military districts. Thus the burden of war was not equally shared. The Volga Germans lived in military districts that were mobilized. For example, in 1904 six of the ten Saratov Province districts, including Saratov and Atkarsk (where colonists lived), received mobilization orders, whereas Kamyshin District reservists faced mobilization in 1905.[50] Yet peasants in neighboring districts and adjacent provinces were not mobilized. Likewise, male villagers who had never been drafted were not called, because the trained reserve was not exhausted. Thus some colonies and colonists were affected more than others. The authorities of

Grechinaia Luka, in Atkarsk District, complained that all colony reservists had been recalled, including blacksmiths.[51] Reports from Iagodnaia Poliana, in Saratov District, stated that mobilized reservists' families had been disastrously affected: "Some of the families could not even sow, but had to lease out their allotments."[52] Zemstvos reported that the war had greatly excited the colonists, who feared the loss of sons, brothers, and fathers, and the economic hardships caused by a shortage of male labor.[53] The inequity of the Russian mobilization procedures must have caused considerable consternation, as the following example attests:

A man forty-two years old and the father of a large family, transferred to the first ban [rank or tier] of the territorial force after he had completed, in time of peace, his active service and his term in the reserve, might have been called out on the sixth day of mobilization; and, shortly after, he might have been sent to the front. In the meantime his son, twenty-one years old and single, might have been exempted on grounds of family status (if he was the only son) and enrolled in the second ban [rank] of the territorial force, which did not call him into active service.[54]

No better evidence of the unpopularity of the Russo-Japanese War among the Volga Germans remains than the recollections of some of their descendants in America. Although most colonists knew little Russian history, other than having heard of "Kaiser" Nicholas and the Romanovs, still comments, anecdotes, and stories about the Russo-Japanese War abound. The crooked General Kuropatkin mismanaged the army, lost the war, caused untold hardships for the soldiers, and even allegedly betrayed his army for the favors of a Japanese woman.[55] Soldiers did not receive the proper clothing and food, often being forced to live unsheltered and to eat dog meat, which caused terrible swelling and pain. Soldiers killed in action were not returned home, but instead were interred in the wilds of Siberia without a proper religious service. The colonists learned of these things mainly from letters sent from the front, although officials also reported a noticeable increase in newspaper reading and discussion of the war. Consequently, as one former colonist stated, it was no wonder that many colonists preferred to go to America rather than Manchuria.[56]

Until 1905, the Volga Germans obediently accepted the many reforms introduced during the reign of Alexander II. Exempted from military service for over a century, the colonists did not challenge the introduction of universal military conscription in 1874. Parents, elders, and religious authorities enjoined young men to fulfill their military duties if drafted. Tsarist officials remained pleased and impressed with the colonists' strong sense of duty to their adopted motherland. While individual incidents of draft evasion occurred among all draft-age citizens within the empire, including the Volga Germans, tsarist authorities never disparaged the Volga Germans' honorable record of military service to the Russian Empire. Massive mobilization of reservists in 1904 and 1905 for an unpopular war seriously tested colonists' loyalties and resulted in a noticeable emigration of ex-Volga German servicemen. Yet even then, most of the Volga German reservists returned to the ranks and served loyally.

From the vantage point of modern state building, the law of June 4, 1871, abolishing the special status of the colonists, could be interpreted as a progressive measure that placed all rural classes within a uniform administrative and legal framework. To the colonists, who now became "settler proprietors" (*poseliane sobstvenniki*), however, it was a regressive and seriously flawed act. Colonists' criticisms of the Saratov Kontora's interference notwithstanding, the Kontora was a much more adequately staffed, responsive, enlightened, and efficient institution than the notoriously corrupt provincial government. Its beneficent guardianship and regular inspections of the colonies had resulted in fairly honest, accessible, and open government in the colonies themselves. The corrupt and venal bureaucratic administration that succeeded it could claim no such record of accomplishments. The former colonists' juridical and administrative condition had deteriorated to the level of the peasantry, the only class still subject to punishment by flogging, whose local officials, although nominally elected, were entirely dependent on and subservient to the land captain. In 1905, the Volga Germans would publicly air these grievances.

Chapter Three

Society

The Volga Germans lived in a small, parochial world supported by the pillars of traditional society: the family, the church, and the local community. The identity of a colonist was defined in terms of his or her parents, place of birth, and religious affiliation. "He came from Grimm," "She was a Dienes," and "They were evangelicals" were frequently heard personal descriptions of Volga Germans. Usually only the person's village name was given, for neighboring villagers would know by the name of the village the religion of the colonist. Religion was a natural and unquestioned part of one's life. A former colonist best described the place of religion in Volga German life:

> The Lutheran faith permeated every facet of my life from the time I was a baby. Our lives revolved around it much the same as the Russian's life was centered about the Greek Orthodox Church. But since it was such an integral part of life, one was never called upon to declare his belief or reaffirm his faith. Belief was assumed. If a man lived in the village and was a German he also was a Lutheran. We accepted it as simply being a part of our lives—as a man's liver is part of his body.[1]

Although all three societal pillars proved durable, the last years under tsarist rule witnessed a weakening of their authority over individual lives as each was divested of many of the functions that once justified their existence and bound individuals to them.

The church played a vital role in the lives of the Volga Germans and, of all their institutions, displayed the greatest resistance to change and Russian influence, even though it differentiated rather than united the colonists, who were adherents to three different Christian creeds—Lutheranism, Calvinism, and Catholicism. The church stood as the most impressive structure in each village, and villagers prided themselves on their churches, particularly the imposing stone edifices of the largest colonies in the "Kontora style," so named because they imitated the classical style of architecture of the Saratov Kontora building—until 1871 the government agency supervising the colonies. Visitors often marveled at the enormous churches that stood in the village squares of even the smallest colonies, a few even having onion domes adorning their steeples. Protestantism prevailed in 72 of the original 104 colonies, with four-fifths of these recognizing the Lutheran Augsburg confession; the few Reformed or Calvinist colonies were found chiefly on the meadow side. The 32 Catholic parishes were scattered on both sides of the Volga. Although the ethnic differences of the original settlers would diminish, the religious distinctions remained, for there was never to be a mixing of the faiths. Custom and doctrine reenforced the common refrain, "Wife and husband must be of one faith." Even in the twentieth century, intermarriage, which rarely occurred, still carried the stigma of social ostracism. It was practically unheard of for a colonist to marry an Orthodox Christian, because an 1832 law, although not always rigorously enforced, required that the non-Orthodox spouse sign a pledge to baptize and raise all children in the Orthodox faith.[2]

Too few clergy to minister to the spiritual needs of the Volga Germans remained a perennial problem. Pastors served several parishes, and some colonies had the services of a clergyman only a few times each year. There was such a scarcity of Protestant clergy that priests sometimes performed the sacraments in Protestant communities. In 1861, a parish served by one minister averaged 6,592 people, and by 1905 it had swelled to about 13,000. The situation had not improved significantly by 1914, when only seventy-nine clergymen served a population of half a million.[3] Under such circumstances, it was quite unlikely that the colonists could develop a close relationship with their spiritual leader. The backwardness and remoteness of the colonies tended to discourage clergy from coming to stay. As a result, particularly until the late nineteenth century, the laity assumed a large role in the conduct of religious services.

The clergy made up in power and influence what it lacked in numbers. Not only did it hold the power to determine the fate of men's souls, welcoming them into this world and ushering them into the next, it had the full authority of the state behind it. As the religious leader, the minister had awesome moral and social authority which extended to all public affairs in the parish. As the most educated individual in the parish, the cleric assumed intellectual dominance and guidance. The pastor or priest was a regularly compensated government official whose salary came from a special tax assessed on the colonists, for the Russian government expected more from the clergy than just the spiritual leadership of the colonies. In an autocratic state such as Russia, state officialdom could exert immense pressure on religious leaders, including threatening their livelihood, to exhort political loyalty and patriotism. Since they were constantly required to listen to pastoral letters and homilies urging them to love and honor the tsar, some Volga German parishioners—no matter how personally repugnant the message—perhaps recognized and empathized with the uncomfortable and delicate situation of their holy fathers. Clerics were also delegated complete control over churches and schools, including control of the monies, and instructed to maintain order, keep vital statistics, supervise morals, discipline misfits, and report at least annually about general colony conditions. The combination of ecclesiastical and governmental authority ensured that the clergy remained very powerful, if not popular, figures in the colonies. This was not lost on the colonists, causing one former colonist to remark: "The Russian government paid the salaries of the ministers. So they had certain privileges and honors, and anyone that abused a minister, he would have to answer to the government, and so he made himself liable to punishment."[4] The dual nature of the clergy's functions also placed them in difficult predicaments, such as in the 1890s when the provincial governors persistently "encouraged" the clergy to support Russian language instruction in the parish schools.

Unlike the Orthodox clergy, who socially and economically resembled the peasantry they served, the Volga German clergy were clearly differentiated from their parishioners by ethnic and material distinctions. The clergy remained a predominantly foreign element within the colonies because few native Volga Germans could enter the ecclesiastical profession, not having the requisite financial resources and classical education. The Protestant colonies never had a nearby seminary to train needed clerics; for them, the University of Dorpat (Tartu) in Estonia was the nearest source. The Catholics experienced the same predicament until 1857 and relied on various Polish seminaries; in 1857, the government installed the Tiraspol Catholic seminary in Saratov, which began to train native sons for the church. Consequently, Polish priests, theological students (of various national backgrounds from the Basle Evangelical Mission School in Switzerland), and Baltic Germans trained at the German-language University of Dorpat for a long time filled most Volga German pulpits; even by 1905, only about half of the Volga clergy could claim native roots.

Although the Baltic German pastors and foreign priests remained strangers to their parishioners, finding themselves more comfortable with better educated urban dwellers, the native sons also felt alienation. Having grown up among them, they could more easily understand the spiritual needs of their communities, but their education, social standing, and wealth marked and isolated them; living in an intellectual vacuum, even the most sympathetic became inured.[5] Such ethnic differences, as well as the significant social and intellectual distinctions, created insuperable barriers between the clergy and their congregations. Except for the native sons, even language posed an obstacle and source of ill will, since the shepherd spoke High German or another foreign language (with Latin used in the Catholic services) while the flock used the local dialect. The most blatantly insensitive were the Baltic clerics who despised, belittled, and publicly ridiculed the local vernacular, further widening the rift. The high salary, rent-free stone parsonage, the sixty dessiatina land allotment which was usually leased out, and receipts from official clerical acts such as baptisms, marriages, and funerals, made the pastor a prosperous man of means, whose great wealth became the target of criticism. Pre–World War I clerical salaries ranged from 1,500 to 3,000 rubles depending on the parish, whereas a schoolteacher averaged 120 rubles.[6] Consequently, the great disparity between clerical and teacher salaries was a major source of enmity, jealousy, and bitterness between these two groups, who were expected to work closely together.

Religious antagonism frequently disrupted the harmony of the colonies and remained a source of friction and division. Besides the expected dissonance between Protestants and Catholics, there developed in the nineteenth century a serious rift within Protestant ranks. Because of the shortage of pastors and the monotonous formality of traditional religious services, the pietistic Moravian Brethren colony at Sarepta directed several missionaries to the Volga settlements. The Pietists' spirited revivals, emotional speakers, pious life-style, and insistence on being reborn grated on the sensibilities of more traditional Lutherans, and, although the Pietistic movement never gained a sizable number of adherents, it would make up in spirit and energy what it lacked in numbers. Despite government attempts to curb the Pietists, the movement never completely died out, because the laity illegally formed a brotherhood and continued to hold private prayer meetings which attracted those not moved by traditional Protestantism. Later, another pietistic movement, Stundism—taking its name from the *Stunde* or devotional "hour" during which its adherents would gather in homes for singing, prayer, and Scripture reading—also spread to the colonies from southern Russia.[7] Much like Pietism, Stundism was a revival movement emphasizing individual moral and spiritual regeneration, cultivation of an inner spiritual life, and rejection of material pleasures. The movement also formed brotherhoods as a reaction to the coldly formal nature of the colony churches and hostility of the Volga German clergy. Pastor Wilhelm Stärkel, who served Norka parish between 1878 and 1908, was the only cleric to give aid and support to the Stundists, or *Der Bruderschaft*, as they were more commonly known. Intolerance and reprisals against the growing Brethren movement in the 1870s resulted in the emigration of many of their families to the United States, although many remained within the parish churches but continued to hold private, informal devotional hours. In 1888, the tsarist government banned Stundism and prosecuted its believers.[8]

Divisions within Catholic ranks also led to dissension, although not on the scale of the Protestants. Between 1861 and 1892, because of disputes with the local church, about 140 Catholic families abandoned their Volga homes and migrated to the northern Caucasus region, where they formed the colony of Semenovka in the Kuban region. These so-called religious fanatics deplored the latitudinarianism of the times and despised Lutherans, whom they called "dogs" in private conversation and considered unclean.[9]

In 1819, the government attempted to erase, if not reconcile, differences between Lutherans and Calvinists by placing all Volga German Protestant parishes under the jurisdiction of the newly established Protestant Consistory in Saratov. Under the energetic leadership of a former priest and orientalist, Ignatius Fessler, the differences in the practices and liturgy of the two denominations narrowed as a common hymnal and liturgical manuals were adopted and annual synods convened to discuss church affairs and to resolve problems. The Reformed Church had become so administratively integrated within the Lutheran parishes, and the two denominations' liturgical differences were so inconsequential, that in 1832 the consistory was renamed Lutheran and incorporated into the distant Moscow Lutheran Consistory, which supervised scattered congregations in various parts of the empire. Until 1917, the Moscow

Consistory was represented in the colonies by two superintendents, one responsible for the mountain-side parishes and the other for the meadow-side ones. This arbitrary division of colony churches for the sake of centralization and bureaucratic efficiency was one more administrative barrier that obstructed cooperation and stifled development of a well-defined and united religious community.

The diminution of clerical authority is one phenomenon of post-1860 Volga German society. The clergy's basis of official authority altered, as well as its role within the colonies. As mentioned elsewhere, in the 1880s, partly in response to the clergy's opposition to Russian language in the church schools, the government began to curb the clergy's educational authority by placing schools under secular government inspectors.[10] The Pietistic and Stundist Brethren rejected the legally sanctioned Volga German churches for their perceived shortcomings and the worldliness of their clergy. As will be discussed later, the failure of the clergy to march in political step with the Volga Germans also widened the abyss separating laity and clergy, as village elders, Russian-speaking ex-soldiers, and teachers, more closely attuned to public opinion, assumed leadership of village politics. Because of their religious principles and attachment to the government hierarchy, the clergy generally espoused respect for the status quo and established order. Increasingly, the admonitions of the clergy and their minions, who were regarded with envy if not contempt, were simply ignored. Yet the colonists did not direct their anticlerical feelings toward the church itself, which remained the key social institution within each colony.

Although rarely mentioned, another Volga German social phenomenon, clearly manifested in the latter half of the nineteenth century, occurring simultaneously with the clerical erosion of authority. This was the emergence of a bilingual, intellectual, and elite leadership, from within the ranks of colonists, which would become the master of those who could not read and write. The terms "intellectual" and "intelligentsia" as used here in the context of the Volga German situation should not be confused with the meaning "intelligentsia" had in Russia at that time. After the 1860s, among Russians "intelligentsia" implied that section of the educated class opposed to the government and the existing order. As used here, the term means those with education beyond the primary level and facility in both written and spoken Russian and the Volga German dialect.

This secular elite came mainly from the two "central schools" created in the 1830s at Lesnoi Karamysh and Ekaterinenstadt, which produced almost all teachers, village clerks, and colony and township leaders—in other words, practically the entire intelligentsia of the Volga colonies. It is ironic that the initiative for such an idea came from the Volga Germans themselves and that the conservative bureaucracy long resisted the notion of introducing Russian language instruction within the colonies, wishing to preserve the wholly ecclesiastical nature of the parish confirmation schools. The genesis of a Russian language preparatory school beyond the primary level in the colonies came in 1825 from Reverend Karl Konrad, pastor of Lesnoi Karamysh, who, responding to parishioners' complaints about ill-prepared teachers and elders, pledged to build a school for the study of Russian which would annually enroll fifty to sixty colonists' children to fill the growing ranks of local officialdom. Because of government intransigence—bureaucrats argued that there was no need for such a school—a decade elapsed before his dream was realized.[11]

In 1833, the imperial government relented and mandated the creation of not one but two central Russian language schools—one at Lesnoi Karamysh and the other at Ekaterinenstadt—to ensure accessibility for children from all the widely dispersed colonies, for the purpose of "preparing teachers for colony schools, who, having studied the Russian language, could sufficiently disseminate knowledge of this language among the colonists."[12] The two schools were to be maintained at the expense of the colonists by means of a six kopeck annual assessment, supervised by the local clergyman, but secularly controlled by the Saratov Kontora (until it was abolished and the Ministry of Education assumed control), which appointed and dismissed the teachers. Each school enrolled twenty-five pupils, selected by village assemblies and approved by the pastor, although children from more populous colonies and orphans were to be granted preference. The original course of instruction was a three-year program beyond the primary level open to children between the ages of fourteen and sixteen, who were literate in their native dialect; by the 1870s the schools offered six-year programs and admitted larger classes. Although religious instruction remained, the curriculum became much more secular, advanced, and practical. Students were expected to emerge from the schools bilingual, since instruction in all subjects except arithmetic and religion was to be in Russian. After completion of studies, students were obliged to teach six years in colony schools alongside the local dialect-speaking teacher. The final result of this process would be that knowledge of the Russian language among the colonists would gradually spread and in time gain general usage.

In fact, these results did not materialize as quickly as anticipated, primarily because of the scarcity of suitably prepared pupils, the delays in construction and acquisition of teaching materials, and, above all, the difficulty in attracting superior faculty. The Lesnoi Karamysh school struggled along until 1857, when it was temporarily merged with the school in Ekaterinenstadt; it reopened in 1864. The caliber of the teaching staff improved, as well-trained teachers—gymnasium graduates fluent in Russian—were hired after officials granted them the same rights and privileges accorded to teachers in district schools.[13] In 1872, courses in pedagogy were introduced. Consequently, it was not until the 1860s, thirty years after the inauguration of the central schools, that significant numbers of soundly educated youth graduated, yet this opportunely coincided with expanding vocational openings that were created as a result of the introduction of the zemstvo and administrative reforms. Facility in Russian and the Volga German dialect became a sure ticket for advancement in business as well, because Lower Volga merchants sought clerks and buyers able to handle transactions with the ethnically mixed population.

Few could have imagined the significance of the two "normal" schools for the Volga Germans. By the 1870s the two schools annually and collectively had enrolled between 200 and 250 students in their programs; thus, conservatively speaking, they had graduated between 2,000 and 3,000 by 1917, supplying the colonies with a functionally literate element glaringly absent in Russian rural communities. As late as 1925, an estimated 95 percent of Volga German teachers were graduates of the two central "normal" schools.[14] But these two schools served the equally important role of main contributor to colony officialdom. Although the schools were chiefly intended to provide teachers for church school classrooms, many teaching posts remained unfilled because central school graduates often preferred to accept more lucrative local government positions. Bilingual clerks were in such short supply before the 1860s that these officials were probably the most mobile element in the settlements as they moved from lower to higher paying posts. The reason for this lies primarily in the amount and form of remuneration. Until very late in the century, parish schoolteachers were irregularly and poorly paid, often in kind, usually grain, and granted a garden plot, whereas township and village clerks and elders received a regular and fairly substantial salary; the zemstvo and cooperative schoolteachers also were salaried employees (though not so highly paid as local officialdom), and their emergence in the 1860s led to intense competition for the bilingual central school graduates. Not only did the rising educated cadre provide the adminis- trative and intellectual leadership for the settlements, they usually advocated general enlightenment by participating in and cooperating with the zemstvos, instigating petitions to the zemstvos for free public libraries and acting as unpaid crop monitors to forewarn district zemstvo officials of harvest failures. Another example would be the alumnus and teacher, Avgust K. Schick, a respected hor- ticulturist who shared the results of his many vineyard and orchard experi- ments in zemstvo publications.[15]

Much less important as a source for local intellectual talent were the Lower Volga gymnasia, whose graduates usually entered the urban professions or im- perial bureaucracy, became Russified, and, having successfully climbed the lad- der of public life, rarely found the way back to their rustic birthplaces. The Saratov classical gymnasium, whose yearly new class of about forty in the 1870s and 1880s usually included three or four sons of colonists, did not train colonists for local employment because most of its graduates aspired to a uni- versity education. Almost all colonists who matriculated at the university level never returned home, thus depriving the colonies of the talents of their most gifted, a phenomenon by no means peculiar to the Volga Germans. Aleksandr Avgustovich Klaus, the former colonist who rose highest in the government bu- reaucracy (attaining in the 1880s one of the top ranks within the Ministry of Communications), graduated from the gymnasium.[16] A Russian classmate had great respect for his colonist classmates: "The Germans, on the other hand, es- pecially in the early classes were the best students. Not known for their bril- liance or quick-wittedness, the German pupils succeeded by their innate discipline, attentiveness, patience, and serious and conscientious attention to their studies."[17]

In 1865, a few wealthy Volga Germans formed a gymnasium in the pros- perous trading colony of Ekaterinenstadt, but its graduates, too, usually sought higher education, civil service careers, or jobs in Lower Volga urban centers, and few colonists could afford the high fees. To join the cooperative cost 150 ru- bles, well beyond the means of any but the most well to do.

Although religion accentuated particularism, out of the babel of dialects the colonists brought with them a distinct Volga German dialect was evolving, a mixed language of German and Russian, which created a more homogenized colony society but also contributed to its distinctiveness. *Kolonistendeutsch*, the name most commonly ascribed to the dialect, consisted of a blending of Russian and various German dialects, of which the Hessian was said to predominate.[18] The colonists' long cultural and historical isolation fostered the formation of a peculiar phonetics system which sounded quite unfamiliar to that uttered by native Germans or Baltic Germans. As early as the 1850s one authority expressed his amazement at the development of the Lower Volga regional dialect: "One can see quite clearly that the language of the Volga colonists differs from the popular dialects used by the common people in Germany, and from those dialects which are ordinarily called Plattdeutsch and Hochdeutsch."[19] However, he also observed that although the dialect was still essentially a spoken dialect without literature, no standard pronunciation had yet emerged, causing notable intercolonial variations.

Of all the German-speaking peoples in the empire, the Volga Germans most came under the influence of the Russian language. According to V. M. Zhirmunskii, a brilliant Russian linguist who completed the most exhaustive investigation of Volga German dialects: "The influence of the German literary language and, in general, German culture, is much more strongly observed in the south [Black Sea Germans] where the population is more prosperous; on the other hand, the influence of the Russian language is more noticeable among the Volga than the Black Sea Germans, who, naturally, due to their prosperity, were more isolated from the neighboring population."[20] Since the remotely situated Volga settlers had more contact with Russian speakers than native German speakers, quite naturally Russian lexicon entered the dialect—over 800 words as counted by one researcher—and particularly words and phrases frequently used in ordinary conversation.[21] The adoption of over 800 Russian words in about a century and a half seems quite remarkable; Serbo-Croatian Slavicized about 3,000 Turkish words during almost five centuries of Ottoman rule. Russian forms of greeting were quite common, and, even more striking, the colonists adopted the Russian form of address, using both the first name and patronymic in addressing each other, which sometimes completely distorted the German names. Two German visitors to the colonies in 1924 were surprised to still hear eighteenth-century dialects, the major differences being the infusion of Russian words and phrases and numerous phonetic changes; one sarcastically and bitterly lamented that the settlers' mother tongue had been supplanted by German-Russian gibberish.[22]

Few scholars have recognized the "catch-22" language dilemma confronting the Volga Germans. *Kolonistendeutsch* at this time was a spoken, not a literary language, still in its formative stage. Through criticism and ridicule, intellectuals, whether German or Russian, convinced Volga Germans that their language was inferior, a bastardized hybrid certainly incapable of becoming a literary language. However, to adopt Russian meant forsaking one's traditional way of life.[23]

The Volga Germans' oral tradition, which formed a foundation for their ethnic identity and remained their only source of history, also succumbed as the settlers adapted to the hostile, frontier environment. Even though oral traditions often were not historically accurate, through them the colonists chiefly preserved their Russian experiences and gradually forgot what happened before the 1760s. Themes of popular tales included the hardships of the early settlers, the Cossack rebellion led by Pugachev, the Kirghiz raids (with numerous variations on the number of captives slain or sold into slavery), brigandage by neighboring Kalmyks or robber bands, and Empress Catherine's special appeal to "her" people to come live with her in Russia. As integration quickened in the late nineteenth century, even original folktales and fables began to disappear and to be replaced by adumbrated or new ones with Russian or nomadic motifs and settings; for example, the savage Kirghiz and Kalmyk frequently usurped the role of the wicked witch as the nemesis in folktales. The folk wisdom that the young male who fattened his horse thereby contemplated marriage—to give his bride a first-class ride—had its origin in stories the colonists had heard about the steppe nomads. Oral traditions, such as folktales and fables, survived so long because the great majority of colonists remained functionally illiterate and studied no history in their schools, the Bible being the only available, if inadequate, historical source.

Even Volga German usage of Russian had become much more common by the turn of the century, although it varied considerably by age and sex as well as by location. Knowledge of Russian, according to one colonist, was especially high in large colonies with weekly markets and vigorous implementation of Russian language instruction in schools; while small, remote colonies remained untouched. A 1901 survey taken of Golyi Karamysh, a large trading and manufacturing center, revealed widespread use of Russian; the chief reading material of the settlers consisted of twelve publications, six in German (mainly religious in nature) and six in Russian (Saratov provincial newspapers).[24] In smaller farming colonies, only a few subscriptions to the locally published religious magazine were discovered. Although official statistics are often unreliable, according to the 1897 census, 47 percent of the meadowside colonists claimed literacy in their own dialect, but only 15 percent declared themselves literate in Russian. However, a much different picture appears when comparison is made by sex and age: one of every five males claimed Russian literacy whereas only one in ten women did so. The male cohort ten to twenty years old had the highest Russian literacy rate of all—33 percent; their female counterparts had an impressive 19 percent.[25] Thus a good proportion of Volga German males, except perhaps for the most elderly, had gained enough practical knowledge to use Russian as a second language, although women, except for the youth, generally remained monolingual because of their very limited involvement in the outside world, making the learning of Russian difficult as well as superfluous. Military service and economic intercourse facilitated and necessitated the male population's basic familiarity with Russian, while the smaller educated elite, taught to scorn *Kolonistendeutsch*, preferred to use Russian. Similarly, a more mobile population, especially in the form of transient labor, brought Russians and colonists into frequent and prolonged contact. Russian instruction in the schools is probably the chief reason for the advance of bilingualism among women. Inasmuch as the strongest supporters of German culture and ethnicity among the colonies were the Protestant pastors educated at the University of Dorpat, it would appear that they were engaged in an insuperable struggle.[26]

The post-1860 spread of literacy, familiarity with Russian, and worldliness also contributed to a subtle but palpable intergenerational tension previously unknown within the settlements. While recognizing the distortions implicit in generalizations, one might nevertheless say that the elder, preform generation remained more conservative and traditional, being more respectful of established authority, such as the church and patriarchal elders, and valuing obedience, even submissiveness, to accepted practices and mores. Similarly, for the elder generation reading and writing were, quite simply, unnecessary luxuries in their isolated farming communities, where knowledge passed chiefly by word of mouth from parent to child. Subjected to sweeping and radical government reforms, especially military conscription and administrative integration, the postreform generations gradually realized the importance of reading and writing in a society and economy increasingly more complex and interconnected. For them, literacy was becoming a matter of necessity, not luxury, and not just in one language but *two*.

While it is difficult to discover and impossible to measure the changing processes at work in reshaping the Volga German generational Weltanschauung, by the turn of the century perceptive sources clearly recognized the social processes at work. A former pastor noted that indeed colonists, like most peasants, were generally quite conservative and tradition-bound, having remained so long isolated from the outside world, yet "When they get out of their colonies, they very soon transform themselves into men, whose origins or descendancy is hardly noticeable in the first generation." However, he found custom and tradition still quite strong, because as soon as the Volga German returned to his settlement, the conservative patriarchal nature of society quickly exercised its coercive authority. Another source concurred with most of the pastor's comments, except he discerned that returning colonists were not as compliant or as easily intimidated by their elders; also, although still not considered independent members of the community, being by tradition still subordinate to their fathers, these youthful, literate, and more secularized returnees commanded a great deal of respect, their voices even being heard in the village assembly, allegedly because they knew the law.[27] As I have documented in Chapter 8, on the Volga German political awakening, the 1905 revolutionary events afforded Volga German youth the opportunity to express itself freely and in some cases even radically.

As a result, a very slow, imperceptible metamorphosis was taking place among the Volga Germans; and it remained far from complete by 1917. As long as the Volga Germans retained their physical segregation and isolation from the larger culture around them, their chances for the preservation of ethnic identity seemed positive; however, those Volga Germans who had become urbanized had already lost most of their distinctiveness. The Germans living in the towns of Saratov and Kamyshin had become almost completely Russified by 1917, and well integrated into the social and economic life of the community; many had married Russians. The urban Volga Germans' knowledge of Russian was well advanced as early as the 1870s, as noted in a zemstvo report that stated: "In Kamyshin one meets many Germans knowing Russian. . . . "[28] Although the rural colonists managed to preserve their villages and neighborhoods, they were not immobile but increasingly moved up or out very gradually, thus assuredly weakening ethnic and community ties. A case in point is how one prosperous colonist agonized over the education of his son. He wanted the boy to have the best education, but he fretted over what effect secular education would have on his son's religious beliefs and values.[29] The students, recruits, wage laborers, domestics, village and township officials, zemstvo functionaries, "third element," and many other individuals experienced broader horizons than their less mobile ancestors. A sympathetic scholar remarked of the Volga Germans at the turn of the twentieth century: "The colonists realized that although they wished to be left alone on the Volga, the world around them was changing at an incredible pace."[30] Similarly, new forces and ideas penetrated the colonies, also eroding insularity and traditionalism.

Gradually but voluntarily the Volga Germans came to accept their "Volga homeland," or *Wolgaheimat*, as they fondly referred to it. The lack of official immigration lists, the passage of time, and a dwindling of interest took their toll as colonists forgot or could not confirm their families' exact eighteenth-century West European origins. As early as the 1870s the Volga Germans' attachment and affection for their adopted but benevolent fatherland was clearly pronounced in a popular farewell melody sung when emigrants departed for America:

> At the borders of Russia
> We will fill our hands with earth
> And kiss it with thankfulness
> For giving us care, food, and drink
> You dear, dear Fatherland.[31]

It is sadly ironic that at the time the Volga Germans had become accustomed to and identified with their adopted homeland, it was not willing to adopt and accept them. After a century of almost benign indifference, the general attitude toward the Volga Germans underwent a profound and disappointing change. The assault on minorities began in earnest with Alexander III and continued unabated under his son, Nicholas II. The government curtailed most of the privileges and autonomy enjoyed by the non-Russian population and embarked upon a vigorous policy of Russification, especially in the borderlands of the empire. The chauvinistic press and organizations such as the Slavic Society fanned popular feelings. Minorities became suspect and distrusted. It is noteworthy that, until World War I, the government's Russification of the Volga Germans was not as ruthless and extreme as that applied to the Poles, Jews, Finns, and Baltic peoples, for although the Volga Germans were intimidated, they were never subjected to violence.

Although the Volga Germans remained oblivious to its nature, power, and appeal, the storm of late nineteenth-century nationalism cast a pall over their future existence in Russia. These eighteenth-century emigrants had departed from small West European states long before the beginning of the linguistic and cultural revolution that eventually came to be transformed into political nationalism. The "Germany" they had left was so particularist and separatist, and the individual states so small, that patriotic sentiments did not inspire the masses or upper classes. In the eighteenth century, the courts and royalty of the numerous German states imitated French civilization, particularly French classicism, while intellectuals promoted the cosmopolitan ideas of the Enlightenment. For the peasantry, the word "national" was incomprehensible, and "Vaterland," though rarely used, implied one's own particular state; they had been reared to do their duty toward God, those in authority over them, and neighbors, but had never been inculcated with any idea of "German" patriotism.[32] Although nominally German by blood, they never imagined themselves as "German" culture bearers or as participants in the creation of "German" history and folk culture—attitudes that arose after the French Revolution and Romantic movement and were rapidly absorbed in the nineteenth century. That the Volga colonists had no deep patriotic attachment to imperial Germany is further corroborated by the scant Volga German emigration to Germany between 1870 and 1917; most emigrants preferring the economic opportunities of the Americas. The widespread and intensified nationalism that swept Europe, the United States, and Japan after 1870, though of varying intensity, fueled intolerance of ethnic minorities everywhere. Like the Irish, Catalans, Basques, Bretons, and Flemings in Western Europe, the Volga Germans also came under attack and suspicion.

Both external and internal forces contributed to the intolerance and chauvinism that swept Russia. Unfortunately, officialdom's and educated society's toleration and acceptance of minorities deteriorated because of external events of no direct concern to the Russian Empire's numerous ethnic groups. The

Polish rebellion of 1863, the Balkan campaigns of the 1870s, and the conquest of Central Asia all had the adverse domestic effect of inflaming Russian nationalism, which manifested itself in imperialism, fanatical Orthodoxy, and aggressive Pan-Slavism. The rise of a united Germany and the emergence of an aggressive German nationalism are often cited as the primary causes for the growing suspicion tsarist bureaucrats and Russian nationalists had of the Volga Germans.[33] Germany's spectacular post-1870 industrialization and armaments program, as well as Bismarck's "Germanization" policies directed at the Poles residing within the Reich, made all Germans in Russia a more likely target of attack. The state of German-Russian foreign relations can be used as a fairly accurate barometer of the Russian government's attitudes toward the Volga Germans. However, it can also be convincingly argued that the tsarist suspicion of the Volga Germans was prompted by the nineteenth-century surge of national feeling among the many minorities *within* the Russian Empire; in the minds of Russian officials, who desired integration of all minorities, the idea germinated and spread that all minorities were potentially disloyal and dangerous, and ultimately harbored separatist tendencies. The growing unrest in the Russian borderlands, the Western provinces, Poland, the Baltic provinces, Finland, and the Caucasus generated considerable uneasiness among Russian nationalists and bureaucrats, who gradually came to regard *all* minorities as unreliable and divisive elements whose interests were incompatible with the general welfare of the empire.

This misguided association of the Volga Germans with the discontented borderland nationality groups should have been rejected because of fundamental differences, for it drove the Volga Germans into the ranks of the discontented. The Volga Germans had no noble or intellectual elite to generate nationalist ideas or to rally them into a cultural or political movement; the few intellectuals produced by the colonies quickly deserted their villages, consciously adopted Russian culture, and embarked upon government careers. As a transplanted people to a new land, the Volga Germans formed an amorphous mass divided into two opposing faiths with no fully developed sense of ethnic identity. They had no history of separate institutions and traditions to jealously guard as did the Poles, Finns, and Baltic Germans. They had not developed beyond a village "Weltanschauung" when the event of World War I and the 1917 revolutions inundated them. Finally, the social and economic integration of the Volga Germans into the Russian Empire had proceeded much further than had that of the borderland peoples. Even though the Volga Germans did not look and think like Russians, by the end of the century they had become economically and politically integrated into the Russian state. The Volga Germans were a small, culturally backward minority living in a sea of Slavs in the heart of Russia, and posing no threat to the state. Thus Russification policies only stimulated the drive for cultural autonomy.

During the last three decades of the nineteenth century, the Russian press transformed the Volga Germans from a privileged but insignificant economic nuisance into a politically subversive element that posed a grave threat to Russia's security, and eventually led to the call for punitive actions against the Volga Germans during World War I. The earliest articles critical of the Volga set-tlers appeared in 1868 in *Vestnik Evropy*, which joined the chorus of reformers advocating the abrogation of special privileges granted by Catherine II.[34] The fallacious argument used to justify revocation was that the unproductive and parasitic colonists had always been an economic drain on the state and de-served no better treatment than the peasants, inasmuch as they had contributed nothing to the well-being of Russia, but more specifically to the improvement of agriculture in the Lower Volga. Just a few years later, newspaper opinion changed radically.

In October 1872, only a year after Bismarck's establishment of the German Empire, the Volga Germans came under a blistering attack for being seditious, dangerous, and racist nationalists. *Russkii mir*, a conservative St. Petersburg newspaper which condemned liberalism, espoused Russian nationalism, and denounced Western influences, published three scathing articles written by "M." entitled "The Germans on the Volga." Armed with a full array of Pan-Slav arguments, the author emphatically declared that the Volga Germans were part of the German messianic movement historically related to the *Drang nach Osten*. He described them as "sons of Germany," Pugachev radicals, German nation-alists, and ruthless exploiters of the magnificent Russian land and people. Among the almost endless list of alleged "crimes" by the colonists included fre-quent open battles with Russians for land and resources; creation of a state within a state with German courts, police, and administration; the seizure and control of the district zemstvo; Germanizing the city of Saratov to make it their cultural and political center; and attempting to gain economic control of the Lower Volga. Racism and Social Darwinism entered into the article when the author claimed that the "revived" German race sought primacy over all others, citing the Prussian military conquests of the last decade as evidence, and warned of the dangers of mixing races. The author reached the limits of credulity by suggesting a hypothetical but ludicrous conversation between the Russians of Kamyshin District and the Saratov provincial governor in which the Russians said: "You, a Russian prince, must save the Russians of Kamyshin District from German predominance: the Kamyshin Germans, according to the horrible theory of the godless Darwin, are devouring the Kamyshin Russians." M. ominously concluded by warning against further penetration of German influence lest the Russians of the Volga region end up like the Prussians (the native people of thirteenth-century Prussia exterminated by the crusading Teutonic Knights).[35]

Even the more progressive press, such as *Otechestvennye zapiski*, which had been in the vanguard of the 1860s reforms, succumbed to the chauvinistic and Pan-Slavic winds sweeping over Russia. In a baseless article provocatively entitled "What Is Healthy to the German Is Death to the Russian," the unidentified author seriously questioned the Volga Germans' patriotism and loyalty by alleging that they had begun to think about returning to Germany. Although this author did not attribute the difference between colonists and peasants in level of economic development to racial superiority, he made the foreign settlers appear to be ingrates by attributing their economic advantage to the beneficial privileges granted the original colonies; he failed to mention that the Russian peasantry had been retarded economically by serfdom and neglect. Having their privileges revoked, the colonists allegedly now sought to maintain their superiority over the neighboring Russians through education, seeing to it that "all receive a higher [*vysshee*] or at least a secondary [*srednee*] education."[36]

The harshest press campaign against the Volga Germans occurred between 1890 and 1894, as relations between Germany and Russia reached their nadir before the outbreak of World War I. Anti-German feeling swelled after the German foreign office announced that it would not renew the so-called reinsurance treaty of 1887, which called for neutrality if either power became engaged in war, and granted Russia certain privileges and promises in the Balkans and the Straits. George Kennan noted, "The anti-German tone of the Russian press was no longer confined to those papers that customarily pursued the Panslav-Germanophobic line: it pervaded the entire spectrum of Russian journalism."[37] Not restrained by the demands of truth and accuracy, the press attempted to arouse Russian society by declaiming that all Germans living in Russia posed a grave threat to national interests.

The flagship of the anti-German campaign and most relentless persecutor of the Volga Germans, printing numerous alarmist articles, was the journal *Russkii vestnik*, which forecast that if war erupted between Germany and Russia, there would be savage, bloody battles between the Russian and German settlers of the Lower Volga, so strong was their animus.[38] Founded by Mikhail Katkov, a prominent publicist who later became one of the most influential nongovernment figures in Russia during the reign of Alexander III, *Russkii vestnik* and the newspaper *Moskovskiia vedomosti* represented the progovernment reactionary vanguard of nationalist and conservative opinion. Their articles were quite damaging, because much of the Russian press applauded them; in addition, they were widely circulated and frequently failed to distinguish clearly the various German elements residing within the empire.[39] For an unenlightened society ignorant of the multitude of ethnic groups in the empire, such articles blurred to the point of invisibility the differences between the Baltic, Black Sea, and Volga Germans. This press-propagated guilt by association confused many Russians into believing that the Volga Germans were wealthy, large estate owners as well as impassioned German nationalists. It also made the colonists easy scapegoats to conceal government failures, particularly in the area of land reform, because articles suggested that everywhere colonists were acquiring land at the expense of the gentry and peasantry.

In 1893, A. Velitsyn wrote a tirade against the Volga Germans which he claimed was based on personal observations made during a trip to the colonies in 1890. Although there is no evidence that he ever visited the Volga settlements, his apparent firsthand observations lent the article great authority. Velitsyn filled the article with virulent invective against the Volga Germans. According to him they were all active members of a large German nationalist movement which included the Germans in southern Russia and the Baltic region; he asserted that the Volga pastors from Dorpat University were the chief masterminds of this nationalist conspiracy. The original colonists, he said, were the scum of Germany who predatorily destroyed the vast, lush Russian lands they occupied. The Volga Germans despised and callously exploited the Russian peasantry, squeezing every kopeck out of them by paying low wages and prices for peasant goods and services, and milking them of zemstvo taxes without any return of services. He concluded with a flourish of demagogy: "Moreover, having lived in Russia 125 years, feeding on its lifeblood and flourishing under its protection, they not only did not get accustomed to the country of their refuge, not only did not learn to love and consider it their motherland, but what is more there began to appear still more strongly and sharply their dislike of everything Russian."[40]

Unquestionably, these anti-German press campaigns permanently destroyed the pre-1870 image of the Volga Germans as hardworking, thrifty, loyal, and obedient, if somewhat privileged, Russian subjects. Since the Volga Germans had no public defenders to refute the baselessness of the outrageous charges hurled against them, the upper levels of Russian society came to regard them as German nationalists, anti-Russian, and therefore untrustworthy. Even the most respectable encyclopedia of Russian geography forsook its objectivity; the 1901 edition, whether maliciously or not, thus maligned the Volga Germans:

> Because of their character, the colonists live a completely isolated life and jealously protect their *nationality* [my emphasis], keeping themselves as much as possible from any contact with the life of the surrounding peoples, frequently reacting hostilely or defensively against all things Russian . . . . They have lived here over a century, not coming into contact with the life of the Russian people, not having put down roots in the country which received them, and they have not learned to love it or consider it their motherland. [Is it not curious that the last line of this article is practically a paraphrase of Velitsyn's article quoted above?][41]

Public acceptance of the government's planned expropriation of the Volga Germans in World War I, as well as their forcible evacuation from their homes in 1941, reveals how well public opinion had been molded by the pre–World War I press.

The situation of the Volga settlers after the 1880s is truly ironic, because in effect they became a people without a nation. The Russian government believed they were still Germans, while the recently established German Empire labeled them Russians. Rejected by the tsarist government which suspiciously viewed them as a pliant tool of the German Empire, they were never considered German by Bismarckian Germany. Few German nationals even knew there were ethnic Germans living on the Lower Volga. The pillorying of the Volga

Germans in the Russian press brought the settlers to the attention of the German diplomatic corps, which dutifully alerted Bismarck regarding their potential economic and political benefit to Germany. Bismarck, quite correctly, considered the Volga Germans to be Russians and Russian subjects, having long forgotten the eighteenth-century German lands they deserted. At Bismarck's directive, the German government washed its hands of the Volga Germans.[42] Interest in them would not appear until 1924 and the establishment of the autonomous Volga German republic.

Had the writers of such bombastic literature occasioned to visit the homes of their Volga victims, they would not once have seen a picture of Bismarck or the German emperor, a German flag, or German political publications—not even Edward Hartman's rabid anti-Russian *Zwei Jahrzehnte der deutschen Politik* (1889), which urged war against the Slavic East so that Germany could annex southern Russia. A frequent visitor to the Volga German settlements observed in 1894 that the colonies did indeed have a German appearance and character, but of a distant past—right out of the medieval Holy Roman Empire![43] There were no works of Fichte, Schleiermacher, Goethe, Schiller, or Herder on the shelf with the family Bible, and not even a copy of the Grimm folktales lying on the table. Mentioning the name of any of these great figures of German civilization would only have drawn blank stares, and those educated few who could understand these classics would have learned them in Russian! The only "Kaiser" they knew was Alexander or Nicholas, whose picture hung in the schoolhouse and sometimes adorned the walls of private cottages. Even the small minority who departed the Russian Empire were not stirred by German national feelings; they deliberately rejected their original motherland as a place of domicile and embarked for the New World. Instead of discussing politics and nationalism, when time permitted, the transplanted settlers in their typical peasant garb huddled to chat about family and colony happenings and to commiserate over land prices, crops, harvests, and livestock. In no way could one logically conclude that these common folk posed a threat to Russia.

Although religious prejudices never allowed for close social intercourse, at the regional and local levels Volga Germans continued to live amicably alongside their peasant neighbors. They were woefully ignorant of the hostile anti-German propaganda being directed against them from St. Petersburg and Moscow. While the nationalist press accused the colonists of shunning and exploiting the Russian peasantry, there is no evidence to support the contention that the Russian peasants despised their alien neighbor. In 1890, a Russian observer familiar with the Lower Volga scene emphatically stated that the Volga Germans and Russians "get along well," and that business ventures between them were not uncommon.[44] Even during the violent and turbulent rural unrest in the Lower Volga in the revolutionary years 1905 and 1917, manifested in illegal seizures of land and destruction of property, the angry peasants never vented their frustrations or directed their attacks against the lands and homes of the Volga Germans, but against the private estates of the region. The story was quite different, however, for the wealthy Black Sea German estate owners, who were targets of peasant outrage.

On closer examination, the oft-cited social distance or "differences," too frequently mistakenly identified as bad feelings or ill will, between colonists and peasants do not turn out to be that substantive. As Stephen Steinberg wrote: "If there is an iron law of ethnicity, it is that when ethnic groups are found in a hierarchy of power, wealth, and status, then conflict is inescapable. However, where there is social, economic, and political parity among the constituent groups, ethnic conflict, when it occurs, tends to be at a low level and rarely spills over into violence."[45] Between the Lower Volga colonists and peasants, there was no significant hierarchy of power, wealth, and status; and during the last years of tsarist rule, the differences that existed narrowed even more. While various factors, such as language and traditions, militated against the development of close social ties among the rural elements of the Lower Volga, religion— much more so than any feeling of economic or social inferiority—posed the biggest obstacle to social intercourse. Although economic differences existed, as they do in all societies, the fact remains that both colonists and peasants were small landholders who found it increasingly difficult to make a steady and adequate living after the 1860s. Both groups remained politically powerless and, after the 1860s reforms, found themselves subject to and governed by the same administration and laws.

Although Russian influence was stronger on the Volga Germans' material culture than on their language or customs, the differences in material culture, in my estimation, were seized upon by most outside observers to exaggerate the apparent disparate economic conditions between Russian peasants and Volga German settlers.[46] But in the observations of travelers and visitors to the Lower Volga, it is clear that what struck them most about the Volga Germans and Russian peasantry was the difference in life-styles, not economic differences.

Invariably, the colonies were described as being colorful, clean, quiet, and orderly, with modest but embellished whitewashed or painted houses and outbuildings. While devoting little attention to the physical description of the colonies, a 1913 geography textbook deemed it important to state, "The Germans live cleanly . . . ." The well-maintained, steepled church or prayer house added to the charm of the village. Observers admired the rectangular grid-patterned settlements, which the government had originally ordered, and marveled at the periodic sweeping of colony streets and fire protection measures (which unknown to them, were originally instituted and enforced by the Saratov Kontora authorities). Even in 1904, the daughter of Governor Stolypin fondly remembered them as the "accurate" Germans.[47]

The colonists themselves were depicted as humble folk—sober, industrious, thrifty, religious, family oriented, and law abiding. In 1894 a Russian observer wrote of the colonists: "All life consists of is the satisfaction of only the necessary human needs: not to be indebted to anyone else, to be fed, clothed, and shod, to live in cleanliness, and for all this to be thankful to the one and only God by praying to Him daily in the home and in church on the sabbath and holy days."[48] Another praised their civil obedience, stating that they would appeal to the highest authority for redress, yet they always treated authorities and courts with respect and heeded their decisions.[49] While these traits are admirable, none of them necessarily equate with wealth, education, progress, or material prosperity, for the same traits could be seen today in the Amish communities in America.

In contrast, the neighboring former state and Crown peasants were criticized for being intemperate, unruly, disheveled, lazy, spendthrift, irreligious, and not family oriented. Besotted, cigarette smoking, coarsely bearded Ivan Ivanovich suffered disparaging comparisons with the sober, pipe-smoking, clean-shaven Wilhelm Avgustovich.[50] Although the physical aspect of the Russian village varied enormously, as a rule all the houses were more dispersed, each with its own garden plot, and fronted and lined a single very broad dirt street, all but impassable in spring and autumn, when rain and melting snow transformed it into a bog. The smaller, drab Russian villages of the Lower Volga had no regular arrangement, and were noisy and dirty with unadorned houses that were unpainted and in disrepair. Dilapidated sheds attached to the houses added to the appearance of poverty and neglect. The irony remains that most bureaucrats disdained the Slavic peasants, attributing their backwardness to a naturally weak, flawed moral character rather than to generations of oppression, and failed or refused to recognize that the peasants were what they were because of centuries of serfdom and government neglect. Thus they remained ignorant, improvident, and hard-drinking because of the insurmountable conditions that had blocked their development into a sound farming class.

The Volga Germans, as is clearly evident in their oral tradition, came to fear and hate the nomadic Kirghiz and Kalmyk, and to dislike and distrust gypsies, who always seemingly absconded with colonists' property; yet their attitude toward the Russians was not one of animosity or jealousy, but more one of sympathy or pity for a people who seemed to be less fortunate. The absence of any genuine social intercourse between the foreign settlers and Russians evidently contributed greatly to Russian ignorance and misunderstanding of the Volga Germans and vice versa. Practically every Russian-Volga German meeting involved an economic transaction or an official function or service obligation. Yet trade is based on a degree of trust and sentiment, and the fact that we have no evidence of economic friction in the marketplace indicates that amicable relations existed. The seemingly trivial but innumerable market transactions, whether the Russian sale of dried fish, the colonists' house-to-house marketing of eggs, or the Russian peddlars' trade in miscellany, helped form a bond of trust between the two peoples. The itinerant Russian merchants who regularly visited the colonies were popularly called "Grandfather," certainly a term of endearment, not enmity. There were also numerous Russians, mainly craftsmen, coming to live part of every year in the colonies, another example of friendly relations between colonists and Slavs. The Volga Germans did have a saying—"Der Russ hat noch einen Russen in Busen"—which implied a certain social reserve toward Russians by emphasizing the strength of blood and kinship ties. A Russian writer in the 1890s commented favorably on how well the colonists and neighboring Russians got along, and a colonist fondly remembered New Year's Day as the time Russian children from a nearby village came to the colony singing and expressing wishes of good will.[51]

While it is difficult to determine what the peasants thought of the colonists, nothing indicates that they viewed them as a foe or with envy, and despite bureaucratic hopes to the contrary, they never adopted the colonists' life-style. This life-style contrasted so markedly with their own that the peasants often referred to their transplanted neighbors as dull, queer, and strange, a common peasant phrase being the "odd foreigners" (*chudaka nemtsa*).[52] Seasonal peasant laborers preferred working for a colonist, who paid better wages, supplied the best food, ate the same meal in the field with the hired hands, and worked alongside the seasonal workers. It was said a colonist would not ask a laborer to do anything the colonist would not do himself.

Simultaneously with the foregoing complex social developments, economic differences emerged that distinguished colonies and colonists, shattering the often-held perception of Volga German homogeneity and equality. However, inasmuch as material differences between colonists were often quite transient and fleeting, and never great, no rigid hierarchy evolved among the colonists to obstruct social contact and intercourse. A two-tier social division was plainly evident which consisted of those who were considered hard working, moral, reliable, upstanding, and able to pay their bills and debts, and those who were not. The poor were viewed as moral failures, for economic bounty naturally accrued to the morally deserving. Thus poverty conveyed a moral stigma as well. As one colonist remarked about conditions at the turn of the century, " . . . the poor families lived more to the lower end of the town. The richer ones lived more in the center part of the town."[53]

Because of the unique situation and changing conditions of each colony, it is difficult to examine family economic conditions with any degree of accuracy and specificity. The land-using and the landless elements of the colonies formed the two most distinct economic groups. During years of bad harvests and poverty, the poor tiller was forced to lease his land to a wealthier peasant for a period of several years, often until the next land redivision. To save themselves and their families from starvation, some peasants became indebted to wealthier peasants, such as was reported in 1886 and 1887: "At the present time the Germans, due to the existence of many landless and families without heads of households, find themselves in debt to private persons."[54] Others were forced to perform temporary, seasonal work outside the colonies. In many cases, the repayment of loans to township banks was in default, and the shortage of money meant that the only available loans were from private individuals at high rates of interest.

State loans to famine-stricken peasants also exacerbated relations between rich and poor, because the state granted loans only to individual peasants and prohibited the practice of dividing relief equally among communal members. Under the system of collective responsibility, however, the whole commune was obliged to repay the loans made to its members. According to

Table 2: Draft Animal Holdings as a Percentage of Households, 1888

Number of Working Animals	German	Russian and Ukrainian
None	18.1	20.6
1	12.6	16.3
2–3	23.4	26.3
3–4	12.6	11.4
5–10	24.1	17.1
10–20	7.8	5.9
Over 20	1.2	2.2

Richard Robbins: "This arrangement tended to penalize the hard-working, self-sufficient peasants and reward the shiftless. As a result, in time of need many communes declined to draw up the required agreement [*prigovor*], and hungry peasants went unaided . . . . More common still, the peasants continued the equal distribution of relief funds despite the threat of legal penalties."[55]

Livestock-ownership and landholding data provide the only statistical information on which to base some tentative speculations on the economic diversity in Volga German settlements. The available data do not enable us to compare villages, but simply all households of colonists residing within a district. For example, an 1888 zemstvo report that surveyed livestock holdings throughout Novouzensk District (the trans-Volga region where the greatest part of the Volga Germans lived, which was overwhelmingly agrarian and had little cottage industry) gave a breakdown on draft animals owned by German, Russian, and Ukrainian households (Table 2).

According to this report, people without draft animals were considered "indigent" and those with only one draft animal were in a precarious state described as "not well-off." Therefore, 30.7 percent of Volga German households and 36.9 percent of the Slavic households did not have enough draft animals to plow and harvest their allotments, and presumably most of their male members worked as farm laborers. The report asserted that only those households with four or more draft animals could be considered solidly established and economically sound (45.7 percent of the Volga German group and 36.6 percent of the Slavic group); these families hired the village poor for seasonal and day labor.[56]

Table 3: Landholding Patterns in Novouzensk District, 1908

Category	Colonists	State Peasants	Serfs	Total
Small land users[1]				
Households	2,734	6,761	1,430	–
Dessiatinas per household	18.7	16.8	11.4	–
Percentage of total	11.8	20.3	96.0	21.5
Average land users[2]				
Households	13,864	12,743	27	–
Dessiatinas per household	25.4	25.1	25.9	–
Percentage of total	60.2	38.2	1.8	44.7
Large land users[3]				
Households	6,450	13,868	32	–
Dessiatinas per household	39.2	41.6	36.3	–
Percentage of total	28.0	41.5	2.2	33.8

[1] 1–20 dessiatinas per household.
[2] 20–30 dessiatinas per household.
[3] More than 30 dessiatinas per household.

Table 4: German Landholding Patterns in Novouzensk District, 1908

Dessiatinas	Households	Percentage of Households
15–20	2,734	11.8
20–25	6,735	29.0
25–30	7,129	31.0
30–40	5,009	21.7
40–50	634	3.0
50–100	872	4.0

Two sets of statistics gathered in 1908 on landholding patterns in the same district provide a rough comparison of landholding among the three dominant farming groups (former colonists, former state peasants, and former serfs) and a more detailed breakdown of German land users (Tables 3 and 4). In Novouzensk District, any peasant household allotment of less than twenty dessiatinas was called a "famine ration." Former state peasants were the largest landholders in the district, the former colonists were mainly modest landholders, and ex-serfs lived near the starvation level with their "famine rations." Similarly, 40.8 percent of all German households lived at a minimum level of subsistence, with allotments of between fifteen and twenty-five dessi-atinas. It must be stressed that the Germans had to support much larger families on their modest plots; the average size of German families was 9.5, compared with 6.5 for former state peasants and 6.1 for former serfs.[57]

Based on this livestock-ownership and landholding data, the Volga Germans can be distributed into the usual three peasant categories. It becomes evident that between one-fifth and one-third of all Volga German households could be classified as poor, with a very bleak future. Without sufficient animal power to plow their meager allotments, their harvests were small and the yield low; many of them formed a landless, rural proletariat subsisting through the sale of their labor. The predominant group, consisting of about 60 percent of all former colonists' households, was the so-called middle peasantry, with sufficient draft animal power and crops to live comfortably unless visited by consecutive poor harvests or natural disasters. Approximately 7 percent were very prosperous families or "kulaks," large-scale farmers possessing at least ten draft animals and farming between 108 and 270 acres (40 to 100 dessiatinas).

Comparable socioeconomic stratification in the mountain-side colonies based on land and livestock holdings existed, but this data must be placed in context by noting the presence of a well-developed cottage industry. Although the overwhelming preponderance of the settlers could still be classified as manual laborers, a considerable number had shifted from field work to cottage industry, most of them performing the backbreaking work of weavers. Occupational lines strikingly reflected the peculiar economic spectrum of the Saratov settlements; farmers, weavers, dyers, machinists, ironmongers, carpenters, joiners, pipe makers, and bricklayers represented the rural artisans. In the largest colonies, observers noted the bifurcation of residents into "peasant toilers" and "manufacturers and traders," with the former wielding political power but the latter in the vanguard of social reform as vociferous advocates of education, particularly Russian language instruction in the schools. Many of these settlements had large numbers of textile workers, earning their livelihood from nonagrarian pursuits, and were managed by a small group of merchants and entrepreneurs. In 1885, the big colony of Norka had over half of all adult males working in nonfarming trades and crafts.[58]

In most settlements, at least a few "rich settlers" had accumulated their fortunes either from grain trading, land investing, or textile manufacture. They lived in the impressive brick or stone homes in the center of the settlement, usually near the church. Having surplus capital, they served as local moneylenders, a role that earned them considerable public disapprobation because of the high interest they charged, although their philanthropy to the local community could be noted, especially in contributions to churches and schools. Attentive to business matters, they usually considered themselves too busy to engage in the routine day-to-day affairs of the settlement, yet in times of crisis, such as a famine, local officials usually called upon these "big guns" to act as weighty intercessors with the provincial bureaucracy.[59]

Two separate societal processes were at work in the Volga colonies in the postreform period. One was the process of transmission of culture from one group to another, in this case Russian culture to the Volga Germans. The colonies, segregated and isolated but never completely closed, experienced continuous and generally friendly contact with the immediate outside world, especially as the Lower Volga rapidly filled with Slavic peoples. As the duration and intensity of that contact increased, so did social intercourse and cultural diffusion. Cultural diffusion transmitted words, practices, and attitudes from one people to another, facilitating the development of a new hybrid language and tradition. Although the government had originally segregated the Volga colonies physically and administratively, the boundaries were not impenetrable. Sweeping economic developments (such as regional and long-distance trade, seasonal labor, urbanization, and socioeconomic stratification), as well as the numerous post-1860s integrationist government policies (such as military service, secular education, administrative integration of the colonies, and creation of zemstvos), thrust an alien world into Volga society and removed many of the Volga Germans from the village and introduced them to new ways of doing things, new ideas, and new products. Knowledge of the larger world grew with more frequent mail service; one of the most popular government services was weekly mail to the larger colonies, which afforded communication with distant relatives as well as the opportunity to gather at the post office and gossip with other villagers.

Yet along with this cultural diffusion, albeit proceeding slowly, we see the emergence of a Volga German ethnicity. They identified as a group or people conterminous with a given rural land area and common past, shared a culture with a common set of beliefs and values, and came from a common racial stock which obliterated physical types. Although the details had been distorted or forgotten, all could remember their special calling as homesteaders on the Russian frontier. *Wolgaheimat* had become their new spiritual homeland, which was a physical part of the Russian fatherland, and they sometimes were simply referred to as the *Volgauers*. Religion still stirred their passions, abetting intolerance and dividing society, yet it instilled endogamy and a common core of Latin Christian belief. Although for the Volga Germans the tenuous ties with their ancestral past had grown very weak and their parochialism crumbled as the outside world rushed in on them, religion served to strengthen their premodern, perhaps even medieval, traditional values, which still formed the basis of their ethics. The evolution of *Kolonistendeutsch*, with its peculiar lexicon and pronunciation patterns, contributed to the feeling of a common peoplehood or ethnicity. The government's repressive efforts to limit the use and study of their language further stirred ethnic feeling. Religious practices, holidays, songs, musical tastes, and folk recreational patterns distinguished them from their neighbors. Therefore, religious feelings, not national stirrings, most strongly fueled mutual suspicion, intolerance, and aloofness among the peasant communities of the Lower Volga. Clearly, the Volga Germans were a people in transition, having long ago left the medieval Western world from whence they came, but having barely entered into the culture of the land they now called home. They were increasingly torn by three conflicting loyalties: faith and devotion to their church as Protestant and Catholic Christians, duty and service to the state as subjects of Russia, and recognition of and respect for their nascent ethnic personality.

Chapter Four

Tillers of the Soil

The Volga Germans, a people of the land, cherished the soil like craftsmen treasure their tools. A field, some seed, draft animals harnessed to a plow, and a scythe were the essential instruments of the Volga German settler, who remained a traditional peasant grain tiller under Romanov rule. A Ministry of State Domains report on the economy of the Volga colonies in 1855 could just as well have been written and issued in 1917:

> It is clear that here fields predominate over meadows and pastures; as a result of this the chief occupation of the local colonists is agriculture, and livestock raising does not form a significant part of their economy. Agriculture itself is limited primarily to tillage, the cultivation of grains, and only a few colonies in Samara Province cultivate tobacco, although recently a few have attempted to grow tobacco in Saratov Province, and only two colonies in Saratov Province grow sugar beets; but these branches of agriculture, like crafts and manufacturing, are the exception; the primary occupation of the local population consists of tillage.[1]

Colonists measured time and remembered the past in terms of harvests, with temporal benchmarks registered not by decades but by the intervals between bounteous harvests and crop disasters.

The adherence to traditional, outdated farming practices remained a hallmark of Volga German life. Although post-1860 events revolutionized the colonies in many often unforeseen ways, the colonists continued to practice in only a slightly modified form the primitive and backward farming methods brought from the West, for the scientific agricultural concepts and techniques initiated by Arthur Young in England did not spread to Germany until the nineteenth century. Arriving in a markedly different environment with little but the clothes on their backs, the colonists by necessity slowly adapted their native methods and equipment, frequently borrowing ideas and practices from noncolonist settlers to accommodate Lower Volga physical conditions. Several authors at various times commented on the intractability of the colonists. Describing the situation in 1865, a colony village elder resignedly admitted the sorry state of farming: "Our people farm the way they learned from their fathers because they don't know anything better." Referring to conditions in the 1890s, another colonist declared, "The development of agricultural techniques in the colonies went along at the same snail-paced tempo as that of the enserfed Russian village." Writing in 1906 to urge the abolition of communal landholding and strip farming, a colonist encountered the age-old retort of the Volga Germans when asked to change: "Our forefathers have so farmed and so we will farm to earn our daily bread; we don't need to change. It is all God's blessing; if our Heavenly Father doesn't will it to be, then all is in vain." On the eve of World War I, a zemstvo agronomist once more echoed the common refrain: "They [the colonists] are so immersed in the vestiges of their past, that their well-being can only be raised by a strong and consistent pressure directed at replacing old and outdated agricultural methods with new ones which correspond to present conditions."[2]

Although the system of communal landholding contributed to the apparent uniformity of the colonists' farming, natural resources such as soil type and quantity of cultivable land generally determined or conditioned the cultivation methods and crops of the farmers, which came to differentiate the colonies themselves. The diversity found among the colonies, particularly between those on the trans-Volga steppe and those in Saratov Province, was primarily a result of the peculiar physical factors each experienced. Thus, as the zemstvo reported in 1890: "Field cultivation in Kamyshin District, while noted in general for its primitive nature, is not noted in any way for differences between the two chief national groups who settled the district—Russians and Germans. Differences in field cultivation depend clearly on soil conditions, the system of land use, farm implements and so forth, and not on the ethnic composition of the population."[3] Consequently, both peasants and colonists used a wood plow (*sokha*) in the southern part of Saratov Province, not because they were more backward but because draft animals could not pull the heavier iron plow on the hilly, rocky, clay-baked terrain; this partly explains why the Volga German iron plow industry naturally began in the northern colonies of Saratov Province, which had heavy but not as hard soils.

For most of the nineteenth century, the colonists and peasants of the Lower Volga clung to a backward, extensive cultivation, instead of devoting their labor and resources to a small bit of land; they practiced a most primitive and wasteful fallow farming method, often called the *perelozhnaia* or *zalezhnaia* system, which lacked the features of any system but particularly of any sensible crop rotation. Yielding abundant harvests with very little effort, virgin fields were sown with the same crop until exhausted, and then left as fallow pasture or hayfield for long periods to restore soil fertility. With the rapid population expansion and the influx of new settlers into the region, which created greater demands on land, the fallow periods became shorter and shorter, resulting in the progressive exhaustion of the soil, the growth of poorer quality wheat, and the decline of the harvests. By the last two decades of the century, the best types of wheat could no longer be grown on these once-rich soils.

Until the last two decades of the century, when colonies began to adopt a three-field system with regular crop rotation, there was no systematic and uniform field system within the colonies. Until then, the colonies divided their lands on the basis of soil quality, distance from the colony, and other factors; this resulted in a diverse, mazelike, multifield system of cultivation with some colonies having as few as three fields and others having over thirty fields, from which individual strips were allotted to each household.

In the decade after 1874, the redivision and apportionment of colony lands on the basis of the number of male colonists, discussed in the next chapter, radically altered the configuration of colony fields and prevented rational field use. In most colonies, a radical land redivision had not been completed in almost twenty years (since the 1858 census); during that time, the colonies had experienced phenomenal population growth. A deleterious effect of the new redivisions was to worsen strip farming in the colonies. To ensure a fair and acceptable redivision, fields had to be more punctiliously surveyed and demarcated into narrower strips. For example, in 1858 Golyi Karamysh (Balzer) had only 1,860 males or revision souls; in 1880, when it implemented the new allocation, its male population had almost doubled to 3,465, yet the amount of available land remained the same. Now, instead of each field having at least

1,860 strips, it had to be divided into at least 3,465 strips. The settlement of Ust' Kulalinka (Galka) had seven large cultivable areas which were broken up into thirty-one smaller fields. Each field had to be subdivided into strips in multiples of 1,560, the number of males entitled to an allotment.[4] Each male was entitled to at least one strip from each of the thirty-one fields, and the distance between the two farthest fields was nineteen miles! In the most land-pressed older settlements, a household might plow ten to fifteen strips six to eight feet wide and two to four miles long in each field.

Except for the more recently founded daughter colonies, few villages had compact holdings; thus scattered fields often lay considerable distances from the colony, in some cases 20 to 30 miles. The colonies of Nikolaevsk District, squeezed closely together along the Volga, suffered greatly from these long distances to fields. The *average* distance of the fields from the homesteads in *all* the colonies was 32.3 versts (21 miles). Pastures for the livestock lay some 20 versts (13 miles) away, understandably harmful to an efficient form of agriculture. The original colonies in Saratov Province also suffered from widely dispersed and broken holdings, the result of tardy as well as deficient land surveys and encroachment, so that all had at least one land section over 7 miles from the settlement. Popovka (Brennig) had four sections, two of which lay 9 to 12 miles from the village; Ust' Griaznukha (Goebel) had five sections, three of which lay 9 to 11 miles from the village center.[5] Questions of access rights frequently caused tensions and exacerbated relations with neighboring settlements. Until the 1840s land crunch, some of the colonies leased these inconveniently located fields to settlements nearer to them, rather than attempt to farm them.

As in eighteenth-century England and other countries of Western Europe, where the agricultural revolution was largely promoted by private enterprise on gentry lands, so it was in Russia. The open-field system of scattered strips seriously impeded the introduction of any advanced pattern or system of cultivation. Therefore, the introduction and implementation of the superior three-field system with annual crop rotation in the Lower Volga did not originate with the colonists.[6] First introduced on the gentry estates, the three-field system of crop rotation was then adopted by former state peasants with badly depleted soils in the more thickly settled northern part of Saratov Province, in order to prevent the further deterioration of the land; from there the system gradually spread southward. While the state peasants quickly divided their lands into three large fields of roughly similar size and quality, the colonists were much more reluctant to adopt a radical and swift conversion to a three-field system, often trying to impose a "system" on the existing multifield land division before they resorted to a true three-field configuration. The colonists also did not always rigorously adhere to the crop-rotation system. While the most frequently followed rotation was winter rye, spring wheat, and fallow, it was not uncommon, because of the higher wheat prices, that spring wheat was substituted for rye, so that a field had two consecutive plantings of wheat. Thus, during the 1880s, the northernmost colonies of Saratov Province and those of Nikolaevsk District in Samara Province, earliest settled and overpopulated, became the first colonies to develop a rational field and crop system for the improvement of grain farming. The colonists, however, showed no great haste in adopting scientific farming. By 1900, only twenty-seven of the fifty-seven Saratov colonies had instituted a three-field system; in Samara Province, only the older colonies bordering the Volga had made the conversion, and only about half of the daughter colonies had made the change by 1914. Writing in 1899, a zemstvo agronomist reported, "The three-field system used by the German colonists in essence is no different from the three-field system of the neighboring Russian settlements."[7]

Although the field systems of the peasants and colonists did not notably differ, as the century progressed the colonists developed a technical superiority over the peasants in the use of agricultural machinery. Complex machinery, such as reapers and threshers, was not extensively used in the colonies because of the availability and cheapness of manual labor. Thus we are not discussing complex and expensive machinery, but simple technical changes which when introduced made farming easier, more efficient, and more profitable: a durable iron plow, the scythe, the winnowing machine, and other simple devices made by the tinkerer rather than the inventor. The simple Russian wood hook plow, originally used by the colonists, gradually disappeared from Volga German fields, although not entirely from Russian villages. The colonists also produced and widely used a scythe with rakes and hooks, which was technically more efficient and superior to the backbreaking and laborious peasant sickle. The basic, no-frills Volga German manufactured winnower separated a cleaner wheat, which brought a higher price on the grain market. As is discussed in Chapter 6, the Volga colonists became widely known for their skills in the innovation and manufacture of simple farm implements. These generalizations should not be drawn too tightly, however, because state peasants adopted many of these implements, but the colonists were clearly technically superior to the former serfs in the use of farm implements.

The Volga colonists' field work also was not any better than that of the neighboring Russian peasants, as indicated by a zemstvo survey of 1895, which stated, "Manuring is not done anywhere in the German settlements and the field work is not any better than in the Russian settlements."[8] The colonists had departed Western Europe before many of the great agricultural innovations of the eighteenth century had gained common acceptance, and there had been no continuing links with the homeland. The only smallholders singled out for exemplary field work were the approximately 1,000 Mennonites settled in nine colonies in Samara Province, who carefully plowed and harrowed their lands, achieving yields in the 1880s double those of neighboring Volga colonies and peasant villages. A writer quite familiar with the Lower Volga region called the Mennonite colonies "an oasis in the desert," strikingly contrasting them with the "unattractive and unimpressive Russian settlements and German colonies."[9]

Because of the Lower Volga's short growing season and the colonists' dedication to grain farming, summers in the colonies were hard. While the foreign colonies in the southern Ukraine and Bessarabia could begin their spring planting between mid-February and mid-March, the Volga colonists could not venture to their fields until late March at the earliest. Similarly, fall planting in the Lower Volga had to be done in August, whereas it could be delayed until mid-September in the regions mentioned above.[10] Planting, whether wheat in the spring or rye in the fall, was the most arduous and frantic field task, requiring a total village and family effort, which usually meant spending entire weeks in the fields away from the village. The only family members left at home were those unable to work—the elderly and usually children under ten. The evening before departing for the fields, the community gathered in the open to offer public prayers for the planting. Villagers liked to leave together early on a Monday morning in order to make camp before nightfall. Food, and sometimes water, had to be carted to the fields—a simple diet of wheat kasha, bread, and potatoes. If any sausage or meat was left over from winter, which was rare, it might be taken along. Those farming in the treeless steppe had to cook over fires fueled by dried manure and plants. This necessitated bringing children along to be fuel bearers. Until the completion of the planting the settlers went home every Saturday afternoon for Sunday religious services, and returned to the fields Sunday evening.

Soil preparation and planting were haphazard and superficial. The iron plow and harrow were the only machinery used, yet they constituted a technical superiority that some Russian peasants did not enjoy. Most colonists lacked the resources, chiefly animal power, to prepare the soil carefully; the devastation and sale of livestock herds during famine years brought unmitigated disaster to the peasantry. In fact, until the onset of severe land shortages, the biggest fault in tillage was the effort to cultivate too much land with too few resources. This resulted in shallowly plowed, clump-filled, and weed-infested fields. Deep plowing was extremely time consuming and exhausted the livestock, and anyway age-old tradition dictated that deep plowing was not only unimportant but harmful and unnatural. The land-short northern colonies in Kamyshin District prepared their lands better, either plowing their richer soil with a heavy iron plow or harrowing before planting, and they practiced seed selection. The colonies in the southern half of the district and in the steppe Novouzensk District, with larger but less fertile allotments (clayey with little humus), might only harrow unsorted seeds with no preliminary soil preparation. The clayey southern region of Kamyshin District was called *Ochsengrund*, or "oxen soil," because, unless one just scratched the surface with a stick plow, the hardened earth required four teams of oxen to draw an iron plow through it whereas in other parts of the district plowing could be done with a team of horses.[11] Hand broadcasting the seed resulted in uneven distribution, which not even a harrowing could correct. Seed drills and applicators did not come into use until just before World War I. The settlers often did not regularly rotate their crops in any beneficial manner, sometimes leaving no fallow areas and planting the same crop on a field in consecutive years. Likewise, no efforts were made to improve the land, such as by fertilizing and replowing after the harvest to increase water absorbency and retention, and weeding was rare.

Haying and gardening occurred between field crop planting and harvesting, but again there were differences between regions. In Saratov Province, haymaking began in early July. On the steppe of Samara Province, haying could not begin until mid-August in the midst of field harvesting, because low-lying meadow grasses did not begin to grow until late June when the waters finally receded on the Volga floodplain. Since neither side of the Volga supplied enough hay to feed livestock through the winter, colonists had to rent additional meadows or purchase hay from neighbors and limit the size of herds.

The typical spring planting spectacle in the colonies was repeated in the summer during the harvesting, with the village again becoming deserted. Harvesting extended well into the fall and often right up to the first frost (thereby making it impossible for the colonists to replow their lands). The cut wheat was bound in sheaves and formed in stacks on the threshing floor. Threshing had changed very little since the founding of the colonies. It was done in the fields by horses, sometimes drawing a wagon, but most commonly a stone or wooden-pronged roller, led in a circle around a prepared threshing floor. The sifting of chaff from the grain was done by hand, using the wind. The introduction of the winnowing machine in the 1860s enabled the colonists to further clean the threshed grain; this process was normally begun in the fields but completed in the colony. The threshed grain was transported to the village and stored in village-constructed wooden granaries and individual householders' sheds; but other than that needed to feed the livestock, most of the straw had to be left in the fields, particularly if it was a distant field and an early winter. Except for what was milled locally for home consumption, most of the wheat was sold to grain merchants.

The post-1860 Volga German harvest record was bleak, unfortunately never matching the predictability and regularity of field work. Generally speaking, erratic, feast-or-famine harvests became commonplace, with shortfalls more than twice as likely to occur than surpluses. This contrasted strikingly with the frequent, often consecutive bumper crops of the first five decades of the century. For example, in the 1850s the fortuitous recurrence of beneficent natural conditions produced bounteous harvests, enabling the Volga colonies to accumulate grain and financial reserves. By the mid-1860s, economic conditions had deteriorated in the colonies to the point where crop failures posed a serious problem. A series of poor harvests between 1862 and 1867, combined with the extraordinary expenditures required to resettle the excess population in the trans-Volga steppe, which the tsarist Treasury refused to fund, literally wiped out the prosperity of the 1850s and depleted grain reserves. The heavy costs of resettlement drained the original colonies' treasuries so much that by 1866 they had accumulated a debt of 700,000 rubles. A government official aptly summed up the bleak situation: "The crop failures of the preceding years . . . consumed all the money and grain reserves of the communities, putting the majority of them in a very critical, almost hopeless situation."[12] He predicted a long and difficult recovery for the colonies.

The 1870s began auspiciously with a couple of good harvests, yet the end of the decade witnessed the first famine in the colonies since their founding. For three consecutive years, severe drought and scorching summer temperatures seriously crippled agriculture in Kamyshin and Novouzensk districts. Hunger stalked the colonies in 1879 and 1880. As a result of these crop failures, the Lutheran Church in Saratov opened free soup kitchens for needy colonists. Mounting financial obligations and exhausted grain reserves compelled households to sell livestock, equipment, and even seed grain, causing an amazing 54 percent decrease in the area sown in the fall of 1880.[13] This massive liquidation created an extraordinary indebtedness, as communes and individual farmers attempted to pay off their losses and resume farming by borrowing from various institutions and private individuals at exorbitant interest rates. The 1879–80 hunger shocked and sapped the colonists, but later seemed only a fleeting, minor disaster compared with the series of calamities that struck during the next two decades.

The 1889–92 period was the most dreadful experienced in the Volga German settlements since their founding. In 1891, an appalling famine leading to mass starvation struck Russia, the worst in the history of the empire. Crops failed in twenty-two provinces, with the Lower Volga provinces enduring the greatest adversity. The misery and unbelievable hardship resulting from an almost total crop failure were so debilitating because there had been several previous bad harvests; the last good harvest in the colonies was in 1886. While the bountiful harvest of 1886 had sometimes yielded twenty bushels an acre, in 1891 it took fifteen acres to yield one bushel.[14] The depression and acute deterioration of grain farming in the colonies during the 1880s is clearly indicated by the increasingly alarming reports from the Volga grain market ports between Kamyshin and Samara which received Volga German grain. Between 1883 and 1891, grain deliveries showed a steady decline, so that by 1890 the grain sold at these ports amounted to only half of that delivered in 1883—23 million puds compared with 48 million puds.[15] This period posed the greatest crisis and challenge to the Volga Germans, and was reminiscent of the 1760s trials and tribulations of their forefathers who struggled to survive on the harsh frontier, and of the Old Testament story of the seven famine years in Egypt.

Unfortunately, there was no Joseph in the colonies to order the colonists to fill their granaries during the good years, a role that the now defunct Saratov Kontora had forcefully played.[16]

The merciless famine of 1891 forced colonists to resort to every measure simply to survive. Settlers consumed anything edible, including roots found along streams and ponds; and, although unverified, rumors of cannibalism were rife in the Lower Volga.[17] Thousands had to beg and even steal food. Many families moved together into one house to save fuel, while numerous others abandoned their homesteads and fled to other parts of the empire, some tragically. For example, many Basle households hastily sold all their belongings for a pittance to move to the Far East Amur region. However, the township elder, backed by the police authorities, refused them permission to leave, so that the "situation of these poor folk" was "absolutely horrible."[18] Thatched-roof houses had their roofs stripped and fed to livestock, yet one-third of the horses died, and almost all the rest had to be sold. Even the wealthiest colonists could not obtain fodder for their livestock, and slaughtered them instead. Not until the 1894 bumper harvest were the colonists able to make much recovery from the horror of 1891, yet, as an article from the conservative St. Petersburg newspaper *Novoe vremia* clearly indicated, the region had not fully recuperated when disaster struck again: "They had suffered during the famine of 1891–1892. The years 1893–1896 had good harvests, but grain prices were low and the peasants had not paid their debts contracted during the last famine, and therefore could not remedy their past troubles. In 1897, the harvest of spring crops was again very bad; finally, this year there is a very bad harvest of cereals and no fodder."[19] The two general Lower Volga crop failures in 1897 and 1898, as indicated in this quotation, effectively derailed a weak economic recovery and plunged the colonies into another cycle of debt and despair.

A Zoloturn colonist described what seemed to be a recurring nightmare: "The people have lived through one of the worst winters since 1891. Grain prices are very high, there is no work and no credit even from wealthy individuals. One-fourth of the households are without any draft animals."[20] An embittered Basle colonist reported pessimistically to the government: "The people are so impoverished that it will take 4–5 good harvest years to restore them to the position they were in before 1898." The futility and frustration of eking out a living on their godforsaken lands was also reflected in a Schaffhausen comment: "The results of the last year on the population are such, that many residents expect the government to permit them to resettle to other, unsettled parts of Russia." Similar reports circulated from all parts of the region, including Kamyshin District, where colonists inundated the zemstvo with requests for grain.

Although the general farming situation in Russia appears to have improved significantly between 1900 and 1914—the net harvest of all grains increased by an impressive 37 percent and grain exports rose by 55 percent, stimulated in part by an improved international market and higher grain prices—several factors attenuated the beneficial implications for the peasantry, thereby yielding most of the benefits to large-scale private landowners. Peasant grain yields still were among the lowest in Russia and Europe, and peasant households marketed a much smaller share of their harvests. Rising wheat prices, which on the eve of the war averaged 109 kopecks a pud and were 30 kopecks higher than those for rye, occasionally improved the profit margins of Volga wheat growers when nature cooperated. But nature's cooperation was increasingly rare as famine continued to wreck budgets and devastate peasant households. Other factors also clouded the peasant horizon. The population increase outran the growth of productivity; estimates of the 1914 population of European Russia indicated an increase of 37 percent since the census of 1897. And spiraling land prices and rents made it prohibitively expensive to expand crop cultivation; in European Russia, land prices rose by about 50 percent and lease rents skyrocketed 70 percent between 1900 and 1914.[21]

A succession of two natural catastrophes, compounded by revolutionary upheaval, brought on the last but very grave prewar agrarian crisis in the Volga colonies. According to zemstvo reports, the colossal 1905 and 1906 crop failures rivaled the disaster of 1891, far surpassing in magnitude the shortfalls of 1897 and 1898. Scant spring rainfall followed by dry, unusually hot summers parched young plants both years. In the trans-Volga colonies soil exhaustion contributed to crop destruction: "Since that year [1905] agriculture began to decline because of a series of crop failures. The land became soft from being plowed too often; it became badly pulverized and, therefore, less resistant to the arid winds, at the very time that drought and dry winds increased. For all these reasons partial and general crop failures increased all over the district [Novouzensk]."[22]

For two consecutive years, zemstvo statisticians heard nothing but "eine vollkommene Missernte" from the colonists, who reported yields closely approximating those of 1891. Both years' yields amounted at best to no more than one-half of an average harvest, and at worst only one-fifth. The zemstvos discovered that most colonies had already consumed their meager grain gleanings by mid-November when hordes of peasants turned to them for grain loans from their inadequate reserves.[23] Widespread famine conditions forced colony officials to appeal to the zemstvos, which opened soup kitchens in several colonies. Shortages of grain caused their prices to skyrocket by as much as 60 percent. Fodder shortages resulted in soaring costs; straw and hay prices quadrupled. Livestock had to be sold or slaughtered, flooding the market and causing prices to plummet. In Kamyshin District between April and October 1905, livestock prices declined 40 to 60 percent. Indebtedness grew, undermining the already fragile economic position of households, particularly the poorer ones. Poorer households had to lease out part of their allotments to pay off obligations or because they had inadequate seed and livestock. Likewise, meager harvests required no additional hired help, leading to unemployment among local day laborers and seasonal migrant workers. Earnings also dropped in all nonfarm supplemental work, but the zemstvo reporters noted that the decline was not as great in the Volga German sarpinka weaving industry because it sold on the larger national market, not just locally and regionally.

The prewar years witnessed no remarkable recovery in colony agriculture, and confirmed the risky nature of farming in the Lower Volga, as evidenced by the year-to-year wild fluctuations in harvests, a long-held dubious distinction of the region. Not only was the Lower Volga the driest region of European Russia with the lowest yields, but it also experienced the greatest variations in yearly crop yields, averaging 28 percent for the period between 1895 and 1912.[24] Although its climatic conditions most closely resembled those of Italy and the Danubian countries, yields were less than half the yields of those regions. Lower Volga peasant yields of spring wheat averaged 7.5 bushels per acre for the period 1883–1913, compared with yields of 18 bushels in Italy and Hungary. In the United States, farmers harvested 30 to 40 bushels an acre. While primitive methods prevailed in the Lower Volga and contributed to such low yields, low and invariable rainfall was the chief foe of peasants and colonists. One year there would be famine, the next a bounteous harvest. With the exception of two bumper harvests in 1909 and 1913, all other wheat harvests—the chief grain—yielded below average returns in the colonies, forcing the consumption of the meager economic resources households had laboriously accumulated.

Table 5: Annual Wheat Yields: Kamyshin District

Year	Yield (puds per dessiatina)
1907	18.4
1908	13
1909	47
1910	21.1
1911	7.5
1912	8.5
1913	55
1914	17

The 1911 and 1912 harvests were so poor that even prosperous colonies reported that colonists had only potatoes to eat. A year-by-year comparison of wheat yields for Kamyshin District (Table 5) shows that all but two fell below the 1900–1914 average of 21.9 puds per dessiatina.[25]

Nature did not cooperate to make the colonists' last years under tsarist rule easy or productive. Fear and uncertainty gripped the colonists—the fear and uncertainty of getting the household back on its feet after the forcible sale of draft animals, equipment, and seed grain; and the fear too of not finding temporary work to sustain the household until the next harvest. A 1909 zemstvo report succinctly summarized the gloomy situation in the Lower Volga: "The peasantry believes more in crop failures than in harvests."[26]

Generalizations about Volga German agriculture present a neat and coherent picture, but they mask striking regional differences that developed within agriculture and farming in the post-1860 period between the mountain- and meadow-side colonies, as well as notable intraprovince distinctions between the older and newer colonies. In the following two sections of this chapter, it will be helpful to detail some of the more marked differences in order to emphasize the considerable heterogeneity.

The Diversity of Saratov Agriculture

Although the colonies in Saratov Province devoted their agricultural efforts to cereal cultivation, chiefly wheat and rye, they also maintained a more diverse, balanced farm economy and never became as dependent on one grain crop as their compatriots did in Samara Province. While wheat remained their chief crop, normally comprising about 45 percent of sown area in the pre–World War I period, they maintained a mixed grain economy, with 25 percent of the sown area in rye and another 5 percent in oats.[27] Market prices and deteriorating soil conditions fostered a two-grain economy; per acre yields of rye and wheat were almost identical, and depleted soils no longer produced top quality wheat that commanded the highest prices. Therefore, although in Saratov Province wheat generally returned a larger profit, the wheat-rye price differential was not so great as on the meadow side, which still yielded superior grade wheats.

After 1850, barley, millet, and sunflowers became important but secondary cash crops. Although grown in all colonies, sunflowers became the specialty of the three colonies in Iagodno-Poliana township, which had begun growing them at midcentury; one-sixth of the land was blooming with sunflowers by the end of the century.[28] Valued for their total utility, sunflowers were marketed in Saratov, where the seeds were processed into a cheap but edible oil. The mash left after oil refining was an excellent fodder; the stem of the plant was a good source of potash; and the husks could be used as fuel, which was in short supply. The mixed cereal farming of the Saratov Province Volga Germans made them less susceptible to famine conditions, for rarely did all crops fail. The only exception was Ilovlinskaia township, which adopted a cropping pattern similar to the meadow-side colonies, becoming almost totally dependent on single-grain cultivation and therefore more subject to famines.

Although not intended for the marketplace because of the low price they brought, numerous noncereal crops were also grown by the mountain-side colonies, usually on garden plots but frequently in fields. These crops proved to be highly beneficial to the health and well-being of the colonists. Grown in the largest quantities, the ubiquitous yet much maligned potato became the staple of the colonists' diet, but was rarely sold as a commercial crop, except by a few colonies near the city of Saratov, whose residents provided a steady demand. Although they had not been grown in any sizable amount in Saratov Province until the 1840s, when the government vigorously promoted them, and despite initial, stiff peasant resistance, potatoes quickly became a mainstay in all Lower Volga peasant plots.[29] The potato was also widely used as livestock fodder. Fruits from small orchards, chiefly apples and cherries, were also consumed rather than marketed. The greatest fruit producers in the area were Russian settlements, not the colonies, but the large colonies were excellent markets for Russian produce. Melons and pumpkins were raised as field crops; the former was a source of additional income, while the latter was used as an autumn fodder product. Watermelons, though widely cultivated and one of the lowest priced foods in the area, produced a strong sweet syrup (*Latwerge*), which was used as a popular sugar substitute in the Lower Volga region. Sugar beets, which had been a small commercial crop grown in seven colonies until the 1850s, when the sugar mill operated by Count Bobrinskii closed, were boiled and pressed to provide a home sweetener.[30] The fruits and vegetables mentioned above were not grown in large amounts on the steppe side, with the exception of some of the meadow colonies along the banks of the Volga.

The Saratov settlements also enjoyed more favorable conditions to tend livestock. It may seem obvious, but the chief determinant of the amount of land sown was the number of draft animals. Of great difficulty for the peoples of the Lower Volga was the maintenance of livestock herds, particularly during times of drought and famine. The mountain siders fared better than others in the preservation of their herds because they had diverse crops that could be used as fodder, and also because there were lush meadows along their more numerous rivers, streams, and lakes.

Another interesting and unique feature of Saratov colony farming was the assessment of pasturage fees, reflecting again the egalitarian nature of these colonies. Generally, in Russia the peasants could freely pasture all of their livestock on the village pastures and any other harvested areas opened up for such use. In the 1860s, several colonies began to assess fees on those colonists who grazed livestock in excess of a colony-established norm (such fees went into the village treasury).[31] The object of this innovation was to deter overgrazing and to reduce the financial advantage free grazing provided the better-off households with large livestock holdings.

Even though agriculture predominated in the Saratov colonies, beginning in the 1880s many households had surplus labor which they hired out as wage laborers. The expansion of the grain trade and the emergence of capitalist agriculture in the colonies created a market for seasonal hired labor which had not existed much before 1880. Until the turn of the century, the Volga German farm wage hands, unlike their Russian counterparts, generally refrained from seasonal work (*otkhozhii promysel*) distant from their own village, because they could usually find local work as regular hired hands or day laborers:

"Thanks to significant tillage on their own and leased lands, ordinarily they [the colonists] hire additional laborers from other households in the settlement."[32] Hired hands worked for daily or weekly wages and food, especially to help with the wheat harvests. Large growers usually hired seasonal workers at the markets of the largest settlements, the biggest being at the two colonies of Golyi Karamysh and Ekaterinenstadt and the two Russian settlements of Zolotoe and Balanda. The size of the agreed-upon wage was largely dependent on the number of available seasonal workers and the size of the harvest.

As economic conditions deteriorated and the population soared, the colonists ventured farther and farther from home to seek temporary work. The first transient workers became stevedores and carters. Between 1890 and 1905, when increasing numbers of poor peasants from Penza and Tambov provinces came looking for work in Saratov Province, many more Volga Germans ventured farther from their homes, crossing the Volga and Don rivers to help farm vast steppe wheatfields to the southeast and southwest of the colonies. Responding to depressed field work wages within the colonies, each year hundreds of young males would spend from April to September in neighboring districts and provinces planting, haying, harvesting, and threshing. By 1899, an annual rite of spring in the colonies was the sorrowful departure of about 3,000 colonists solemnly taking leave of their families. Whether the colonists were "pushed" or "pulled" out of Saratov Province is debatable. Some argue that the poorer peasantry from Penza and Tambov worked for less and therefore depressed the summer wages, while others pointed out that the higher wages paid on the steppe lands attracted the colonists and other Saratov peasants to seek employment there. However, even the trans-Volga steppe became less and less attractive for wage laborers "because everywhere they are introducing machines."[33]

After 1905, the Saratov colonies conformed quite closely to the Russian practice, and exported many of their men to distant areas for all kinds of work. More than anything else, the 1905–6 crop failures in Saratov Province contributed to the decline of "local" seasonal labor. While these seasonal migrants still chiefly sought agricultural work, although in much more distant fields such as the Don Forces Oblast and the northern Caucasus region (since the wheat crops had also failed in Samara Province), a sizable number found nonfarm work in such distant cities as Baku, Tiflis, and Astrakhan. Attracted by rumors of higher pay, ever larger numbers of Ilovlinskaia township colonists trekked farther into the Don region for summer work. Colonists from Sosnovskaia township boarded Volga boats in search of summer construction work in Tsaritsyn, Astrakhan, and Baku; a number even accepted temporary winter factory work (*zimnii otkhod na manufakturnuiu fabriku*).[34] The settlement of Elshanka (Husaren or Husary) reported that about one-half of the village had left to seek work in Baku, but had been disappointed because widespread strikes there had crippled most economic activity. Some colonists looked for railroad work while others simply headed for a city, willing to accept any type of job. Unfortunately, the strike and revolutionary events of 1905–6 seriously darkened their prospects and dampened their hopes. Yet in the immediate pre–World War I years, the large-scale temporary migrations resumed.

The Specialization of Samara Agriculture

The post-1860 economic crisis of the trans-Volga colonies, which deepened as the century progressed, was caused by their almost total dependence on agriculture for their livelihood and, in time, on one cash crop: wheat.[35] Nature forced this choice on the colonists, for the semiarid conditions of the steppe required the cultivation of drought-resistant grains, economical in their use of water. Dryland farming also required the practice of fallowing in alternate years to allow for the buildup of moisture in the subsoil. Fallowing posed serious problems on light, sandy soils when winds could easily blow away the topsoil. Wheat best filled these requirements for dryland farming on the Samara steppe. However, market factors, particularly the greater demand and higher prices for hard spring wheats, encouraged an even greater crop specialization. The Volga Germans' growing preference for and dependence on spring wheat compounded the risks and dangers of dryland farming. Winter wheat was the more suitable and traditional wheat crop sown in Russia, because although commanding a lower market price than spring wheat, it produced, on the average, higher yields and was much more resistant to drought. Sown in autumn when there is adequate moisture in the soil, winter wheat has a much longer growth period than spring wheat, enabling production of a greater number of reproductive stems from a single seed, and therefore a higher yield per seed sown. Protected by adequate snow cover, the wheat accelerates growth during the spring, when again there is ample soil moisture. Because the crop matures and is harvested in midsummer, the summer drought has little effect. On the other hand, spring wheat yields a valuable, high-protein hard grain, but its greatest growth occurs during midsummer; thus summer droughts, depending on their severity, can either sharply reduce yields or ruin the crop entirely. To avoid the dangers of winter kill, spring wheat is only sown after the last spring frost and comes to maturity in August.

Commercial wheat farming swiftly dominated the entire trans-Volga steppe of Samara Province. In 1851, a traveler in the colonies remarked that several cereal grains were grown there, although wheat was most common; by the late 1870s, wheat was supreme, even driving out cultivation of some grains such as millet.[36] Wheat had quickly become "king" in Novouzensk District. A survey in 1887 revealed that colonists and settlers had 70.2 percent of their sown lands in wheat, the highest rate in all Russia. As late as the 1840s wheat had made up less than 40 percent of the harvests in Russia; the figure for Nikolaevsk District was 57 percent, fourth highest in the empire.[37] This growing specialization meant that a poor harvest unequivocably spelled disaster. Thus the trans-Volga peasantry suffered the greatest distress and hardships during such natural calamities as drought, blizzards, and storms, which frequently created famine conditions.

The dramatic shift to commercial wheat farming brought short-term gains but long-term problems. The simultaneous expansion of wheat farming in the fertile plains of the Ukraine and the United States eventually resulted in formidable competition for Volga wheat growers. While yields increased in the better endowed plains of the United States and the Ukraine, they actually declined in the marginal Volga steppe. By 1900, yields in some parts of Novouzensk District were half their 1870 level. Repeated wheat cultivation produced lower quality grain, which received lower prices on the grain markets. Hoping to compensate for a lower price per bushel, growers attempted to maximize production. This had the negative effect of hastening soil exhaustion and contributing to an even larger wheat glut.

Of course, as long as land was cheap and plentiful, no systematic or rational farming was necessary. Until the 1870s, the wasteful farming of marginal steppe lands could still provide a bountiful livelihood because of the availability of large tracts of unsurveyed state lands. In 1837, A. M. Fadeev, later governor of Saratov Province, toured the colonies and attributed the prosperity of the meadow-side colonies to the surplus of steppe lands.[38] The land was there to be exploited, not conserved. Peasants and colonists pursued every means, even illicit, to gain access to much-coveted virgin steppe; they leased state lands cheaply and frequently trespassed on state lands by planting without obtaining permission of the authorities.[39] They farmed wherever it pleased them to farm, practiced no crop rotation, and even ruined beautiful meadows. When inexpensive lease lands began to be unavailable in the late nineteenth century, either because peasants had settled on them or they were in long-term lease to wealthy merchants and landowners, many colonists faced economic ruin.

Sober-minded observers early warned of the pitfalls of relying too heavily on agriculture in this region and, in particular, of zealously specializing in grain farming. Concerned over the enormous inflow of new settlers, a surveyor warned that great care and attention would be needed to preserve the fertile but fragile soil of southern Samara Province.[40] In 1865 Jacob Wagele, village elder in the meadow-side colony of Weizenfeld, studiously examined the Volga colonies and concluded that the colonies in Saratov Province had a more diversified agriculture, as well as many different crafts and nascent but robust cottage industries, whereas the meadow-side colonies had become solely committed to grain farming. He warned that such cereal grain particularism did not bode well for the colonists, especially since their harvests were abundant only because the land was still fertile not because of careful cultivation. Later in the century, another local peripatetic observer encountered many more impoverished and landless colonists in the Samara colonies than in those of Saratov Province, attributing this phenomenon to their one-sided agrarian economy.[41]

The more amply endowed, newer colonies in the steppe practiced the most primitive farming methods right up to the end of the Russian Empire. Their farming practices closely resembled the predatory and rapacious farming methods of the neighboring state peasants. Irrational farming techniques, excessive exploitation of the land leading to soil depletion, and lack of a systematic method of crop rotation contributed significantly to the declining harvests and frequent famine. Until the 1860s, the abundant, rich, unplowed virgin steppe lands provided the peasants with large harvests for very little effort. The *zalezhnaia* system was widely practiced, with a field being sown continuously for several years and then left as a hayfield or pasture for long periods until it regained its fertility. With the influx of new settlers into the region and the rapid population expansion, the abundant land reserves diminished, and lands had to be tilled more often. Because of the increasingly short fallow intervals, the land became soft and badly pulverized from being plowed too often, and therefore less resistant to the arid winds that blew away thousands of acres of topsoil and created dust bowl conditions.[42]

The older settlements proved the maxim "Necessity is the mother of invention" by introducing more efficient farming methods. The land-short, densely populated original settlements could no longer continue to practice the wasteful fallow-field system of farming. To maximize the amount of land under cultivation, a four- and even five-field system had been implemented along with regular crop rotation. Some older settlements had even advanced to plowed fallow; instead of simply leaving the fallow land idle or scattering rye seed among the wheat stubble, farmers plowed the fallow land, seeded rye, and then plowed it under in the spring as a green manure crop.[43] In areas of little rainfall, like the Lower Volga, fallowing conserves the moisture in the soil. The accumulated precipitation of two seasons might raise a crop that would not have survived with just one season's rainfall. By 1908, farmers in the older, original settlements were attempting to reduce the effects of drought by erecting snow screens or plowing snow into ditches, and later spreading it over crops. Farmers introduced drill sowing with interrow cultivation to preserve moisture, and planted drought-resistant grasses to provide for livestock during droughts. The more recently settled German villages lagged behind the Volga settlements in implementing advanced agricultural techniques. Some of them continued to follow the more wasteful *zalezhnaia* system; others, allegedly practicing the *zalezhnaia* system, actually left only a small part of the land fallow, repeatedly planting a field with the same crop or leaving it fallow for a very short period, sometimes only a year.

The dromedary, introduced to the colonists by steppe nomads, became a unique but common draft animal on the drier, sparsely vegetated trans-Volga steppe. The swifter, one-humped camel needed little water and could survive on Russian thistle, which was gathered in the summer, dried, and used as a fodder during the winter. Although temperamental and unable to pull heavy loads, camels were good draft animals, and their broad, splayed hooves made them surefooted in the snow. The women prized the beast for its hair, which grew thick and luxurious in the winter cold; they wove wonderfully soft, warm garments and blankets highly valued for their durability and heavy weight.[44]

The twenty-four colonies of Nikolaevsk District enjoyed an economic prosperity and diversity atypical of the other meadow-side colonies, which most observers attributed to their cultivation of tobacco. The introduction of tobacco in 1772 is credited to some families from Holland who planted it in Ekaterinenstadt and neighboring colonies. Tobacco cultivation spread to other meadow-side colonies, but never became a significant crop in the mountain-side colonies, despite efforts by tsarist officials to introduce it there. Although tobacco was being produced in sufficient quantities by 1805 to gain the attention of St. Petersburg officials (the colonists harvested 1,400 tons in 1804), its low quality and the limited market for it resulted in low prices and modest profits. Most tobacco was sold locally to peasants or shipped down the Volga to Astrakhan for sale to nomadic peoples.[45]

Tobacco as a profitable commercial cash crop for the colonists could not have been important much before 1830, but by the 1860s the colonists themselves acknowledged, "Cultivation of tobacco is one of the most important branches of agriculture in the Volga colonies."[46] Only in 1828 did the Ekaterinenstadt Stahf family open a tobacco factory in the city of Saratov. Tobacco curing and processing quickly developed in the colonies in the 1830s, during which time the Stahf family also introduced better grades of foreign tobacco. In the 1850s, with tobacco prices double those of 1830, tobacco farming brought in almost as much revenue as grain cultivation, benefiting greatly from expanded military sales during the Crimean War and the Caucasus campaigns. But the best indication of the lucrativeness, and therefore expansion, of tobacco cultivation was that the average annual tobacco harvests for the 1830s were almost double those of the preceding decade: 3,870 tons compared with 2,010 tons. This expansion continued until the late 1870s. Between 1845 and 1878, harvests of over 5,000 tons were common, with the 1860s seeing harvests closer to 6,000 tons.[47] As cultivation of better quality tobacco spread, the colonists' tobacco attracted foreign markets. In 1855, the first batch of cigar tobacco from the colonies was shipped to Hamburg, and in 1857 a shipment reached England.

While tobacco growing remained a vital aspect of colony agriculture, a decline began about 1878 from which there was no full recovery. Large yields per acre and a high-quality product are necessary to make tobacco farming profitable. Beginning with the 1878 harvest, which was 450 tons smaller than those of the 1860s, tobacco production embarked on a long decline. The colonists attributed the decline to the costliness of tobacco growing, declining tobacco prices, and inflated wheat prices; many chose to raise the more profitable and higher priced wheat.[48] Since tobacco is one of the most soil depleting crops, repeated or frequent tillage alters the soil composition. The Civil War disrupted American production, thus contributing to much higher colony tobacco prices in the late 1860s and early 1870s, which also led to overplanting and serious soil depletion, thereby resulting in lower grades and yields of tobacco.

Because of the great amount of hand labor and manure involved in cultivation, tobacco was an expensive crop. It required many field workers to meticulously prepare the soil; to plant, top, and sucker the seedlings; to hoe the fields; and to harvest the crop. Consequently, many tobacco fields were sown with wheat, which was much easier to raise and generated more profits. Finally, government fiscal policies as set forth particularly in the new 1881 tobacco tax (*Ustav o tabachnom sbor*), enacted allegedly to improve tax collection on tobacco products, also hurt the financially weakened planters by further depressing tobacco prices. The tax law stipulated that leaf tobacco could only be sold wholesale to tobacco factories or warehouses; since a few tobacco merchants monopolized the Lower Volga trade, they could arbitrarily offer low prices to the growers, who legally had no one else to sell to.[49] However, lax enforcement and the development of a black market in tobacco mitigated the effects of the new tax regulation.

Even before the 1881 tax reform, tobacco growers had been at a serious disadvantage in the disposal of their harvest because of the timing of contract negotiations. The buyers from the few tobacco factories intentionally arrived in the colonies in November, when growers were most vulnerable, to arrange prices and contracts for the coming year. By November, most growers were financially strapped and needed cash to pay taxes and obtain items for next year's planting. The buyers took advantage of this by "coming at the end of the year and tax time, and trying to lower it [the price] as low as possible."[50] After haggling with the growers and settling on a price, the buyers would leave an advance amounting to about one-third of the value of the agreed purchase, with the remainder payable after the harvest.

Tobacco farming survived the setbacks and made a partial recovery after 1900, but the nature of the industry had changed remarkably. The Nikolaevsk District colonies now harvested a low-quality tobacco (*Nicotiana rustica*) used mainly on the domestic market as loose tobacco in pipes and *papirosy* (low-grade cigarettes made out of newspaper or writing paper). By 1900, only two of five Saratov tobacco factories remained in operation, processing almost exclusively *makhorka*, a strong, coarse, shredded tobacco consumed by the lower classes. However, between 1900 and 1908 the expanding domestic economy generated a healthy demand for colony tobacco. Between 1891 and 1904, factory revenues had increased from 279,000 to 730,000 rubles, and the plant work force had increased from 206 to 360; further expansion occurred to meet higher demands from the soldiers in the Russo-Japanese War. Tobacco cultivation slumped again after 1908 when land sown with tobacco amounted to less than two-thirds of the pre-1905 area.[51]

Tobacco cultivation proved to be of great if ephemeral importance for the colonies. For the tobacco-producing colonies, the years between 1850 and 1878 were unquestionably the most prosperous ones ever experienced. At the peak period, approximately 20 percent of colonist households in Samara Province cultivated tobacco and hired large numbers of hand laborers. In 1853, an experienced Russian observer noted the commercial importance of tobacco: "Look at the colonist: he sows wheat, oats, barley, and also potatoes and tobacco; the former provides him with an additional food source, and the latter always gives him a net profit."[52]

The Saratov Kontora, the government agency that supervised the colonies, was also duly impressed with the profitability of tobacco: "This [tobacco] revenue is enormous, if taken into account that it was distributed between the inhabitants of only a few colonies."[53] Thus great wealth was generated within the colonies; during peak years, a tobacco-growing colony earned between 30,000 and 40,000 rubles in total revenues. And tobacco also created a more diverse economy which could cushion the blows of wheat failures: "The famine of 1873, which was so disastrous for the peasants of Samara Province, did not affect very much the German colonists, who reaped an abundant tobacco harvest but suffered like everyone else the complete failure of its grain harvest."[54]

The post-1880 decline led also to the impoverishment of many colonies and the even greater concentration of tobacco wealth. The agricultural depression of the 1880s ruined hundreds of colony households that had become indebted to merchants and buyers for seed and advances: "This curtailment of tobacco cultivation, caused by the unprofitability of tobacco farming, had as its consequence the impoverishment of the German colonies, reflected in the accumulation of arrears and widespread indebtedness of the colonists to private individuals."⁵⁵

Such indebtedness placed growers under the complete control of the lenders. As a result, tobacco wealth became concentrated in the hands of a few families, such as the Rothermel family of Orlovskaia, which had accumulated enormous capital from the tobacco trade and loans. The wealthy trading families of Orlovskaia often bought up 80 percent of the tobacco crop of the surrounding colonies. As tobacco declined, many of the wealthy tobacco families invested their money in the flour milling industry or steppe lands.

The almost complete dependence on cereal cultivation, the overspecialization in wheat, the use of marginal farmland, and the agricultural depression that dominated so much of the period all contributed to the deterioration of the standard of living of the trans-Volga colonists. Forces beyond their control, the whims of nature, and the fluctuations of the grain market, as well as human desires to earn a decent living, intensified the already precarious nature of their existence. Pessimism, resentment, frustration, incomprehension, and even resignation heightened as a result of their precarious economic situation.

Development of the Grain Trade

Although the methods and practices of Volga German farming appeared stubbornly to resist change and innovation, agriculture in Russia and the colonies went through a profound transformation beginning in the 1860s. The change was from a subsistence peasant farming to a market agriculture. Gradually the subsistence farming and barter economy gave way to a money-based economy and a surplus-producing agriculture based on greatly expanded trade with the outside world. In his study of the development of capitalist grain farming in Russia, A. S. Nifontov, using official government harvest figures, concluded that grain commodity farming began in the 1860s, but only became clearly discernible in the 1880s and 1890s with the appearance of larger areas in grain crops, bumper harvests, and rising grain sales.⁵⁶ Grain trade, both foreign and domestic, became a lucrative business for grain merchants, who had small profit margins but handled enormous grain sales. At this time, regional specialized grain farming emerged in Russia, with the frontier or borderlands, such as the Lower Volga region, becoming major grain producing areas and the less suitable central provinces reducing areas sown to grain crops, although such farming did not develop evenly and simultaneously in Russia. It began earliest in the central, black earth provinces and only in the last two decades of the century in the black earth borderlands (which included Saratov Province) and steppe regions (which included Samara Province). However, the black earth borderlands and steppe eventually became the chief grain growing areas of Russia, while the older central agricultural provinces became secondary grain growing areas.

The nineteenth century witnessed a tremendous expansion of European and New World lands under crop cultivation. This expansion began to slow in many parts of Europe during the last decades of the century, but not in the United States, which witnessed a period of enormous agricultural growth unparalleled in its history, with 430 million acres of land settled in the westward expansion by settlers who moved into the Great Plains. The rapid population increase was the most important factor contributing to the expansion of agriculture. In Europe alone, there were more than 200 million more mouths to feed in 1900 than in 1800, while in Russia the population more than doubled in the five decades preceding World War I.[57] Rapid urbanization and industrialization also created a much greater market for food as more and more Russian and American grains began to nourish European workers. Until the late 1870s, Western Europe enjoyed a general prosperity and easily absorbed these ever-increasing grain exports, with world grain prices remaining high and fairly stable.

A prolonged agricultural depression began in the late 1870s. The two decades between 1877 and 1897 were years of ruinously low farm prices, not only in Russia but elsewhere in the world. World grain prices tumbled and a serious international agrarian crisis developed as a result of abundant grain harvests and exports, and the economic depression that hit Europe. In the United States, the decade of the 1880s was a time of growing agrarian discontent as farmers vigorously reacted to the precipitous drop of farm prices and swift accumulation of debts; wheat dropped from $1.05 a bushel in 1870 to 49 cents in 1896.[58] The price of Russian exported grains plummeted; between 1871 and 1875, the export price of Russian wheat reached an all-time high of 90 kopecks per pud (36.113 pounds, or about half a bushel), but by 1886 had dropped to 64 kopecks, and in 1894 reached its nadir, 46 kopecks. Domestic grain prices also fell, in the 1890s to about half their 1870 levels. Only after 1900 did the agricultural market rebound.[59]

The post-1850 period also marked the opening of more Russian domestic markets to Lower Volga grain producers. The colonists had benefited from the food supplies sold to meet the dietary needs of the Russian soldier in the Caucasus wars, which had been fought intermittently for nearly half a century, and in the Crimean War (1854–56). Of even greater importance for the colonists' agricultural resurgence was the stationing after 1856 of a 300,000-man army just 600 miles south of the colonies, a result of Alexander II's decision immediately following the Crimean War to launch an all-out military campaign to complete the pacification of the Caucasian tribes. Although Shamil, the leader of the largest resistance element, was captured in August 1859, other groups resisted Russian forces until the mid-1860s. Large quantities of colony farm produce were easily sent southward on the Volga to Astrakhan, where they were purchased and distributed by military quartermasters to supply the mountain troops. Thus, because of the post-1856 continuation of the Caucasus campaigns, the general military demobilization after the Crimean War did not noticeably diminish colony sales.

The opening of all Russian markets to the colonies occurred somewhat later. T. M. Kitanina, who has written the best study on the Russian grain trade, stated that not until the 1880–1900 period was a single grain commodity market fully formed in Russia.[60] Until the 1880s and the development of improved transportation systems, Russia had no single grain commodity market, but there were numerous local and regional markets, each with its own locally determined prices and fairs. The colorful and immemorial Russian fairs, such as the giant one at Nizhnii Novgorod, attested to the backwardness of the Russian Empire and its inadequate transportation network. The major grain market of the Lower Volga was the city of Saratov, where, because of the glut of regionally grown grain and the inability to transport it to other markets, grain prices were badly depressed and approximately 40 percent lower than grain sold in St. Petersburg or Rybinsk, a major grain market on the northern Volga with rail connections to Moscow and St. Petersburg.[61] With the formation of a national market, domestic grain prices moved fairly uniformly. Thus the price of grain in St. Petersburg and Moscow began to approximate closely that of grain sold in Saratov, because better transportation resulted in increased domestic demand, especially from the fast-growing urban industrial centers, and higher prices for grain sold in the markets of the producing regions, such as Saratov and Samara Provinces.

The Volga River remained the chief artery for grain shipments because of its easy navigability and cheapness over railroads. Although large quantities of wheat were locally marketed and consumed, the leading authority on this subject stated that most of the wheat grown in the Lower Volga was shipped north from Saratov, Ekaterinenstadt, and Rovnoe to Rybinsk, where it was transshipped to St. Petersburg for export or on to the northern provinces (Vologda, Archangel, Olonets, Novgorod, and even Finland) for domestic consumption.[62] A few of the southernmost Volga shipping ports, such as Rovnoe and Ekaterinenstadt, shipped some of their grain south to Astrakhan for milling. With the development of the milling industry, larger quantities of wheat remained in the region for processing and later rail shipment as flour.

The type of wheat generally determined its destination and use. For this reason, the higher quality grains marked for foreign export came chiefly from the meadow-side colonies of Samara Province, while the lower quality wheat harvested in the colonies of Saratov Province ended up on the local markets for domestic consumption. The major kinds of wheat grown in the Lower Volga were Saxony, Russian, and durum, or hard wheat varieties. The first two were high-quality and high-priced soft wheats grown chiefly for export; they grew well in Samara Province. In fact, the excellent Saxony wheat was cultivated almost solely in the Volga colonies of Samara Province and sold to grain merchants in Ekaterinenstadt and Rovnoe for export abroad. In the early 1880s, about 75 percent of all the wheat shipped from these two colony ports was Saxony intended for foreign export.[63] Russian wheat was rarely grown in the colonies because it sold for a cheaper price than Saxony. Hard durum wheats grown in the region included the prized *beloturka* (White Turkey), the excellent *kubanka* (Kuban), high in gluten and superb for macaroni, and *pererod* (a lower quality degenerated durum with a certain amount of mealy kernels). It is difficult to classify these hard wheats, because since they were extremely sensitive to changes in soil quality, the White Turkey and Kuban quickly degenerated into the lower quality *pererod*. By the 1860s, the long tilled soils of the mountainside colonies produced only lower quality durum wheats. The best kinds of White Turkey grew only on the virgin soils of Novouzensk District in Samara Province.[64] The hard wheats brought lower prices than the better quality soft wheats; and the *pererod* was the cheapest, intended for domestic sale and use.

Although the Lower Volga region became the primary wheat-growing region of the Volga basin, only a few Volga German settlements played important roles in the wheat trade. By 1870, seven colonies had emerged as grain ports: Ekaterinenstadt, Rovnoe, Privalnaia, Skatovka, Tarlyk, Iablonovka, and Sosnovka (the only mountain-side port), but the first two dominated the colony grain trade, accounting for almost 90 percent of the colonies' trade.[65] In fact, Ekaterinenstadt and Rovnoe became major grain shipping points, consistently ranking in the top five Volga grain ports between 1875 and 1917, annually and collectively shipping between 15 and 20 percent of all Volga grains.

Ekaterinenstadt, or Baronsk, the largest meadow-side colony with a population in the 1860s of over 5,000 (making it larger than most Russian district towns), developed into a thriving trading colony, the commercial hub for Nikolaevsk District. Travelers to the colony came away impressed. Fine stone and wood houses, many with two stories, and the immense, stone Lutheran and Catholic churches visibly represented the prosperity of the community, while the imposing wood church serving the Russian Orthodox parishioners of the town confirmed its cosmopolitan nature. In 1870, sixteen stone and eighteen wood shops offered a variety of goods and services. Three secondary schools, two of which were stone and two-storied, attracted students from neighboring settlements. Although the wharves and grain merchants dominated the economy of the colony, the Stahf family tobacco factory and other smaller handicraft industries contributed to the economic prosperity of the colony and attracted several hundred outsiders to settle there either permanently or temporarily.[66]

Conveniently located on a deep, wide bend of the Volga, Ekaterinenstadt was well suited for commerce. Early on, Ekaterinenstadt traded in timber floated there from the upper Volga for use and sale in the treeless, trans-Volga steppe. In the 1860s, with the rapid expansion of wheat farming, it began to trade largely in grain, quickly transforming the town into a huge grain warehouse. By the late 1870s, over 95 percent of all grain brought to Ekaterinenstadt was wheat, carted overland from colonies, settlements, and villages in Samara Province or ferried across the Volga from villages in Saratov Province. The colony served as the grain market for an area of over 800 square miles.[67] In the 1880s, colony grain merchants annually purchased approximately seven million bushels of wheat. Although widely renowned as a major wheat market, Ekaterinenstadt's reputation rested on the export of high-quality wheat. The higher quality wheats, Saxony and Russian, comprised over 80 percent of grains shipped from Ekaterinenstadt, compared with only 57 percent for all other Volga ports.

Even though Russian grain firms had their buyers and offices in Ekaterinenstadt, the grain trade remained highly concentrated in the hands of a few wealthy colony families.[68] In fact, five families were the major grain purchasers: the Raushchenbachs, Lipperts, Sieferts, Liebigs, and Feidels. Before becoming grain merchants, most of these families had been important town merchants dealing in a variety of commodities. Originally the wheat trade was a barter arrangement, with the peasant or colonist giving grain in return for goods provided by the grain merchants. The grain buyer would transport the grain to market and sell it there, or the growers might transport the grain themselves to a grain collection point. As the grain trade developed it became monetarized, and the merchants built warehouses and granaries where they could store the grain until shipment.

Rovnoe, also known as Seelmann, remained a small, sleepy, dusty frontier town until the expansion of the wheat trade. With a population of just over 2,000 in 1860, the site looked like most other steppe colonies except for its unique location on a great bend of the Volga which branched into a deep, slow-moving channel of the Volga, making it the best port in the vicinity. Located over 90 miles downriver from Ekaterinenstadt, Rovnoe eventually became the chief grain outlet for southern Samara Province.[69] The wooden Catholic Church reflected the modest means of its inhabitants. The weekly Friday bazaar interrupted the regular routine of the town, attracting traders and buyers from neighboring settlements. The large September livestock fair created a circuslike atmosphere as Ukrainians, Russians, Kirghiz, and Kalmyks journeyed to Rovnoe to market steppe cattle. Although the din and turmoil of man and animal disrupted the tranquility of the community, the colonists derived considerable supplemental income by hawking goods and produce and providing lodging, provisions, and stables.

Prosperity came quickly to Rovnoe in the 1870s when it developed into a major grain market center. The population had quadrupled by the outbreak of World War I. The town soon outdistanced the few neighboring grain outlets and by 1900 even surpassed Ekaterinenstadt to become the third largest grain shipment point of Samara Province, handling over 10 percent of the province's grain. By the 1890s, visitors to Rovnoe marveled at "this rich German colony served by all Volga steamship lines."[70] Rovnoe even boasted of its fine Muir and Merrilees department store, one of many established by the Scottish firm all over Russia.

Aside from its natural location as a port, other factors contributed to the growth of Rovnoe. First, the recent colonization and settlement of Novouzensk District by state peasants and colonists brought many virgin lands under cultivation in the environs of Rovnoe. As wheat farming moved farther into the steppe, hauling the harvested grain to Rovnoe became more convenient and cheaper. Second, two eminent and reputable Russian grain dealers based in Nizhnii Novgorod, the Bashkirovs and Bugrovs, decided to open branch offices in Rovnoe. Grain farmers who had previously delivered their crops to other ports switched to these two recognized firms. Many other grain dealers and even some flour millers soon followed the example of the two grain giants and built offices in the town. By 1885, forty grain purchasing firms were operating in Rovnoe. But in Rovnoe, unlike Ekaterinenstadt, Russian grain merchants dominated the wheat market, although colony grain dealers continued to garner a small share of the business.[71]

Another factor promoting the economic growth of Rovnoe was the availability of inexpensive overland transport necessary to haul grain, sometimes over 150 miles, from the steppe to the Volga. Cheap transportation became available in the 1870s when the salt haulers of Astrakhan Province lost much of their business to the railroads. Seeing the opportunities of grain hauling, many shifted their activities to Novouzensk District and Rovnoe. "The number of carters at this port amounts to tens of thousands," a government official reported in the 1880s.[72] This meant low-priced ground freight to Rovnoe, which was essential for the wheat growers because colonists and peasants themselves could not transport sixty-pound bushels of wheat in large loads by horse or oxen over long distances on dirt roads and trails. About the only hauling done by the steppe farmers was a "horse load" of wheat (about three bushels) to a mill for grinding. Food for the draft animals also had to be taken along, otherwise they had to forage off the land or be fed expensive fodder along the way. Finally, Rovnoe's favorable location allowed receipt of considerable grain from Kamyshin District in Saratov Province via boats in summer or horse-drawn sledges in the winter.

The Volga ports bustled from autumn to winter as grains inundated them. Every August, Ekaterinenstadt and Rovnoe became transformed as thousands of wheat-laden wagons streamed into the towns and delivered grain directly to barges for transfer and immediate shipment. Since the Volga closed for shipping about mid-October, much grain arrived too late for fall shipment and had to be stored in the merchants' large granaries, because, until the advent of the railroad, long-distance grain movement ceased in winter. In Ekaterinenstadt, over two hundred such granaries with a capacity of three million bushels stretched along the edge of the colony on the banks of the Volga. Shipping resumed in spring when the flooding of the Volga allowed barges to dock at the granaries and load directly from them. In the two-month period between April 15 and June 15, the winter-stored grain would be readied for shipment as the grain merchants worked round the clock to load barges. As the waters receded in late June, grain handling costs trebled when hundreds of extra laborers had to be hired to carry wheat from the granaries to small wagons, which were then put on small boats and taken to barges anchored in midchannel, where the wheat was unloaded.[73]

The colonies of Saratov Province did not have easy access to Volga grain ports, although grain could also be shipped down the Medveditsa River to the Don. Unlike the Samara Province colonies, many of which were clustered compactly along the banks of the Volga, few of the mountain-side colonies lay on or near the great river, most being situated some twenty to fifty miles away and separated by a hilly, rocky, north-south ridge. Only one colony—Sosnovka (Schilling)—developed as a grain port, but by the 1880s it had become a minor grain outlet, accounting for only 1 percent of all grain shipped from Saratov Province.[74] Many years later a former colonist remembered well how, on the eve of World War I, her grandfather had traveled to distant markets checking on grain prices and arranging sales: "He had a horse, and each fall he would go to a market miles and miles away."[75] Transporting grain to riverine markets was also more difficult and expensive in Saratov Province, where carters encountered dirt roads, swollen streams, and hilly terrain as they moved grain to markets in Saratov, Kamyshin, Sosnovka, or Rovnoe. Dirt roads became impassable during the rainy autumn and the spring thaw, so that deliveries had to be made in early fall or during the winter when the ground froze. Transportation costs cut into grain profits; to offset these costs, wheat buyers paid less for grain purchased in interior villages than for grain delivered to ports or collection points.[76]

Substantial ground transport of grain in the Lower Volga was possible with the coming of the railroad, but it never eclipsed the hegemony of the Volga

River. Although the first railroad to the Lower Volga, the Tambov-Saratov Railroad, opened in 1871, collapsing the borders of the local economy and opening up new markets, the Volga colonists did not reap the full economic benefits of the "iron road" until the 1890s.[77] In the beginning, railroads could not compete profitably with water transport, whose rates were seven times less than rail freight. The only savings the railroad offered was time, taking only fifteen days to complete the trip between Saratov and St. Petersburg, whereas a Volga boat took three months. In 1877, Ekaterinenstadt grain merchants moved 20 percent of their grain via the Tambov-Saratov line, but because of the high freight (based on distance), little more was sent by rail until the 1889 reform of railroad tariffs.[78] This new system made rail transport more economical by establishing a differential system which offered lower rates for long hauls. The rise of the Saratov flour milling industry and expanded rail network greatly benefited the Saratov Province Volga Germans. The opening of two other lines in 1894 brought the railroad and markets much closer to the colonies. The Atkarsk-Balanda branch line of the Tambov-Saratov mainline made rail transport accessible to the northwestern mountain-side colonies of Walter, Norka, and Frank; and the Riazan-Uralsk railroad linked Kamyshin with Tambov and Riazan, passing close to several southern colonies. Thus the Volga Germans did not feel the full impact of the railroads as early as the American frontiersmen.[79]

Flour Milling

Between 1860 and 1917, the Lower Volga changed from a predominantly grain exporting region to a major flour exporting region, with the Volga Germans playing a vital role in the rise and expansion of the flour milling industry. Originally, most Lower Volga wheat had been shipped up the Volga River as grain to the northern regions of Russia, where it was milled for domestic sale or exported as grain. This changed profoundly with the coming of the steam engine and improved transportation systems. During the 1880s, there arose an extensive and sophisticated steam-powered flour milling industry, concentrated in the city of Saratov, which milled regionally grown wheat and transported the flour via the Saratov-Tambov railroad to the central provinces of Russia.[80] Large-scale flour milling in the Lower Volga region began in the 1860s; until that time, only small, water-powered flour mills ground grain.

Even until 1917, flour milling in Russia was almost equally divided between the large, commercial, mechanically powered mills, which supplied flour for the urban centers, and the small, rural wind and water mills, which served the local markets.[81] The simple country mills survived because peasants and colonists found them more to their advantage. It was cheaper to mill your own grain than to sell it and buy flour produced in commercial mills; likewise, the common folk did not mind the coarse ground local flour. Also, inadequate roads made long-distance transport difficult. Milling was a profitable business because the customary price for grinding flour was one scoop per pud (a pud is about 36 pounds). A powerful "scooper" was the miller's most valuable hired hand: "There were always stories about a good mill scooper being able to scoop almost as much flour out of your grind with his stiff large sleeve as he got for the house in the scoop."[82]

The city of Saratov became the Minneapolis of the Lower Volga, and the Volga Germans the Pillsburys of the flour milling industry. Although the first steam-powered mill opened in 1857, the decade of the 1880s was the great expansion period of flour milling in Saratov, by which time the city had become firmly established as an important flour producing center, second only to Samara on the Volga, and known for its fine-quality *"krupchatka"* flour, so called because of its high content of durum wheat from the trans-Volga steppe. By 1885, twenty-five flour mills were operating in the vicinity of Saratov, five of which were large, steam-powered concerns. Saratov's favorable location on the Volga River had been substantially enhanced in the 1870s when the railroad arrived and converted the area into a superb land and water route intersection. As a result, the city became the terminus for grain not merely from the Volga basin but also from the trans-Volga steppe (the supplier via Rovnoe and Ekaterinenstadt of over half of Saratov's needs), the Urals region, western Siberia, and even Central Asia, where milling was not well developed. If harvests failed in those regions, Saratov millers carted grain from the Don basin.

Growth continued in the 1890s as flour milling became the fastest growing food processing industry in Saratov Province, reflecting the wheat-growing dominance of the region and enabling Saratov to emerge as the premier milling city on the Volga. Saratov flour sold domestically along the Volga and in the central and northern provinces of the empire.[83] Between 1895 and 1905, because of increasing competition and demand, Saratov millers renovated and installed the latest equipment; all mills were converted to steam power, thus quadrupling production capacity. Between 1891 and 1904, the number of workers employed in the milling industry increased by 552 percent (594 to 3,480) and the value of production multiplied threefold, from 6,005,782 rubles to 20,229,735 rubles.[84] By 1909, ten huge, modern commercial flour mills annually ground between 300,000 and 400,000 tons of wheat. By the time war broke out in 1914, Saratov had emerged as the greatest flour producing city in all the empire, with flour mills accounting for 60 percent of Saratov's industrial production.[85]

The history of the Saratov milling industry is really but a chapter in the history of the Volga Germans. In 1857, the Siefert family, colonist grain dealers from Ekaterinenstadt, constructed the first steam-powered flour mill in Saratov, which initially ground 5,500 tons of grain. The wealthy Schmidt family, five brothers from Ust' Zolikh (Messer) who earned their first fortune as manufacturers of inexpensive cotton cloth (sarpinka), later acquired it. The Schmidt plant was the sole commercial, steam-powered mill until 1877, when a Russian by the name of Uvarov built a steam mill which was soon sold to the prosperous Golyi Karamysh colonist, Emanuel Borel, another sarpinka manufacturer.[86] Between 1877 and 1885, three more steam-powered mills were established, which pushed annual flour production to approximately 100,000 tons! Four of the five Saratov steam-powered mills belonged to colonists: the Schmidt Brothers now had two mills, the Borels had one, and during this time the Reinach (also spelled Reinecke) family—Conrad and his sons, Constantine and Vladimir, from the colony of Kutter—became the third great Volga German milling family.

On the eve of World War I, four Volga German-owned mills produced over two-thirds of the city's total output. The two prewar decades witnessed an incredible economic boom for the four commercial millers, transforming their mills into the largest industrial plants in Saratov with a capital stock valued at 4.2 million rubles.[87] Production had more than doubled from a daily average of 500 tons of ground grain in 1895 to 1,200 tons in 1912, the latter figure representing 68 percent of the city's total output. The combined work force of the four mills increased from about 400 in 1895 to 900 in 1912, making the mills the largest employers in Saratov.[88] The mills operated six days a week the year round, unless poor harvests reduced grain shipments, with double shifts from six in the morning until eight o'clock in the evening.

The Volga German commercial millers continued to be the innovators and pacesetters of the industry. They had been the first in the region to convert to steam power, and by 1917 two mills even used dual power sources: steam and electricity. In the 1890s, they introduced grain elevators, which had been developed in Chicago and Milwaukee in the late 1850s and early 1860s, to facilitate the transfer and storage of grain. Industry publications lauded their model plants and displayed their sturdy, tall brick structures as examples of fireproof buildings. The Schmidts expanded their successful milling operations to St. Petersburg, Rybinsk, and Astrakhan. Since two-thirds of the Saratov mills' grain arrived via the Volga, the millers established a shipping branch; the first firm in this regard was that of the Schmidt Brothers, which had quickly acquired five steamships and thirty barges.[89] After 1905, the Schmidts began to use American conveyor belts to move grain from barges to their large grain elevators, and then to the mills. They also participated actively in the All-Russian Congress of Flour Millers, founded in 1888, which sought government assistance to increase the export of flour; Fedor Petrovich Schmidt was a longtime member of its executive council. The wealthiest Volga German flour mill owner, Schmidt lived in a palace in Saratov and financially supported the *Saratower deutsche Volkszeitung* and the liberal Kadet party.[90]

While the spectacular rise of the great Schmidt, Borel, and Reinach flour magnates and their vast, Saratov-based commercial empires fascinates and stirs the imagination, another interesting, but unknown episode of the Volga Germans' past is their control of the smaller, rural water and later steam mills that serviced local markets in Saratov and Samara Provinces. Most of these mills could be found on the mountain side in Saratov Province, which had better streams, rivers, and waterways needed to power the mill. In 1855, 157 mills operated in the mountain-side colonies, while only 13 existed in Samara Province.[91] No matter what indicators are examined, they clearly reveal that the colonists had greatly broadened the local scope of their milling operations to become the chief millers in Saratov Province. An 1872 survey confirmed that colonists milled 45 percent of the province's flour and owned or leased 17 of the 50 largest water mills found on its rivers.[92] The origins of this local industry are difficult to trace, but many of the millers began as colony millers and grain dealers. Originally, each colony had a water or wind mill to grind villagers' grain; the mills, being communal property, were contracted out to colonists for operation and maintenance. The leasing miller, who in fact was also the local grain dealer, paid an annual rent granting him the right to grind his neighbor's grain. Left to accumulate, these locally generated profits could be invested in other mills and grain operations in other parts of the province. As early as 1866, the short-lived regional German newspaper noted that several foresighted colony millers had become "mountain-sider capitalists" (*die Bergseiter Kapitalisten*), having expanded their grain operations beyond the colonies and concentrated a "great part" of all the province's flour milling in their hands.[93] Probably the best example of such financial success was that of the Reinachs, a family that began as local grain entrepreneurs but became great Saratov magnates.

These local millers eventually built or leased mills in the biggest colonies (Golyi Karamysh, Norka, and Linevo Ozero) and towns (Balanda, Rudno, Kamyshin, and Atkarsk) in the province, as well as at rail-water intersections, such as the junctions of the Medveditsa River and the Riazan-Uralsk railroad in Atkarsk District. They remained a permanent feature of the rural landscape, not threatened by the Saratov urban-based mills because they did not compete for the same markets. Their millstones turned out a cheaper, coarser grade of flour, some of which was rye, intended for local peasant markets. In the process, the smaller, village mills decayed or were driven out of business as rural folk took or sold their grain to the larger steam-belching mills in the districts (the colonists referring to them as *die Feuermuhlen*). Two examples of highly successful local millers were the Eckhardts and the Reissigs. Johannes Eckhardt, offspring of a milling family in Medveditskoi Krestovoi Buerak (Frank), moved his family to Balanda in Atkarsk District, which lay northeast of the enormous estate of the Sheremetev family, where he established one of the largest and best mills in the area. The neighboring peasantry flocked to the mill because "Eckhardt flour and Eckhardt bran were better than those of the neighboring Russian mills."[94] Although Volga Germans dominated milling in Kamyshin District, owning twelve of the twenty-one mills, the Reissig family had no equals, owning eight of the largest mills. Most of the Reissig mills were located in or around the important grain port town of Kamyshin, and their output comprised over one-third of total district production.[95]

Flour milling did not develop to any degree on the meadow side until the advent of steam power, because the steppe rivers which flowed into the Volga were unsuitable for harnessing water power. Most were gentle rivers with little water in the summer, but which recurrently flooded over their low banks in the spring, demolishing the mills and dams constructed by the original colonists. Ekaterinenstadt, as in so many cases, proved the exception to the meadow-side pattern. Although it remained a major grain port, the town never rivaled Saratov as a major flour milling center because of unfavorable natural conditions and the preference of its wealthy colonists to invest in steppe lands. In 1876, a steam-powered flour mill opened which locally marketed its product in Lower Volga towns, but whose annual production in the 1890s amounted to only a month's output of the Reinach mill in Saratov.[96] By 1914, Ekaterinenstadt housed four of the thirteen steam- or combustion-engine powered mills constructed in the meadow-side colonies, yet accounted for about half of their production. Compared with the four large commercial mills in Saratov, these thirteen mills were quite small and very new. They employed 134 workers and their maximum daily production amounted to one-fourth that of the four Saratov mills. Interestingly, these mills had not been in operation long; half of them had begun milling since 1907.[97]

Besides creating fortunes for a few Volga German families, the grain trade and flour milling industry had profound effects. It created many salaried jobs which colonists filled to supplement their farm incomes. The best educated could aspire to office clerking. Grain merchants scurried around the provinces acquiring needed grain for the numerous mills, enlisting the aid of numerous salaried local colonists and peasants in larger settlements to arrange purchases there and in smaller neighboring villages. In time, the grain *Kaufmann* became a ubiquitous figure. Some of the local salesmen and wealthier peasantry also became small-scale grain dealers, purchasing the grain of their less well-off neighbors and then reselling it to other grain merchants. Many new, lower wage jobs opened up in such agriculturally related areas as milling, carting, river and rail transport, and construction. Grain hauling became a thriving full-time business, except, of course, when weather prevented it, as considerable land hauling was required to move grain from colonies and villages to the nearest granaries and depots, and to link river and rail routes. For example, flour on the mountain side was hauled as far as forty-five miles from rail-serviced mills on the Medveditsa River to ports on the Volga, a five-day trip; on the return trip, the carters transported lumber.[98]

Conclusion

The nineteenth-century agricultural transformation and modernization of Russia wrought many changes to the peasant economy, in particular linking rural communities to the world. The natural and largely self-sufficient peasant economy yielded to the market economy. Rents, wages, and prices penetrated the peasant consciousness as land, labor, and crops became commodities leased, bought, or sold for the purpose of increasing output and ultimately reaping larger profits. Producing for the market divorced production and consumption, weakening economic ties to the once remote, isolated villages which no longer could provide an adequate livelihood for all residents.

A superficial glance at Volga German fields would not elicit much wonder or enthusiasm, because they did not contrast significantly with those of other, Slavic settlements in the region. Such heterogeneity in field work as did evolve emerged as a result of varied physical conditions rather than ethnic background, with the rural dwellers of Saratov Province and those in the southern reaches of Samara Province adopting notable cropping and cultivation variations. When it came to tilling the land, tradition still gripped the Lower Volga peasantry, including the Volga Germans, who only slowly and reluctantly abandoned the practices of their forebears. By the turn of the century, the Volga Germans had emulated the gentry example of a three-field crop rotation; however, they did not consolidate their lands into a few fields, but out of a sense of equity maintained numerous fields meticulously divided into hundreds and even thousands of narrow strips. In assessing the historical role of the Volga Germans in Russian history, exaggerated appraisals have described them as model farmers. In this earnest if distorted effort, historians have overlooked the substantial contributions of the colonists to the grain trade and flour milling industry. Similarly, the Volga Germans did have more farm tools in their sheds, especially compared with ex-serfs, but the real significance of Volga German machinery lay in its importance as a cottage industry, to be discussed later, which nurtured a beneficial economic diversity and a thriving artisan element, able and eager to manufacture for the Lower Volga market.

Cruel and fickle environmental and economic conditions victimized the Volga Germans, as a lengthy agricultural depression, crop disasters, and fluctuating market prices made them participants in complicated circumstances often beyond their control. Their agriculture adjusted—not so much in farming

practices as in the types and ratios of grains cultivated—to broader market opportunities, although a protracted global agrarian crisis and recurring natural
catastrophes made the adjustment a difficult and, for many, an unhappy one.
The post-1860 expansion of the colonists' grain farming came in response to
the opening of domestic and foreign markets. The result was specialization in a
region unsuitable for such one-sided agriculture. As the colonists grew increasingly dependent on cereal grain cultivation, life became hard and precarious,
even though the altered economy, especially with its larger urban markets,
offered opportunities and investments in other areas. In the nightmare years of
1886–99 and 1905–6 the colonists repeatedly faced horrendous natural catastrophes, making Volga German life bleak indeed. The worldwide agricultural
depression, and later war and revolution, only worsened conditions. Economic
differentials widened and a dichotomy formed between the land rich and the
landless poor. Yet out of these crises, agriculture made a limited, if not vigorous,
recovery which lasted until World War I. However, the reality of a crippling
crop failure persisted, exacerbated by a growing scarcity of land, an issue discussed in the next chapter.

Chapter Five

The Land Question

Land became the crucial issue in the perennial dilemma confronting the Volga Germans up to the time of the 1917 revolutions: could a rapidly growing population living on a fixed amount of land survive and progress? As indicated in the previous chapter, although great changes occurred to disclose economic opportunities for the Volga Germans, the post-1860 history of their agriculture is rather one of decline and deterioration. In fact, land represented the key variable in the colonists' "means" versus "ends" standard of living equation—the "end" in daily life being a livelihood, food, and income, adequate to sustain a bloating population. For most Volga Germans, the "means" to this end was agriculture, more precisely bounteous grain harvests, which required adequate amounts of land, labor, and capital. Unfortunately, labor, manual not animal, was the only resource existing in plenitude; capital, except for that amassed by a few households, was scarce as a result of depressed prices and fluctuating harvests which wiped out any accumulated balances; land remained fixed for the communities and costly to increase. The growth of cottage industries and emigration eased the land squeeze somewhat, so that conditions among the Volga Germans never became as serious as experienced by the Russian peasants living in the central provinces. Agricultural innovation offered little hope for a better life, because it challenged tradition and thus was difficult to introduce. One can only understand the Russian peasants' and foreign colonists' concerns for additional lands by recalling that until the "green revolution" of the twentieth century, with its use of fertilizers, improved plant strains, and improved crop techniques, the only way to grow more crops was to cultivate more land. In this regard, both the peasant and colonist suffered a similar fate: they failed to resolve their "land problem."

Of all the post-1860 government policies imposed on the colonies, the most pernicious and damaging pertained to land. The imperial government refused to assist the Volga Germans in alleviating their land scarcity. In 1840, little did the overcrowded colonists realize that the act promulgated that year, appropriating additional trans-Volga steppe lands for resettlement, would be a landmark act, the government's last transfer of land to them. That realization did not occur until 1871, when officials denied to colonies the allocations necessary to meet government-established peasant land norms. Thus the 1860s and 1870s witnessed the onset of a gradual but irrevocable shift in the government's century-old, generous land policy—a shift caused by the scarcity of vacant state lands, the ever-increasing Russian peasants' clamor for land, and also, in part, by the press-generated chauvinistic and anti-German feeling that swept government and social circles. Beginning in the 1880s, the authorities not only turned a deaf ear to the colonists but even obstructed efforts to purchase new lands by refusing them credit. Ultimately, during World War I, the tsarist regime launched a plan to dispossess the Volga Germans. However, the "land question" also referred to matters of tenure and distribution, which must first be addressed to place the question in perspective.

In eighteenth- and nineteenth-century Russia, excluding the gentry class, the concept of private rural landownership was totally alien, because all peasants were members of communes, which were legal entities controlling the lands that collectively belonged to them. Except for garden plots and the lands on which the villagers' dwellings were located (which were considered permanent, hereditary household property), the arable lands were regularly redistributed among the member households, with most rural dwellers practicing two basic forms of communal landholding: (1) communal repartitional tenure, or *mirskoe vladenie*, which was the most common in Russia, called for the peasants to redistribute land allotments periodically among the members of the community; (2) household tenure, or *podvornoe vladenie*, granted the family household hereditary use of the land in perpetuity with no redistribution; this form of tenure was found mainly in western European Russia, and it was never very extensive. To ensure each family an equitable share of lands of varying quality, all arable land under both forms of land tenure was originally divided into fields and subdivided into strips, with each household receiving strips in the various fields in proportion to the number of male members or labor force. Thus peasant family holdings, no matter what form of land tenure, were scattered in open fields in more or less numerous strips.

By the early nineteenth century, the Volga foreign settlers were disregarding the government's initial landholding prescription and, instead, were subscribing to practices common among the Russian peasantry. In the original land directives of March 19, 1764, the government of Catherine II in effect stipulated communal household tenure, with each family promised thirty dessiatinas of land "in indisputable and eternal hereditary possession," which would pass indivisibly to the youngest male member not as personal property but as the common property of each colony. Thirty dessiatina allotments—consisting of fifteen dessiatinas of arable land, five of meadows, five of forests, and five for the homestead, garden plot, and pastures in or near the village—were thought to be adequate to support a family of four males.[1] This policy, it was thought, would prevent the fragmentation of the household estate into numerous, small, nonsustaining plots and would induce older sons to learn a trade or craft, or to hire out as day laborers on farms lacking sufficient manpower. While the foreign colonists of the southern Ukraine or the Black Sea region, particularly the Mennonites, accepted the indivisible and hereditary estate, or farm, with inheritance going to the youngest son, the Volga colonies never adopted family land tenure, vesting control instead in the collective community with periodic redistribution among the adult males. With the exception of the few Mennonite colonies in Samara Province, which practiced hereditary nonrepartitional tenure, the Volga colonies adopted communal tenure with frequent repartitions on the basis of the number of males—a method typical of the Russian village. In 1814, colony officials in Saratov reported: "The Saratov colonists hold all their land in communal ownership. No master and family has a certain plot forever or for a set period of time. Each community divides its land generally into the good, average, and poor, and the land parcels are allotted on the basis of the number of heads of households or souls in the community. Allotment assignment is decided by lot, and this distribution is performed every year."[2]

Each family separately tilled its strip allotments, but the intermingling of strips and the custom of livestock grazing on fallow and harvested fields necessitated coordinated field work and crop rotation, with the village assembly setting the dates for planting and harvesting. The Volga Germans would divide and redistribute their lands with a vengeance, even more frequently and narrowly than the Russian peasantry.

Several factors explain why the foreign settlers in the Lower Volga failed to adhere to the government's original land directive. First, it was physically impossible to allot each family the promised pasturage, forests, meadows, and croplands in any type of compact and contiguous acreage, ensuring at the same time that each family would receive land of equal quality. Likewise, the government failed to impose a system of family holdings, because the Volga lands had not been surveyed; this made it not only impossible to allocate lands by families but even to grant measured lands to individual colonies. The second reason was that population increase resulted in land shortages in large families, while small families could not work their entire household allotment. Redistribution resolved a pressing social problem by providing lands for elder sons, many of whom had families to support. The undeveloped frontier region of the Lower Volga could not provide sufficient craft opportunities and trade outlets to absorb the disinherited sons, forcing them into farming instead. Another well-documented view is that a simple administrative directive, introduced by a colonist official as a fiscal measure, inadvertently led to the changeover by assessing equally on all working males between sixteen and sixty the long overdue collection of the colonists' government debts. Thus the colonists decided that with males sharing an equal debt burden, all should have equal shares of land. Communal repartitional tenure also was a fair, if cumbersome, way of equalizing land use among males who were equally and collectively responsible for the payment of the community's taxes. Since the law required each foreign settler to pay the same amount of tax, each should have equal amounts of land both in quantity and quality. In conclusion, the introduction of communal repartitional landholding was seen at the time to be in the best interests of both the colonists and the government, especially the latter's fiscal needs, and explains why the government made no rigorous representations to rectify the colonists' willfulness.

Later, communal repartitional landholding seriously inhibited sound farming methods, but considerable clear-sightedness would have been required to imagine the problems this system would create in the last half of the century. Adopted at a time when colony population was small, the virgin soil so fertile that it almost provoked exhaustive cultivation, and the prospects of land shortages unimaginable, periodic redivision seemed a just, if not extremely practical, system. That the system would engender population growth, become an obstacle to agricultural innovation, hinder the intensification of agriculture, discourage individual incentive, and reenforce the patriarchal, large extended family (*die Grossfamilie*) as a strong economic unit became apparent only later.[3]

The essence of the commune was redistribution, at fairly lengthy intervals, of land among households which were guaranteed use but not ownership of land. Provided they owed no significant arrears of taxes and dues, each household was entitled to receive a land allotment. In fact, any household in good standing had no right to refuse its allotment, the alternative being that the household could request to leave the colony but the land would remain with the commune with no compensation. Until the early 1870s, the allocation of land in Volga German villages, as well as most peasant communities, was usually based on the taxed or "revision" male soul, which the colonists referred to as the *Seelenlandsystem*. To reflect accurately the new taxpaying base of the colonies, villagers regularly demarcated and reapportioned all their field lands (known as a radical redivision, or *korennoi peredel*) after the government completed its census or revision, because the revisions were used to prepare new tax rolls. The land to which each family was entitled then depended on the number of male household members registered during the last tax census. The government executed these male statistical enumerations about every fifteen to twenty years between 1718 and 1858, when the last one was conducted.

In the 1870s, partly in response to government inactivity as well as initiatives, egalitarianism once again triumphed over pragmatism. Most Volga German communities boldly effected practices that resulted in the worsening of the already deleterious strip farming discussed in the previous chapter, and in more frequent land redistributions based on the actual number of males residing in the colonies, not just on those registered on the outdated, often grossly unrepresentative, tax rolls. Rapid population increase in the colonies had heightened the anticipation for the next government revision and land redistribution, which, of course, never came. The government's vacillation in undertaking another census created worsening land imbalances, as once-large households continued to hold disproportionately large shares of land, while other families fortunate enough to have multiple male births after 1858 resented their small parcels. Although implemented by a few colonies before

1874, the new system was adopted by most of the colonies during the decade after 1874, with the primary impulse arising almost incidentally from two unrelated government actions. In 1873, "family lists" were drawn up everywhere as part of the government land reform, which will be discussed later in this chapter. The colonists regarded these household enumerations as accurate and reliable, like the earlier revisions. Second, the introduction of military conscription in the colonies in 1874 prompted many colonists to support the idea of military liability as the basis for land use. Families with sons born after the 1858 government census, who would soon be subject to the military draft, demanded that every male should receive an equal share of the land based on the 1873 family lists, since all sons henceforth would be equally liable for military service. Thus the coincidence of the 1873 enumeration and the introduction of universal military conscription in 1874 helped bring about the swift modification of the Volga Germans' land allocation system.[4]

Despite the apparent fairness of the new system and its rapid adoption in most colonies, in a few settlements considerable opposition surfaced and raged for more than a decade. Opponents initially urged patience and moderation, spreading unfounded reports hinting at the immediacy of a census. These arguments lost their cogency and opposition diminished when proponents learned that the authorities had no definite plans for an official enumeration in the near future. The more stalwart and strident opponents warned that adoption of the new system would seriously disrupt farming by introducing more frequent radical redivisions of the colony lands, inasmuch as the government census, undertaken about every fifteen to twenty years, would no longer dictate matters to the village assemblies, and they would be able to initiate redivisions at their discretion. In fact, the opposition's prediction proved correct, because under the new system the Volga German communities usually executed radical redivisions every two to twelve years, with the most common interval being six years.[5] These intervals were not rigid, and often the colony assemblies voted to shorten the interval between redivisions. Even the government's efforts to check land repartitions had little effect; in 1886, it required communes to muster a two-thirds vote for land redistributions, a step that proved ineffectual. The Russian government, in the law of June 8, 1893, ordered land captains to supervise all redistributions and mandated that they should be no more frequent than every twelve years, believing that peasants would be more likely to improve their holdings if held longer; the colonists lodged protests, citing rapid population increase and the extreme diversity of the land as their reasons for preferring more frequent partitions.[6]

A land "crisis" was first mentioned in the colonies on the mountain side in Saratov Province when, as early as 1808, an official inspection of these colonies reported overcrowding and shortages of arable land, exacerbated by the fact that the settlements were "limited on all sides by settlements of state peasants and gentry [*pomeshchick*] estates."[7] In characteristically deliberate bureaucratic fashion, the tsarist government finally redressed this situation by drafting the 1840 legislation providing for additional lands in the trans-Volga steppe. This resettlement program, described in an earlier chapter, temporarily eased the pressure on land, but could not meet the needs of a rapidly growing colony population. Various measures taken to alleviate it proved inadequate, and so the "land question" festered slowly until the collapse of the Romanov dynasty.

In the 1860s, a serious public debate of agrarian issues surfaced within the colonies, in part stimulated by the expectations aroused by the emancipation of the serfs and state peasants, which focused most attention on land use and availability. In 1865 and 1866, the short-lived *Saratowsche deutsche Zeitung* served as the forum for this debate, which the editor had launched by warning of the dangers of the colonists' total dependence on agriculture and exhorting them to develop crafts and trade, otherwise "It will not be long until the population in the colonies is so great that a shortage of land will be felt." Considerable public comment and documented reports of village officials persuaded the editor to admit that land scarcity was already at hand: "The complaint of shortage of land is an almost universal one of all our colonies and it has been placed in perspective many times in this newspaper." A report of the Saratov Office for the Guardianship of the Colonies on May 6, 1865, corroborated that the colonies had reached the limits of landholding, noting that the days of migration and resettlement had ended, and concluded that the future prosperity of the colonies depended on better farming methods and higher yields.[8]

In 1867, the St. Petersburg authorities, having already enacted legislation to resolve the status of serfs and state peasants, addressed the future status of the Volga Germans, charging the Ministry of State Domains with the drafting of regulations to implement land and administrative reforms for all colonies in Russia, the ultimate objective being the complete amalgamation of the colonists

with the peasantry in all areas—social position, administration, and government.[9] After lengthy review and approval by the State Council and Alexander
II, the regulations proposed by the Ministry finally became law on June 4,
1871. The rumors of reform and a land windfall heightened the expectations of
the Volga Germans, but reality dashed their hopes. Like the peasantry's reaction, disappointment with the reform soon pervaded the colonies.

The land reform of 1871 did not ameliorate the colonists' land problems. In
principle, the land reform of 1871 reflected the legislation of both 1861 and
1866, addressing the situation of the serfs and state peasants by preserving the
status quo and thus failing to alleviate the colonists' land anxiety and refusing
even to acknowledge a scarcity. Each colony received only the land resources
previously granted to it, with colonists entitled to the continued use of their existing land allotments, provided they met or did not exceed the regionally established norm of fifteen dessiatinas per male. In fact, the 1871 land directives
paralleled almost precisely those set forth in the November 24, 1866, statute,
which established land norms and regulations for the state peasants ultimately
intended to nurture a rural class of free landowners.[10] In the meantime, collective ownership prevailed, and the communal assembly emerged unscathed
as the functioning agent for the control and redistribution of land, requiring a
two-thirds vote of members to effect any major land change, such as conversion
to household nonrepartitional tenure and consolidation of individual plots. The
colonists, however, made no use of the authorization to alter the traditional
form of communal landholding.

Official confirmation of each settlement's holdings was in the form of the
vladennaia zapis', literally "possessional record," which verified the number of
settlers in the community, type and amount of land under its possession, description of the settlement's boundaries, and amount of annual rent to be paid
until the assembly agreed to land purchase. As the term clearly implied, only
land possession, not ownership, was conferred on the colonists. Ownership
would come after completing a lengthy redemption phase; the colonists had
twenty years, until June 4, 1891, to agree to begin the actual purchase of their
land. Until agreeing upon redemption, they would pay the government a fixed
land rent or "state *obrok* tax," which could not exceed by more than 15 percent
what they had been previously assessed by the government. Rent and land payments for the land were to be guaranteed by the collective responsibility of all

members of the community. The only new assessment was a collection to support the newly created local peasant administrative organs.

During the fall of 1871 and the spring of 1872, the land arbitrators, who inspected the colonies and granted the *vladennye zapisi*, certified that all but four colonies possessed their prescribed allotments.[11] The land-short colonies of Pobochnoe, Sevastianovka, Golyi Karamysh, and Gololobovka requested that additional allotments in Saratov Province be added to their landholdings; the government denied these requests but permitted families from these colonies to settle on unclaimed state lands in Samara Province which had been granted the colonists in 1840. Despite protestations from most colonies that the prescribed allotments were inadequate, the Volga Germans roused no disturbances on the scale of those manifested by deeply disgruntled serfs following their emancipation a decade earlier. Overall, however, the former colonists, like the state peasants, received land on more favorable terms than the former serfs, who often lost their forests and common lands.

Nevertheless, the Volga Germans, like the serfs and state peasants, experienced bitter disappointment with the 1871 land redemption, fervently believing they were entitled to their lands without compensation. Consequently, few settlements rushed to initiate repayment of their collective debts. Impatient with the peasantry's reluctance to redeem their lands, the government promulgated the law of June 12, 1886, arbitrarily converting the *obrok* land rent into redemption payments, which were to be collected in one annual sum over the next forty-four years. Thus title of land ownership would not be received until January 1, 1931. The state peasants and colonists both resented the arbitrary conversion to land purchase, which resulted in a steep increase in their annual obligations, because redemption payments on the average were 45 percent higher than the former land rent.[12] These higher payments, coming on the eve of a series of disastrous harvests and culminating in the catastrophic famine of 1891, forced many colonies into arrears. By 1902, 20 percent of the colonies in Saratov Province had accumulated arrears, compared with a provincewide figure of 17 percent for all rural settlements.[13] Although redemption payments technically applied toward the purchase of land, the colonists, as well as the state peasants, disdainfully regarded them as simply a greater tax to replace the poll tax abolished in 1885, because payments were so high and some places exceeded the value of the land. Redemption payments also generated resentment because they strengthened ties to the community: with higher financial obligations and community indebtedness, the communal assembly would take whatever actions considered appropriate to ensure payment from the individual households, such as taking an allotment from one household and giving it to another. Also, since the colonists knew that redemption payments were the last step of the former serfs to full emancipation—a kind of personal redemption payment—it seemed a step backward for the colonists, who had never regarded themselves as anything other than free men.[14]

Although the ramifications of the 1871 land decree, particularly the imposition of rigid limits on Volga German landholding, would not be fully felt for another generation, except in the few under allotment settlements, its intent was clear. The government would no longer rescue land-hungry colonists. Their privileged days had come to a close. The full impact of the decree was delayed because the colonists resorted to another solution which temporarily alleviated land pressures: leasing.

Leasing proved to be a short-term solution that postponed a critical Volga German crisis until the two decades before World War I. After 1860, population growth and expanded markets, encouraging the shift to capitalist farming in Russia, fostered among the peasantry a frantic rush for additional lands to exploit, a phenomenon particularly widespread in Saratov and Samara Provinces. The Volga Germans participated in this stampede, leasing lands to increase their production of the highest priced grain, wheat. In the 1880s, one out of every four dessiatinas of allotment lands in the colonies in Kamyshin District was farmed on lease. Yet the colonists' practice of generally leasing lands within the colonies initially differed from that of their peasant neighbors because of internal developments unique to the Volga German settlements. First, the proportion of Volga Germans engaged solely in agriculture decreased. Between 1860 and 1917, the ratio of colony families farming full time dropped, as many turned to crafts and trade, leasing their entitlements to other colonists. Similarly, recurrent crop disasters magnified the indebtedness of marginal households and necessitated the liquidation of livestock and consumption of grain reserves, preventing them from sowing their allotments. Finally, emigration and migration, swelled by the 1879 and 1880 crop disasters, also relieved land pressure within the colonies, as is clearly indicated in this zemstvo report: "Ten to twelve years ago [1874–76] the colony [Hussenbach] experienced a great demand in the leasing of outside lands, but thanks to the emigration and redivision of lands on the basis of individual male souls, this demand has been significantly curtailed."

Zemstvo officials noted that the colonists might miss the emigrants, but they benefited by the lease of their former allotments.[15]

In the 1880s, the coincidence of agricultural crisis in Russia and agricultural opportunity in America stimulated a significant Volga German exodus. The attraction of abundant land and a better life in America, not oppression, proved the greatest impetus for Volga German emigration.[16] Certainly one of the most important reasons for the Volga German exodus to the United States was the availability of abundant land and the favorable land legislation of the federal government. In 1862, Congress passed the Homestead Act, which gave any settler at least twenty-one years old, whether a citizen or an alien, 160 acres of land in exchange for the payment of a small fee and the promise to live on the homestead or cultivate it for five years. For the wealthier settler, unlimited quantities of public lands could be obtained at public auction or at the closest land office. The railroad companies were another source of valuable and well-located lands available on easy credit terms; colonists acquired considerable lands from them at very cheap prices. Between 1850 and 1871, the federal government had given land grants to railroads totaling 155 million acres; the Northern Pacific received land grants almost the size of all New England. Railroads were great promoters of United States colonization, eager to sell their lands and to transport settlers, thereby building up settlements and increasing freight traffic. In fact, according to an eminent American historian, the great post-1870 expansion of United States agriculture was largely attributable to the railroad companies of the Great Plains: "They carried forward on a vast scale the work that had been done on a lesser scale by colonizing companies on the seaboard in the colonial period."[17]

In their widespread and competitive recruitment of foreign settlers, the railroads frequently misrepresented the nature of the Great Plains. Enthusiastic and exaggerated advertisements reached all parts of Europe, including the remote Lower Volga valley. The Northern Pacific Railroad circulated 800 agents throughout Europe to distribute promotional literature written in all major languages and to assist prospective emigrants.[18] Hundreds of railroad agents worked in New York City to receive and also recruit new arrivals; they offered special rail rates to those who agreed to settle on company lands, and advice on how to go about settlement. It is no exaggeration to state that the Atcheson, Topeka, and Santa Fe and later the Burlington railroads initiated and organized the colonization of Kansas, Nebraska, and the Dakotas from the numerous

Germans from Russia—the Mennonites, the Black Sea Germans, the Bessarabian Germans, and of course the Volga Germans. Many Volga Germans later worked for these railroads. Similarly, the Northern Pacific recruited most of its immigrants from Scandinavia to settle mainly in the Dakotas and Montana. The fact that U.S. railroad colonization and the tsarist government's revocation of the colonists' privileges occurred coincidentally in the 1870s has contributed significantly to the long-held views that the Volga Germans fled Russia to escape military conscription and other forms of discrimination. In fact, they did not flee unbearable conditions in Russia; they were attracted by visions of land and a better life in America.

There are other indications that conditions in America, chiefly the importance of railroad colonization, rather than conditions in Russia, played a more significant role in influencing the decision of the Volga Germans to emigrate. There is little indication of significant Volga German emigration in the 1870s, the period of the revocation of privileges, yet emigration picked up in the 1880s. There are several possible explanations for this. On September 15, 1873, the United States experienced a devastating economic crisis with the collapse of the Philadelphia banking empire of Jay Cooke. Railroads figured largely in this economic crisis and suffered disastrously from its effects. Railroad colonization efforts and lands sales slumped until 1879. Railroad expansion surged forward in the 1880s. Between 1880 and 1887, the Chicago, Burlington and Quincy Railroad Company, which attracted so many colonists to western Nebraska, laid more new rails than in any other seven-year period in its history.[19] Interestingly, the last great surge of expansion and colonization by the Burlington lasted from 1901 to 1915, a time when many colonists left Russia. Coincidentally, between 1882 and 1887 the Great Plains experienced an extended period of higher than average rainfall; the five-year average for Kansas, Nebraska, and South Dakota was almost twenty-two inches, with most rain falling during the growing season.[20] Settlers rhapsodized about abundant precipitation in their letters to their friends and families in Russia, who were experiencing a dry period. Railroad recruiters boasted of this and the abundant harvests in their promotional pamphlets, with some even asserting that the climate was changing. Naturally, this sparked the interest of prospective foreign settlers, who had been aware of the dryness of the plains and therefore had been reluctant to proceed to the Great American Desert. Consequently, the Volga German movement to America temporarily eased land pressures at home.

Inasmuch as each *Gemeinde*, or communal assembly, determined the lease terms of lands at its disposal, the nature of the agreement varied. In many cases, indebted colonists had no choice but to lease their allotments because of the collective responsibility of paying taxes (*krugovaia poruka*). If the family could not pay arrears by selling goods or personal property, the communal assembly commanded that its allotment lands be leased. In Iagodnaia Poliana, for example, the village assembly repeatedly directed the village elder to seize the field allotments of all households that had not paid state and village assessments. The elder was empowered to lease these allotments to other households for cash (to retire the tax arrears) or to transfer them to "sound" households who would assume all the outstanding and future financial obligations.[21] This forcible or coercive leasing arrangement generated considerable animosity and tensions among households, especially in those cases of alleged collusion between the village elder and prosperous lessee households. For instance, an unpopular but effective stratagem that wealthier colonists employed to gain a lease was to request a long-term one, generally until the next land redivision, promising in exchange to pay in advance in one lump sum the total rent and taxes due. Understandably, this so-called squeezing of the poorer colonists happened most commonly in the settlements with the severest land shortages, such as the colonies in Iagodno-Poliana township. Sometimes, particularly if there was a great demand for land, the indebted family might privately arrange its own lease arrangement, pay off the debt, and earn a few extra rubles in rent.

The communal assembly also arranged for the lease disposition of other lands it controlled, the first and, by far, the largest of these being the so-called emigrant allotments. After the lapse of the ten-year, 1871–81 emigration grace period (provided for in the 1871 reform of the colonies), during which emigrating colonists formally and permanently could legally renounce their colony membership and land claims, colonists could exit Russia only on temporary passports (*po pasportam na vremennuiu otluchku*), granted at the office of the provincial capital only after the traveler received a two-thirds vote of approval from the *Gemeinde* and written approval of township and district authorities. These official documents limited the holder to six months abroad, but that term could be extended. Consequently, most colonies gave emigrating households a grace period to reclaim their allotments (usually until the next land redivision); during that interval, the commune leased these lands to the highest bidder. Similarly, most colonies also leased out lands of families who had moved but "still belonged to the community." These households had sought work in Russian towns or had leased state lands in the Don or Kuban regions. The so-called orphan lands also remained at the disposal of the *Gemeinde*. Since orphaned children could not farm their parent's allotment, it reverted to the commune for lease. Widows' allotments were handled in the same manner.[22] Therefore, depending on the circumstances, a commune might have a sizable amount of land at its disposal, thus temporarily easing land pressures.

Much less common was another type of private lease arrangement involving a mutual understanding between two debt-free households. This situation usually arose when a household decided to abandon agriculture and pursue a craft or trade. A household might lease all or part of its allotment; it usually never completely forsook tillage, but farmed only part of its allotment in order to conduct other economic endeavors. Such arrangements were most common in the mountain-side colonies where there were developed cottage industries; however, they were also noted in the land-short colonies of the meadow side, where labor-short households leased all or part of their allotments for very high rents. The terms of this kind of lease arrangement reveal considerable diversity, but generally stipulated a fixed cash rent and a long-term lease with the lessor also paying all taxes due on the land. The lease usually lasted the length of a land repartition, commonly undertaken every six years. In-kind payments were rare, as was sharecropping or tenant farming, both considered to be quite risky in this marginal agricultural region; should crops fail, which was not unlikely, the renter, not the lessor, lost economically. In addition, the nature of the harvests played a vital role in establishing rent levels. A bountiful harvest boosted demand for lease lands, because farming households had abundant seed, adequate livestock and equipment, and some extra cash. Thus rents would soar. Crop failures could cut land rents in half, as they did in 1905 in Kamyshin District, where financially strapped peasant households had to sell livestock and deplete seed reserves. Garden plots, as well as cabbage and potato allotments, were not leased, as is evident from the stipulation that the rentee provide the lending household a horse to plow its garden plot.[23]

The unsatisfactory results the Volga Germans had with land renting were much like those in other parts of the Russian Empire, as rents outstripped grain prices; rents skyrocketed 53 percent between 1887 and 1914 while grain prices rose by only 10 percent. The Lower Volga provinces experienced much worse rent inflation when rents rose 76 percent on the average.[24] A fixed supply of available lands, combined with the peasantry's population explosion, caused rents to soar, with meadow rents triple those of field land. As the land hunger worsened, land rents rose, length of leases shortened, and lease lands had to be sought outside the colonies in distant parts. Having fully exploited the leasing possibilities opened up by cottage industries and emigration, the Volga German settlements around the turn of the century began to lease sizable amounts of outside lands, particularly vacant state lands in the trans-Volga steppes of Novouzensk District. However, as will be explained later, the government finally closed this land outlet. Thus the pressure or demand for land remained, only it came to a head later in the colonies than in the neighboring villages of state peasants and former serfs.

Rents rose more dramatically in the Volga German settlements of Saratov Province than in those of Samara Province, although, once again, intercolony differences complicate generalizations about leasing. In Kamyshin District, where most mountain-side colonists lived, high rents became the norm. Having the highest percentage of peasants in the entire province, the district felt a tremendous demand for land, and it could not be satisfied by the rental or purchase of state or gentry lands. Kamyshin District rents were highest in the northern colonies and lowest in the southern, yet by 1904 districtwide they averaged about ten rubles per dessiatina, a 73 percent increase since 1882.[25] Railroads also fueled the inflationary spiral and, because they had appeared earlier in Saratov Province than in the trans-Volga steppe, pushed Kamyshin District land values even higher. As early as 1872, the Saratov Kontora reported the surge of rents in Saratov Province colonies: the majority of localities witnessed the doubling of lease rents between 1862 and 1872, and those settlements adjoining the Tambov-Saratov railroad actually saw rents treble.[26] Lower Volga land rents rose significantly everywhere between 1880 and 1917, yet they were also subject to wild, short-term fluctuations, which primarily reflected the highly fluctuating harvests, and varied from colony to colony. The highest rents were found in the most overpopulated original colonies in Iagodno-Poliana, Ekaterinenstadt, and Panin townships. In 1883, colonists in Iagodnaia Poliana township leased allotment lands for nine rubles per dessiatina, double that of other colonies in Saratov Province. In 1898, zemstvo surveys discovered that rents in these three townships were five times higher than in surrounding areas. They were highly inflated because of the absence of state and private lands in the vicinity. The closest available lands were those in the steppe of Novouzensk

District—at least forty-five miles from the nearest of these colonies. In 1889, demand was so great that nonfarming households could clear five to ten rubles per dessiatina with leases running for only one or two years: "There are no longer term leases anywhere." Lowest rents could be found in the colonies of Novouzensk District, where state lands were plentiful and leasable, yet even here rent differences were significant. In the late 1880s, rents for state lands ranged from a low of 3.75 rubles to a high of 8.1; within the colonies the range was 2.2 rubles to 5.4 rubles.[27]

Unfortunately, leasing proved to be a panacea, not a solution, ruining once fertile soils and only temporarily delaying the onset of a serious land crisis. Yet at the time it seemed the only solution. Leased lands were never rotated or fallowed, but repeatedly plundered by constant plantings of spring wheat. Lands leased for eight to ten years usually became so depleted as to be completely worthless. Why had the colonists during the 1860s failed to heed the numerous warnings of their leaders, who advocated, instead of leasing, the purchase of land at whatever cost? Cost, of course, was one of the reasons. Land was expensive, and, except for individual colonists, the Volga German communities did not have the funds to make land purchases; and, as will be seen later, the government would not assist the colonists in land acquisitions. No one could have predicted the confluence of factors—rapid population growth, influx of new settlers, rise of commercial farming, and so forth—which so greatly inflated the cost of land in the Lower Volga. Nor could they have foreseen the harsh, anticolonist government land policies that would begin during the reign of Alexander III; no doubt, many colonists long hoped for another government resettlement like that announced in 1841.

Augmentation of Volga German landholdings through purchase never materialized, because the 1881–1917 land policies of Alexander III and Nicholas II turned decidedly anticolonist, and contributed to more straitened land conditions within the colonies and the decision by many Volga Germans to leave Russia.[28] Equally important, however, was the chronic absence of credit to finance individual householders' long-term land transactions. Although there were over a thousand savings and loan associations in Russia by the 1880s, including a few in the colonies, they could not serve as a source for land purchases because of their small amount of capital, but above all because they did not grant long-term loans. Their loans were mostly for a year or less, and loans for five to ten years were unheard of.[29] Skyrocketing land prices and plunging grain prices, during the last two decades of the century, posed insurmountable obstacles to land purchase, which required large amounts of mortgage credit. From a midcentury average of 12.6 rubles per dessiatina, land prices in Russia had risen to over 100 rubles in 1910. In 1882, a dessiatina of Saratov land sold for 45 rubles; in 1887 for 53 rubles, approximately one-third higher than comparable land in the Samara steppe.[30] The depressed foreign and domestic grain prices, coupled with the peasantry's higher monetary obligations of the 1880s and 1890s, led the Volga Germans to conclude that the only solution to their economic quandary was to plant more, which meant additional land. However, little land was readily available, since the tsarist government, beginning in the 1860s, more carefully monitored and closely regulated state lands in the Lower Volga; in the 1880s these lands were reserved for resettlement of peasants from the land-scarce central provinces. Ironically, while the government would pursue a paternalistic policy to secure peasants more lands, it would not allow this solution to the Volga Germans. These policies initially made it impossible for colonies to purchase land, then placed restrictions on their leasing of land, and finally, in 1915, expropriated colony lands.

The Peasant Land Bank acted as the paramount credit agency for peasant communes in the huge transfer of gentry and state lands to the Russian peasantry, yet not a single one of the hundreds of thousands of acres of gentry and state lands would enter into the possession of the Volga foreign settlers. The regulations of the Peasant Land Bank, founded in 1882 to promote peasant land acquisitions, permanently deprived the former colonists from the credit of this institution, even though bank rules were repeatedly amended and liberalized to include other rural groups. Although they were technically excluded on the grounds of being "settler proprietors" rather than "peasants," the exclusion in truth resulted from the rising xenophobia, particularly the anti-German feeling fueled by the press, the rampant nationalism, and the Russification policies of the government of Alexander III. The bank's blatantly discriminatory policy against the non-Russian peasantry reflected the opinions of the highest government circles, such as Minister of the Interior D. A. Tolstoy, who in a letter to Finance Minister Bunge enthusiastically avowed that the Peasant Land Bank would counteract the expansion of colonists and advance Russification by increasing peasant landholdings, thereby strengthening their economic conditions.[31] The government's position never wavered, because a February 28, 1905, Ministry of Finance directive denied a petition of the Nikolaevsk District zemstvo assembly requesting that the former colonists of the district be allowed to use the Peasant Land Bank to purchase badly needed lands. The ministry lamely justified its decision on the grounds that approval would set a precedent that would encourage petitions from other colonists. It also explicitly revealed a long-held, anticolonist bias: "The Bank's granting of assistance to increase the landholdings of the settler proprietors, former German colonists, does not correspond to the main task of the Peasant Bank—to promote land acquisitions for peasants of Russian origin."[32] Although the bank could not single-handedly resolve the land crisis, as is evident in the numerous unfulfilled peasant requests for funds, the fact remains that during a single decade (1895 to 1905), peasants *annually* acquired 530,000 dessiatinas through the agency of the Peasant Land Bank, while the Volga Germans obtained nothing.[33] Ironically for the Volga Germans, the government's plans were best realized in Saratov Province, where between 1883 and 1901 the peasants purchased 317,453 dessiatinas of land through the Peasant Land Bank.

While deprivation of essential credit required to purchase lands proved injurious to the colonists, particularly after the 1905–6 jacqueries, when so many gentry estate lands in the Lower Volga went on the auction block, a little-known government land directive in 1906 dashed all hopes colonists had of increasing their landholdings. As developed earlier in this chapter, leasing of state lands in the trans-Volga steppe had become the chief method colonists had used since the 1890s to expand crop cultivation. Until 1904, large amounts of state lands in Novouzensk District had been leased out for periods of eight to nine years to peasant and colony communes, as well as wealthy individuals. State leasing of these frontier lands ceased with the law of June 7, 1904, which designated that all state lands in Samara, Orenburg, and Ufa provinces were for sale to landless and land-short peasants for settlement. Although alarmed at the clouded future of these lease lands, the Volga Germans thought they saw a silver lining. Judging that they qualified for the resettlement program, many of the older, land-short Volga colonies expeditiously drafted documents depicting their critical land situation, received the official sanction of the district zemstvos, and finally petitioned the government. Over two years, the Volga Germans nervously awaited the government's reply. Finally, on April 12, 1906, the Ministry of Agriculture announced the crushing blow, categorically prohibiting all colonies and colonists from purchasing or settling on these lands.[34] Even a public outcry in the chief Volga German newspaper, aimed at enlightening the government about the serious land shortage in the colonies, failed to persuade the government to reconsider its decision. One writer pleaded, "There are entire communities which have a total of only one-half dessiatina of farmland per male in all three fields."[35] While short-term leasing for one to two years would continue until all the lands were claimed, the crucial significance of this directive was readily apparent to the disillusioned colonists. There was no more room for them in Russia! The ban on Peasant Land Bank credit and the land directive of 1906 literally ended all hopes of the colonies' obtaining more land in Russia. The Volga frontier had closed. Lacking funds, deprived of credit, and now prohibited from further leasing, there was no future for them in Russia. The result was a resurgence of emigration that stopped only with the outbreak of World War I, when the Russian borders were closed.

The constant accusations made in government documents and in the censored, chauvinistic press to the effect that the Volga colonists enjoyed more prosperity because they were great landholders do not stand up to scrutiny. The unfair and untrue assertions that the colonists were "land rich" grossly distorted reality, especially since the history of Volga German landholding during the post-1860 period was one of sharply shrinking allotments. In fact, Volga German allotments closely approximated those of the entire Lower Volga peasantry. In Samara Province, former state peasant allotments slightly exceeded Volga German holdings, whereas the reverse occurred in Saratov Province. Likewise, even though Lower Volga allotments exceeded those of the land-starved peasantry of the central provinces, the common refrain heard in the Lower Volga was that because of primitive farming methods, the marginal nature of the soil, and the fickleness of nature in this region, rural allotments were inadequate to sustain a healthy peasant economy.

As both individual and household allotment statistics show, the majority of the Volga colonists did not belong to the largest peasant landholding group in the Lower Volga and bravely faced an endless contraction of their farm plots. In both districts of Samara Province, where approximately 60 percent of the Volga Germans resided after the 1860s, the state peasants possessed larger landholdings. A thorough zemstvo land survey conducted in the late 1880s disclosed that in Nikolaevsk District the average land entitlement of a state peasant was 12.7 dessiatinas, compared with 10.6 dessiatinas per colonist; in Novouzensk District, an average allotment for a state peasant was 16.1 dessiatinas, compared with 14 dessiatinas for a colonist.[36] The trans-Volga peasantry experienced a

Table 6: Average Size of Household Allotments in Samara Province (dessiatinas)

District and Household	1877	1905
Nikolaevsk District		
State peasants	33	26.6
Colonists	33	20.7
Novouzensk District		
State peasants	41.9	30.4
Colonists	40.5	27.3

near-catastrophic constriction in landholdings during the next three decades; for example, on the eve of World War I, in Novouzensk District the average holding of male state peasants had shriveled to 3.1 dessiatinas, the colonist's holding to 2.2 dessiatinas, and the former serfs to only 1.3. Surveys based on size of household allotments also confirmed the peasant group disparity, miniaturization of holdings, and especially sharp shrinkage in the colonists' allotments in the prewar period (Table 6).[37]

It is true that colonist holdings considerably exceeded those of the former serfs residing in central Russia. But compared with the peasants neighboring them, the Volga Germans were never regarded as large landowners, such as the colonists in the southern Ukraine, whose holdings in 1905 were between two and three times larger than those of the comparatively well-endowed neighboring peasants, and whose private family estates were quite common—over 1,000 large estates possessing over 4,000 dessiatinas (1,500 acres).[38] But simply diagnosing the economic health of the peasantry based on allotment size is misleading. Considering the marginal natural conditions and the primitive, exploitative methods of agriculture, even large allotments were not enough. Describing Novouzensk District in the 1890s, the writer quoted below claimed that even using sound farming practices, which only the Mennonites observed, a household needed 30 to 50 dessiatinas to sustain itself; therefore, except for the Mennonites, all settlements suffered from inadequate holdings: "For this reason [backward, predatory farming practices], it would be difficult to find one settlement in the district, in which there would not be complaints of land shortages . . . even though allotments reached 15 to 20 dessiatinas per soul, or from 45 to 60 dessiatinas per household, and even in some district settlements with allotments of 30 dessiatinas per soul!"[39]

In Samara Province, great landholding disparities existed between the original Volga German settlements and the new colonies established in the post-1840s resettlement, primarily from the excess population of the overpopulated mountain-side colonies. The tenth revision taken in 1857 revealed that the new settlements had allotments three times the size of the original meadow-side colonies and five times larger than those in Saratov Province. Because the colonists were unable to obtain additional state lands, this disparity in the size of landholdings between the original and daughter colonies was never erased; by 1905, none of the original settlements in Nikolaevsk District had allotments over 30 dessiatinas per family, whereas in Novouzensk over 80 percent of the colonies, all daughter colonies, had allotments larger than 30 dessiatinas.[40] Therefore, the demand or pressure for land was always felt much more intensely in the older settlements.

In Saratov Province, as in Samara Province, the size of colonist landholdings closely approximated those of the former state peasants, but significantly exceeded those of former serfs. The size of individual male allotments in 1886 in Kamyshin District, where 80 percent of them resided, was between those of the state peasants and the former serfs: 8.9 dessiatinas for state peasants, 8.2 for colonists, and 3.9 for ex-serfs. A provincewide survey taken over a decade later revealed similar results, while also noting the sharper decrease in Volga German holdings: 7.9 for state peasants, 6.1 for colonists, and 3.4 for former serfs. Data from an 1899 land survey of Saratov Province revealed that over one-third (twenty out of fifty-seven) of Volga German settlements failed to meet the norm of 4.5 dessiatinas per male regarded as essential for farming, and in 1906 some colonies alarmingly reported that the last land redistribution had yielded allotments of less than 2 dessiatinas, even though almost half the male population lived and worked outside the colonies.[41]

Comparison by households appears to place the colonists in a better light as landholders, while also revealing that notable extremes existed among the colonies themselves, with about 10 percent of the families having less than 10 dessiatina allotments while 7 percent of the households had allotments triple that size (Table 7).

The allotments of these two groups seem enormous when compared with the 7 dessiatinas the former serf households of the province averaged in 1877, which shrank to just a little over 5 dessiatinas by 1905. Two important caveats must be kept in mind concerning these figures. First, colonist families were the

Table 7: Average Size of Household Allotments in Saratov Province (dessiatinas)

District and Household	1877	1905
Saratov District		
State peasants	17.4	11.7
Colonists	12.5	9.3
Atkarsk District		
State peasants	20.4	14.3
Colonists	23.4	19.3
Kamyshin District		
State peasants	22.8	15.6
Colonists	29.9	19.7

largest in the region, thus they fared less well when allotments per individual male were used as the standard of comparison. In 1886, the average sizes of households for colonists, state peasants, and serfs were 8.14, 6.82, and 5.46 respectively. Larger households only meant that the colonists had ample manual labor to farm, not that they had more land per capita. Second, although the Kamyshin District allotments were larger for both groups, the quality of soil was not as good as that of the other districts, for it contained little chernozem. By the 1890s, yields of both rye and wheat on humus-rich state peasant lands in the northern half of Saratov Province were one and half to two times greater than those in Kamyshin District. Consequently, the Russian peasants had little reason to envy the colonists; rather they envied the rich lands of the gentry estates found predominantly in the northern half of Saratov Province, which was the area of greatest peasant unrest during 1905–6. Yet the overall trend was unmistakable. In 1905, households farmed much smaller allotments. Some allotments, such as those of the colonists of Kamyshin District, were only two-thirds of what they had been in 1877.[42]

Curiously, as will be seen in a later chapter, land failed to emerge as a major issue during the revolutionary events of 1905, primarily because coincidental, more compelling issues overshadowed the land question; and there were still ways of easing land pressures, such as growth of cottage industries, temporary seasonal labor, emigration, and, above all, leasing—particularly, until April 1906, the leasing of lands in the trans-Volga steppe. The panic and hostility generated by mobilization of reservists for the Russo-Japanese War translated into a general, consuming obsession not assuaged until the demobilization of Volga German soldiers, which was not completed until the end of 1906. Distasteful Russification policies imposed on Volga German schools, threatening the social fabric of the community, fired public opinion to fever pitch. Finally, the disastrous harvest of 1905 dissipated peasant energies and tended to deflect enmity away from government policies and to focus it on the vagaries of nature and environment. Police officials reported that many households resignedly decided that the land situation in the Lower Volga was utterly hopeless, and emigrated.[43]

Inasmuch as the Volga Germans and Russian peasants aspired more to be larger-scale farmers than to be private, independent ones, it is not surprising that the Stolypin land reform, issued as an imperial decree November 9, 1906, failed to excite enthusiasm among the colonists, particularly coming so soon after the April 12, 1906, directive prohibiting Volga Germans from purchasing or settling on state lands in Novouzensk District. Generally, the Stolypin reforms elicited muted response, because the peasantry, enduring what they felt to be unjust and critical land pressures, craved additional lands, especially those of the parasitical gentry, which Stolypin regarded as inviolable. Few peasants could understand how receiving a scrap of paper, confirming title of private ownership to what they considered grossly inadequate plots, would make life more tenable.

After forty-five years of upholding the commune, the Russian government resolved to destroy it, primarily for the restraints it imposed on able and enterprising peasants. Aimed at the dissolution of communal landholding and the establishment of a class of independent farmers, this last major land reform of the tsarist regime reluctantly resurrected the long defunct emancipation goal of private ownership of land. Stolypin, the executor if not the architect of the reform, had concluded that communal land tenure, which the government had bolstered in the 1880s and the 1890s, was incompatible with agricultural progress and the improvement of peasant life. With the cancellation of redemption payments effective January 1, 1907, the peasantry also would no longer have any financial liens on their lands. Specifically directed at imparting peasant respect and desire for private ownership, consolidating and enclosing scattered strips into compact holdings, and abolishing joint family ownership, the reform was truly revolutionary except in one respect. The reform offered the colonists nothing new in the most crucial area—land. All it promised was private ownership of land that they already had in their possession, which was too little. Likewise, the Volga Germans were barred from access to the primary agency involved in transfers of private and other nonallotment lands to the peasantry, the Peasant Land Bank, which arranged sales of state lands to peasants, provided credit for the purchase of gentry estate lands, and offered mortgage loans on allotment lands. As one scholar recently noted, the Peasant Land Bank played a crucial role in the realization of Stolypin's objectives: "In a variety of ways, then, the Peasant Land Bank made departures from the commune advantageous and gave important financial support to the establishment of the new rural class envisaged by the reformers."[44] Unfortunately, as discussed previously, the Volga Germans did not share in the bank's largesse.

The conversion to private landownership was simple. The November 6 decree abrogated joint family ownership and granted the household elder sole ownership of the family's allotment lands, dispossessing all other males still living in the family. In rural communities, such as the colonies, which engaged in periodic land redistribution, every individual householder could at any time request the communal assembly to grant him all lands to which he was entitled in personal ownership. An entire colony could abolish the commune and proceed to private ownership with a two-thirds vote of its householders. Consolidating the numerous scattered plots was a much more time-consuming matter, requiring a complex land surveying operation. A householder could press the commune to grant him land in a single location. This had to be done if the request was made during the time of a general redistribution of the land or if the request was made by one-fifth of the total number of householders; otherwise, the community had to meet such a request only "insofar as possible." Thus an individual householder's petition for private ownership, without consolidation, resulted in no practical consequences except that he could sell his still scattered holdings.[45]

While the procedural aspects of the Stolypin reform were clear-cut, the socioeconomic consequences and inconveniences of conversion to private landownership were much more complex and uncertain. Each colonist householder was perplexed by several unresolved but vital questions. What assurance was there that he would receive an equal and fair share of the land? Would the household still have access to scarce water resources? Knowing the diversity of the colony's lands, how would it be possible to consolidate holdings and also ensure an equitable apportionment based on the quality of the soil? What would happen to his use of the common lands for pasture, gardens, orchard, and meadows? Since he already was short of land, how was the reform supposed to make large enough allotments to support his family? He probably would either have to sell what he received and move elsewhere or try to buy or lease extra lands from other colonists, which would cost dearly because of high land prices. What would happen to his sons, most of them married but still living under one roof, who heretofore were entitled to a share of the land? How would the family be treated by villagers if it separated from the commune? If the entire colony decided on private ownership, with all the land to be broken up and sold, and the communal assembly abolished, how would the community itself survive? If "outsiders" purchased former colony lands, the community would eventually be ethnically and socially transformed. If colonists respected the urgings of the government to establish individual farmsteads on consolidated plots, the colony faced physical liquidation. These and many other questions inexorably forced every colonist to conclude that the proposed land reform would radically alter his way of life, and threaten the socioeconomic foundations of the colonies.[46] To a peasant society that cherished tradition and resisted change, a social revolution was not an attractive prospect. The colonists also resented and resisted the strong-armed tactics of the land captains, to whom the government had entrusted implementation of the reform, and who used force if necessary.[47]

Despite the vigorous implementation of the reform, the commune survived in Russia as well as in the Volga colonies. When Stolypin began his land revolution, about 77 percent of peasant households (83 percent of all peasant allotment lands), except in western Russia, were on communal tenure. On the eve of the 1917 revolution, 60 percent of all peasant households (71 percent of all peasant allotment lands) still adhered to communal tenure. The aforementioned factors led the colonists to resist stubbornly the Stolypin land reforms, above all in those colonies where the commune was strong or had been in existence for a long time, and where there were land shortages. While exact figures are lacking, the reform came to be generally accepted only in the more recently founded daughter colonies, especially those in the Novouzensk District steppe, where land was more abundant, land prices lower, the commune less strong, and land redistribution less engrained.[48] By 1910, the land organization commissions in Saratov Province reported that only six colonies (out of fifty-seven) had managed the two-thirds vote in the colony assemblies necessary to convert the whole colony to private ownership and had completed the land survey; all six were small, averaging only 250 households, and had been founded as daughter colonies in the 1850s. None of the original, older colonies had completely forsaken communal landholding, and fewer than 400 households had individually requested private title to their land.[49] By the eve of World War I, only two more colonies (Galka and Nizhniaia Dobrinka), both southern but original colonies not far from the other six, are known to have adopted private land tenure.

In Samara Province, of the 27 colonies (out of about 150 settlements) that converted wholly to private landownership by January 1, 1912, two-thirds (18) were daughter colonies settled in the late 1850s and early 1860s. Approximately 1,100 other individual households had requested and separated themselves from their respective communities.[50] However, less than 10 percent of all colony lands converted to private ownership on the meadow side of Samara Province were located in Nikolaevsk District, which included only original colonies founded in the eighteenth century and where there was severe land pressure. Looking at only entire colonies adopting private landownership, we find that 18 percent of the meadow-side colonies had converted to private landowning, while only 12 percent of the mountain-side colonies revoked communal land tenure. In 1913, a colonist who had followed closely the progress of the reform reported that communal landownership still overwhelmingly predominated in the colonies.[51]

No evidence indicates that the colonies deviated significantly from the general response to the reform elsewhere in the empire. They reacted in much the same way as the peasants living near them, suggesting that local economic and geographic conditions may have been the crucial determinant in acceptance or rejection of the land reform. For example, a regional scarcity of water made access to water or water rights a major concern of all households. There is general agreement, depending on what statistics are used, that by the outbreak of World War I between 15 to 25 percent of formerly communal households had completed their legal withdrawal from the commune and adopted private landownership.[52] Roughly speaking, this held true for the colonies, but a closer examination revealed considerable diversity among the colonies—a diversity that conformed to local Lower Volga variations. The best figures we have on the colonies would appear to support a comparable figure for the meadow-side colony households in Nikolaevsk District (about 21 percent), but a considerably higher one (44 percent) for the recently settled Novouzensk District, where the infant commune was weak; a much smaller figure (10 percent) is found for the more hard-pressed, land-short mountain-side colonies, where there was considerable opposition. How closely the colonists conformed to the local norm can be seen in Kamyshin District, where all but a handful of the Saratov colonies were located; the district zemstvo reported very little support for the reform, with only 6 percent of the district's peasant households having separated from the commune, compared with 7 percent of Volga German households.[53] A similar pattern developed in Novouzensk District. Of all peasant communes in Samara Province, those in Novouzensk District responded most enthusiastically to the reform; likewise, the best colonist response to the reform occurred in Novouzensk District.[54]

Similarly, I. V. Chernyshev found that in the Lower Volga the reform was best received and accepted in the comparatively land-rich settlements with few households (under 175). This pattern also held true for the colonies, where the small colonies most enthusiastically embraced the reform, whereas the old, established, large colonies, most having over 500 households, rejected a complete conversion to private ownership. While whole village conversions to private land use prevailed in the colonies and peasant villages of Samara Province, this happened much less frequently in Saratov Province, where householders individually requested private holdings and withdrew from the commune, suggesting personal factors at work.[55] For example, family size may have prompted a family to separate; a family having lost several adult members might wish to separate, fearing a much smaller allotment during the next land redistribution, or simply to sell its allotment and give up farming. Finally, the initial rush to private ownership had slowed by the time the shots were fired in Sarajevo. In the Volga German settlements, the greatest land activity occurred between 1908 and 1910, but it had slowed drastically by 1911, causing the governor of Samara Province, for example, to order land captains to use all their considerable authority to "promote" the reform.[56]

Although World War I intervened to blur the final results of the Stolypin reform, the last major effort of the tsarist government fell short, certainly not alleviating the Volga Germans' land hunger. Forced to redivide only those lands in their possession, precluded from using Peasant Land Bank funds to augment holdings, and excluded from government-sponsored migration, the colonists found that Stolypin's agrarian reforms offered only the opportunity to sell their land and leave the community. Yet the implications of these conditions paled in comparison to the announced expropriation of the Volga Germans during World War I, to be discussed later. The revolutionary events of 1917 allowed the colonists to vent their feelings openly and freely. That the reform did not stifle the colonists' clamor for land was unmistakably manifested in the actions of the Volga colonists, who, after the overthrow of the Romanov regime, called for the expropriation of all large landholdings so they could be divided among smallholders and landless.

hapter Six

Cottage Industries in the Colonies

The seasonal nature of peasant farming, with its long days of spring and summer work and long periods of winter inactivity, facilitated the development of cottage, or *kustar* industry (or *Hausindustrie*) in the colonies, although such opportunities were limited. As late as 1905, a zemstvo study of Saratov Province reported that peasant farming required about one hundred days of hard labor, leaving two-thirds of the year with not enough work. Considering that the Orthodox peasants celebrated about a hundred holidays, the non-Orthodox colonists had even more spare time.[1] Individuals involved in *kustar* industry were small, rural producers of manufactured goods, who usually worked with simple hand tools in their homes during the nonfarming months. As industries developed, some workers did their manufacturing in small shops and sometimes used machinery. On the whole, the practice of combining agriculture with subsidiary earnings in industry, either as *kustar* or factory workers, was a reflection of the backwardness of both industry and agriculture in Russia.

Kustar industry long played a vital role in the Russian economy, supplying enormous quantities of goods, especially to the rural markets, and creating fortunes for those with the capital and entrepreneurial skills to organize such industries. It augmented peasant pocketbooks with an important supplemental source of cash. Even the development of the factory system failed to eliminate Russia's cottage industries. According to Olga Crisp, factors contributing to the durability and longevity of Russian cottage industry were the particularly seasonal nature of Russian agriculture, the significant price differentials between regions and seasons, the low overhead for such industries, and finally the high value the *kustar* worker attached to his independence: "In most cases there was no competition between him and factory industry, because they concentrated on different products or worked for different markets."[2] Finally, even as late as World War I, the wages of the *kustar* worker compared favorably with those paid factory workers.

The Volga German economy, especially of the mountain-side colonies, became remarkably diversified in the second half of the nineteenth century with the substantial increase in peasant handicrafts and trades. A government report attributed growth of *kustar* industry chiefly to the "increase in population in the colonies. The colonists' families are very large and they feel very strongly the shortage of land, consequently, each year outside [nonfarming] earnings become more and more necessary."[3] Such a need developed overwhelmingly in the less fertile, nonchernozem Volga settlements, where peasants and colonists turned to *kustar* industry when making a living from farming became increasingly difficult and precarious. *Kustar* also developed where there was access to larger markets, meaning proximity to a major trade route, in this case the Volga River via Saratov and Kamyshin; railroads also opened up new markets.[4] And the Volga German colonists brought with them various skills and crafts essential for the development of *kustar* industry.[5]

The "putting out" system for weaving cotton cloth became the largest and most important cottage industry in the Volga German settlements, but it was concentrated almost exclusively in the colonies of Saratov Province, and more particularly those in Kamyshin District. During the second half of the nineteenth century, cotton products were a significant part of Russian domestic trade, becoming the chief article of trade at the great Nizhnii Novgorod fair and accounting for one-third of all its trade; in fact, cotton goods surpassed wool, linen, and other cloth products to become one of the most important trade items in towns and fairs. Although the colonists did not introduce the production of cotton textiles to the Lower Volga region, they were excellent learners and would eventually dominate the industry. The origins of the industry can be traced to the followers of Count Nicholas von Zinzendorf, who, in the 1760s, formed a small, secluded Hutterite mission at Sarepta, over a hundred miles southwest of the Volga colonies. These Moravian or Bohemian Brethren originally were members of a sect deriving from John Hus, but under Zinzendorf's influence they created a strict communal life in which they willingly submitted themselves to discipline, perpetual supervision, and public criticism and censure. Among the Hutterites were several weavers who first wove silk and wool but soon switched to cotton, or *sarpinka*, as the cloth became commonly known, taking its name from the nearby Sarpa River. In time, throughout Russia this cloth became synonymous with sturdy calico.

The Hutterites' missionary activity among the Volga colonies was considerable, but most beneficial was the skill of weaving that the Volga Germans learned from the Brethren during the first quarter of the nineteenth century as a result of the expansion of the Sarepta weaving operations.[6] Originally, the Hutterites performed all functions (spinning, warping, dyeing, and weaving), but because of a shortage of labor and the strong demand for the cloth after 1800, the Brethren consigned the spinning of thread to Volga colonists. Simultaneously, a few colonists sent children to Sarepta to learn the weaving craft, and they later introduced it into the colonies. Spinning of thread gradually ceased within the Volga German settlements, as more cheaply produced thread from England and Moscow became available, and as weaving began to spread among colonist households.

In 1816, the Sarepta weavers moved their operations to the town of Saratov. Sarepta proved to be a poor location, distant from population centers and transportation routes. After two devastating fires in the community, the weavers decided to move closer to a large weaving workshop they had established in 1810 in the Volga German colony of Norka, thirty miles southwest of Saratov. The Saratov weaving mill on German Street struggled along until the early 1830s, when it finally went bankrupt. Even the financial and technical assistance of the Schechtel brothers, who imported master weavers from the West, failed to save the concern.

The collapse of the Saratov weaving mill was not peculiar, but paralleled the experience of the entire Russian cotton-weaving industry. According to a leading authority, "The first half of the 19th century was characterized by a struggle between cottage and factory weaving which resulted in a decisive victory for the former."[7] Many factors contributed to the failure of the Saratov weaving operation. The Schechtel brothers had become financially overextended. The higher costs of town production, entailed by the payment of the requisite fees and imposts, placed it at a disadvantage. The Lower Volga provided a limited market for the superior quality but high-priced cloth, and competition from the nascent colony cottage weaving played a part too. Peasants and nomads of the region wove their own cloth or could only afford the coarse and cheaper cottage-woven cloth. The full-time master weavers required higher wages than the part-time cottage weavers, who also had livelihoods from farming. Thus, as M. I. Tugan-Baranovksy asserted, "Large-scale capitalist production decidedly lost its place, and independent *kustar* cottage weaving, the direct offspring of the factory, won out."[8]

The Schechtel brothers' unfortunate financial fiasco proved a boon for the colony hand weavers. The closure of the Saratov weaving mill and spread of weaving skills in the Volga colonies quickened the development of the sarpinka putting-out system in the 1840s and 1850s. The unemployed master weavers left Saratov and traveled about the colonies, instructing colonists in the finest and latest weaving techniques. A few even settled in the colonies. The spinning and weaving of cotton were technically simple operations easily and eagerly learned by the Volga Germans. The weaving of plain cloth could be learned in about a month, and the loom was an inexpensive tool. By 1837, there were already about 1,000 weavers in the colonies who had earned an estimated total income of 716,400 rubles.[9]

The Volga German weavers worked alone in their homes, mainly between October and April, but actually any time they were free from field work. Originally weaving was a male craft, but by 1900 half of the weavers were women. The interior of the weaver's home looked like a small mill with one or two large, simple looms—depending on the number of weavers in the household—abutting a wall or partition. Nearby were benches on which children or elderly household members sat while they wound thread on spools. Parents frequently kept children out of school to augment the family's livelihood. The long hours and backbreaking work took their toll on the weavers, some of whom labored sixteen hours a day in dimly lit houses. An unnatural working position placed tremendous strain on the back muscles: the weaver's unsupported feet were constantly in motion as they raised and depressed the treadles, and arms and hands moved swiftly to operate the shuttle and beam. Humped, or weaver's, back and arthritic hands were painful and common physical afflictions.

Whereas weaving was a wearying but fairly simple skill, the organization of cloth manufacturing represented a much more complex process. The absence of local materials, the necessity of having to prepare thread for weaving, and the need to find ways to market the woven cloth led to a capitalist form of production and the rise of cloth merchants, called *fabrikanty*, or capitalist intermediaries, who established *fabrichnye* and *razdatochnye kontory* (mills and shops) that prepared and distributed raw materials to the colonists. Former weavers themselves, the cloth merchants purchased thread and indigo about 600 miles upriver at Nizhnii Novgorod, the great trading city at the junction of the Volga and Oka, or Moscow (eventually going abroad to England and Elberfeld, a Rhenish town, for the finest thread), dyed and warped the thread, and then "put it out" to other colonist families for weaving.[10] Dyeing and warping were completed in the mill of the *fabrikant*, who performed these operations himself or employed hired help. The weavers received a piece-rate wage based on the type of cloth and amount of work completed. The *fabrikant* had to examine closely the quality of cloth, to guard constantly against embezzlement and wastage, and to see that orders were completed on time. An 1870 visitor to the colonies described the sarpinka industry in this way:

Now you will find in almost every colony several sarpinka factories, but these factories are nothing like those built on a large scale by wealthy manufacturers. Expecting to come across buildings where the latest machines are working and where hundreds or thousands of hands are employed, you will be sadly mistaken. The manufacture of sarpinka here is done in a completely different manner: at the home of the cloth merchant [*fabrikant*] is built a dye-works for bluing yarn, where the master himself works, and in some cases hired help. The *fabrikant* then gives the blued yarn to the weavers, who work at home on their looms of simple construction. Each *fabrikant* has about 150–200 looms working for him. You will not find in colonies having sarpinka factories one home where they are not weaving sarpinka, excepting the home of the *fabrikanty* or wealthy individuals working in trade or commerce. The weavers are paid by arshin—a rate of 3 to 5 kopecks per arshin. It is said that the very best weavers and female weavers (women weave, but men predominate) can weave up to 16 hours a day maximum.[11]

The high concentration of the sarpinka industry in a few hands and areas (four townships in Kamyshin District) remained a notable characteristic of this cottage industry. While it is not possible to resolve the competing claims of Golyi Karamysh (Balzer) and Ust' Zolikh (Messer) for the title of "founder" of the sarpinka industry in the colonies, obviously these two settlements dominated the industry. Most of the dyeing and warping of thread was done in the mills of these two colonies, which sometimes employed thirty to fifty full-time workers; and as late as 1911 fourteen of the twenty-seven dye and warp works were in Golyi Karamysh.[12] Weaving was done in colonists' homes in these and surrounding colonies. By 1888, twenty-four colonies in Kamyshin District monopolized the industry with 7,000 looms and 5,742 weavers.[13] Similarly, a few colonist families controlled the industry and accumulated great wealth, which would later be invested in other ventures. By the 1850s, three families dominated the industry—the Borels, Schmidts, and Reinachs, who lived and operated in Golyi Karamysh, Ust' Zolikh, and Popovka (Brennig), respectively.[14] The profitable sarpinka trade at the great Nizhnii Novgorod fair, the largest in all Russia, which lasted from July 15 to September 10, remained under the complete control of the Borel and Schmidt families. These leading merchant families eventually opened branches and worked with many smaller middlemen in other colonies, but particularly in Gololobovka (Donnhof), Lesnoi Karamysh (Grimm), Splavnukha (Huck), and Norka. Even though most of these original sarpinka merchant families would later sell their sarpinka interests and leave the trade to invest their capital in the lucrative grain and flour trade, the sarpinka industry would remain in the hands of a few. On the eve of World War I, only seventeen families controlled the sarpinka business, and just five families employed 60 percent of the weavers.[15]

A brief survey of the history of the sarpinka trade reveals that sarpinka became available in the 1840s as a locally marketed, cheap, coarse cloth manufactured in one or two colors, desired and consumed exclusively by peasants. By the end of the century it was a nationally marketed, high-quality, durable, and colorful cloth, purchased by urban dwellers as well. Sarpinka production began to expand rapidly in the 1860s as the cloth gained popularity among peasant women for summer dresses (*sarafan*). In 1866, according to official Saratov Kontora figures, sarpinka statistics were truly impressive: sixty-nine sarpinka dyeing and warping enterprises (a fivefold increase since 1855) prepared 30,000 puds of thread for 6,000 looms, which produced revenues of 1,156,000 rubles.[16] This rapid expansion of the industry resulted in an oversupply of cloth in the 1870s, glutting the local and regional markets, which included the settlements and fairs of Saratov, Samara, and Astrakhan provinces, the Don Cossack region, parts of Simbirsk and Kazan provinces, and the Nizhnii Novgorod fair. In 1874, revenues dropped to 800,000 rubles, largely because of the poor harvests of 1872 and 1873. As profits continued to fall in the 1870s with reduced sales, due in part to more bad harvests and the appearance of cheaper, machine-made, multicolored, and patterned Moscow cloth, the Borel family made an abortive effort to form a stock association of sarpinka producers which could purchase thread and dyes in quantity and on better terms, therefore making sarpinka prices competitive with the cheap Moscow chintzes.[17] The other producers suspected Borel was scheming to gain control of the industry by forcing them into heavy indebtedness in order to buy them out.

The arrival of the railroad in the Lower Volga revitalized sarpinka industry in the 1880s and boosted sales by opening up the national market. According to one source, "The strong stimulus to sarpinka production came in the 1880s when the Saratov region became joined to the Moscow region by railroad."[18] Sarpinka sales spread, with extensive marketing in the Ukraine, Central Asia, and even the Moscow region. One foreign observer noted, "Sarpinka could still be bought at fairs throughout Russia at the beginning of the century."[19] This growth pattern generally continued until the outbreak of World War I. In 1900, there were eighty sarpinka factories supplying materials to over 7,000 weavers.[20] The strong demand for thread led to the establishment in 1901 of the *Fabrika Saratovskoi manufaktury*, which soon supplied half of all the Volga German weavers' needs. An observer optimistically asserted: "*Kustar* weaving, with the correct arrangement of production—weavers being supplied with good quality thread and improved types of equipment—has a secure future, especially in localities far from the industrial region."[21] Another reason for the viability of the industry was that the home weaver could and would work for less than the factory weaver. Even on the eve of the 1917 revolution, sarpinka sales remained strong because sarpinka cost three to four kopecks less per comparable unit of factory cloth.

The 1904–5 strike and revolutionary movement in the Russian Empire not only did not disrupt sarpinka production, inasmuch as the weavers did not work in factories and had no workers' organizations, but in fact the strikers' shutdown of textile factories in Moscow, Lodz, and Ivanovsk increased the demand for sarpinka. In 1905, factory inspectors reported that employment in the manufacture of sarpinka in the Volga colonies and neighboring Russian villages had soared to 10,000 workers.[22]

The increased used of Central Asian domestic cotton rather than foreign, chiefly American and Egyptian cotton, also benefited the Volga textile mills because of cheaper transport costs and the high duties imposed on cotton imports; by 1906, Central Asian cotton supplied almost half of Russia's needs. In 1911, sarpinka sales soared to 3.5 million rubles.[23] The outbreak of World War I badly disrupted sarpinka production by creating raw material shortages, less demand for the cloth, and the need to seek more local markets; most dyes came from Germany, and the Central Powers' blockade of Russia dried up the dye supply. Interestingly, conscription did not decrease the number of weavers, because other family members assumed the work of the drafted weavers.

In the 1880s and 1890s, the Volga German *fabrikanty* implemented some astute improvements in weaving, dyeing, design, and product diversification to advance and promote the industry. The chief result was a lighter, more colorful and patterned sarpinka. The Borel family manufactured eighty different colored and patterned fabrics, some quite embellished and decorative. An official in the Ministry of State Domains observed, "Such concern of the *fabrikanty* [for improved cloth] has promoted strong sales of sarpinka."[24] Sarpinka won honors and awards at several major textile exhibitions, while sarpinka scarves and stockings became popular trade items.

Sales and marketing underwent profound but sophisticated changes also. Several sales offices opened in Saratov, and a few of the *fabrikanty* established sales offices in Ekaterinoslav, Kharkov, Orenburg, Baku, and even distant Tashkent. About a decade after Richard Sears sent out his first mail-order catalog in 1886, mail-order sales and free illustrated catalogs were introduced, largely as a result of the aggressive and innovative marketing of Ivan Kuznetsov and Andrei Stepanov of Saratov, both of whom became partners in the Borel enterprises.[25] These two entrepreneurs studied foreign and domestic fabric designs and colors, and encouraged the *fabrikanty* to produce more colorful fabrics, which the Russian peasants preferred. They mailed their price and cloth lists to merchants and likely buyers, in some cases even sending along cloth swatches, promising to honor all orders. Their goal was to familiarize people with sarpinka so that they would request it from merchants, who in turn would send in large orders. By the turn of the century, all the large *fabrikanty* were using illustrated catalogs to advertise their wares.

Cutthroat competition occurred in the 1890s, when smaller *fabrikanty* eagerly expanded production in the hopes of garnering a larger share of the rapidly growing sarpinka traffic. The wealthier entrepreneurs tried to squeeze out the smaller ones by luring away their weavers with higher pay. This led to an unexpected but extraordinary development. In 1898, one *fabrikant* paid 7,500 rubles to 100 weavers of a competitor as an enticement to switch employers; the victimized *fabrikant*, V. P. Merkel, stubbornly refusing to buckle under, recruited Russian weavers in the settlement of Potapovka. He provided looms on time and offered free instruction by Volga German weavers. Until that time, sarpinka weaving had been exclusively in the hands of the Volga Germans. By 1902, this Russian settlement already had 806 looms, and weaving had spread to neighboring Russian settlements, thereby ending the Volga German sarpinka monopoly.[26] Even though sarpinka businessmen competed bitterly, relations between the Volga German and Russian weavers, who continued to live in their separate settlements, remained peaceable and businesslike; in fact, in 1918 they amicably and voluntarily formed a joint weavers' cooperative.[27] Thus, curiously and unexpectedly the Volga Germans did serve as models for their Slavic neighbors, providing skills, technical assistance, and economic benefits to some Russian peasants, though not in the area of cultivation and animal husbandry as so often cited.

Although earnings from weaving remained low, they were an excellent and vital source of supplemental income for many colony households. Piece-rate wages prevailed in the manufacturing of sarpinka: weavers were paid by the length of cloth and children by the number of spools. The rates, which fluctuated widely from year to year, were primarily dependent on sales and market demand. Since sarpinka was sold mainly to peasants, the volume of sales was directly related to the size of harvests. In the 1870s, during a bountiful harvest year, a weaver could earn between 60 and 84 kopecks a day; in a poor harvest year, such as 1872, earnings dropped to between 36 and 48 kopecks a day. Wages became more depressed in the 1880s because of the competition of factory cloth, the growing number of colonists who were turning to weaving, and the onset of a serious agricultural depression. In the 1880–1914 period, an average daily wage of between 33 and 45 kopecks was common. An average weaver could weave thirteen and one-half arshins a day (one arshin equals twenty-eight inches), and normally received 3 or 4 kopecks per arshin. Thus an average weaver earned about 58 rubles a year, based on a working year of 150 days and an average rate of 39 kopecks a day. Children generally earned about 7 or 8 kopecks a day. Therefore, a typical weaving family could expect to earn about 75 rubles a year.[28]

Scholars have not adequately assessed, understood, and stated the significance of the sarpinka cottage industry in the Volga German settlements. Without doubt, most of the Volga Germans in Saratov Province enjoyed greater prosperity and less socioeconomic stratification than neighboring peasants, not because they were "model" agriculturalists, as is often asserted, but because they had well-developed cottage industries, chief of which was the manufacture of sarpinka. A 1903 zemstvo survey of the Volga German sarpinka industry concluded as much: "Therefore, the populations of Sosnovka and other manufacturing townships enjoy prosperity and an absence of overwhelming poverty [*podavliaiushchei bednosti*], as well as comparatively less sharp differentiation among the people than is observed in neighboring townships with a purely farming population."[29]

The earnings from sarpinka gave some colonies in Saratov Province a measure of security, which not even the wheat-growing colonies in Samara Province enjoyed. The fact that one-fourth to one-third of a family's earnings came from a second income spared them from total dependence on unpredictable harvests. Reporting how sarpinka earnings saved many mountain-side settlers from hunger, a government official wrote, "If such [peasant] industries existed in Samara Province, serving as a supplemental source of earnings to farming, then they would not suffer from hunger."[30] The colonists themselves recognized the critical importance of sarpinka to their survival. Jacob Fritzler, village clerk of Rossoshi (Franzosen), acknowledged that earnings from weaving saved colonists from terrible hunger: "If we had had to live off of the 1898 harvest alone, then the people would have starved [*to naseleniiu prishlos' by golodat'*]." Similar reports from other colonies corroborated his conclusion: "In Vershinka [Kautz] shortages were felt from December to February and were fulfilled partly by loans [of grain] from the communal granary, but *most of all from earnings from sarpinka weaving*" (italics mine). And from Ust' Zolikh (Messer): "Thanks to sarpinka production, well developed in our settlement, the people did not need food provisions [from the zemstvo]."[31]

The sarpinka industry also relieved the acute land problem in the colonies, because many weaving families leased out part or all of their land allotments to other households. Zemstvo observers noted: "In general the production of sarpinka to a significant degree neutralizes [*paralizuet*] the demand for land."[32] It is noteworthy that the mountain-side colonies with the most serious land shortages were the sarpinka manufacturing ones, which were also generally regarded as the most prosperous ones. This is clearly stated in the above-mentioned 1903 zemstvo report of the Volga German sarpinka industry. This distinction between the poorer farming colonies and the better-off colonies with cottage industries was also discerned by the colonists themselves. Talking about the colonists of the farming colony of Walter, a former resident perceptively observed: "That's why they were a poor colony. Walter as a colony were [*sic*] primarily farmers. Some of the larger colonies had some industry."[33]

Finally, the sarpinka trade had created a vast wealth of technical know-how and expertise in the Lower Volga of great value to the state. The sarpinka dyeworks turned out brilliant, fade-resistant colored yarns and fabrics considered among the best in the empire. Observers praised the weavers' diligence, discipline, and work ethic, and recognized the exquisite mastery of the weavers who could skillfully and swiftly perform all weaving functions. Writing in 1918 of the advanced art of the weavers, the national *kustar* industry journal noted: "Many weavers operate 5, 7, and even 8 footboards, which manipulate several shuttles used for the feeding of the weft in multicolored cloth . . . . Interest in their work is so palpable among the men and women that one feels a kind of sporting competition to attain the greatest production and highest quality . . . ."[34] In the rural wasteland of Russia, the Volga Germans created in the textiles field a technical and material oasis of inestimable benefit to the state and society.

The image of colonist craftsmen as simple weavers monotonously transfixed to their looms is incomplete, because although textile weaving was the most advanced and widely dispersed cottage industry in the Volga German settlements, employing thousands of people, several mountain-side colonies developed other significant peasant crafts and industries, including even some small-scale manufacturing concerns engaged particularly in the production of agricultural equipment. By the 1890s, the colonists' skills and reputation as farm machinery manufacturers were well established and widely recognized, as was noted in a multivolume popular reference book: "The production of agricultural equipment . . . is found also in Simbirsk Province, but above all in Saratov Province, where the center of this production is the German colony Lesnoi Karamysh."[35]

The production of simple agricultural machinery originated in the Saratov province colonies as a *kustar* industry, with individual craftsmen and their apprentices creating and assembling all or most parts of the equipment in small workshops. Blacksmithing, an important and widespread occupation in the colonies, laid the technical foundations for the sizable manufacture of agricultural machinery in the post-1860 period. The blacksmith produced the iron parts for the wagons, carts, plows, and wheels which the colonist *kustari* could not produce themselves. The development of capitalist farming in the Lower Volga also generated a tremendous demand for inexpensive, sturdy farm machinery. Iron plows, winnowing machines, and threshing stones produced in the mountain-side colonies of Saratov Province could be found in almost every village of the Lower Volga region and Siberia. In this regard, the Saratov and Samara province colonies became remarkably complementary: hard-pressed Saratov colonists eagerly sought sideline occupations to supplement their marginal farming income, and the rapid expansion of capitalist commodity farming in the trans-Volga colonies created a good market for farm machinery. The only Samara Province colony engaged in manufacturing was the large, bustling trading settlement of Ekaterinenstadt. Thus the equipment industry in the mountain-side colonies broadened its local base and eventually supplied most of the manufactured agricultural equipment used in the meadow-side colonies.[36]

Until the 1890s, the manufacture of plows remained primarily a *kustar* industry. Statistics and details on the production of plows are limited, but colonist skills in this area are frequently mentioned. A zemstvo report noted that in most parts of Saratov Province the iron plow had become the primary cultivating implement by the 1880s, outnumbering the traditional wood plow [*sokha*] by two to one, thus giving rise to the "important farm implement industry in some of the colonies."[37] It said that the expansion of farming in the southeastern parts of Russia had led to large demands for the colonist-made plows because the light and wheelless *sokha* could not cut the soils of the region deeply enough. Another observer noted that colonist implement manufacturers were remarkably adept imitators, who could quickly and precisely duplicate machinery that they saw: "In 1882 and 1883 the original two-plowshare Eckert plow first appeared south of Saratov in Kamyshin District, and by 1885 German blacksmiths in Kamyshin District settlements began to make a similar two-plowshare plow."[38] In 1889, one of the craftsmen, the report continued, had received "very high praise" at the Saratov Province zemstvo agricultural exhibition. The colonists' reputation as skilled machinists grew steadily, and was often mentioned in advertisements for machinery they had produced, an indication of the high regard for their craftsmanship.

The *kustar* plow industry continued to thrive until the 1890s, when it gradually lost much of the market to domestic and foreign factory produced goods. By 1914, imports, primarily from Germany, accounted for about 45 percent of

Russia's farm machinery sales. The capitalist form of production could be seen in the emergence of "machine construction factories" (*mashino-stroitel'nye zavody*) in the colonies. These so-called factories housed their own large foundries, in which all metal parts were cast, and they completed all manufacturing processes under one roof, employed many metalworkers and several woodworkers, required a sizable unskilled work force, and used traveling salesmen to market the finished product.[39] The keen competition of the "factories" gradually forced many individual craftsmen to sign on as wage laborers in these more sophisticated machine shops.

Although machine shops employing a sizable wage-labor force developed in many colonies, two colonies gained preeminence as the home of two of the most advanced plow factories in the Lower Volga region: Bauer and Sons of Golyi Karamysh and F. F. Schaeffer and Brothers of Ekaterinenstadt. Simple but business-minded blacksmiths founded both enterprises. The original Bauer, whose first name is unknown, was described as being "sharp" (*smetlivyi*), for he not only repaired foreign machinery but learned to copy it, and became particularly renowned for perfecting his plows; because he made several plows (including the popular Eckert foreign model) which were adapted to different soil conditions, his reputation spread and business boomed.[40] In 1888, his steam-powered plow factory, which stamped and cast all its parts, began to manufacture fire-fighting equipment that was marketed as far away as western Siberia. Similarly, although originally founded as a plow factory in 1880 by a metalworking wizard, the Ekaterinenstadt-based F. F. Schaeffer Brothers' Factory of Agricultural Machinery and Equipment on the eve of World War I was making all types of sophisticated, motor-powered machinery and was heavily involved in the construction and renovation of steam-powered flour mills which used complex grain-grinding machinery.[41]

Artisans in the colonies also replicated unsophisticated and inexpensive tools particularly well suited to the cultivation methods of the peasants. What the cotton gin was to cotton, so the winnowing machine was to wheat. The simple, time-consuming, and inefficient old ways of manually winnowing the wheat from chaff, dirt, and weed seeds could never completely separate out the small nongrain particles. Cockle seed and chess, or cheat, in particular could not be separated by primitive winnowing methods. This lowered the price of the marketed grain considerably, and, if the grain was sent to the mill unseparated, of the flour itself.

By the end of the nineteenth century, most peasants in southeastern Russia and western Siberia were chattering about and were quite familiar with the so-called *kolonisty*, which they greatly admired and appreciated. The ever popular *kolonisty* were seemingly omnipresent, for they were very sturdy, simple, but marvelously efficient winnowing machines. M. A. Shevchenko claimed that the Volga Germans crafted about 25 percent of all winnowing machines sold in Siberia.[42] Curiously, it might be argued that the Volga German colonists became best known and respected among the peasant farmers of Russia for their manufacturing and not for their farming, especially since the term *kolonist* gained common parlance associated with a type of winnowing machine. Many winnowers later bore the trademark *Kolonistok* or *Kolonistin*, as producers recognized the popular connotations of the term and had it wood-burned on their machines to promote sales.

The origins of the *kustar* manufacture of winnowing machines, or *Putzmaschines*, as the colonists called them, are to be found in the colony of Lesnoi Karamysh (Grimm), and corroborate again the skill of the colonists in copying equipment. According to several sources, in 1874 a certain D. Leonhardt, a large sower in Grimm, purchased a winnower from Mennonites in Samara Province, which two Grimm joiners serviced and repaired. Despite many problems, particularly the difficulty in finding good cast metal parts, by 1875 the joiners Faas and Brunhardt had produced their first model winnower. The new, no-frills machine quickly gained acceptance among local colonists and peasants. The great demand for the machine led to the dispersion of the industry to many Saratov Province colonies as village craftsmen sought to meet local demand, but Lesnoi Karamysh remained the leader of the industry. In 1890, about one-tenth of its households were engaged in the manufacture of winnowers.[43] Norka and Gololobovka (Donnhof) also became major producing centers. The abundant harvests of 1882–85 saw a surge in new shops and producers. Growth in the 1890s continued as sales expanded beyond local markets to the trans-Volga steppe, Siberia, the Don Forces Oblast, and the Ukraine, but weakened after the turn of the century because of factory competition. During the pre-1914 peak years, annual production reached as high as 25,000 machines.[44]

The *Putzmaschine* returned almost a fourfold profit over costs until the turn of the century. Cost of production varied between 13 and 15 rubles, requiring little start-up money. During the last three decades of the century, a machine usually sold for between 40 and 50 rubles, although for several years in the 1880s, prices soared to 70 and 80 rubles. Individual artisans could easily clear 150 rubles annually: "Such high earnings from the craft, on the one hand, and little income from agriculture on the other, caused more and more parts of the population to begin to take up its production. Consequently, thanks to the existence of this craft, a relatively small part of the population of ten settlements extracts very solid earnings, which are a very prominent item in the budget of the local peasantry."[45] Revenues for 1901 yielded profits of over a quarter of a million rubles. The increase in number of manufacturers led to continued improvements and changes in the machine, but reduced profits as well.

As factory or shop production gradually dominated the market and transformed the winnow machine industry, it became increasingly specialized and concentrated, and showed smaller profit margins. This transformation was generally accomplished during the post-1895 decade. Local blacksmiths lost more and more of the metal parts market to the large, modern Strecker Foundry in Lesnoi Karamysh; handcrafted wood parts gave way to mechanical production; and individual *kustari* began to face the rigorous competition of machine shops based on a more efficient division of labor. Zemstvo reports stated that by 1902, just ten colonies in Sosnovskaia township (which also dominated the sarpinka industry) manufactured most of the machines, with annual total production reaching as high as 25,000 to 30,000 units, but that machine shops in Lesnoi Karamysh alone accounted for over half of them.[46] By 1910, the price of winnowers had fallen to only 20 rubles. Even with the marketing assistance of the district zemstvo, the colonist winnowing industry had become stagnant by 1914, and the wartime agrarian crisis only hastened its decline.[47] The industry survived the war and revolution badly crippled, and in 1926–27 the colonists were hoping to be able to manufacture 4,500 machines, a sixfold decrease from prewar production.[48] Whether these production figures were met is not known.

Threshing stones were the last noteworthy farm tool produced in the colonies. Almost all the threshing stones used in the colonies and many peasant villages in the Lower Volga were cut in two Volga German settlements: Nizhniaia Dobrinka (Dobrinka) and Verkhniaia Dobrinka (Dreispitz), located in the southernmost part of Kamyshin District in the vicinity of the Volga River. These two areas shared a sandy vein of rock. Again imitators, the Dobrinka colonists learned the craft from Mennonites; the threshing stone, explained an 1891 zemstvo report, "was first introduced into Kamyshin District about thirty years ago [1860] in Ust' Kulalinskaia township, thanks to the instructions of Mennonites (settlers from Tauride Province going to resettle in Samara Province) who brought along their model [threshing stone], according to whose design the local artisans began to make them out of local stone and to distribute them not only in Kamyshin District, but even in neighboring districts of Saratov and Samara Provinces."[49]

The threshing stone was actually a horse-drawn cylindrical stone-roller three feet wide and two feet in diameter, which was drawn over sheaves of wheat placed on a smooth, hard threshing surface. Much more efficient than the flail, the traditional peasant threshing tool, and much less expensive and complicated than the threshing machine, which came to be widely adopted only in large-scale farming, the threshing stone found a ready place in peasant agriculture. Originally as high as twenty rubles, the price of threshing stones had fallen to six rubles by the 1890s because of several bad harvests. One stone-cutter working full days could finish two stones a week. Although no complete figures are available on the size of this craft, in Verkhniaia Dobrinka alone approximately 150 stonecutters, or one male per household, made threshing stones in the off-season, when the threshing stone trade was at its peak.[50]

Another Volga German *kustar* industry that gained a provincewide reputation—although it was nowhere near as important economically as sarpinka weaving or as well known as the agricultural equipment industry—was the leather tanning industry. In the numerous tanneries, hides were soaked in large vats of solution, then scraped, washed, resoaked, and dyed. The process required considerable skill and precision so as not to make the leather too brittle or too weak. The tanning industry prospered because it was basic to so many other crafts, such as shoemaking and bootmaking, harness making and saddlery, and outer garment tailoring. The hides came chiefly from Saratov Province, but also from Astrakhan Province and the trans-Volga steppe.

The tanning business became highly capitalistic and was concentrated in just two Kamyshin District colonies. Tanning had begun as a locally oriented *kustar* industry, with the colonist household specializing in the craft and family members doing all the work. As the leather trade expanded, particularly in the 1860s and 1870s, the industry changed markedly. Production shifted from the colonist's home to a mill or shop where hired, skilled workers earned a wage from the leather *fabrikant*, who owned all the tools and equipment. This economic development was not peculiar to the colonies, but was observed throughout the Lower Volga. The *kustar* tanner usually specialized in certain aspects of the tanning process, while the capitalist mills performed all tanning processes. Thus, by the 1880s, unlike the sarpinka weavers who worked seasonally in their homes, the approximately 165 tanners had become full-time factory hands employed year-round in twenty-four colony mills.[51] Golyi Karamysh (Balzer) and Sevastianovka (Anton) cornered the trade; they had twenty-one tanning works, which employed 40 percent of all the tanners in Saratov Province. The four tanning mills of Sevastianovka had seen their revenues more than double in eight years, totaling almost 20,000 rubles by 1892; the smaller but more numerous tanning mills in Golyi Karamysh generated revenues only half those of the larger Sevastianovka mills. A zemstvo report stated that the slower increase in the tanning industry in Golyi Karamysh resulted from *fabrikanty* investing in "sarpinka weaving, which, being very profitable compared to tanning, attracted capital and labor to it."[52] As a locally and regionally marketed commodity, leather goods suffered not so much from the competition of Moscow factory-produced goods as from the high prices of raw materials and the depressed economic effects of bad harvests. Nevertheless, "the industry has become so engrained, that the well-being of very many families depends more upon it than upon agriculture."[53]

Finally, one must not forget to mention the colonists' production of tobacco pipes, which began to boom in the mid-1860s. Since the colonists loved to smoke, with many beginning in their teens, and pipes were less a fire hazard than cigarettes, pipemaking developed as an important craft in the colonies, particularly since public cigarette smoking was prohibited in the colonies and many peasant villages as a fire protection measure. One of the things strictly enforced by the colonists employing hired laborers was the ban on cigarette smoking. And all pipes had to have lids to prevent the escape of tobacco ashes.[54] Individual artisans in two colonies, Lesnoi Karamysh and Popovka, specialized in the pipemaking craft, which remained a noncapitalist craft up to the eve of the 1917 revolutions. It took three years to become a skilled pipemaker, and by the turn of the century there were approximately 250 pipemakers in these two mountain-side colonies. There were no pipe factories, shops, or producer artels, each master being the sole boss of his own enterprise. There was not even a division of labor; each artisan purchased his materials locally (maple was most in demand), made all pipe parts (with family members assisting in the cleaning of the wood), and consigned the pipes for sale. Pipe prices varied considerably, depending chiefly on the quality or type of the pipe. Cheap peasant pipes sold for as little as four kopecks, but finely crafted ones could bring as much as four rubles. In one week, a master could make four of the highest quality, ten to twenty of average quality, or fifty of the lowest grade. Most were consigned for sale in Saratov and Samara provinces but some artisans sold their wares in such distant cities as Penza, Orenburg, and Astrakhan.[55] As a rule, the artisan received from the consignee one-half of the selling price.

Pipemaking, though limited to a small number of artisans, was a lucrative occupation in the colonies. According to a government report in 1888, "One must assume that this craft gives undoubtedly large profits to the colonists, since some of them have left farming and begun to work exclusively in the making of pipes."[56] In the early 1870s, pipemaking profits amounted to almost 20,000 rubles. Two late nineteenth-century sources cited annual production figures of over 800,000 pipes, with a value of over 300,000 rubles. This would mean an income of roughly 150,000 rubles for the pipemakers themselves, from which, of course, costs would have to be deducted (although costs were only about one-fourth of the price).[57] This would indicate profits double those of the 1870s.

The post-1905 period witnessed some decline but not the demise of the colony *kustar* industry, which had enjoyed considerable growth since its founding. Factory production brought stiffer competition, but it was not the chief threat to the industry, because cottage workers could and would work for less than factory wages. The two most important retardants were the increasing number of settlers and peasants who took up crafts and trades to help supplement farm earnings (and, in turn, depressed *kustar* wages), and the decline in purchasing power resulting from poor harvests, which sent shock waves through the local and regional economies. The fall in agricultural prices seriously affected *kustar* workers. As long as farm prices remained strong and the costs of production remained low, especially labor and raw materials, the future of the *kustar* industry seemed propitious.[58]

The former colonists who lived in Saratov Province were materially better off than their peasant neighbors, primarily because they had developed *kustar* industries to supplement their incomes. The economic diversification provided by *kustar* industries was a way to ensure their economic survival, because the nature and shortage of land, coupled with an enormous population increase, meant that farming alone could not sustain them. This economic diversification of the Volga German economy in Saratov Province provided a sounder and more secure existence than the more specialized and less-developed economies of the neighboring peasants. We know full well that the peasants' plight cannot just be blamed on vodka, as most critics of peasant backwardness claimed, but was the result of the many adverse conditions of their lives, such as bad weather, pest crop destruction, small land allotments, low grain prices, high rents for leased land, and others. All of these variables applied to the colonists as well; but the absence of an extensive *kustar* industry among the neighboring peasants, which would have given them work and money during their idle winter months as well as easing pressure on their land, made their livelihood more precarious and less prosperous.

As early as the 1830s, outsiders expressed amazement at the large number of trades and handicraftsmen in the Saratov colonies; and in the 1870s it was actually observed that farming by peasants and colonists remained at about the same level, yet the colonists appeared more prosperous, a fact mainly attributed to the colonists' "diverse sideline crafts which act as a supplemental income to grain farming." It was said: "All these crafts have a favorable influence on the welfare of the colonist. First, he does not have to buy and order different things in the town, where everything is much more expensive, and second, he always has some real earnings to put in his purse, making it possible for him to pay his taxes, set aside a kopeck during crop failures, or in favorable times to begin some kind of larger scale trade."[59] Almost forty years later, a zemstvo survey of peasant agriculture of Saratov Province taken on the eve of World War I noted the same striking contrast between peasants and colonists, and observed re-grettably that peasant agriculture had not changed significantly: "The population lives comparatively poorly, since the only occupation is farming—there are no industries; they work only in the summer and there is practically nothing to do in the winter, and they live on only what they can get from summer work and their harvests, which are small, since land is insufficient."[60]

While these statements attest clearly to the superiority of the cottage industries of colonists over the enterprises of neighboring peasants, rudimentary zemstvo statistics also corroborate this. Although considerable variations are found in statistical reporting, the Kamyshin District zemstvo tax roll surveys of enterprises in colonies and peasant villages included enough standard

Table 8: Number and Estimated Value of Village Enterprises

Year	Colonies		Peasant Villages	
	Number	*Value (rubles)*	*Number*	*Value (rubles)*
1867	1,109	266,473	548	88,097
1872	1,216	249,395	588	90,914
1886	913	441,488	451	146,905

categories to be able to make some generalizations. They regularly recorded the number of rural enterprises and their estimated value (Table 8). Over the twenty years represented, the value of colony enterprises remained about three times greater than that of neighboring peasant enterprises, even though the population of both groups remained about equal.[61] In the two years for which estimated income was recorded, income earnings of colonist industries remained treble those of the peasant enterprises.

The development of numerous crafts, trades, and cottage industries transformed many mountain-side colonies into large commercial-industrial towns, but particularly those in sarpinka-producing Sosnovskaia township, where 45 percent of the households did not engage in farming, instead earning their livelihood from nonagricultural work; this figure was twice as high as that of the rest of the province.[62] Lenin himself noted the capitalist manufacturing in the colonies of this township.[63] In the thirteen settlements of this township, which comprised one-third of all the colonists in Saratov Province, the average size settlement was 5,500. Yet by 1910, the four largest colonies were bustling, thriving urban centers: Norka, Lesnoi Karamysh, Golyi Karamysh, and Medveditskoi Krestovoi Buerak, all with populations between 10,000 and 15,000. In 1900, all of Russia had only sixty-five towns with over 20,000 inhabitants; no wonder that Russian travelers marveled at the sight of such unusually large towns so close together. Thirteen colonies had between 5,000 and 10,000 inhabitants. Thus, of all the colonists in Saratov Province, approximately 65 percent lived in towns of over 5,000, whereas in 1897 only 13 percent of the empire's population were urban dwellers and in 1922 only 16 percent of the Soviet population lived in towns.[64] This in itself—such large towns—posed a striking contrast to the smaller peasant villages which retained their quintessentially rural, not to mention their often dilapidated and squalid, appearance.

A healthy *kustar* industry also stimulated and created diverse subsidiary trades and jobs. Salaried agents, who worked as intermediaries between the cottage artisans and the owners of the raw materials, carried out numerous functions. The traveling salesman, plying plows, winnowers, or sarpinka, became a new man on the scene. Nonfarming colonists needed to buy food, fuel, and livestock, even though they kept gardens; the wares of the larger towns enticed them to shop there and to use their few extra kopecks to purchase gifts for family and friends. These newly created jobs and economic opportunities meant that few colonists had to leave the colony to seek outside employment; in fact, the colonists had the lowest rate of seasonal temporary labor (*otkhozhie promysly*) in the region.[65] Simple homespun wool and linen goods gave way to store-bought sarpinka and other cloth materials, which stimulated the demand for buttons, lace, ribbons, and broaches to add decorative touches to the clothing. Tailors, cabinetmakers, and shoemakers were but a few of the craftsmen who benefited from cottage industry. For example, decorative stove tiles made at the Selivanov pottery factory in Saratov were one of the luxury items that the colonists liked to buy at fairs and in the towns.

Finally, the colony cottage industries spawned a thriving, dynamic, and civic-conscious middle class. The original wealth of the great colony families came primarily from their earnings in the sarpinka cottage industry. Many of these families would later invest their money in larger commercial and industrial enterprises, particularly grain trading and flour milling, but some would also become land investors. For example, the Reinach family became one of the largest grain dealers at the Nizhnii Novgorod fair and built a large, modern steam-powered flour mill in Saratov, while the Borel family diversified even more by also becoming large landowners.[66] This group of men also served in the zemstvo; although most did not assume active leadership roles in the zemstvo, they participated along with the land captain in the practical work of the zemstvo, such as supervision of the construction of hospitals, clinics, and schools.[67] Although the richest families had permanent residences in the city of Saratov and spent a part of the year in one of the capitals, St. Petersburg and Moscow, they rarely cut their ties with the home colony. The most important family events—baptisms, weddings, and burials—were performed in the colonies. The colonies shared in the wealth of their most successful families. Colony churches received a considerable part of the largesse. In 1906, the Borel family gave 10,000 rubles to Golyi Karamysh to establish a preparatory school (progymnasium); when the patriarch of the family, Emanuel Borel, died, part of his estate was left to the colony.[68] It should be mentioned again that it was these entrepreneurial colonists who hoped to broaden the horizons of colonists. They initiated Russian language instruction for their children and actively supported its introduction in colony schools; while originally encouraged for reasons of utility and perhaps necessity, such instruction helped the colonists to participate more fully in the events of their adopted motherland. Thus cottage industry resulted in significant economic, social, and even physical change within the colonies.

The Volga Germans and
the Zemstvos

As a result of the 1861 emancipation, the peasants remained isolated legally, economically, and administratively from all the rest of Russian society. Tied to the land by their communes, judged in their separate courts, and ruled by their township and village administrations, they had few contacts and little in common with the provincial gentry and townspeople. To assist in the management of local affairs and to aid the peasants' transition from gentry dependence to independence, the government created assemblies of the land, or zemstvos. The zemstvo reform promoted the principle of rural, local self-government and established the only institution in which all three estates—nobility, peasantry, and merchantry—came together on a regular basis. This chapter examines the role of the Volga Germans in the zemstvos and the impact these organs of local self-government had on the colonists themselves. My twin objectives are to assess the influence and impact of the zemstvos on the Volga colonists and to ascertain the attitudes and reactions of the colonists toward the zemstvos. As will be seen, the Volga German zemstvo experience was unique, thus attesting to the considerable district-to-district diversity that evolved and exemplifying the influence of local conditions on the composition and activities of each zemstvo.[1]

The law of January 1, 1864, establishing zemstvo institutions at the district and provincial levels, defined the duty of these organs as the management of local affairs. Zemstvo deputies were elected for three-year terms from three curiae based on property qualifications. No single curia could have an absolute majority and thereby control the zemstvo, except for about forty districts that had so few gentry landowners that the peasantry controlled at least 50 percent of the district seats; most of the Volga Germans would be constituents of these rare but relatively unexamined "peasant" zemstvos. Elected zemstvo deputies served without pay, posing an economic hardship for some of the peasant members. Because the zemstvo assembly met once a year for no more than a week to ten days, the body elected an executive board to carry out decisions and also empowered it to hire a staff and the professionals required for the zemstvo's many programs.

The 1864 zemstvo reform endured over five decades, but not without alteration. The most significant change came in the form of the law of June 12, 1890, which intended to give the nobility greater control of the zemstvos. Despite the seemingly retrograde nature of this legislation, the years 1890–91 do not mark a sharp break in the nature and scope of activities of the peasant-colonist dominated zemstvos of the Lower Volga valley, even though the peasants lost their right to elect their deputies; instead, they were only allowed to nominate candidates, the peasant deputies being selected by the governor from the list of peasant nominees.[2] Thus the "character" of these zemstvos and their policies and programs did not change appreciably because of continued peasant-colonist majority control and cooperation, and their more regular attendance and participation. Another factor contributing to zemstvo continuity was the larger role and importance of the "third element" by the 1890s—teachers, doctors, veterinarians, and agronomists employed by the zemstvos, many of whom came from peasant-colonist ranks. Whereas before 1890 most of the commissions and boards consisted only of zemstvo members, after 1890 the zemstvos increased significantly the number of these commissions and invited the "third element" to sit on them.

The commonly held view that the Volga Germans remained indifferent to and inactive in the district zemstvos is entirely without foundation. Boris Veselovskii propagated this historical myth by asserting that "in Kamyshin and Novouzensk [district zemstvos] the German colonists did not take an active role [*aktivno ne vystupali*]."[3] In fact, a Volga German element was active throughout the history and existence of the Kamyshin and Novouzensk district zemstvos. Only in Nikolaevsk District, where the colonists formed only a small minority (12 percent), did the Volga Germans play no influential role in the zemstvo.[4] For the Volga Germans, the zemstvo was an interesting if curious institution of local government, because it was the first regular meeting place and joint forum of peasants and colonists, who had remained administratively segregated for over a century, never permitted to cooperate in matters of local interest and mutual concern. While day-to-day relations between peasants and colonists remained peaceful and decent, if distant, the working relationship within the zemstvos came to be a closer one, if still businesslike, based on common socioeconomic interests.

The Kamyshin and Novouzensk district zemstvos were unique not only for the large number of rural colonists participating in them but also because a partnership of former state peasants and colonists controlled them between 1865 and 1917. These two zemstvos belonged to the so-called peasant zemstvo ranks—the forty-odd district zemstvos, out of the 360 in Russia, in which the peasant element held a majority; most of them were in the northern part of European Russia (in Viatka, Perm, Olonets, and Vologda provinces) where serfdom had never prevailed. Serfdom never took root in Kamyshin and Novouzensk districts. In Novouzensk District the peasant element was divided almost evenly between former state peasants and colonists, with former serfs comprising only 2 percent; ethnically, 42.6 percent were Volga German, 35.3 percent Great Russian, and 18 percent Ukrainian.[5] In Kamyshin District, the former colonists were the largest peasant and ethnic group; they constituted 49 percent of the district population, with the former state peasants following close behind, and former serfs and Crown peasants forming less than 10 percent of the district peasantry.[6] There were very few gentry estates in either of these districts, thus the peasants dominated the district zemstvos.

Peasant control of zemstvos did not necessarily imply homogeneity of policies, programs, and methods. Population density, type of peasant (serf, state peasant, Crown peasant, or colonist), the nature and health of the peasant economy, and geography were but a few of the important influences on the development of peasant zemstvos. Such variables were present in the districts settled by Volga Germans and influenced zemstvo development. About all that can be safely asserted is that peasant zemstvos differed from gentry-dominated ones, particularly in spending more on public education than on health and medicine. Much more research is required to provide definitive answers to the questions first raised in the 1880s concerning the peasant zemstvos.[7] What can be stated with certainty is that the Kamyshin and Novouzensk district zemstvos were among the most progressive zemstvos in Russia, noted for their willingness to spend large amounts of money on zemstvo programs, to improve the health and welfare of the peasantry, and to promote the local economy.

Until 1891—in other words, over half the lifetime of the zemstvos—the colonists of Kamyshin District elected a majority to the district zemstvo assembly, dominated the executive board, and provided the chairman to the board. The forty-six member Kamyshin District zemstvo assembly was about average size for the empire, but still not a large body; twenty-three deputies were elected from the landowner curia, eighteen from the peasant curia, and five from the town of Kamyshin. Colonist majority control of the zemstvo came about because of the small number of gentry landowners in the district and the tripartite electoral division based on property qualifications. Because of the ambiguous nature of article 23 of the zemstvo legislation, the Volga German textile merchants were able to elect a majority of their number from the landowner curia. This article allowed owners of nonurban industrial or agricultural enterprises (with an annual production valued at not less than 6,000 rubles) the right to vote in the first curia, normally dominated elsewhere in Russia by the gentry, who had to hold under private deed a stipulated amount of rural landed property.[8] Thus the wealthier entrepreneurs of rural cottage industries, especially the leaders of the sarpinka weaving industry, a cottage industry widespread in Kamyshin District colonies, were able to play a decisive role in the elections of the landowner curia. Of the eighteen-member peasant curia, the colonists elected eight members and the Russian villagers ten. The town of Kamyshin sometimes elected one colonist to the zemstvo. Thus, with the eighteen or nineteen seats held by the colonist entrepreneurs from the landowner curia, which was the number most often held by them until 1891, and the eight peasant colonists, the colonists elected a majority of their members to the Kamyshin District zemstvo assembly.

For the first quarter century of its existence, the Kamyshin District zemstvo and colonist Peter Egorovich Louck were synonymous, for Louck served as the only chairman of the district board between 1866 and 1891. Louck, a former township elder from Talovka, was eight times reelected to this important post. Zemstvo members recognized Louck as the prime mover and organizer of the Kamyshin District zemstvo, and petitioned the Saratov Province zemstvo and provincial governor to reward or decorate him for making the district zemstvo an efficient and effective institution. He was effusively lauded for his excellent management of the zemstvo budget, vigorous promotion of public education, successful organization of village granaries stocked with grain in case of crop failures, initiation of the zemstvo insurance program, and maintaining harmonious relations within the zemstvo by reconciling and mediating the interests and concerns of the Russian peasantry and Volga Germans.[9] Louck's courage and political independence, particularly his refusal to be intimidated by the district marshal of the nobility (who chaired the zemstvo), also earned him great respect. Although embittered by his loss of the chairmanship as a result of the 1890 zemstvo legislation, requiring that the post be filled by a person eligible for state service, he continued to play an active role in that body.

The Volga Germans literally ran the district zemstvo because of their positions on the executive board, which, unlike the assembly, labored year-round to supervise zemstvo activities, manage zemstvo finances and records, and hire zemstvo employees. Besides controlling the chairmanship of the Kamyshin zemstvo board, the colonists actively participated in other ways. With the exception of but a few years, colonists usually filled two of the three-member board positions, elected one of their members to be secretary of the board, and placed at least one colonist on each of the commissions created by the zemstvo assembly. Colonists frequently chaired these commissions, which studied board proposals and prepared reports and recommendations for the assembly's consideration. It is no exaggeration to state that colonists living in Kamyshin District actively participated in their district zemstvo.[10]

Unlike their brethren living in Kamyshin District, the colonists of Novouzensk District did not have majority control of their district zemstvo, but worked closely with Russian and Ukrainian peasants to ensure peasant control. This peasant-colonist coalition faced no serious gentry landowner opposition, because the landowner curia of Novouzensk District consisted of few noblemen, but mainly merchants and wealthy peasants who had bought large amounts of state land and devoted most of their efforts to individual economic gain and little to civic duties, such as zemstvo participation. Such a figure we see in Ermolai Alekseevich Lopakhin in Chekhov's *The Cherry Orchard*. Usually the colonists elected one-fourth of the zemstvo delegates, but with the absence of large landowners normally active in zemstvo affairs, the peasant-colonist delegates clearly controlled the Novouzensk District zemstvo. The colonists' regular attendance at zemstvo assembly meetings, and the notoriously poor attendance of the members of the landowner curia, meant that the colonists constituted one-third of the delegates in attendance. Colonists sometimes chaired the board but more frequently provided a significant contingent of the board members, who in effect ran the zemstvo. Only in the seventh term

Street scene in Ust' Zolikh
(Messer). Wood homes were typical
in the mountain-side colonies.
(Kamyshin District, Saratov Province)

The whitewashed, sod-brick, and straw-thatched houses shown on the right were most common in the meadow-side steppe colonies. The, however, is a street scene in Karamyshevka (Bauer). (Kamyshin District, Saratov Province)

A group of village elders in Ust' Zolikh (Messer). These heads of households participated in the village assembly. (Kamyshin District, Saratov Province)

Volga German soldiers in cavalry uniforms.

Wedding procession leaving the church in Karamyshevka (Bauer). The church played a vital role in Volga German life. (Kamyshin District, Saratov Province)

In the Samara steppe colony of Stepnoe (Stahl) the small wooden church was centrally located. (Novouzensk District, Samara Province)

Typical Volga German family in the early 1900s.

Midday domestic scene in a Volga German home.

Threshing grain in Ust' Zolikh (Messer) in 1910. (Kamyshin District, Saratov Province)

A camel-drawn wagon in Rovnoe (Seelmann), a major grain trading colony. (Novouzensk District, Samara Province)

Colonist tobacco field in Nikolaevsk
District, Samara Province.

The thriving trading colony of
Ekaterinenstadt (Baronsk) boasted of
several fine churches, two of which can
be clearly seen in the distance.
(Nikolaevsk District, Samara Province)

The granaries of Ekaterinenstadt
(Baronsk) stored vast quantities of wheat.
(Nikolaevsk District, Samara Province)

Fedor P. Schmidt flour mill in the city of
Saratov.

Emanuel I. Borel flour mill in the city of
Saratov.

Reinach family flour mill in the city of
Saratov.

Steam-powered flour mill of Emanuel I. Borel in the Russian settlement of Nizhniaia Dobrinka situated at the intersection of the Medveditsa River and Riazan-Uralsk railroad. (Kamyshin District, Saratov Province)

Grandmother spinning thread for sarpinka in the colony of Ust' Zolikh (Messer). (Kamyshin District, Saratov Province)

Sarpinka weaving in an Ust' Zolikh (Messer) family cottage. Textile weaving was the major cottage industry of the Volga German settlements. (Kamyshin District, Saratov Province)

Interior of a sarpinka merchant shop in Ust' Zolikh (Messer). (Kamyshin District, Saratov Province)

Street merchant selling leather goods during market day in Golyi Karamysh (Balzer). Leather tanning was an important cottage industry among the Volga Germans.

Volga German women buying the popular sarpinka cotton cloth from a street vendor in Golyi Karamysh (Balzer).

Wheat gleaners in 1910 in the steppe lands of Samara Province carefully finish the work of the harvesters.

Workers and oxen-drawn wagons begin the trek to distant fields in the steppe lands of Samara Province.

A wood house and outbuildings in the steppe of Samara Province.

A small, sod-brick, thatched-roof shed typical of buildings in the meadow-side steppe colonies.

An unusual team: horse and camel.

Camels watering at a small stream in a
meadow-side colony before the summer
heat dried it up.

The town of Kamyshin, shown here, was
a Volga port and government seat of the
district in which most mountain-side
colonists lived. By the turn of the century
many Volga Germans lived and worked
here.

Mill workers of the Schmidt brothers'
sarpinka factory in Golyi Karamysh
(Balzer) sit in front of the buildings
where thread was dyed and warped.

Pipe making became an important craft
in the colonies. All pipes had to have lids
to prevent the escape of tobacco ashes.
Here village elders in Ust' Zolikh
(Messer) light up.

(1883–86) did the colonists elect a chairman and majority to the zemstvo board.

Consequently, the zemstvos provided outlets for Volga German civic participation and growth, especially after 1889 with the institution of the land captains and the curtailment of the colonists' autonomy. The land captains became the chief judges and magistrates of the countryside, exercising broad powers over the colonists and their elected village and township elders, including the right to impose disciplinary punishments. In the 1890s, several Volga German township elders "fled" (*sbezhali*) the arbitrary actions of the overbearing and meddlesome land captains by resigning from their administrative offices and seeking elective positions in the zemstvos.[11] Heinrich Khristoforovich Schellhorn served six years as a township elder before resigning in protest because the land captain had overturned several of his decisions. He then entered zemstvo service, serving eighteen years in the Novouzensk District and Samara Province zemstvos, where he gained prominence that led to his election as a deputy to the First Duma in 1906. Similarly, Konstantin Nikolaevich Grimm, because of service to the state, became a member of gentry class and large estate owner. As a Volga German his career is unique, as are his conservative political credentials. In December 1905, he helped found the conservative Party of Legal Order, which eventually linked up with the Octobrist coalition. Between 1906 and 1917, as a result of the rightward shift in provincial zemstvo politics, he was twice elected chairman of the important provincial zemstvo board. In 1907, he was elected a Saratov provincial delegate to the conservative Moscow Zemstvo Congress. His outstanding management of zemstvo affairs and correct political beliefs led to his selection as chairman of the wartime Saratov Province Food Supply Council.[12]

Surveying the publications and programs of the Kamyshin and Novouzensk zemstvos tells a great deal about the philosophical outlook of the peasant-colonist deputies. For want of a better term, their credo could best be described as "pragmatic realism." Having no precedents to follow, and conscious of the suspicion and opposition of the government and the ignorance, stubbornness, and tradition-mindedness of most of the peasantry after centuries of oppression, the zemstvo members expected no quick and easy solutions to the local problems confronting them. Lacking the necessary staff and revenues to quickly remedy the onerous and multiple obligations imposed on them, the zemstvo members became frugal and scrupulous watchdogs of zemstvo monies, keeping a strict account of everything from hospital bandages to teachers' salaries. They were apparently devoid of any strong ethnic feelings, because no ethnic rivalry or animosity surfaced. The Russian, Ukrainian, and Volga German delegates seemed most concerned with the local peasantry and economy. Thus zemstvo members were parochial, and jealously defended the best interests of their district. Rarely did class animosities arise, and they usually involved complaints against merchants and townspeople for their meager financial support of the zemstvo. They expressed no strong political views, narrowly devoting themselves to local economic and social concerns as prescribed by the 1864 zemstvo law. None of the "colonist" zemstvos became involved in the zemstvo political movement which began in the 1890s. Even during the revolutionary disturbances of 1905–6, they expressed confidence in the tsarist regime's promises of reform. The most hotly debated issues usually involved economic, not political matters, such as the debate over more government financial support of primary education.

Colonists who actively served in the zemstvos were not typical Volga colonists. They generally came from the hardworking, prosperous, and most enlightened ranks of colony officialdom, because zemstvo members received no salary, except for the chairman of the board and board members, and because members had to be able to read and write reports. Their education ranged from home instruction and self-education to the equivalent of a high school education. All had some facility with Russian, because all zemstvo business was transacted in Russian, and most were serving or had served in some leadership post in the colonies. In fact, most of the "active" zemstvo members—those who served on the executive board—invariably had served in some township administrative capacity, suggesting that participation in peasant government nurtured administrative skills and resourcefulness, as the examples of Louck and Schellhorn attest. There was another reason for the dominance of township and colony elders in the zemstvo. The elders were quite powerful and influential figures at the local level, for they represented the authority of the government, and it was the township assemblies that elected the zemstvo deputies. An unfortunate consequence of the elders' position as zemstvo power brokers was that colonists and peasants, initially at least, looked upon the zemstvo as simply another state administrative organ rather than as a bona fide organ of local self-government. Although the elder zemstvo deputies were drawn from and felt beholden to the peasant constituency who had elected them, and had deep roots in the locality they represented, the peasant electorate long remained confused whether the deputies served the basically local economic interests of "society" or the essentially political matters of the "state."

Quite curious was the behavior of the sarpinka manufacturers or colonist "middle class" deputies to the Kamyshin zemstvo, which was marked by an aversion or inability to take a leadership role. The colonist zemstvo leaders, such as Peter Louck, came from the ranks of the "peasant" colonists—that is, those elected from the peasant or small landholding curia, the village communities with communal property ownership. Although the *fabrikanty* served occasionally on commissions, they rarely served on the time-consuming executive board. Possibly the extensive time requirements of burdensome leadership posts deterred these busy entrepreneurs from assuming such posts. While it might be argued, as Veselovskii does, that the *fabrikanty* in fact controlled and manipulated the zemstvo and its leaders, there is no evidence to support this contention. In fact, the frequent and bitter squabbling among the *fabrikanty* would seem to indicate disunity rather than unity of purpose. This might also explain why they never elected one of their own to a top zemstvo post, agreeing instead on a neutral coreligionist. In the 1870s, the number of sarpinka entrepreneurs significantly increased, and they constantly tried to undercut each other by enticing away the weavers of their competitors.[13] Class consciousness did not seem to be particularly strong among the *fabrikanty*.

Despite the wide-ranging significance of the zemstvo reforms, the lower Volga populace did not respond enthusiastically to the organs of local self-government. Initially, the zemstvo (or *Landsamt*, as it came to be known to the colonists) was viewed by many as just another government agency, simply a replication and extension of the central bureaucracy. The individual colonists had no tangible input in the zemstvo elections, because the elections of deputies took place in the township assemblies, which consisted primarily of the village elders. The colonists never saw the zemstvo, because it met infrequently and in the main district town. Also, in the 1860s and 1870s, there were few people working for the zemstvos, so they long remained somewhat nebulous organizations. However, there were other reasons for the lukewarm responsiveness of the colonists.

The zemstvos had no executive powers and depended on the police and other government officials, over whom they had no control, to execute their decisions and to collect zemstvo taxes. Frequently, the zemstvos protested police discriminatory tax collection methods, as the Novouzensk District zemstvo did in a May 1906 complaint to the Samara provincial governor, accusing the police of discrimination against poor taxpayers by more vigorously demanding payments from them than from well-to-do taxpayers: "In our [the zemstvo board's] opinion the poorest people of the district are much more dependable in paying zemstvo taxes than the more well to do, since they [police] don't stand on ceremony with them: once they don't pay, then they [police] inventory the property and force them to pay, but the police don't dare to act so energetically against the rich . . . ."[14]

After 1889 and the institution of the position of land captain, the zemstvos had to work closely with this despised government official, who became the "boss" of the area over which he governed. The fact that the colonists deeply resented the land captains, therefore, meant that any persons seen with the land captain would have aroused distrust. When Kamyshin District zemstvo officials in 1910 spoke favorably of "energetic" assistance rendered by a land captain in support of zemstvo measures, they revealed insensitivity or blindness to the distrust and enmity felt by colonists toward land captains.[15] As long as zemstvo personnel had to work in tandem with the land captains, the rural people would look with suspicion on the zemstvos.

The zemstvos also had to contend with the traditional colonist-peasant distrust of all "outsiders," which made the lot of zemstvo employees—the teachers, agronomists, and doctors—quite difficult. A teacher in one of the Kamyshin District colonies wrote of the mistrust the colonists held toward zemstvo employees: "There still prevails a darkness among the people . . . . There is still not education; only during the last six years has it [education] begun to improve; consequently, the people still don't understand the benefits of schooling, medicine and veterinary medicine, etc. and because of this the population, not being in a condition to discern who are their friends and enemies, treats the Russian teachers, doctors and in general all persons not a member of the village, badly even with hostility."[16] Praetorius also noted that an agronomist frequently came to the colony of Galka, but the colonists for a long time remained distant and unreceptive to his ideas.[17] These zemstvo "professionals" eventually earned the respect and admiration of most colonists, but only after forty years of hard work.

Generally, throughout most of their history, the peasants and colonists of the Lower Volga looked upon the zemstvos with indifference and skepticism. The major reason for this attitude was that the peasantry did not really understand the purpose and functions of the zemstvo, commonly mistaking it for another state administrative unit. A survey of Saratov Province in 1905 reported that after forty years of zemstvo existence: "It is very sad, but it is a fact, that a significant part of the peasantry up to this time considers the zemstvo a bureaucratic or government institution, not a public institution . . . . The people make very little distinction between the zemstvo and the government."[18] Incredible as it may sound, many peasants could not and did not differentiate between the zemstvos and land captains. Another reason the peasants thought of the zemstvo as a government agency was that there was much duplication of effort among zemstvos and government agencies in such areas as education and agriculture. Thus the peasantry might quite easily and understandably confuse the zemstvo school inspector with the Ministry of Education school inspector, or the agricultural instructors sent out by the Ministry of Agriculture with the zemstvo agronomists, both of whom might be accompanied by the land captain, especially at agricultural demonstrations.

The peasant-colonist zemstvos of Kamyshin and Novouzensk districts earned high praise and had a recognized record of accomplishments despite general public apathy, government suspicion, inadequate funds, and an absence of executive powers. The official provincial newspaper, *Saratovskiia gubernskiia vedomosti*, publicly praised the Kamyshin District zemstvo as the most active and effective one in all of Saratov Province in studying and meeting the needs of the rural peasantry.[19] It was also recognized as the best example of a district zemstvo trying to develop peasant agriculture by employing agronomists and other trained agricultural specialists. By 1910, the Novouzensk District zemstvo employed more doctors than any other district zemstvo in Russia and consistently ranked first in Samara Province in zemstvo expenditures and second in per capita zemstvo expenditures.[20]

On the question of education, the Volga colonist zemstvo members aligned themselves with the "forces of change"—a few clergymen, colony leaders, the Saratov Office of Foreign Settlers (until it was abolished in 1871), and a sizable element of the colonists (especially those who dealt and traded with Russians)—in advocating basic literacy and Russian language instruction in colony schools, but never attempted to impose these solutions on the colony church schools as the tsarist government did at the end of the nineteenth century. The Volga German deputies did not want to Russify the colonists, but agreed that the colony church schools needed to offer Russian language instruction to enable the colonists to survive in an increasingly Russian environment, and to reduce greatly the amount of time devoted to religious instruction and invest that time in reading, writing, and arithmetic instruction. They felt that pupils should be taught to be literate and not simply to gabble the catechism. In the 1860s, considerable colonist public expression called for the gradual introduction of Russian language instruction in the church schools, its proponents asserting that it was the only hope of the colonists to progress and to enter fully into the society in which they lived. Many admired the educational project conceived by the last director of the Saratov Kontora, Peter A. Shafranov, who proposed that colony parish schools should continue their primary function of religious instruction but gradually broaden the curriculum to include practical knowledge to promote farming and trade, and Russian language instruction.[21]

The conservative or status quo forces included most of the clergy and the majority of the colonists, who wanted their children to work and contribute to the family budget. To them the sole purpose of school was to prepare children for their confirmation, a crucial rite of passage. As a result, they were satisfied with the traditional colony church school, with its emphasis on preparation for confirmation and with religious instruction in the colonists' dialect. The conflict between the supporters of secular and religious education was not confined to the colonies, but became acute throughout Russia during the last two decades of the nineteenth century.

Witnessing the great reforms and changes sweeping Russia in the 1860s and 1870s, the "forces of change" realized that the colonists would have to change also, and believed that the best way for colonists to accommodate themselves to new circumstances was through education. In 1869, the colonist-controlled Kamyshin District zemstvo unsuccessfully petitioned the Ministry of Public Education for permission to introduce compulsory primary education in the district. Alarmed by closures of village and colony schools, some of which received zemstvo subsidies, the zemstvo realized that, left to local discretion and initiative, primary education would fail because of the unwillingness of the rural communities to assume the burden of supporting schools.[22] However, the ministry refused the petition for financial reasons, chiefly the shortage of capital to carry out the program.

Although the Volga colonist zemstvos could not embark on a bold and radical educational program because of government intransigence, the lack of funds, their own inexperience, and peasant-colonist tradition-mindedness, for almost the entire period of their existence they assigned it their highest priority.[23] The Novouzensk District zemstvo always spent more on education than public health, and until 1901 led all districts in Samara Province in the percentage of budget allocated to education. Likewise, the 1864 zemstvo legislation and the primary school act of July 14, 1864, limited zemstvos to the economic aspects and financial management of education, entrusting educational policy to government ministries. While more an indicator of intent than success, the following figures showing the percentage of zemstvo expenditures spent on public education attest to the concern of the zemstvos for education.[24]

	1877	*1890*	*1901*
Novouzensk District	22.7	24.1	30.2
Kamyshin District	18.4	20	26.1

Thus, in 1877 these zemstvos assigned three times as much to primary education as did the other zemstvos, whose allocations averaged only 7.7 percent of expenditures.

Confronted with the many constraints, the zemstvos, until the 1880s, played a limited, nonactivist, and indirect role in education. The provincial zemstvos assumed responsibility for teacher training and secondary education, while the district zemstvos directed their efforts to primary education. The district zemstvos offered "encouragement" (*pooshchrenie*), usually in the form of undesignated but equal subsidies, to local bodies and existing schools, yet they expected the initiative for opening new schools and most financial support to come from the village communes. While various types of primary schools (church, colony, and state and Crown peasant) existed before 1864 and the zemstvo reform, they were notoriously bad and few in number. Thus the Volga German district zemstvos attempted to work with the existing church schools (*die Kirchenschulen*), found in almost all colonies; the private schools (*die Gesellschaftsschulen* or *tovarishcheskiia shkoly*), found almost exclusively in the colonies of Kamyshin District; and the new zemstvo schools (*zemskie shkoly*), established in the largest numbers among the more recently founded daughter colonies of Novouzensk District, which had fewer schools (the first opened in 1866 at Tonkoshurovka).[25]

Disappointed with the lack of progress and pitifully low teacher salaries in the village schools receiving zemstvo funds, the zemstvos abandoned the undesignated subsidy system in the mid-1880s and earmarked zemstvo monies exclusively for teacher salaries. Heretofore, the zemstvos had hoped that their grants would be used to supplement village school funds, but in fact many villages and a few colonies accepted the funds and then *reduced* the village appropriations to the schools! When teachers received pay from two sources— zemstvo and commune—the villagers frequently did not provide their share. As long as the teachers' salaries came wholly or partly from the villagers, their authority was undermined, because the peasants looked upon and treated them as hired hands. The new system aimed at strengthening the "soul" of the school—the teacher—and ending the teacher's dependence on the villagers. Beginning in 1887, the Kamyshin District zemstvo doubled education appropriations to 15,000 rubles to provide 250-ruble salaries to sixty teachers in thirty-two peasant schools and twenty-eight colony schools in return for the villagers' assumption of all other school costs.[26] In 1894, they raised teacher's salaries to 300 rubles and granted a 60-ruble bonus to teachers with five years of district service.

The Volga German zemstvos found it almost impossible to exert influence on the colony church schools, because, according to the 1864 primary school law, public funds could be granted only to schools offering Russian language instruction, and the clergy-dominated colony church schools stubbornly resisted teaching Russian. Colonies did not request zemstvo monies for their church schools until the 1890s, when the government enforced mandatory Russian language instruction on them. The zemstvos also lacked any authority over the *Kirchenschulen*. A brief survey of the administrative history of the colony church schools reveals the predicament of the zemstvo authorities. Between 1819 and 1881, the colony clergy had a monopoly over colony education, and this monopoly had a legal basis in the *Ustav inostrannykh ispovedanii* of 1832, which recognized the confessional nature of the colony school, whose purpose was religious and moral instruction, and whose ultimate goal was preparation of pupils for confirmation. The colony church school remained almost throughout its entire history a religious school, patterned after the catechism schools that had arisen during the Protestant Reformation in the sixteenth century. Thus the government granted the clergy of the colonies monopoly over education; in return, the clergy promised to "educate" (actually, "confirm") all children in

Christian principles and to bring them up to be obedient, God-fearing people. According to article 322 of the *Ustav*, every father was obligated to send all his children to church school from age seven until confirmation or else be fined three kopecks for each day of classes missed.[27]

Although the village commune could still choose the teacher or *Schulmeister*, the local clergyman had to approve the choice, thus giving him a veto over teacher selection, and thereby making the teacher dependent on the local clergy. The clergy had to visit the school in their own community once a week and the other schools in their parish every other week. They recorded their observations in school record books, and determined the curriculum and methods of instruction. Until 1881, the clergy held the church schools firmly in their hands.

Another phase in the administrative history of the *Kirchenschulen* began May 2, 1881, when the government transferred all colony schools to the jurisdiction of the Ministry of Public Education. The colony church schools became part of the public education system of Saratov and Samara provinces and subject to the appropriate secular administrative authorities in those provinces. The clergy lost their preeminence to the public school inspectors. The school function of the clergy was narrowly defined as the supervision of the religious and moral instruction in the schools. A government directive of September 24, 1891, in effect brought parish schools under Russian government administration by making the public school inspector the dominant figure in parish school administration by giving him the power to appoint and dismiss teachers in the village schools.[28] It should not be presumed that after the 1890s the clergy lost all control of education in the colonies. Even though appointed by the public school inspector, the village teacher had to remain on good terms with the minister, who enjoyed social status and influence in the village. For example, a minister could put considerable public pressure on the teacher by simply failing to confirm some pupils attending the teacher's school. In such instances, the community would direct wrath at the teacher, not the minister. In fact, it would be quite difficult to stop a minister from getting rid of a teacher he disliked if he really set his mind to it.

Unable to penetrate the clergy-controlled church schools, the zemstvos furthered their educational activities in the Volga German colonies by funneling zemstvo monies into new zemstvo schools and into private schools, found in Kamyshin District under the name of *tovarishcheskiia shkoly*, loosely translated as "cooperative schools." Both offered superior instruction and had by World War I surpassed the parish schools in quality of instruction and, in some areas, number of students enrolled. It must be stressed that the requests for zemstvo funds to establish zemstvo schools and to aid private cooperative schools originated among the colonists themselves, not the zemstvos, because of the felt need to learn Russian and the failure of the church schools to teach the fundamentals of reading, writing, and arithmetic. This Volga German initiative for "functional" or "survival" literacy corresponded to a similar phenomenon notable among the Russian peasants, but particularly those in Saratov Province; according to Ben Eklof, the peasants themselves "were the driving force behind the progress in literacy" between 1864 and 1890.[29]

The zemstvo school, authorized by the 1864 primary school law, represented a new type of primary school offering a more secular curriculum, which posed a real threat to the church school's monopoly over colony education and even to the social fabric of the colony. The zemstvo school was free, whereas colonists had to pay nominal fees to attend the church school and high tuition to enroll in the private, cooperative schools. Introduction of this new school in the colonies brought with it Russian language instruction, which soon gained a reputation for its quality. One of the first pupils fondly recalled his teacher, Olympiada Ivanovna Skvortsova, who "spent much time with the children so that many of her students became fluent in Russian."[30] Although not explicitly described in the law and far from being fully realized, the zemstvo school offered a general education course of study which introduced pupils to their own native language, instructed them to read for comprehension, instilled a love of learning (especially reading), acquainted them with the world around them by studying geography and history, and developed skills to think and express ideas clearly.[31] While religious instruction was not excluded from the zemstvo school, and often encouraged, it did not enjoy the place of preeminence or perhaps dominance that it held in the church schools. Consequently, in the struggle over schools and education, which became quite bitter in the two decades before World War I, the "forces of change" defended and promoted the new zemstvo school over the older colony church school.[32]

The zemstvo school was a mutual undertaking of the colony and the district zemstvo. Only by a majority vote of the village assembly could the colony petition the district zemstvo for a zemstvo school. In 1866, the first colony, Tonkoshurovka (Pfannenstiel), successfully petitioned the Novouzensk District zemstvo to open a school, and the zemstvos continued to receive colonists' petitions up to the eve of World War I. Zemstvo schools spread rapidly among the colonies of Novouzensk District. In 1872, fifteen schools had been opened in colonies within the district, with an enrollment of about 600 pupils; by 1886, forty-one zemstvo schools existed, with an enrollment of over 2,000, in the meadow-side colonies.[33] While colonists willingly accepted zemstvo monies to pay teachers, yet often failed to provide acceptable school and teacher accommodations, the Novouzensk District zemstvo remained convinced that these schools offered the best instruction in the district, and continued to expand the system.

The main reason colonists requested the zemstvo school was because the school taught Russian, which the colonists badly needed. The 1891 request from the colonists of Friedenfeld exemplifies this, inasmuch as the colonists stated that their children needed Russian: " . . . because most are afraid upon entering military service and are confronted with problems stemming from not knowing the state language, which, in addition, is also necessary for daily life, for constantly mingling among the Russian people, who do not know German, inevitably contributes to misunderstandings, mistakes and so forth."[34] Other colonies, such as Alt Weimar, petitioned for a zemstvo school because of its superior education: " . . . the zemstvo school gives a better education than the church-parish school, and also affords the opportunity to study Russian."[35] Some colonies long resisted the introduction of zemstvo schools, but often financial exigencies brought on by recurrent crop failures forced them to abandon the church school. Thus, in 1906, after two successive crop failures, several colonies requested the conversion of their church schools to zemstvo schools.

The primary school act of 1864, permitting zemstvos, village communes, and private individuals to open primary schools, got a welcome response from some Kamyshin District colonists. Well-to-do colonists took the initiative and founded private schools, which the zemstvo (with a large well-to-do colonist contingent) soon recognized and granted annual subsidies. So, after 1864 there existed alongside the *Kirchenschulen* and zemstvo schools in Kamyshin District the cooperative schools, privately founded and financed by groups of individual households because of the poor quality of instruction and absence of Russian language training in the colony church schools.[36]

Three factors contributed to the creation of these cooperative schools. First, some families recognized that their children, especially boys, needed Russian to advance economically, educationally, and socially. As early as 1866, the short-comings of the *Kirchenschulen* were apparent: "A striking example of this [little learning in the church schools] is the fact that if it is at all possible, many of the more prosperous colonists have their children educated not in the church schools but in private schools in the country or in the city."[37] Second, the trans-fer of the colonies to regular government administration as a result of the June 4, 1871, law, which required the use of Russian in township and colony gov-ernment, "prompted parents to turn special attention to the study of this lan-guage [Russian] by the younger generation."[38] Third, the main reason for the rapid expansion of Russian language training was the 1874 law subjecting the colonists to military conscription. Before 1871, only five cooperative schools had been opened. By 1877 twenty existed, and by 1886 there were twenty-eight (compared with fifty-four church schools), with about 1,000 pupils en-rolled, or 8 percent of all pupils enrolled in Kamyshin District.[39] By the late 1890s, such schools had spread to almost all colonies: "A long time ago the German population recognized the necessity of learning Russian. Particularly it began to penetrate with the introduction of military service upon them. From that time the Russian-German cooperative schools began to open in the Ger-man settlements, the number of which grew from year to year and by the time Russian language instruction was introduced in the colony church schools [1897], cooperative schools were in almost all the German settlements."[40]

While not without their problems, the cooperative schools quickly gained an excellent reputation. In his 1874 inspection of the province the Saratov pro-vincial governor praised the private school established by colonists in the Rus-sian settlement of Zhirnoe, which enrolled fifty colonist and peasant children.[41] By 1887, the district school inspector judged them the best of the district's pri-mary schools. He attributed much of their success to their being in session ten months of the year (not just five months, as in the church schools) and having enthusiastic parental support. The majority of the teachers were colonists who had been educated at the colony central teacher training school in Lesnoi Karamysh, and whom the school inspector praised for speaking and teaching Russian correctly.[42]

Although the cooperative schools had no standard curriculum or rules, they did share several characteristics. Prosperous heads of households joined to-gether and organized these schools (*hat eine Gesellschaft der bemittelteren Hausvater*).[43] Instruction was offered for two to four years in Russian and

German, the school having one or two teachers depending on the availability of qualified teachers. If there were two teachers, the Russian teacher usually taught Russian, arithmetic, geography, and general history; the German teacher taught religion, German, and also arithmetic. Usually there was only one class with two sessions, morning and afternoon, and each school enrolled between thirty and forty pupils. The schools were open to all pupils who could afford the monthly tuition, which varied from two to three rubles.

The Kamyshin District zemstvo began to fund the private schools in 1871 out of fairness and equitability, because the zemstvo had approved peasant requests to open five zemstvo schools in Russian settlements, while only one request had been approved for a colony.[44] The zemstvo had decided to divide education funds equally among all schools in the district that offered Russian language instruction. Since the only colony schools that did so were the private schools, the zemstvo granted them funds to be used as tuition stipends for poor children (which was cheaper than if the zemstvo opened its own school). By the 1880s, the zemstvo began to pay the entire teacher's salary, provided that the private school admitted five tuition-free pupils.[45] Zemstvo funding of the private schools contributed to the expansion of the educational system, promoted Russian language instruction in the colonies, and enabled a small minority of poor colonists' children to obtain an education.

One of the few secondary schools opened and funded by a district zemstvo was the Kamyshin *real'noe uchilishche*, or *Realschule*, which opened in 1877, the brainchild and pet project of the colonist and Kamyshin District zemstvo board chairman, Peter Louck.[46] Concerned with the limited educational outlets for the colonists' children beyond the primary level, the zemstvo petitioned the government in October 1873 for funds to open a three-year *real'noe uchilishche*, later to be expanded to a six-year school, which would be jointly financed by the Kamyshin zemstvo and the city duma.[47] In 1876, when the Ministry of Public Education refused to grant a large subsidy to the school, Louck persuaded the zemstvo and city duma to raise their annual subsidy from 5,000 to 14,000 rubles, at which time the ministry consented to the opening of the school.

Colonists' sons immediately enrolled in the Kamyshin *Realschule*, and by 1885 they comprised 15 percent (21 of 140) of the student body. But until 1888 they were at a distinct disadvantage, because the ministry had refused to allow a Russian language preparatory class (which Louck had championed to improve colonists' Russian language skills), simply because preparatory classes were not mentioned in the March 15, 1872, *Realschule* legislation.[48] In 1888, the ministry relented, provided that the zemstvo covered all costs of the preparatory course. The introduction of Russian language training facilitated a rapid expansion of Volga German enrollment; by 1908, half of the students enrolled in the Kamyshin *Realschule* were Volga Germans![49] This zemstvo-initiated school offered the bright colonist child, who might attend on a zemstvo stipend, and the child with affluent parents, who could afford the high tuition, educational and career opportunities available to very few youth living in the Russian Empire.

The most successful aspect of the zemstvo educational program was the creation of a small cadre of trained, dedicated, and essentially bilingual primary teachers in the colonies. The zemstvo teachers were the earliest, most numerous, and most influential of the hired zemstvo professionals, or "third element," to work in the colonies. The zemstvos considered teachers the "soul" of the school and chose to pay their salaries as the means to nourish this vital element. These selfless and indefatigable teachers, Volga-German and Russian in ethnic background, struggled to overcome the customs, traditions, and superstitions of their wards by offering a full primary education (not just limited to reading and writing). They risked being labeled government agents, atheists, "Russifiers," or dangerous propagandists of alien notions. Zemstvo payment of teachers' salaries encouraged the poor, frugal, and tradition-bound peasants and colonists to request zemstvo assistance and to open more schools, and also enhanced the social status of the zemstvo teachers and made them more financially secure by lessening their dependence on the village communes, which had a notorious record of nonpayment of teachers' salaries. The zemstvo payment of a regular but modest salary to teachers improved their material conditions, yet also contributed to the colonists' perceptions of the zemstvo-paid teacher as a government agent and instrument of Russification. However, by the eve of World War I, this distrust had largely dissipated, and the teachers had gained the esteem and respect of most of the colonists. Thus, in February 1912, the Catholic colonists of Kopenka (Volmar) publicly mourned the death of their teacher, A. F. Morozov. Similarly, Strassburg colonists received permission from Orthodox Church officials to hold a non-Orthodox graveside service for their zemstvo teacher, a young Russian woman.[50]

On the Volga German zemstvos' list of priorities, the extension of professional medical care to the rural areas ranked second only to the implementation
of primary education. Before the 1864 zemstvo reform, the colonies had only
a few rudimentary medical services, but by 1917 the zemstvos had extended
basic health care services to the remotest colonies. In 1864, only one full-time
doctor in Ekaterinenstadt and one part-time doctor in Gololobovka (Donnhof),
both on state salary, served all the colonies; but they rarely ventured into the
countryside. The nearest hospital was in Saratov. What "medical" care the colonists received came from the ubiquitous midwives, the itinerant but medically
untrained "vaccinators," and about a dozen generally well-intentioned but
poorly trained feldshers, or paramedics, who, according to a zemstvo doctor
serving the colonies in the 1880s, "understood as much about medicine as I did
about Chinese grammar."[51] Most every colony had its traditional but quite popular healers, who resorted to faith healing or folk remedies. Medical treatment
of most serious maladies consisted primarily of bleeding, with the only medi-
cation being the occasional ingestion of quinine for fever.

The popularity of folk medicine and the zemstvos' concentration on education retarded the implementation of rural health programs, with the greatest
expansion of zemstvo medicine occurring only during the first decade of the
twentieth century. Health services spread quickly, however, as medical care facilities staffed by physicians were established in various district settlements; by
1910, all Volga Germans were within a day's travel of the much-improved,
low-cost medical services. The two zemstvos employed a medical staff of fifty-
three doctors (nineteen in Kamyshin and thirty-four in Novouzensk), and operated eighteen hospitals and numerous dispensaries and pharmacies.[52]
Because of the more even distribution of the heavily populated colonies, where
most doctors and hospitals were located, the Volga Germans in Kamyshin District had easier and quicker access to medical services than the colonists on the
eastern steppe, where the few populous settlements lay close together along the
Volga River.

No statistics are available that could be used to measure the effects of the
zemstvo medical programs on the Volga Germans, but a few examples will suf-
fice to show how vital these services became. Zemstvo doctors first diagnosed
and treated trachoma, so common among the large, overcrowded Volga German families.[53] The doctors warned of the dangers of this highly contagious

inflammation of the inner membranes of the eyelid if left untreated, and prescribed hygienic measures and isolation of the infected individual. The zemstvo doctors also detected a high incidence of bone tubercles among the Volga Germans, which they thought might in part be caused by the frequent intermarriage of close relatives. The medical "third element" also persuaded the zemstvo boards to publish most health brochures in Russian and German. Concerned about the frequent problems of communication arising between colonist and zemstvo physician, the Kamyshin zemstvo in 1886 successfully entreated the former colonist and recent graduate of Dorpat University medical school, Peter Karlovich Haller, to enter zemstvo service and practice medicine in Golyi Karamysh (Balzer); later, in memoirs of his childhood years, Haller indicated the indebtedness of the colonists to the zemstvo doctors.[54] When Haller resigned, Anna Ivanovna Sukhodeeva, the first woman doctor hired by the Kamyshin zemstvo, replaced him and soon "met with the approval of the residents."[55] In 1911, a zemstvo doctor stopped a serious scarlet fever epidemic in Gololobovka and nursed fifteen seriously ill youth back to health. Anna Erhard, a young girl living in the colony of Rozenberg, owed her life to a quick-thinking zemstvo doctor, who rushed her to a zemstvo rabies clinic in Saratov. The Volga Germans of Verkhniaia Kulalinka (Holstein) township prided themselves on their zemstvo doctor and thirteen-bed infirmary, while other colonies, jealous of such facilities, also requested zemstvo support, if nothing more than a feldsher.[56] Indubitably, if the zemstvos had not provided the means, leadership, and organization, few physicians would have ventured to the remote and isolated colonies of the Lower Volga, no hospitals would have existed to treat the seriously ill, and the health care of the ordinary Volga German would have been immeasurably poorer.

The Volga German zemstvos staunchly supported measures whose purpose was the overall economic growth and integration of each district. In 1867, the Novouzensk zemstvo, "expressing the wishes of the people," petitioned the State Council to remove the district from Samara Province and to make it again a territorial-administrative unit of Saratov Province (which it had been until 1850 and the creation of Samara Province), claiming this to be in the best economic interests of all. This peasant-colonist initiative declared that the Volga River imposed no major physical barrier between Novouzensk District and Saratov Province, but actually linked the two, and that as a result the district had most of its economic ties with the river towns and settlements of Saratov

Province, and especially with the provincial capital, Saratov. Unfortunately, these arguments failed to sway government functionaries, often woefully ignorant of the Lower Volga region.[57]

No less ardent supporter of economic integration, the Kamyshin District zemstvo consistently backed the construction of a "southern" railroad in Saratov Province. In September 1868, the Kamyshin zemstvo adopted the position of the district zemstvo railroad commission—chaired by none other than the indefatigable Peter Louck (half of the commission's members were colonists)—which favored a Tambov-Borisoglebsk-Kamyshin railroad over the proposed Tambov-Saratov line.[58] The Kamyshin District zemstvo and its deputies to the Saratov Province zemstvo ardently fought, but failed to prevent, the provincewide zemstvo partial funding and loan guarantees for the private construction of the Tambov-Saratov Railroad, claiming that a railroad constructed 120 miles from Kamyshin towns and villages would bring Kamyshinites few benefits. Finally, in 1913 the Kamyshin District zemstvo urged that a branch line of the Riazan-Uralsk Railroad linking Saratov and the large former colony of Golyi Karamysh was not only feasible but necessary for the economic development of the district.[59] Consequently, the peasant-colonist zemstvos steadfastly placed district economic interests above those of the province and state.

Inasmuch as these Lower Volga districts were predominantly peasant and agrarian in nature and the zemstvos were directed to promote local economic needs, the zemstvos devoted considerable attention and resources to the development of agriculture. The methods and programs differed, but the sole aim was to improve the livelihood of the peasantry by raising farm output. In September 1865, the Novouzensk District zemstvo, consisting "almost exclusively of peasants and colonists," launched one of the earliest and boldest initiatives for improving peasant agriculture by requesting the Ministry of State Domains to sell the vast state landholdings in the district, amounting to about 1.2 million acres of unoccupied state lands, to the peasants, with the district zemstvo acting as the sales intermediary. This imaginative scheme even caught the attention and gained the support of the influential capital newspaper *Sanktpeterburgskiia vedomosti*.[60] Foreseeing the agricultural potential of the vast virgin lands of the trans-Volga region, many wealthy individuals, particularly merchants, had succeeded in the 1850s in obtaining long-term leases on the best state lands in Novouzensk District for nominal rents. These large, wealthy leasees in turn rented the lands to peasants and colonists. Peasant and colonist communes were unable to lease these lands directly from the government, because the state leased only large tracts requiring a sizable outlay of funds, which most peasant communities did not possess.

The Novouzensk zemstvo delegates offered several sound reasons why the government should sell the state lands to peasant and colonist communes. The Treasury would make much more from the sale of these lands than it would earn from the existing low-rent lease program. The peasants and colonists needed more lands, but the wealthy leasees were gouging them by charging exorbitant rents sometimes twenty-five times higher than the rents the merchants paid the government! Finally, the zemstvo urged the end to the lease program to prevent the complete exhaustion of the state lands. Faced with high rents and scarce lands, the peasants practiced the most exploitative farming methods to squeeze the last kernel of grain from the leased state lands. Frequent and repeated wheat sowings quickly depleted the soil. The government rejected the proposal and continued to use these land tracts as a resettlement area for land-short peasants from central Russia. If the government had shared the foresight of the Novouzensk District zemstvo and accepted this proposal, the colonies and peasant communities might have been spared the land-scarce conditions that first became felt in the 1880s.

Rodents posed one of the greatest crop threats to the peasants of the Lower Volga. In the spring and early summer, the voracious and prolific *suslik*, a burrowing field rodent, invaded wheat fields and devoured the young, green wheat plants. Seeing the ineffectiveness of individual village rodent extermination efforts, the Kamyshin District zemstvo in 1868 launched one of the first districtwide rodent control programs in Russia.[61] The zemstvo established a mandatory bounty system of thirty *susliki* per taxed male, and failure to supply one's annual quota resulted in a maximum fine of ninety kopecks. By 1905, the zemstvo had created a sophisticated poison program offering free, professionally instructed application of carbon bisulfide.[62] On the eve of World War I, the rodents no longer posed such a serious threat to the crops, and in some places they had been almost eradicated.

Beginning in the 1890s, the district zemstvos significantly augmented the holdings of small agricultural machinery in the local peasant economy by acting as nonprofit middlemen between machinery manufacturers and the peasants. The zemstvos early realized that a rapidly expanding peasant population and a finite land area, fast approaching the limits of agricultural cultivation, meant that the days of peasant "extensive" cultivation were numbered. Traditionally, the peasants and colonists had expanded crop output simply by cultivating more land. The zemstvos felt that if the peasants had greater access to small agricultural machinery—chiefly iron plows, harrows, and winnowing and sowing machines—crop yields per acre of land could be increased. Since peasant plots were small and there was an overabundance of cheap manual labor, such labor-saving machinery as threshing machines and hay mowers were superfluous to peasant farming. The zemstvos generally purchased the farm implements from the manufacturers and then either resold them to the peasants or communes at cost on easy credit terms, with a small down payment, or rented them for a nominal fee. Zemstvo machinery distribution points were established in most locales to afford easy peasant access.

The Kamyshin District zemstvo, in particular, had a very impressive record in agricultural equipment transfer, placing it in the top 10 percent of all district zemstvos. During the 1904–14 decade, its sales of farm machinery jumped over 300 percent, from 96,500 rubles to 330,972 rubles.[63] By 1908, it annually purchased over 1,000 units, or about 7 to 8 percent, of the total Volga German production of the winnowing machine known as the *Kolonistok* In this way, the zemstvo aided the local peasants, but also promoted colonist *kustar* industry (discussed later in this chapter). In 1910, Volga Germans living in Kamyshin District increasingly rented seed-sowing machines from the zemstvos and reported favorably on the even seed distribution and improved yields.[64] Impressed with how quickly the peasants and colonists had adopted the use of agricultural machinery, zemstvo agronomists in 1915 reported a "remarkable" increase in peasant-colonist use of farm machinery furnished by the zemstvos.[65] Although machinery sales and distribution remained one of the best and most appreciated zemstvo programs, machines alone could not solve all the peasants' farming problems.

To the Kamyshin and Novouzensk district zemstvos belong the credit and honor for the introduction, promotion, and advancement of scientific farming methods in the Lower Volga. Zemstvo dissemination of agricultural information to the colonists and peasants brought their first real awareness of the benefits and advantages of systematic crop rotation, careful soil preparation, manuring, cultivation of grasses and legumes, planting of row crops, and seed selection. Despite frequent claims to the contrary, the Volga Germans were not "model" agriculturalists and long practiced traditional, peasant farming methods not markedly different from those used by the neighboring Russian peasants.[66] Before the advent of the zemstvos, the only farm units in Saratov and Samara provinces adopting and adhering to advanced farming practices were a few gentry estates and the nine, small Mennonite colonies in Samara Province.

The two zemstvos were among the first in Russia to employ agronomists to be the disseminators and promoters of progressive agricultural ideas and practices. The agronomist with specialized and advanced training in crop production was an invaluable resource to the predominantly grain-growing peoples of the Lower Volga. Russia did not educate and graduate many agronomists until the 1890s (there were only twenty-two district agronomists in all Russia in 1890), and that is the main reason why the Kamyshin and Novouzensk district zemstvos did not hire their first agronomists until 1898. Soon, however, the two zemstvos had expanded their staffs of agricultural specialists until they were among the largest in Russia. Boris Veselovskii, author of the best zemstvo study, cited the Kamyshin District zemstvo as an outstanding example of a district zemstvo that promoted agriculture by employing agronomists and other agricultural specialists; it had one of the lowest per capita agricultural specialist ratios in the empire.[67] By 1914, the zemstvo had a full-time staff of twenty-five specialists (seven of whom were agronomists); this was a larger staff than some provinces had. Similarly, by 1912 the Novouzensk District zemstvo employed more agronomists—seventeen—than any other district zemstvo in Russia, with five of them having their main office in Volga German settlements.[68]

The peasants and colonists received the zemstvo agronomist with much less hostility than the zemstvo teacher, though initially they were indifferent to the agronomist's approaches. After all, having farmed all their lives, what more could any outsider teach them? The zemstvo agronomist thus found the peasants to be obstinate foes of agricultural innovation, suspiciously viewing the agronomist at best as a well-intentioned but inexperienced and inept, book-educated city-slicker, and at worst as simply another government bureaucrat meddling in peasant affairs. The agronomist encountered rigid peasant-colonist customs and traditions, which valued the old over the new ("the older the better"), and in almost every village he heard either in Russian or the Volga German dialect, "We live like our forefathers, and our fathers and grandfathers did not know this and they did not hunger."[69] Finally, language differences slowed and sometimes blocked the exchange of information between the agronomists and Volga Germans.

The agronomists did not let all these obstacles deter them from their mission, and their competence, diligence, and dedication eventually earned them the grudging respect of the peasantry and brought tangible change in the lives of the peoples of the Lower Volga. They traveled around the districts demonstrating plowing, seeding, and harvesting techniques. Unquestionably, the agronomists' machinery demonstrations contributed significantly to the success of the zemstvos' agricultural equipment sales programs. The agronomists also instructed the people in the application of carbon bisulfide in the zemstvos' rodent-control program. The agronomist-directed reforestation projects stopped serious erosion of valleys and ravines in several Kamyshin District colonies.[70] The agronomist-manned experiment station in the colony of Ust' Kulalinka (Galka), one of seven in Kamyshin District, distributed seeds and conducted various crop experiments on its fields, especially the cultivation of grasses and legume crops. In this colony, the agronomist cooperated closely with the zemstvo schoolteacher, Alexander Schick, to persuade other colonists to plant vineyards and to sow with a seed drill.[71] After 1906, upon agronomists' recommendations, both district zemstvos issued regular agricultural publications in Russian *and* German.[72] The zemstvo agronomists could not perform agricultural miracles, but by 1914 they had begun to have a noticeable influence on peasants and colonists: "The introduction of new and different, heretofore unknown, machinery and techniques into the peasant economy clearly indicates that the peasants and former colonists have not remained deaf to the advice of the agronomists and already are trying to implement different technical methods recommended by the latter."[73]

Although they expended the preponderance of their resources and efforts to rectify "local economic needs" through the improvement of peasant agriculture, the peasant-colonist zemstvos did not neglect peasant cottage industry, because they saw in it a means to alleviate the colonists' economic problems resulting from the deteriorating agricultural situation in the Volga German settlements. On February 28, 1903, zemstvo agronomist Aleksandr Loginov reported the findings of his study of the Volga German cottage industry to the Kamyshin District zemstvo:

We see that farming is already unprofitable and under the best of conditions barely yields enough to cover regular needs let alone special needs. Such a sad agricultural situation, leaving no hope for its immediate improvement in the future, coupled with the population increase which only worsens the matter, shows that ultimately farming will become almost impossible.

. . . .

It is for these reasons, and also many others, that lately the populace is seeking another way out of this dilemma and is trying to find ways for its excess population to make a living in occupations other than farming. Therefore, we see that in Sosnovka township and others cottage industry is penetrating, developing gradually, and improving, and as a result gives more or less regular income to an entire group of people . . . .[74]

Healthy cottage industries provided supplemental income, alleviated colonist pressures on the land, offered excellent work during the slow winter months, and sometimes meant the difference between hunger and starvation during years of crop failures.

The Kamyshin and Novouzensk district zemstvos followed different approaches to cottage industry—approaches that corresponded to the peculiar nature of such industry in the two districts. The Kamyshin District zemstvo attempted to generate ways to increase sales of an extensive, diverse, and long-established *kustar* industry manufacturing primarily cotton cloth, small farm machinery, tobacco pipes, and leather goods. The Novouzensk District zemstvo sought ways to nurture a quite small, fledgling colony cottage industry consisting basically of sarpinka weaving and wattle basketmaking. While *kustar* industry already existed and was fairly well developed in Kamyshin District colonies when the zemstvo came into being in the 1860s, in Novouzensk District peasant industry in Volga German settlements did not begin until the late 1890s and never reached the size, scale, and significance of Volga German industries in Kamyshin District.

In the 1890s, the Kamyshin District zemstvo attempted to arouse peasant-colonist interest in trades and crafts by setting up weaving and machine-manufacturing workshops in settlements, but even the zemstvo admitted that this experiment had been a miserable failure. As a result of these unfortunate experiences, the zemstvo remained reluctant to undertake any "artificial inducements" (*iskusstvennyia nasazhdeniia*) to aid cottage industry, claiming that solid peasant industry occurred only when initiated and established by the peasants themselves. Thus, in 1910 it refused to accept three free stocking knitting machines, offered by the Saratov Province zemstvo, to be placed in new workshops. The reasons it gave were that the district zemstvo would have to cover maintenance and housing costs, the new workshops would not be able to compete with existing ones, and, above all, "any development of *kustar* production requires that the initiative come from the local population, and any artificial inducements are fruitless."[75]

The Kamyshin zemstvo did not remain unsympathetic to the plight of colonist industries struggling to survive. While the Volga German sarpinka industry remained in excellent economic health, competing successfully with factory-produced goods up to 1917, such was not the case with the Volga German winnowing machine industry, which had stagnated. Founded in the 1860s, the small Volga German workshops were losing out to Russian and foreign factories by 1900 because no basic changes had been introduced in the simple Volga German machine. The zemstvo attributed the stagnation to the colonists' inability to implement costly new production methods because of a shortage of credit. What was needed, the zemstvo thought, was a zemstvo bank to provide low-interest, small loans to peasant manufactories. But inasmuch as none existed and the zemstvo always lacked sufficient financial capital, the Kamyshin zemstvo attempted to bolster lagging sales by acting as a sales agent for the Volga German *Kolonistok* winnower, selling as many as 1,200 machines some years.[76]

The few, nascent colonist industries of Novouzensk District seemed destined to provide only seasonal, part-time, and low-paid jobs. Low profits, caused by such things as scarce natural resources, high costs of materials, distant markets, and lack of capital and a marketing organization, provided colonist artisans with only small, supplemental incomes. Even with such dim prospects, the district zemstvo realized that the crisis of agriculture and the absence of factories and mills in the district necessitated the development of *kustar* industry to augment shrinking peasant family incomes, and by 1905 zemstvo expenditures on *kustar* promotion placed it among the top twenty district zemstvos.[77]

In 1905, the Novouzensk zemstvo encouraged thirty sarpinka weavers in seven Volga German settlements to form a cooperative, known as the Friedenfeld *tovarishchestvo*, by lending them interest-free, start-up capital.

Colonists resettling in the district from Kamyshin District in the 1860s brought with them looms and weaving skills, but until the late 1890s weaving was done chiefly for home consumption. In 1899, the weavers began to produce for the local market; however, they could not compete with the larger and better organized sarpinka industry in the colonies of Kamyshin District, because until the formation of the cooperative, the individual weaver bought his dyed thread from a middleman and had no sales outlet to market his cloth. The new cooperative purchased thread directly from Saratov and Moscow spinning mills and entered into agreements with merchants to market the cloth. By 1911, the cooperative had over 300 members, and its success had prompted other colonist and peasant communes to petition the zemstvo for weaving workshops to be opened in their villages.[78]

The abundance of brushwood on the Volga islands and riverbanks led to wattle basket and furniture making in a dozen colonies adjoining the Volga River. The bad harvests of the late 1880s forced them to take up wattle weaving as a sideline. Kustarevo-Krasnorynovka (Neu Kolonie), Krasnopol'e (Preiss), Berezovka (Dehler), and Kazitskaia (Brabander) became the major centers. Adoption of better techniques, such as cleaning and stripping the wood, and weaving of better-quality items enabled the industry to progress from simple basketmaking for the region's fruitgrowers to large baskets, trunks, children's wagons, and even furniture. But profits remained abysmally low, with a master sometimes earning twenty to fifty kopecks per fifteen-hour day! One problem was the high cost of brush, which was often bought up by middlemen and then sold at high prices to weavers. Consequently, during the winter of 1906, only about seventy weavers wove.

The Novouzensk District zemstvo tried to revive this cottage industry. In February 1903 it opened a basket-weaving workshop in Kazitskaia, hired an experienced weaver from Kamyshin District, and supplied inexpensive and high-quality materials. The purpose of the workshop was to instruct local weavers to weave more valuable articles. In 1906, the zemstvo employed another master weaver from Moscow to hold workshops throughout the district. Finally, in 1910 it founded a three-year weaving school in Kazitskaia, which had a master teacher and offered zemstvo stipends to a dozen students each year.[79] War and revolution intervened before the results of this zemstvo program could be discerned. At best, the program indicated the zemstvo's commitment to expand job opportunities for the Volga Germans.

Brief mention needs to be made of the less successful zemstvo efforts to provide villagers with food and grain after crop failures. The so-called food provisioning (*prodovol'stvennoe delo*) of the populace remained a zemstvo function until June 12, 1900, when it was transferred to the central government. The 1864 zemstvo law had assigned to the zemstvo the responsibility of "supervision" (*nadzor*) of food provisioning.[80]

The Volga colonies generally fared better than neighboring peasants during crop failures. Since 1800, the government had imposed upon each colony an emergency grain reserve system (each colony had a granary filled with a specified amount of grain), which was closely supervised and enforced by the Saratov Office of Foreign Settlers.[81] In 1834, the tsarist government imposed a similar system on the entire peasantry, but it was inadequate and badly supervised. Many colonists also had supplemental earnings from cottage industry to help them survive bad years. The more prosperous colonies could purchase grain with community monies. Of course, during general harvest failures, such as 1890–91, little grain was available and all peasants hungered.

Despite bureaucratic interference, administrative bottlenecks, scarce financial resources, and inadequate policing authority, the Kamyshin and Novouzensk zemstvos endeavored to alleviate peasant hunger and misery during crop disasters. In 1882, the Novouzensk zemstvo initiated a public works program, consisting of drilling and digging wells, to assist beleaguered peasants; it was one of the first of its kind in Russia.[82] Later the zemstvo supported and organized "soup kitchens" in the neediest settlements.

The Kamyshin District zemstvo quickly established a type of harvest early warning system. Because of the remoteness of the Lower Volga region and an inadequate transportation network, a bad harvest could easily turn into a disaster for the peasants unless swift action was taken. Even though grain might be available in other regions of Russia, it was difficult to move supplies to the Lower Volga. Food relief via the Volga had to be received before the river froze and closed around October 1. Long-distance ground transport of food supplies was all but impossible during famine years because of fodder shortages and the weakened condition of livestock. The zemstvo board had only two months, between mid-July or early August (when crop yields could be ascertained) and October 1, to arrange and deliver famine relief. Under Peter Louck's leadership, the zemstvo established an efficient and invaluable crop-reporting system.[83] Each settlement in the district had a designated reporter, such as the village elder, teacher, or clergyman, who immediately and directly reported to the zemstvo board the size of the local crops and, in case of crop failures, careful estimates of food and seed provisions needed from the zemstvo. Although the zemstvo frequently could not provide sufficient food provisions, the organization's efforts were commendable.

Not until the 1890s did the Volga Germans begin to feel the full impact of the zemstvo reforms, with the great increase in the size of the zemstvo "third element." The term "third element" was coined in the late 1890s to apply to the experts and professionals (teachers, physicians, agronomists, and statisticians) employed by the zemstvos to distinguish them from the other two elements of provincial and district government, the appointed government bureaucrats and the elected zemstvo members. Until the appearance of the zemstvo professional "third element," the colonists had little contact with or knowledge of the zemstvos, chiefly because no zemstvo unit comparable to the district zemstvo existed at the township level, the zemstvo convened in the district town center, and the district usually covered a large area. During the 1890s, the size of the zemstvo "third element" greatly increased, and by 1910 it numbered over 700 in the two districts. These zemstvo employees forged a tangible and vital link between the district zemstvo and the Volga Germans.[84] The success or failure of the zemstvo schools, hospitals, and agricultural and economic endeavors largely rested on the shoulders of the "third element." The "third element" directly touched the lives of the former colonists.

Indubitably, the zemstvos improved the quality of life of the colonists and brought them many tangible benefits, a fact to date largely unmentioned in the historical literature of the Volga Germans. Countless specific cases could be cited as examples of zemstvo success stories. The colonists of Galka, Dreispitz, and other settlements owed much to the zemstvo for helping them build bridges over deep ravines and earthen dams to control the flooding Kulalinka River. In 1910, the zemstvo advanced Galka settlers 11,000 rubles to drill wells, saving colonists from driving their cattle long distances every day to the Volga River for watering.[85] By 1894, villagers of Shcherbakovka had a small library because of the efforts of their zemstvo teacher, David Vollert, who requested library funds from the district zemstvo. The zemstvo doctors and feldshers gave the colonists their smallpox vaccinations. Numerous Volga German youth, including many young women, continued their education beyond the primary level, thanks to zemstvo stipends.[86] Finally, but most important, the countless zemstvo publications remain rich and invaluable sources of information that has immeasurably enriched the historical legacy of the Volga Germans.

The zemstvos serving the Volga German settlements were not unmitigated successes. Limited and fluctuating revenues, coming primarily from a land tax borne by the peasants and colonists, forced the zemstvos to restrict and, in times of crop failures such as in 1877–80, 1891–92, and 1905–6, to curb completely some of their programs. Lacking administrative authority, the zemstvos had difficulty enforcing and monitoring policies. While no criminal behavior on the part of zemstvo officials was uncovered, elected zemstvo members were not entirely altruistic. Cronyism was sometimes an element in the awarding of contracts for zemstvo concessions (such as way stations and horses), the granting of zemstvo jobs, the allotment of student stipends, the determination of zemstvo salaries, and the approval of requests to open village bazaars and fairs. The zemstvo delegates protected their own local economic interests by denying other settlements the right to open weekly bazaars.[87]

Only a small minority of Volga colonists, chiefly the well-to-do entrepreneurial element and colony officialdom, immediately applauded the zemstvo reform, quickly enrolled in zemstvo service, and participated actively in the zemstvos. But this initial active zemstvo participation indicated that as early as the 1860s a number of Volga Germans were capable of functioning effectively in a Russian milieu. The zemstvos gradually broke the colonists' isolation, fostered a sense of broader community interest, and became a major conduit for new ideas and change. By the 1890s, more Volga Germans had become a part of the zemstvo network, first as students in the zemstvo schools and later as members of the rapidly growing "third element." Through the efforts and dedication of the "third element," the ordinary settler became more familiar with the outside world. Although most Volga Germans long remained suspicious of zemstvo support, in the long run the zemstvos brought them much assistance and many essential services, particularly in the areas of education, health, and agriculture.

Chapter Eight

The Political Awakening of 1905

The Volga Germans' long pent up and deeply felt resentment finally erupted during the revolutionary days of 1905, when they were swept up in the euphoric liberation movement which attracted all elements of the Lower Volga. Reform was the hope of all groups of society, and a spirit of compromise fostered a political unity which lasted for most of 1905. Differences were muted and common aims stressed. Not only did zemstvo liberals cooperate with socialists, but Social Democrats shared the platform with Socialist Revolutionaries, radicals tempered their rhetoric, the "third element" associated with peasants and urban workers, and the Volga Germans joined the chorus of society in urging reform and political cooperation.[1]

The revolutionary events of 1905 also revealed the grievous nature of the "national problem," the situation of the non-Russian peoples of the empire. The aggressively enforced assimilation policy of blatant cultural and religious Russification aroused extreme resentment among the minorities, which manifested itself fully in 1905–6. The demands of the various nationality groups ranged from nonviolent requests for cultural autonomy to violent outbursts for national autonomy. The nineteenth-century political awakening of minorities in the Russian Empire was connected closely with the national awakening of these groups. The strength of ethnic consciousness—that is, the degree of development of an ethnic group's native language, religion, and culture—generally varied directly with the group's political demands and methods. Thus groups with an old, well-developed civilization, such as the Poles, Armenians, Finns, and Georgians, agitated for political autonomy and in some cases

independence; those minorities with less well-formed ethnic identities and consciousness respectfully petitioned for recognition of their cultural particularity—
usually the right to study their history, language, and culture openly and freely.
The Volga Germans belonged to this last category.

There was nothing revolutionary about the Volga Germans' political aims
and methods, which corresponded closely to those of the state peasants living
near them. Volost and colony authorities sought the reform of local government by requesting greater autonomy and reduced bureaucracy; there were no
popular outcries for political autonomy, constitutional monarchy, a national
zemstvo organization, or any other political bodies. Zemstvo elements, primarily the teachers, sought a radical reordering of education to enhance popular
enlightenment. Moreover, the colonists adopted nonrevolutionary means to
achieve their goals, which contrasted strikingly with the anarchic outbreaks of
arson, pillage, and land seizures committed by former serfs with small allotments. The massive agrarian disturbances so characteristic of Saratov Province
were, in fact, generally concentrated in the former serf and large gentry estate
strongholds of the northwestern districts, where agrarian problems were much
more severe. The economic crises and exploitative arrangements, which so exacerbated peasant-gentry relations, were largely absent in the southern districts
of Saratov and Samara provinces, inhabited overwhelmingly by former state
peasants and colonists. Accordingly, while the northwestern tinderbox burst
aflame on gentry estates in the summer and autumn of 1905, the south remained quiescent with no violence directed against the Volga Germans, reflecting the comparable socioeconomic conditions of the colonists and neighboring
peasantry and generally good relations between the two communities.[2]

Although the turbulent days following the senseless January 22, 1905,
Bloody Sunday massacre elicited no mass Volga German uprising on the scale
of the former Russian serfs in the northwestern districts, the lapse of governmental authority allowed for unparalleled scattered acts of defiance and protest
in the colonies. While it is difficult to generalize, most acts were directed not
against neighboring landlords but against depressed economic conditions and
local officialdom. The only major reported violence broke out in the Volga port
colony of Rovnoe, erupting over low wages and scarce jobs. In May 1905 when
the spring thaw set in, time came to move the winter-stored grain. Hearing of
the growing strike movement in Russia, the local workers, who hauled grain
from the granaries to docked barges and most of whom were Volga Germans,

protested their low wages by going on strike and forcing the grain merchants to grant wage increases. The sudden appearance of large numbers of poor, distressed nonlocal seasonal workers threatened to destroy the strikers' recent wage agreement. The press reported, "The German haulers feared the outside workers as competitors for their jobs, and as soon as the nonlocal workers appeared on the riverbank the Germans drove them away."[3] Unfortunately, several of the nonlocals did not manage to escape and were badly beaten. With the local authorities unable to control the belligerent Rovnoe dockworkers, the government finally dispatched a seventy-soldier detachment to quell the disturbances and restore order.

In response to the decree of February 18, 1905, granting communes the right to appeal directly to the tsar, several colonies petitioned for local autonomy and the reform of the colony assembly as a classless (*bezsoslovnyi*) one in which all male residents could vote and participate, instead of only the heads of the farming households.[4] Heretofore, all other village adults—adult sons, clergy, teachers, artisans, merchants, and any noncolonist, such as a Russian merchant or trader residing in the colony—remained totally excluded from local government. Therefore, vital issues affecting agriculture, education, and the welfare of the colonists were discussed and resolved by the eldest, often more backward and tradition-minded of the farming colonists. The Volga Germans also asked that local village government be given control of the police, who were despised for their dishonesty, idleness, drunkenness, and failure to preserve order.

There soon followed petitions for a classless township government and court which would end the political segregation and second-class citizenship of all peasant rural dwellers, into which category the colonists fell after the 1871 reforms. The lack of legal rights was also a major grievance repeatedly expressed by Saratov and Samara peasants in their petitions to the government. Until 1917, the township, as a territorial-administrative subdivision of the district, remained an organization of the peasant class; landed proprietors, urban residents, and all other nonpeasant elements remained free and apart from township government. Likewise, township courts handled disputes and litigation only between peasants, whose decisions were resolved on the basis of custom and tradition, not law. Illiterate judges often presided in these courts.

By the summer of 1905, most colonists were extremely war-weary and deeply troubled by revolutionary agitation, although the major topic of conversation was the fickle weather—drought followed by severe hailstorms. Many perhaps felt like the colonist who wrote, "We are living in a very difficult period in which human life is placed in great danger."[5] The demands of an unpopular war still weighed heavily on the colonists, causing considerable economic distress. The drafting of many zemstvo doctors and the fear of another cholera epidemic like the one in 1903 stirred up many rumors and much uneasiness. The mobilization of the menfolk and requisitioning of horses and wagons resulted in a decline in the amount of land sown.

Despite the administrative and bureaucratic problem, the most emotional, explosive, and divisive issue in the colonies from the 1890s until 1917 unquestionably revolved around the changes taking place in the colony parish schools, the *Kirchenschulen*. The deep colonist resentment erupted into public view in the autumn of 1905. In fact, between 1905 and 1907 the Russified elementary schools became the object of most protest among all social groups of the non-Russian peoples of the Russian Empire.[6] Under the leadership of Count Dmitrii Tolstoy, minister of education from 1866 to 1880, the tsarist government embarked on new education policies. Tolstoy recognized Russia's need for a literate population, but sought to reduce the threats of literacy to autocracy by advocating bureaucratic centralization and Russification of primary schools. The primary school he envisaged was to be financed by the local community and zemstvo, instructed by clergy qualified to imbue education with the spirit of religious truths, but centrally directed and supervised by the Ministry of Education. Tolstoy had nothing against a role for clergy in the primary schools, but it was to be a limited and not decisive role. The introduction of Russian language instruction in non-Russian schools, especially during the last two decades of the nineteenth century, was based on the notion that knowledge of and respect for Russian history and literature would integrate the non-Russian borderlands more closely into the Russian part of the empire, narrowing the gulf dividing Russians from non-Russians.[7]

The intrusion of secular authorities and Russification into the *Kirchenschulen* in the 1890s deeply disturbed and confused the colonists, because tampering with the schools raised many serious religious and social issues. The decree of September 24, 1891, placed the church schools under the direct control of the Ministry of Education and its agent, the public school inspector.[8] A reduction in religious instruction to make time for other secular subjects threatened to corrupt beliefs, contribute to a decline in knowledge of basic doctrine and tenets, and ultimately place in jeopardy one's hope for salvation. The Protestant colonists also believed very fervently that they had to speak to God in their tongue, thus their alarm about learning Russian.[9] The changes threatened to undermine the position and influence of the pastor, the intellectual as well as spiritual authority in the village. The introduction of an educated teacher (*Lehrer*) to replace the barely literate *Schulmeister* would challenge the pastor's intellectual hold over the colonists.

The turbulent school question reflected the limited cultural or ethnic awakening that had occurred over the last two decades. The reform of the church schools threatened to undermine the capacity of the colonists to transmit the Volga German dialect, customs, and traditions to their children, because the more Russianized and secularized the schools became, the less effectively they functioned as transmitters of Volga German ethnicity. The church schools' emphasis on religion and traditional values fostered continuity and ties of the pupils with the community, inasmuch as schooling got one into the church, and therefore into full membership in the village community; the more Russianized and secular the education Volga Germans received, the greater likelihood they would leave the colony, because rarely could educated colonists find suitable employment in the colony. Likewise, the more people learned about the outside world, the more likely they were to become dissatisfied with the backward, boring, and isolated life of the village. Literacy threatened to undermine the traditional order of the community by bringing more people into the mainstream of society and political life. The emergence of a better educated and Russian-speaking youth could pose a leadership challenge to their elders.

To make matters worse, the tsarist government badly bungled the implementation of the educational reforms, producing disastrous educational and political results, and even losing the support of that segment of colonists who had long advocated school reform. Scarce financial resources and an overambitious program led the government to impose the new program of mandatory Russian language and secular instruction on the existing colony church schools, a program they were not designed for and could not fulfill. Russification, not reform, prevailed, inasmuch as the only major change was the addition of a Russian-speaking teacher. Overcrowding and poor facilities remained serious problems. Overzealous school inspectors sometimes expelled qualified Volga German teachers and appointed Russians. Many colonists, like, Peter Sinner, felt betrayed: "This would have been good [school reform] if they [school inspectors] had not begun to propagate Russification policies, expelling the German teachers and appointing Russians, against the will of the master of the school—the people."[10] Some of the new teachers were often barely more literate than the teachers they replaced. The inspectors threatened and cajoled teachers to devote more time to teaching Russian at the expense of other subjects. In 1898, the Kamyshin District zemstvo reported that Russian language instruction was "extremely bad" and that "the local population was dissatisfied with the inspectors and the extremely low level of education possessed by the inspector-appointed teachers."[11]

The anti-intelligentsia campaign that surfaced throughout the Lower Volga also penetrated the colonies.[12] The general strike begun in early October 1905, paralyzing the government and bringing the Russian Empire to a standstill, prompted a marked increase in Volga German defiance and protest directed chiefly against the government's irksome Russification policies. Ironically, the object of the colonists' wrath was not the land captains, local police, or school inspector, but the symbol of Russification, the Russian language teachers, or "Russifiers" (*obrusiteli*) as the Volga Germans often called them, many of whom were Volga Germans; these teachers were still highly suspect because of the widespread suspicion that the government secretly instructed them to convert children to Orthodoxy! Generally speaking, by this time most colony schools had at least two teachers, one a Volga German and the other a Russian. The issue of Russification was also often connected to that of secularization. As colonists lamented: "The school has stopped fulfilling its purpose . . . . Our clergymen were in charge of the school and children left the school as true believers . . . . Now the Russian teachers read the children various fables and fairy tales about mice, birds, and monkeys, rather than from the Bible."[13] This last statement also reveals the tension between church and zemstvo, clerics and teachers, which pervaded the Russian countryside in 1905.

By the end of October, twenty-eight communities in Saratov Province and thirty-five in Samara Province had voted to expel the Russian language teachers from their schools.[14] Some teachers narrowly escaped bodily harm, while others were locked out of their lodgings and schools. All received no salaries. In one school, pupils, at the instigation of their parents, threw down their Russian books, screamed they would not study Russian, and fled from the classroom. In other colonies, public furor became so explosive that officials closed schools for fear that enraged colonists would destroy them. Many teachers remaining on the job carried weapons for self-defense.

Sporadic and unrelated incidents of other types of illegal acts intensified in the Volga German settlements throughout the month of October as political authority collapsed. The only known instance of Volga German participation in an attack on private estate lands happened in mid-October in the meadow-side township of Paninskaia, where the Volga Germans joined with peasants in stealing straw from an island belonging to the wealthy Shuvalov family.[15] Both provincial governments received reports of Volga German tax protests and defiance of police authorities, as the resolute populace refused to submit meekly to the small, but long dominant, well-to-do conservative leadership. With the harvests collected and order collapsing, lawlessness accompanied the last fading days of autumn on the Volga.

There was no apparent organization or effective leadership of the growing unrest within the colonies, for no peasant or teacher unions propagandized there; but, for the first time, Volga German zemstvo elements and youth appear to have wielded considerable influence, and in some settlements challenged the more conservative leadership of the elders. Many zemstvo teachers admittedly pursued that career for political reasons, because it was one of the few outlets through which one could conduct public propaganda and establish contacts with like-minded professionals. Although radicalization of the teachers was evident and attracted the attention of the police, notably their letter writing campaigns in the local press urging political activism, they lacked SR political indoctrination and organization more readily apparent in the northwestern settlements of Saratov Province. Taking advantage of the political crisis and resultant weakening of traditional order, many youth tried to arouse parents and fellow colonists. For example, in five meadow-side settlements, returning soldiers from Manchuria and young teachers agitated in the village assemblies for the nonpayment of taxes, which they claimed had been set too high by the land captain. In the colony of Kazitskaia, the police reported that young males, many of them ex-soldiers, and the poor disrupted the communal assembly and refused to pay taxes. The Rovnoe police reported that students were in a revolutionary mood, which was exhibited in their attempted takeover of the teacher-training academy.[16]

But the appearance of the "third element" and youth as agents of reform should not be exaggerated; in a few instances, the traditional village authorities, the elder and the minister, sensitive to the long-suppressed grievances of the Volga Germans, agitated for change and urged disobedience of the law. The police charged village elder Koenig of Obermonzhu with inciting not only his own constituents but also the residents of Ekaterinenstadt. In the colony of Tsug, Father Bach, the Catholic priest, inveighed against the wealthy colonists' exploitation of the poor and called upon his parishioners "to beat the police and authorities like mad dogs [*beshenykh sobak*]."[17] On the other hand, in Rovnoe, complaints had arisen against the Catholic priest for his obsequiousness toward the authorities. While unrelated, these incidents clearly revealed the gradual weakening and even breakdown of local government that had occurred by late summer in the Lower Volga.

The issuance of the October Manifesto of 1905 by Emperor Nicholas II, granting the basic civil liberties of freedom from arrest, freedom of opinion, of the press, of assembly, and of association, and promising the creation of the State Duma, prompted a wild outburst of enthusiasm and resulted in a gradual ebbing of colonist agitation. The Volga Germans greeted the October Manifesto with much hope, believing it to be the start of a new order. Very quickly they made use of the newly granted civil and political liberties to express their views and promote their goals. As a result, Volga German grievances took on a more distinct form, and various elements came to perceive the need for political action and organization. The "days of freedom"—the eight months between the issuance of the October Manifesto and the beginning of government repression in the summer of 1906—remain very important to the study of the Volga Germans, primarily because it was the only period of their life under the tsars when they could freely and openly profess and disseminate their views.

Although the turbulent period from October 1905 to April 1906, when elections to the First Duma were held, was the most bloody and violent in Saratov Province and not conducive to measured and reasonable political debate, the Volga Germans remained relatively immune to the urban and rural violence, and enthusiastically engaged in heated but nonviolent political activities. The jacquerie in the northwestern districts terrorized the landowners, some of whom became reactionary in their politics while others remained too disillusioned to act, and led to the liquidation of estates as owners flooded the Peasant

Land Bank with requests to auction off their properties.[18] Brutal clashes between Cossack forces and peasants, and police and urban radicals, caused numerous casualties, fueled rumors, and unalterably fractured the liberation movement. Politics became polarized as gentry-led reactionary elements and revolutionary forces challenged and attacked the more moderate but still radical mainstream of society, which hoped to stay the reform course and destroy autocracy by legally implementing the provisions of the October Manifesto.[19] Unquestionably, the Volga Germans remained in this mainstream.

The first uncensored Volga German political and secular opinions came to be expressed in three newspapers: *Saratow deutsche Zeitung, Unsere Zeit*, and *Privolzhskaia gazeta*. The weekly Saratov-based newspaper, usually referred to as the *Deutsche Zeitung*, published thirty-four editions between February 1 and September 27, 1906. Its co-owners and publishers were Adolf Lane, a businessman, Heinrich Schellhorn, a Rovnoe grain dealer who also operated a McCormick agricultural machinery dealership in the same colony, and Peter Sinner, a teacher and writer; Sinner, with journalistic experience on the *Odessauer Zeitung*, was the real organizer and editor. Few knew of Sinner's association with the newspaper, because he had fled in disguise to Saratov to escape the police, who sought him for chairing a strike committee in the Ukraine during the October 1905 general strike; although Sinner wrote most of the editorials, Lane signed them.[20] The newspaper's political orientation eventually followed closely the line of the Constitutional Democratic party, or Kadets. Despite recurrent printer strikes and labor problems, the *Deutsche Zeitung* continued publication until September 1906, when its founders decided to cease publication rather than let the governor of Saratov Province dictate the content of the paper.[21]

Unsere Zeit had an even shorter life than the *Saratower deutsche Zeitung*, appearing thrice weekly between March 5 and May 17, 1906. Published in the town of Kamyshin by Johannes Fritzler, its avowed purpose was to raise the political awareness of the Volga Germans. Fritzler believed that the October Manifesto offered great political opportunities and that the Volga Germans needed to be informed citizens in order to participate fully in the new order in Russia. In a veiled attack on the Volga German religious publications, which allegedly shirked all political responsibility and failed to function as vehicles of information, Fritzler stated that the only way a colonist could gain any news of the current political and social situation was to read a Russian newspaper. He urged the colonists "to come out of the house and look after your own interests;" to do so they needed to be well informed.[22]

The only Russian-language newspaper to espouse wholeheartedly the cause of the Volga Germans was the *Privolzhskaia gazeta*, published in Saratov. One of its publishers, colonist Jacob Dietz, wrote numerous articles on life in the former colonies. Not only did Dietz reach the small group of Russian-reading colonists, but he managed to portray and disseminate the Volga Germans' sorry plight and grievances to the general reading Russian public. Dietz also effectively used the paper to mobilize mountain-side Volga Germans for the elections to the First Duma. In the fall of 1906, like other opposition newspapers, it succumbed to the repressive measures of Stolypin.

The short-lived Volga German free press provided invaluable benefits to the colonists. At a time of rapid and critical change, these newspapers filled an important information void, providing the colonists not only with uncensored national and international news but also with local news. While reporting a surge in Volga German emigration, the newspapers attempted to aid those remaining, troubled colonists by reporting on such matters as land prices and soil conditions in the prospective areas open to emigrants.[23] For the first time since the colonies were founded, the colonists became aware of conditions in the other colonies on a regular basis. The "Von den Kolonien" weekly columns printed newsworthy items written by colonists about events and conditions in the Volga German settlements. Although the great mass of the colonists remained directly untouched by these publications, they were the first to address all Volga Germans, whereas religious publications addressed only the respective faithful.

Even though the religious press had wide circulation among the Volga Germans, it became unequivocably clear in 1905 that it was not marching to the same political tune as its parishioners. While the newly formed secular press closely mirrored Volga German antigovernment public opinion, the religious press remained steadfast in its support of the status quo. The clergy had no reason to protest or object. Their positions as state-salaried servitors, and the Protestant clergy's close affinities with the conservative Baltic Germans and Dorpat University, acted to restrict their roles to those of preacher and conservator of religious—and to some extent monarchist or at least conservative—values. Long perceived by many as servile, tsarist functionaries, the clergy became the target of criticism and attack after civil liberties were conceded by the October Manifesto. At that time, the public mood within the colonies took on a definite anticlerical character.

The events of 1904–5 glaringly magnified the clergy's conservative, progovernment sympathies and the ever-widening gulf separating the people and their religious leaders, who offered no viable leadership to their politically naive flock during this uncertain but momentous period of Russian history. The clergy's staunch support of the unpopular Russo-Japanese War clashed with Volga German antiwar public opinion. Ironically, typical of this prowar stance was *The Peace Messenger*, its full title being *Der Friedensbote auf Berg und Wiesenseiter der Wolga*, the most widely circulated and popular religious publication in the Protestant colonies, which Pastor Hugh Günther published in Talovka (Beideck) between 1884 and 1915. Born in the Baltic region and educated at Dorpat University, Günther, whose admiration of the conservative Baltic Germans became quite evident, contributed many articles; most, however, were written by Baltic evangelical ministers and Dorpat University theologians. Besides religious articles dedicated to the "edification, instruction, and support of the Christian family," the illustrated monthly contained a few pages of foreign and Russian news, but nothing about local events. Although government censorship prohibited discussion of the actual nature of military conditions and casualties, thereby preventing the religious press from presenting an accurate description of the war, this journal not only uncritically printed government press releases depicting the alleged heroics and glories of the war but enthusiastically exalted the Far Eastern war, characterizing it as a noble and just campaign which should be fought to a victorious solution, thereby constantly reminding the Volga Germans of something most of them would have preferred not to think about.[24] At the same time, Günther also haunted the Volga Germans with the specter of a bloody socialist revolution.

Most of the colony free press unmercifully vilified the privileged clergy for being indifferent to social reform, caring only about the colonists' spiritual concerns while ignoring entirely their lot on earth. A frequent allegation leveled against the clergy was that their long-standing control over education and their preaching of meekness and subservience had retarded social and economic progress within the colonies. One writer asked how the Volga Germans were expected to function under current conditions when in school they had only to memorize Biblical verses and aphorisms, and were thrashed into submission with regular applications of the rod. Many colonists believed, as did this one, that the clergy retarded the intellectual development of the colonists: "From the very beginning of our schools our clergy did nothing to raise the moral and intellectual level of the schools: instruction was conducted by illiterate peasants—our schoolmasters for over a hundred years . . . . A good schoolmaster only needed a strong voice and no pedagogical training."[25] Although the writer admonished the clergy for its inaction and insensitivity, he urged the church to assume a positive advocacy role in the reform of education, citing as an example the recent proposals of Catholic priests in Saratov Province who called for total zemstvo and/or government funding of education.

Scathing criticism of the clergy's servility toward the government and opposition to reform appeared in the recently created free press. So many complaints against the Catholic priest in Rovnoe had aired that even the Catholic periodical *Der Klemens* had denounced his actions. According to one report, the public felt Father Levenbruch's obsequiousness to authorities had gone "far beyond tolerable limits." Undaunted and incorrigibly reactionary, Father Levenbruch allegedly terrorized his congregations in November by warning of the "threatening cloud" of revolution hanging over them.[26] The newspaperman Jacob Dietz, who traveled among the Volga Germans in 1905 to gauge their mood and problems, corroborated that the Rovnoe priest was by no means atypical. He discovered that many colonists described clergymen as *chinovniki* who, paid high state salaries and decorated with all sorts of government ribbons and medals, unhesitatingly carried out the government's wishes. Similarly, Dietz reported Volga German resentment, which remained until then unexpressed, regarding the clergy's open disdain of the public; being the only educated people in the colonies, the clergy remained aloof from the ignorant populace, surrounding themselves in a halo of mystery by having contact with their flock only at church services, which might only be six or seven times a year. Even then, the priest or pastor offered little hope, for the most common sermon or homily themes—even more frequently heard after the spread of revolution—were resignation, submission to misfortune, and obedience to the governing authorities. Once elections to the Duma were announced, the clergy instructed their parishioners to elect men with strong religious convictions (*die was für die Religion haben*), denouncing revolutionaries as monsters who belonged to the party of the devil.[27]

The elections to the First Duma—the first national election in Russian history—disclosed that the former Volga Germans were neither staunch, conservative defenders of the old regime nor revolutionary fanatics; and they rejected the reactionary political advice professed by the clergy. The Volga Germans' liberal reformist leanings in politics dispelled the often expressed notion that they were confirmed monarchists intent on preservation of the status quo and adherents of pan-Germanism. As late as 1915, one author erroneously wrote: "It will not be superfluous to recall, that the German colonists are confirmed monarchists in their political orientation, standing firmly for the preservation of the present state and social order."[28] To the contrary, their views generally followed class rather than ethnic lines. The political alignment of the Volga Germans with the mainstream of Russian opposition in 1906, as well as the shrewd and skillful political instincts of a few astute Volga German politicians, resulted in the election of two Volga Germans as deputies to the First Duma.

The issuance of the Duma electoral legislation on December 24, 1905, greatly alarmed the Volga Germans. Although it extended the franchise to most adult males and granted large representation to the peasantry, based on the unfounded feeling in bureaucratic circles that peasant deputies would form a conservative bloc in the Duma, the law stipulated indirect elections entitling each township to send two delegates to the district assembly, which would elect delegates to the provincial assembly, and that, in turn, would finally elect the Duma deputies. This procedure placed the colonists at a serious disadvantage, for they had fewer but much larger townships than the peasants. Thus, for example, in the Kamyshin District electoral assembly the peasants enjoyed a two-to-one voting advantage over the colonists because they had twice as many townships, even though the Volga Germans constituted a majority of the rural population. The Volga Germans lived in only eight townships and thus were entitled to elect only sixteen delegates to the district assembly, whereas the minority peasants lived in seventeen townships and had thirty-four delegates. This distressed the colonists, who thought that if they could do well in the Kamyshin District electoral assembly, which sent the largest contingent of delegates to the provincial electoral assembly, they might have a chance to play an influential role, because the law provided that the rural delegates at the provincial assembly could meet separately and elect one Duma deputy. Those colonists residing in Samara Province suffered the same electoral liabilities.

Jacob Egorovich Dietz stood in the forefront of the 1906 political mobilization of the Volga Germans. Born in 1864 in the small mountain-side colony of Pochinnoe, he completed his classical secondary education at the Saratov gymnasium, but because of inadequate financial resources he never pursued formal university studies. In the 1880s, Dietz began to read for the law examinations. Because of the repressive mood of the times, he, like most students, became politically suspect; although he passed the examinations, he had to wage a bitter struggle to practice law. Having won that battle, he relocated to the Don Forces Oblast, where he practiced law in the settlement of Arched and quickly gained a reputation as a knowledgeable, honest, and hard-working attorney. In his spare time, he studied the history of the colonists, utilizing the archives of the Saratov Kontora, and wrote numerous articles about them, which were published in several Russian newspapers. With the new political opportunities offered by the events of October 1905, he returned to Kamyshin, where he practiced law in the district court and soon after became a partner in *Privolzhskaia gazeta*, which shared the political program of the People's Freedom party, later known as the Constitutional Democratic party.[29]

After careful examination of the electoral laws and the problems confronting the Volga Germans, Dietz began an intensive campaign calling for solidarity with the Russian peasants and cooperation with the Constitutional Democratic party within the framework of a reformed state. Traveling widely and writing prolifically, his message was always the same. The peasants and colonists suffered from the same problems: economic adversity (attributed primarily to inadequate landholdings) and bureaucratic oppression. While acknowledging that the Volga Germans had special problems, particularly the much-needed reform of their schools, he said that only through unity with other rural elements would the colonists have a realistic chance of accomplishing their political ends. Although he did not harshly criticize the colony township elders' March 1906 petition to Count Sergei Witte, requesting that the colonists be able to elect a deputy separately, Dietz warned that the rightist parties would excoriate and condemn the Volga Germans for separatism. He suggested that forming Germans into a separate electoral unit, of course, would be interpreted by the rightist parties as "autonomy" for the colonists, thereby endangering the fatherland and bringing about its ruin. He clearly distinguished the Volga Germans' political demands from those of the more belligerent and disaffected nationality groups: "We demand local self-government—not autonomy as in Poland."[30]

Accusing many of the Volga clergy of being in league with the Baltic Germans, the combative Dietz also called upon his constituents to repudiate the appeals for their political union with the German colonists in the southern

Ukraine and the Baltic Germans in support of the Union of October 17. The Octobrists, as they were commonly called, were monarchists who opposed the more extreme political demands of the Kadets, particularly the expropriation of land and ethnic equality. Small and not well organized, they waged a weak campaign for Volga German votes. Initially, the *Saratower deutsche Zeitung* had advocated such a political union of all Germans in Russia (Deutsch-Russen) and implied that there was already strong sentiment for such a union among the Volga Germans: "In the efforts of the Germans along the Volga as well as of those in the south of Russia there has emerged the consciousness of belonging together and of the necessity of a close union of all Germans once and for all."[31] The newspaper urged the Volga Germans to emulate pan-German political organizations that were forming in other parts of the empire, citing as an example the Muscovite Germans who had recently formed the *Moskauer Deutschen russischer Untertanenschaft*.

What disturbed Dietz more were the efforts of the southern Germans to sway his Volga compatriots. Hundreds of copies of an issue of *Odessauer Zeitung* (the southern colonist newspaper which Dietz sometimes referred to as "the Black Hundreds organ of the southern colonists") that contained the Octobrist program had been sent to the Volga colonies. Dietz heatedly argued that the Volga Germans had absolutely nothing in common with the prosperous southern and northern Germans, who were "richly endowed with land and perfectly satisfied with the status quo." Instead, Dietz invoked the memory of close if not cordial relations with the peasantry: "Russians and Germans are compatriots in misfortune, and between them in the course of 140 years there was neither hatred nor antagonism."[32] A colonist from Talovka echoed Dietz's views:

We German colonists have refrained up to now from taking part in any kinds of parties. And now our southern colonists advise us to affiliate with the Union of 17 October which stands for the preservation of the old ways, but these old ways drive us to madness.

We are dying from hunger because of a shortage of land, and they [southern colonists] advise us to join with the Baltic Germans—barons, who enserfed Letts and Estonians on their lands. We are waiting for more land to earn a living, for freedom from bureaucratic arbitrariness, while they, hiding behind the back of the monarchy, tell us: join and support a unified state and a strong monarchy! We supported the monarchy which sent our sons and brothers to Manchuria . . . . No, the old ways brought us no joy.[33]

With the revolutionary parties boycotting the Duma elections, the political program of the Kadets, representing the left-wing of public opinion, most closely mirrored the views of the Volga Germans. Even though it had only organized in October and held its inaugural congress in January, the Constitutional Democratic party waged an energetic Duma campaign to propagandize its program. Committed to the formation of a genuine parliamentary government, the Kadets advocated a comprehensive program of social and economic reforms, including equality for all nationalities and religions, and agrarian reform based on the expropriation of landed estates with compensation (both programs especially appealing to the Volga Germans), as well as equal, direct, and secret suffrage for both men and women. The popular slogan of the Kadets became "Political freedom and social justice." The Constitutional Democratic party was also the result of the joining of the zemstvo movement with the professional Union of Unions (teachers, lawyers, writers, doctors, and engineers). Thus the Volga German leadership, long active in zemstvo work, naturally gravitated to the Kadets.

The cooperation of the Kadets and the Volga Germans was also based on political reality: votes. The Kadets were weakest in the countryside and needed votes in the township electoral assemblies; the Volga Germans wanted a voting deputy in the Duma. The large representation of the districts in which the colonists resided also attracted the attention of the Kadets. Kamyshin and Novouzensk districts sent the largest contingent of delegates to their respective provincial assemblies, and in those districts the Kadets held several political rallies. The Kadets acted swiftly to convince the colonists of their commitment to a political pact. Thus Dietz announced on March 27: "From informed sources we have learned that the People's Freedom party [original name of the Constitutional Democratic party], which appears in all likelihood to do well in the [district] elections, already has allotted one deputy seat for our German colonists."[34] With this announcement, the alliance was cemented.

The Kadet endorsement of a Volga German deputy, combined with the strong showing of the Kadet candidates in the closely watched and hotly contested colony township assemblies (all but two or three of the Volga German township delegates to each of the three district assemblies favored the Kadets), convinced the last colonist holdouts that alliance with the Kadets was the best and only realistic political choice. Eliciting no response to its public appeal for political separatism, on March 29 the *Saratower deutsche Zeitung*, the largest circulating Volga German newspaper, abandoned its call for particularism and a German political union, and announced its support of the Kadets: "For us Germans there is no other way than under the banner of the People's Freedom party."[35] *Unsere Zeit* initially had advocated noncooperation with any Russian parties and formation of a unified colony group, believing that the Russian groups would splinter, thereby enabling the colonists to play the dominant role in the electoral assemblies. In early April Johannes Fritzler, the editor, announced that he now supported the Kadets and urged others to follow his example.[36]

The alignment of the Volga Germans with forces opposing the tsarist regime occurred despite widespread reports of attempted government coercion and intimidation. Police and land captains tried unsuccessfully to manipulate local elections by ordering election methods—anything but a secret written ballot—that would increase the chances that the favorites of the authorities would be elected. Intimidation most often took the form of portraying the Russian peasantry as volatile, vengeful reactionary nationalists who had no love for the Volga Germans and would wreck violent retribution on the colonists if they participated in the opposition movement. Thus, in the Nizhne-Karaman township assembly, the land captain warned the colonists to remain calm because after the first Duma there would be a second Duma, exclusively made up of Russian peasants: "Then the peasant Duma would force the Germans to emigrate back to Germany!"[37]

The greatest success of the Kadet-Volga German coalition occurred in the Kamyshin District rural electoral assembly, which was entitled to send fourteen delegates to the Saratov Province assembly and elected all fourteen with Kadet party affiliation. The fifty-delegate district assembly (thirty-four Russians and sixteen colonists) convened April 6 and unanimously elected Jacob Dietz as the chairman, a recognition of his widespread popularity and respect among both Russians and Volga Germans. In his opening remarks, chairman Dietz urged the delegates not to be intimidated by the attendance of the police and land captains; he also announced his allegiance to the Kadet platform. Dietz then brought to the attention of the assembly the unfair position of the Volga Germans, who constituted over half of the rural population but because of the electoral method were entitled to send only sixteen delegates to the district assembly. Although the details of the political deal that followed are not available, the assembly's near unanimous first action was to permit the Volga

German electors to elect five of their own to the provincial assembly. The strident debate that followed showed that the Russian peasants were almost evenly split between eighteen "conservatives," so called because they allegedly owed their election to the connivance of land captains, and sixteen "progressives," who generally subscribed to the Kadet program. Although all but three delegates officially affiliated with the Kadets, Dietz realized that colonist unanimity would be required to elect progressives to compensate for the less well-developed political maturity of the other peasant delegates. As a result, the progressive Volga German–peasant coalition quickly elected nine progressive delegates, and the time came for the colonists to vote separately on their five delegates. Four had been chosen when the conservative delegates, embittered by their inability to elect one of their own, objected to allowing the colonists to elect the fifth, demanding that the last delegate be chosen by and from the plenary assembly. Fearing a deadlock and hoping to defuse the bitterly contentious situation, Dietz, during a brief recess, persuaded the colonists to concede the fifth delegate. Reconvening the meeting, Dietz magnanimously announced the Volga German decision and then granted the conservatives the opportunity to nominate one of their own for election. After ten conservative nominees failed to win majority, Dietz accepted the nomination of a progressive, who was easily elected. The strategy had worked; the deadlock was broken and all elected delegates were in the Kadet progressive camp. Dietz and the colonists had shown their willingness to compromise and their shrewd political sense. The colonists' magnanimous gesture in the assembly did not pass unnoticed. The press reported that all progressives were pleased to see that the Volga Germans had broken completely with the conservative electors: "It is impossible not to say 'thank you' to the Germans, who deliberately and unselfishly sided with *general* peasant interests. They, satisfied with only four electors from their ranks (although they constitute half of the population of the district), courageously and in a friendly manner entrusted their interests to the best progressive Russian elements, assuming that the latter represented *all* peasant needs" (italics in the original).[38]

The mountain-side Volga German delegates to the Saratov provincial electoral assembly joined the Labor Group (*Trudovaia gruppa*), whose commitment to radical land reform attracted most peasants. The largest voting bloc in the assemblage was the left wing of the Kadet party, which quickly split from it and formed the Duma fraction known as the Labor Group; all of the Kamyshin

District delegates affiliated with it, and Dietz became one of its leaders. The Labor Group represented radical peasant sentiment by advocating expropriation without compensation to owners, and land reform based on established work norms, which favored the small farmer. Although never a strongly united party, it claimed to be the party of "all working people." Six colonists were represented in the Samara Province electoral assembly, but little is known of their political views except that they looked to the Duma for land reform and claimed adherence to the Kadet program.[39]

The two Volga Germans elected as deputies to the First Duma had few things in common, other than a common heritage and experience as newspaper publishers. The more radical Dietz, who enjoyed being called a leftist lawyer, had been absent from the colonies and never held a position in local government. While maintaining ties with his native colony, he became an astute politician who articulated the views of his constituents and quickly built his political base after October 1905. His election to the First Duma is primarily attributable to his steadfast affiliation with the Kadets, his masterful maneuvering at the Kamyshin District electoral assembly, and his skill as a writer and orator. Dietz's program had broad appeal. Not only did he have the support of the village leaders who elected him, but he had the backing of the sarpinka manufacturers, who praised him in the press.[40] The moderate businessman Heinrich Schellhorn, elected from Samara Province, earned his position in the Duma as a result of a long record of public service in village and township government, as well as in the district and provincial zemstvo; Schellhorn was one of the many local officials who had abandoned their posts with the introduction of the land captains and become active in the zemstvo.[41] His position as publisher of the Volga German newspaper with the largest circulation also probably figured in his selection.

The political credos of the two deputies offered some striking differences, because Dietz eventually linked up with the Labor Group, while Schellhorn remained with the more moderate Kadets. Schellhorn largely remained a local issues deputy, whereas Dietz stated that his first priority would be legislation guaranteeing political and civil liberties. Dietz also played an active leadership role in the Duma, through election to its executive committee, which planned the Duma's strategy and agenda. Dietz sought a radical land reform based on the expropriation of estates without compensation and the allocation of land to rural working folk based on established norms. He believed that the land should belong to those who worked it, and unequivocally stated that if that made him a revolutionary, so be it. He added that his views were well known and fully accepted by the 342 of 373 delegates who elected him in his landslide victory in the township election, and were also widely shared by the thousands of colonists with whom he had spoken.[42] Schellhorn, on the other hand, acknowledged that the colonists suffered form severe land shortages, but he did not believe that expropriation was the solution, arguing that primitive farming was the nemesis. Rather, prefiguring Stolypin's reform, he called for the abolition of communal landholding, with its strip farming and periodic redistribution, and the adoption of private individual land tenure, which would facilitate the implementation of improved farming techniques. While Dietz was reticent on taxation, Schellhorn proposed a progressive income tax to replace the numerous, unfair indirect taxes, but especially those on sugar, liquor, and petroleum.[43] On the issues of local self-government and ethnic autonomy, it was a matter of emphasis that separated them. Dietz railed against bureaucratic interference and the paralysis of local government, whereas Schellhorn, when he got before a Volga German audience, constantly denounced the sorry state of colony schools. In fact, he stated that no more pressing issue confronted the colonists than the creation of a German primary school system (*eine deutsche Volksschule*). While Schellhorn's position is unknown, the antifeminist Dietz rejected the Kadets' planned extension of the franchise to women, claiming that women clung more closely to religion and therefore were more conservative than men: "As is well known, women are always for religion and the clergy."[44]

The halcyon days of freedom were to be ephemeral and devoid of substantive political and social change. Although autocracy had foundered, the forces of reaction had regained the initiative by the autumn of 1906, dashing all hopes for reform. By the end of December 1905, the revolutionary forces had been crushed. Just as April election results showed the clear-cut victory of the opposition parties, the government promulgated the Fundamental Laws creating a weak legislative body. The short-lived First Duma, convened May 10 and dissolved July 22, clashed with the emperor and his ministers over a bill providing for radical agrarian reform. Although other Dumas would convene, none aroused the enthusiasm and admiration of the Volga Germans as much as the first.

After the dissolution of the Duma, the colonists, like most inhabitants of the empire became apathetic to new calls to action. The colonists' last significant political statement happened in August 1906, when the government attempted to suppress their popular hero, Jacob Dietz. On August 16, the police appeared at Dietz's Kamyshin apartment with a warrant for his arrest and search of his possessions. The warrant charged Dietz with distributing illegal, seditious literature from his residence in July "which incited people to overthrow the existing social order." The search, however, discovered no such publications. Rumors spread quickly around the town that the police were arresting the people's elected representative, and a crowd soon gathered at Dietz's residence; within a few minutes, it swelled to 2,000 to 3,000 people. The press later reported that the most agitated and rebellious element of the angry mob was "the German part of the population." The crowd began chanting that it would not "give up" Dietz to the police. When the police attempted to speak, the tumultuous mob silenced them with angry, crude epithets. Although reinforced by several Cossacks and at least ten other policemen, the shaken authorities assessed the situation as too volatile to risk Dietz's arrest, declared him to be under house arrest, and hastily fled the scene. Dietz then appeared on his porch and thanked the crowd for defending him, but reminded them: "You are not defending me, Dietz, but your idea-popular government, scorned by the government, the very one in which the people through their deputies expressed distrust and contempt." That evening, a loyal guard of his Volga German followers voluntarily took up positions around Dietz's residence. This would be the last small victory and popular display of the Volga Germans until 1917.[45]

The all too brief "days of freedom" lasted long enough for the outsider to see that the Volga German settlement was not a happy and harmonious *Gemeinschaft*. As in most peasant societies, life was a struggle, and jealousy, hatred, and conflicts of interest came to the surface when the traditional order showed signs of weakness. The revolution of 1905 revealed significant changes in the social dynamics of the Volga Germans, which had evidently emerged as a result of the weakening of government and traditional village authority. The political crisis opened the way for mass agitation and the expression of Volga German opinion, particularly in the village assemblies where agitators and even Duma delegates or their representatives harangued when festering issues flared, and frank and heated political debate followed. Heightened political consciousness developed as a free press presented a diversity of views, which, although not read by all, were orally transmitted and discussed widely. The youth and poor expressed their views for the first time in various forms ranging from tax protests, to lively disputations in the village assembly, to seizure of schools.

The revolutionary events of 1905 witnessed the beginning of the "politicization" and "radicalization" of the colony teachers. Leadership of the teachers generally came from the ranks of the colony zemstvo teachers. The best evidence of the surprising political role of teachers is in the electoral process, where two of the ten Volga German delegates elected to the provincial assemblies were teachers (both bona fide secular teachers and not "catechizers"), who had graduated from teacher seminaries with instruction conducted in Russian.[46] Although we have only incomplete information, it appears that teachers made up the next largest professional element in the composition of Volga German township and district electors, after local government functionaries (village and township elders and clerks). On the other hand, no evidence of clergy electors has been discovered among the Volga Germans, although nine Orthodox priests managed to win election to the First Duma, where they joined opposition parties.

Although outwardly the events of 1905 in the colonies do not appear momentous, the revolutionary experience tells a great deal about the Volga Germans. It is clear that they had rejected pan-German political particularism and remained constant in their attachment to the Russian liberation movement and even the Russian state, albeit in a reconstituted liberal form. While highly concerned with the preservation of ethnic identity, the pragmatic Volga Germans did not let that obstruct their political alliance with Russian liberal-radical opinion. Thus they were quite unlike the Baltic Germans, who, frightened by the large-scale peasant violence directed against them and feeling betrayed by the tsarist government, increasingly looked to imperial Germany as a possible protector of their privileged position.[47] Although the government had conceded reforms at the state level, such as elections to the Duma, religious toleration, and university autonomy, local institutions and conditions witnessed little change. In that respect 1905 was a great disappointment to them, because they chiefly desired to be left alone to administer their own institutions, but above all their schools. The government ignored the colonists' numerous but respectful petitions, thus perpetuating paternalistic administration over the colonists as well as the paralysis and powerlessness of colony government. The bureaucratization of local government remained a sensitive issue among the Volga Germans until

1917. The position of the clergy within the colonies altered dramatically in the aftermath of 1905, for the secular colony leaders, zemstvo officials, and the "third element" capably filled the political vacuum left by the clergy. The co-incidence of a severe natural calamity (consecutive bad harvests), an unpopular war, and revolution made the years 1904 and 1905 the most traumatic ones the colonists had experienced since their founding. Finally, as one prominent historian has noted, "Abortive though it was, the revolution of 1905 initiated the defiance and struggle that in 1917 developed rapidly into the most extreme forms of revolutionary violence."[48]

Chapter Nine

Reaction and Revolution, 1906–1917

Although oppression became palpable in the Volga colonies during the last decade under the Romanovs, the settlements appeared calm and tranquil even while masking deep bitterness and disappointments. The two most pressing Volga German problems were land shortages and political freedom. Frustrated by the unfulfilled and broken promises of the 1905 reforms, the Volga Germans responded to the call for a radical land solution and self-government in 1917. Like the rest of the peasantry, they became revolutionary for the moment. While the Russian peasants seized the opportunity to confiscate new lands, the Volga Germans rebelled against the old regime to avert the expropriation of their lands.

The turbulent years of revolution and unpopular war in the Far East brought much uneasiness to the Volga Germans and raised an obscure threat which weighed heavily upon the Lower Volga. The tension generated by these events subsided slowly, and rumors as well as reports of police harassment swept the settlements, disturbing their usual quietude. The sensational news printed in bold type on the front pages of the newspapers had displaced local news, questions of family, home, church, and village, as the topic of discussion in the streets, meetings, and homes of the Volga Germans. Strikes, party programs, the Duma, expropriation of land, Stolypin, and elections were more frequently brought into the conversation. The traditional and parochial nature of a way of life that had provided so much stability was being boldly challenged and reshaped. How could one be certain anymore that the lawlessness, political agitation, demonstrations, strikes, and mutinies which directly and indirectly touched the traditional peasant farmers would not happen again, particularly since the government refused to grant the reforms desired by most of society? No peaceable and acceptable solution of the crisis facing Russia had been found. It did not bode well for a future amicable solution.

Wars and international crises associated with virulent nationalism and imperialist expansion had seemed remote. Now they unsettled everyday life, troubling the entire family and community. The 1908 Bosnian annexation crisis and ensuing Balkan Wars stirred up alarm and deep depression in the minds of the Volga Germans. The flames of Balkan nationalism threatened to embroil the Russian Empire and disrupt colony life. The fear of another war, so soon after the Russo-Japanese War, haunted the colonies.

The last decade of tsarist rule for the Volga Germans witnessed economic recovery, but otherwise the status quo prevailed. Stevedore and sailor strikes in Baku had crippled Caspian shipping, seriously disrupting oil and kerosene supplies to the Lower Volga so that by the spring of 1907 a fuel famine had taken hold. The revolution physically changed little, yet left a legacy of social divisions. The pressing issues remained unresolved, and the "days of freedom" had opened social and religious fissures which threatened to disrupt the normally tranquil society. The turbulent events of 1905–6 badly ripped the social fabric of the Volga Germans. Only after the reaction had set in did the colonists begin not only to assess the actions of the government but, above all, to ponder the actions of all their compatriots. In particular, the 1905 revolution unmasked the reactionaries as well as the reformers.

For the Volga Germans, the "victory" of government reaction over public reform was visibly and shockingly manifested on August 27 and 28, 1906, in the bloody suppression of civil disturbances by government troops in the town of Kamyshin. Reports of the bloodbath quickly reached the colonies and gravely alarmed the colonists, many of whom had relatives working or residing in the busy port town. On the morning of August 27, a market day in Kamyshin, a government convoy escorting fifty nonlocal criminal and political prisoners to the local prison entered the market square. Hoots and jeers soon passed between the shoppers and convoy guards, and rumors began to circulate about "people's representative" Jacob Dietz, whom the police had unsuccessfully tried to imprison earlier in the month. Although the police kept onlookers at a distance, some people believed they had glimpsed Dietz among the shackled prisoners, while others asserted that the convoy was on the way to arrest Dietz.

Incited by these rumors, the agitated but unarmed crowd pressed in on the convoy, which, unnerved by the angry mob, suddenly fired two volleys, mortally wounding a priest and injuring several others. The shockingly brutal police reaction cleared the mob from the market square and the convoy safely reached the prison, but soon the clanging of the town alarms drew thousands to the streets.

By early afternoon, the now incensed mob had obtained arms and barricaded most of the main streets. Speeches and songs roused the spirits of those manning the barricades. The authorities mustered all available police and mounted troops—they had to do without the company of soldiers garrisoned in the town, which had been dispatched earlier in the day to quell disturbance in another district settlement—and confronted the seething crowds. Initial attempts to incite the armed detachment to join the rebels failed, and for over an hour nothing happened as both sides silently peered at each other. Suddenly, shots rang out—from which side is uncertain—and heavy firing continued for approximately two and one-half hours, when the mob exhausted its ammunition and abandoned the barricades. Intermittent, sporadic gunfire could be heard throughout the town until eleven o'clock that evening. Since many of the victims did not report their injuries, there is some uncertainty about the total number of casualties. The best estimates were seven dead and forty-two wounded; one of the tragic fatalities was a female teacher, in a nearby school, who was shot attempting to rescue two wounded children.[1] By the next morning, the provincial governor and troops from Saratov had arrived to disperse the last holdouts. The government's brutal pacification of the town lived long in the memories of the people of the Lower Volga.

Popular disillusionment, government intimidation, the partial failure of the 1906 grain crop, and preoccupation with Stolypin's land reform all contributed to the political malaise that prevailed in the colonies after the failure of the First Duma. Although the Volga Germans elected eight of their peers to the January 1907 provincial electoral assemblies for the Second Duma (all considered to have a progressive "opposition spirit" and to be dedicated to the promotion of the peasantry's interests and views), the election campaign itself stirred much less public interest and enthusiasm, perhaps in part because the government employed every method short of force and fraud to ensure the election of deputies acceptable to it.[2] The repression practiced during the elections—particularly the disqualification of electors and the bans on meetings and the circulation of political literature—was much more systematic than what was done during the elections to the First Duma. Harsher censorship and the closure of most of the Volga German press effectively stifled most public debate.

Nevertheless, the Volga German electors themselves appear not to have shared the public apathy, and even shifted more to the left, along with the rest of the Russian electorate. The township electors to the Kamyshin District rural assembly were more radical than those of the First Duma, yet were not so well organized. Perhaps they missed the able leadership of Jacob Dietz, who was disenfranchised because he signed the Vyborg Appeal to the people of Russia following the dissolution of the First Duma, calling for them to refuse to pay taxes or serve in the army until the government had announced the date for the election of another Duma. The more leftist Rovnoe township assembly resoundingly rejected moderate incumbent Heinrich Schellhorn, who sought reelection: "The Germans don't like him because he was silent in the Duma."[3] Instead, they chose two electors who were considered more progressive than the reticent and timid Schellhorn, who had not signed the Vyborg protest. At the Samara provincial assembly, Alexander P. Kling, owner of a Singer sewing machine store in the Russian settlement of Pokrovsk and member of the left wing of the Kadet party, was the only Volga German to win election to the short-lived Second Duma, which met from February 20 to June 3, 1907.[4] It is quite likely that, had Dietz not been deprived of his electoral rights, he would have been reelected to the Second Duma, not only because of his great popularity but because the Saratov provincial assembly was dominated again by the Labor Group and other leftist parties.

The unconstitutional promulgation of the complicated electoral law of June 3, 1907, simultaneous with the dissolution of the Second Duma, in effect eliminated the political influence of the Volga Germans by reducing the number of deputies and the representation of the peasantry, as well as of non-Russian peoples, and increasing the representation of large property owners. The electorate was now divided into four groups: landowners (other than peasants and colonists), urban residents, peasants, and industrial workers; representation was heavily in favor of the upper, propertied classes. The indirect elections to electoral assemblies continued, but the assemblies of the landowners sent much larger delegations to the provincial assemblies that elected the Duma deputies, whereas the number of peasant electors was cut drastically—often in half. As a result of these modifications, the landowners' electors, combined with the large property-owning urban electors, constituted an absolute majority in all the provincial assemblies of European Russia. A landowner's vote was estimated to be equal to that of about 260 peasants or 540 workers. Thus, while the ordinary Volga German saw his voting strength diluted, that of propertied colonists increased.

As a result of the government's electoral tampering, the political orientation of the Russian Empire changed dramatically and quickly, as is evidenced in the Saratov and Samara provincial assemblies, which elected only landowning conservative deputies, chiefly Octobrists, to the Third and Fourth Dumas. The two Volga German deputies elected to serve in the "landlord" Third Duma were indicative of the momentous political shift to the right: Nicholas Ivanovich Rothermel and Konstantin Nikolaevich Grimm were both members of the conservative Octobrist party.[5] The wealthy Rothermel, who lived in Orlovskaia and whose family earned a fortune from the tobacco and flour trade, was one of the largest landowners in Novouzensk District. He had completed his education at a private boarding school and was regarded as a shrewd businessman and sound agriculturalist. Konstantin Grimm, whose family gave its name to the mountain-side colony, graduated from military school, served in the military for several years, and returned to Saratov Province, where he inherited a large estate and joined the ranks of the gentry. He had a long and distinguished public career, serving for many years as a deputy in the Saratov provincial zemstvo, as head of a famine relief commission, and even for a time as a land captain.

The political affiliation of the tiny Volga German landowning class with the gentry-dominated Octobrists reinforces the often overlooked point that socioeconomic affinities proved stronger than ethnic ties among the former colonists. It reveals as well that a very small wealthy elite existed within the Lower Volga colonies whose class interests more closely reflected those of the upper levels of Russian society than of their compatriots, whose antigovernment opposition views were too radical and repugnant. The various policies of land expropriation proposed by the Kadets and the other leftist parties threatened their economic survival; as Octobrists, they cooperated with Stolypin in his land program, which excluded expropriation of private estates.

One of the clearest victims of the government repression that began in 1906 was the colony zemstvo teacher, and therefore the Volga German schools. Although not sharing uniform beliefs, most teachers initially called for the right to organize a teachers' association at the district level and to reform the antiquated and overcrowded colony church schools. Following the autumn 1905 "teacher expulsion campaign" that many experienced firsthand and believed to have been tacitly encouraged by the clergy and provincial authorities, many teachers advocated political activism, arguing that political reform was a precondition of educational reform; a very few espoused revolutionary changes. Although there is no evidence that the district zemstvos promoted and supported a political education role for teachers, as was done by some zemstvos in Saratov Province, there is also no evidence that the zemstvos dissuaded the teachers.[6] While the teachers collectively mounted no organized efforts, individual teachers subscribed to periodical literature (which they shared with others), wrote letters to newspapers, translated and interpreted articles, read newspapers to groups, and distributed political pamphlets. That teachers had become a political force is indicated by the colonists' selection of teachers as township and district delegates in the peasant curia to Duma electoral assemblies in the spring of 1906, revealing that political education was effective in combatting the anti-intellectual feeling so common in the fall.

During the fall and winter of 1906, the government launched its attack against now defenseless teachers throughout the empire. Teacher unions were abolished and teachers summarily dismissed from their posts. Following the examples of zemstvo teachers in other provinces, on September 26, 1906, the teachers of the Volga colonies convened their first abortive meeting in Saratov to form a teachers' union, which immediately succumbed to police actions. As the teachers departed, they were rudely warned that such unions and even teachers' mutual-aid societies were illegal and that transgressors would be severely punished; taking the warning to heart, the teachers would not reconvene until April 1917. That the Volga German school cadres had become politically suspect is apparent from the numerous police arrests and interrogations of "third element" zemstvo teachers which began in the fall of 1906. Although statistics are lacking, in terms of dismissals Saratov Province officials waged one of the most vigorous campaigns against teachers.[7] For example, based on the rumor that he had revolutionary literature in his possession, a zemstvo teacher by the name of Schultz, who had taught several years in a Volga German school in Samara Province, was arrested and taken to Saratov for questioning. Although no seditious material was found, Schultz was summarily dismissed.[8] Those not arrested or forewarned became intimidated and demoralized. Teacher activism was completely stifled, and countless successful teaching careers were destroyed. The massive purge victimized the Volga Germans, who lacked any community control over their schools, and already suffered a notorious short supply of teachers.

The glaring deficiencies of Volga German schools came into full view with the government's introduction of compulsory primary education in 1908, which mandated four years of free education for all children eight to eleven years old. District zemstvo surveys revealed the sorry state of colony schools, whose conditions had deteriorated rapidly because of the purge of teachers and inadequate funding.[9] The survey of primary schools by an eight-member Kamyshin District zemstvo commission painted a very bleak picture of the colony schools:

> The conditions of the former German church-parish schools are in all respects worse than the Russian schools. Suffice it to say that 16,625 children attend the German schools which have 113 teachers; that is an average of 147 pupils per teacher, and in some schools there are 300 to 350 pupils per teacher. Instruction is usually conducted in the prayer houses, which have one enormous room, and where there are several teachers the room is divided by simple curtains into several classes; instruction is done simultaneously in all the classes; one class disturbs the other and, of course, it is useless to talk about the productiveness of learning under such conditions.[10]

The zemstvo education commission placed blame squarely on the central government, not on the Russian language teachers or the colonists as the government public school inspector had insisted. The Ministry of Education school inspector unfavorably compared the Volga Germans with the foreign settlers in southern Russia, publicly charging that the underdeveloped and backward Lower Volga colonists placed no value on education and willfully allowed their schools to decline. The eight-member commission accused the inspector of calumny, asserting that the colonists were not antieducation but opposed to the present system of administration which stripped them of control of their schools. The commissioners rebuked the Ministry of Education and its inspectors for demanding reform yet never providing the personnel or financial means to implement it.

The zemstvo commissioners ridiculed government educational policies. They were particularly critical of the assumption that a teacher, without the benefit of sound pedagogical training, suitable classrooms, textbooks, and instructional materials, could be expected to teach Russian to hundreds of pupils who had little formal knowledge of their own native dialect. The zemstvo report concluded that Ministry of Education policies had been the bane of colony education, which had done nothing but deteriorate ever since colony schools had been placed under the control of the central government. They skeptically pronounced that the government would have to appropriate about one million rubles to implement compulsory education in Kamyshin District, if it was to achieve its goal of free primary education with an average school radius of two miles, a fifty-to-one pupil-teacher ratio, clean classrooms, and textbooks and equipment.[11] Inasmuch as the entire zemstvo budget was only 400,000 rubles and almost one-third of it supported education, the central government would have to assume the financing of public education, for it was beyond the means of local government. The commissioners' skepticism was well founded, because the Ministry of Education did not assume chief responsibility for compulsory education until 1911, left maintenance to the local government, and then funded it well below the levels estimated by local officials.

The Volga German public mood of inquietude, resentment, and even alienation resulting from repressive government measures temporarily abated or was forgotten in the wake of the shattering news of August 1914. Few in Europe could foresee the nature or consequences of the "great war," particularly how quickly the pre-1914 illusions and enthusiasms would turn to disillusionment and despair, in turn threatening the foundations of European civilization. The greatest threat to the Volga Germans' survival and way of life during World War I, however, would not be the advancing foreign armies of the Triple Alliance, but the hostile policies and actions of Russian civil authorities. The outbreak of World War I opened the last and worst stage of Volga German history under the Romanov administration, which pursued a policy of rabid chauvinism that gave free rein to intolerance, narrow-mindedness, and repression. Non-Russian groups, particularly any having an affiliation with Germany, became scapegoats for military blunders, economic shortfalls, and general government ineptitude, and targets of public criticism. For the Volga Germans, this was virtually an assault on their economic and ethnic survival.

Although it is difficult to discern the attitudes and feelings of the ordinary Volga Germans concerning the outbreak of World War I, no doubt the chauvinistic mood and patriotic slogan "Faith, Tsar, and Country" which swept the empire stirred many of them too, particularly since popular opinion held that

Germany was the aggressor. The Volga Germans were not torn, as many Russian intellectuals were, between nationalism and internationalism. nor is there any evidence that they succumbed to an antiwar position, which eventually developed among many of the urban working class. The strong tradition of being loyal, law-abiding citizens of the empire probably prompted most Volga Germans to decide that defense of the fatherland was a responsibility from which they could not stand apart. In addition to "significant financial contributions," the Volga Germans were publicly cited for opening hospitals, making bandages, and giving clothing. Wealthy and conservative Volga Germans, such as Konstantin N. Grimm and Friederich Schmidt, served with distinction on provincial provisioning boards.

National unity and support of the fatherland became common themes of the *Volkszeitung*, the only German-language but politically conservative newspaper still published in the Lower Volga. Editorials pledged fraternal cooperation between the Volga Germans and Russians, and predicted valorous conduct on behalf of the 50,000 former colonists on active duty or in the reserves. A much more suspect source, a Lutheran minister, perhaps exaggerated the enthusiasm of the Volga Germans when he wrote the Saratov provincial governor, "Our sons and brothers will now have an opportunity, as never before in their history, to demonstrate gratitude to the Emperor and glorious Fatherland."[12] Although unfounded suspicion later befell the Volga Germans, objectively their loyalty was never in question.

Considerable disagreement still exists regarding the impact of World War I on the Russian countryside. The economic situation has resulted in conflicting interpretations. The Soviet historian A. M. Anfimov asserted that wartime conditions exacerbated the depressed rural economy and contributed to popular discontent, which ultimately led to the revolutionary events of 1917. The émigré historian A. N. Antsiferov, on the other hand, wrote that the peasantry benefited from higher grain prices, government allotments, and military acquisitions.[13] Evidence can be found to support both viewpoints: mobilization negatively affected the peasantry, whereas lower lease rents and higher grain prices served those with the available labor power. In fact, the war touched each region, province, village, and family differently, so that only the outline can be drawn here of the major changes involved.

The mobilization of approximately 15.5 million men, practically every male between the ages of twenty-one and forty-three who had previous military service, had a tremendous impact on the colonists.[14] Families and colonies adversely affected by the mobilization of 1904–6 again suffered. Mobilization of both classes of reservists (representing the ex-servicemen who had become reservists between 1896 and 1910) provoked alarm, but the alternative of emigrating to the West was no longer viable, with the frontiers now battlefields. However, as was not true of the Russo-Japanese War, the demands for troops at the front became so great that most of the first class of the militia, ex-veterans between the ages of forty and forty-three, as well as untrained and poorly armed twenty-one to forty-three year olds whose lottery numbers had never been called, were also activated, affecting even more families. The unexpectedly prolonged war and rapidly mounting casualties finally forced the government to reduce the draft age to seventeen and to extend the military obligation to age fifty, yet the government never fully mobilized the second class of the militia—those males unconditionally exempted from military service. Consequently, inexperienced adolescent grandsons and their elderly grandfathers trooped off to the war while their exempted-generation relatives remained out of uniform.[15] Although precise figures for Volga German soldiers in World War I are lacking, one ex-soldier estimated that 40,000 Volga colonists were activated.[16] Bearing in mind that about half of able-bodied males from the rural peasant class were withdrawn from productive labor and enlisted in the war effort, then the consequences on the Volga Germans were great indeed, although not as devastating as for private landowners dependent on wage laborers. Near the end of the war, 30 percent of peasant households in Saratov Province and 32 percent of those in Samara Province were without male workers.[17]

The massive mobilization of men and livestock resulted in portentous social and economic changes for the rural settlements of the empire. By 1917, women comprised almost three-quarters of the total rural labor force.[18] Although women had always participated in farm work, they now were forced to perform most of the backbreaking field work which had been primarily the domain of their husbands, sons, and fathers. In the textile-producing colonies of Saratov Province, women took over the weaving duties of absent husbands. The inane, nondiscriminatory mobilization policies of the government depleted the ranks of village skilled laborers, as blacksmiths and other craftsmen were sent off to war; thus those colonies that had complained during the Russo-Japanese War of the loss of such vital craftsmen found themselves in the identical situation. Although the Volga Germans lived far from the front and were not involuntarily pressed into labor services by military authorities, they were expected, like all other subjects of the empire, to supply matériel for the war effort. The requisitioning of horses for the army compounded the labor problems of the peasantry, for although they were reimbursed by the government, the payment was below the market price. Livestock requisitioning fell hardest upon the households of the poorer colonists, who might lose their only horse; the more affluent, even with the requisitioning of half their horses, would have three to five left to do their field work, even though the military laid claim to the best horses. By the spring of 1916, two out of every seven horses classified as fit for wartime service had been mobilized in the war effort. Although livestock requisitioning varied from province to province, statistics for the six Volga provinces indicate that 26 percent of households were without draft animals in 1917, less than the national average of 31 percent.[19] Qualitatively, the livestock herds suffered as the military tapped the best of the peasantry's stock.

Those households with the necessary man and animal power found that the war had unexpectedly produced some favorable if ephemeral economic conditions, although generally the total amount of land cultivated constricted by about 12 percent in the empire during the war. The siphoning off of peasant labor reduced the demand for land and caused lease rents to fall; in some regions, sowing of leased lands had decreased by one-half.[20] In 1916–17, grain prices rose as the gross yield of grain amounted to only 73 percent of prewar harvests, while army consumption increased almost sevenfold, for bread was the essential food item of both civilian and military diets. Hence, although peasant sowings contracted, their income might not, because of the higher market price of grain. But the greater inflation in the price of the most essential manufactured goods easily consumed any increase in peasant income. By 1917, however, the Volga grain market became saturated, and prices declined as the railroads became overtaxed and river shipping could not transport the grain to the hungering urban centers of the north. Likewise, fewer manufactured goods became available for purchase, and those one could find commanded a dear price. While this author would not go so far as to accept Anfimov's generalization that "the rich peasants got richer and the poor got poorer," undoubtedly the more prosperous households were better able to weather the strains of a prolonged war than their poorer brethren.[21]

For the Volga Germans' faithful service, pledges of loyalty, and valiant deeds displayed in February 1916 in the bloody and fierce conquest of the Turkish fortress at Erzerum, the government reciprocated with discrimination, repression, and an anti-German witch hunt. Volga German recruits were generally not sent to the Western front to fight against Germans, but shipped via the Caspian Sea to Baku to battle the Turks on the Caucasus front.[22] Shocked by the catastrophic defeats at the hand of the Germans (the Russian army had been routed at the battles of Tannenberg and Masurian Lakes), by early 1915 the government had begun striking blindly at anything German. Most vexing for the settlers was the prohibition of the Volga German dialect in all correspondence with military personnel, which meant for many families and soldiers a complete break in communication for the duration of the war unless they found someone to write and read Russian for them. Colonists traveling outside their settlements carefully avoided speaking the dialect for fear of arousing suspicion and detention by overzealous authorities, and Volga Germans residing in Russian towns and settlements experienced anti-German baiting. The sizable number of Volga Germans residing in mixed settlements of the Don Forces Oblast experienced the brunt of Russian chauvinism. On February 2, 1915, a Volga German described the hostile mood to a relative: "Today at the meeting in Mikhaylovka [a Don Forces mixed settlement], speeches were made against citizens of German origins. They want to exile us. And it has become so strict. They are making a count of Germans in all the region and in the villages."[23] The writer also stated that violence had been committed against former colonists.

The government also banned the publication of all German newspapers and other reading material, requiring the Volga Germans to glean what censored information they could from Russian publications. Not only was the *Volkszeitung* suspended, but also the publication of a sympathetic history written to commemorate the 150th anniversary of the founding of the colonies.[24] Early in 1915, the Ministry of the Interior discussed administrative proposals to lessen the foreign colonists' social isolation, the intent being to hasten their assimilation. That same year, a government rescript ordered the closing of all German organizations. Interpreting this decree as broadly as possible, zealous Samara provincial authorities even forbade the colonists to conduct their communal assemblies in the dialect and to use the German names of the colonies. In some cases, wiser and cooler heads prevailed, as when the Saratov City Duma refused to approve the governor's request that German Street be renamed.[25]

The effects of World War I, particularly the rise of Russian chauvinism and military call-up, hit Volga German schools quite hard. The military law of 1912 abolishing the total exemption of teachers from conscription worsened the already deplorable pupil-teacher ratio. The Council of Ministers' December 24, 1914, decision to vigorously enforce the use of Russian as the language of instruction in all schools using German may not have had a significant impact on the actual Volga German classroom, but it clearly showed the government's anticolonist bent. In 1915, the Ministry of Education ordered the closure of the few remaining church schools, alleging that they had inadequately and poorly trained teachers, and caused them to be converted into public schools. Public school inspectors threatened teachers, whom they felt were not rigorously instructing in the Russian language.

The dormant but prevalent Germanophobia of the 1890s, tempered by the revolutionary event of 1905, erupted malevolently soon after the first shots rang out in August 1914.[26] Once the 1905 revolutionary tide had ebbed and an assessment of recent events had been made, many elements in Russian society could see that the revolutionary forces had not only attempted to reorganize the state administration but had given impetus to a disintegration of the Russian state by stimulating and releasing the aspirations of nationalities whose aim was autonomy or at least self-government. While many Russians desired to create a liberal and constitutional government, even according equal rights to all ethnic groups, few were prepared to accord any measure of autonomy to the non-Russian elements of the empire, such as Poland, the Baltic Provinces, and the Caucasus. An example of this Russian patriotic sentiment could be seen in the strong condemnation by the liberal-minded Second Duma of a project to grant home rule to Poland. Similarly, this was a time of active hostility against the Jews. Any action taken by an ethnic group that could be seen as a weakening of the empire aroused resistance among Russian patriots.

The expropriation of the Germans within the empire is the worst example of the bankrupt nature of tsarism, which seized upon rabid Russian nationalism and anti-German feeling to divert criticism from its own inept conduct of the war. The approximately two million German inhabitants of the Russian Empire became convenient scapegoats for the failures of autocratic rule, and suffered the ignominy of being cast as traitors and sentries of the perennial German *Drang nach Osten*. As one contemporary author stated, "World war broke out with Germany and the Volga Germans had to pay for the failure of the tsarist generals."[27] The measures of economic war initiated by the Russian government to rid the country of the "German yoke," the term frequently used to describe the economic power of enemy nationals within the empire, eventually were broadened to include all Russian subjects of foreign extraction. War was to be waged not only on the battlefield but in the economic sphere, as was indicated at the October 7, 1914, meeting of the Council of Ministers, which raised the issue of foreign property and endorsed the opinion of the minister of foreign affairs that the state should liquidate German landholdings along the western frontier, which had witnessed a large migration of German settlers from Russia's Polish provinces in the 1880s. Very quickly, distinctions blurred as Duma deputies declared that even German colonies should be wiped out for reasons of national security and the rewarding of peasant soldiers, the latter idea enthusiastically promoted by Minister of Agriculture Alexander V. Krivoshein. Consequently, any person or group that had any association with Germany eventually became linked with the "German yoke."[28]

The conservative press and public opinion applauded and supported the Council of Ministers' declarations about enemy nationals, but also urged that they be broadened to include all settlers of German extraction. Initially, the German colonists of southern Russia were singled out by the vocal estate owners of that region, who claimed that the Germans had bought all the best lands of the region, forcing peasants to emigrate to Siberia. In November 1914, Sergei Shelukhin, a Ukrainian landowner, was the first one to propose that the lands of German colonists be expropriated and redistributed to Russian peasants. Although Shelukhin directed his arguments chiefly at the extensive landholdings of the foreign settlers of southern Russia, particularly Kherson Province, where he stated they owned two-thirds of the cultivated area, in fact he did not differentiate landholding patterns of the various German colonist groups within the empire.[29] Shelukhin argued that liquidation of German landholding would not only kindle chauvinism but also create a small land reserve that could serve to divert peasant ill will on to the "German" landholders and away from the natural enemy, the large gentry landowners.

Angered and humiliated by the Russian debacle on its western front, the chauvinistic press attacked the nefarious and omnipresent German "influence" within the empire for causing the collapse of the Russian military machine and for miserable conduct of the war effort. The reactionary but widely circulated *Novoe vremia* again led the anti-German campaign to liberate Russia from the "German yoke." The newspaper made no distinctions between the ethnically and economically diverse Germans living within the empire, but attacked them

all for being disloyal and actively in league with the German war effort, even accusing Volga German grain dealers of planning to supply grain to the German
army through the port of Libau (even though Libau was not then in German
hands). The newspaper published a series of articles accusing the Russian Germans of collusion with Kaiser Wilhelm to transform Russia into a colony of
German, which stretched the limits of credulity.[30] *Vechernee vremia* inveighed
against the ubiquity of the German influence. In one article, an alleged father-
son conversation conveys Russia's dilemma when the father says, "I, your
Papa, will give you two oranges if you can tell me where in our Holy Russia you
cannot find Germans!" When the perplexed son cannot respond, the father re-
plies, "Where, indeed [can you not find Germans]?"[31] The effectiveness of the
anti-German scapegoat campaign in turning the population against the Volga
Germans is attested to in a 1918 Bolshevik report, which stated that one of the
chief tasks of the Soviet government vis-à-vis the Volga Germans would be to
overcome Russian prejudices toward them.[32] One can only wonder what effects the anti-German campaign had on Stalin's suspicious nature and his later
distrust of the Volga Germans.

The pervasiveness and venomousness of anti-German attacks in the periodical press were in striking contrast to the late nineteenth-century anticolonist
campaigns in the press. Everything "Germanic" the press denounced. Newspapers depicted settlers of German origin as "strangling" the peasantry, "seiz-
ing" Russian lands, and "plundering" the natural wealth of Mother Russia. A
scurrilous article on the so-called history of the Volga Germans reached the
lowest levels of fabrication and yellow journalism, the author unabashedly
avowing that the unscrupulous foreign settlers brutally harnessed Russian men
and women to their plows![33] The Volga Germans were invariably described as
the lowest form of humanity, debauched, devious, dishonest, and deceitful,
whose only purpose in coming to Russia had been to exploit the Russian land
and people. Duma representatives repeatedly castigated the internal German
nemesis for destroying the social and economic fabric of Russia, and those remarks even made it into the provincial press. Thus the Volga Germans must
have been uneasy and upset when they read that a Duma deputy had labeled
them the basic evil of Russian life that had to be eradicated. Even the official
press of the Orthodox Church joined the chorus crucifying the Germans of the
empire, who "on every occasion mocked and criticized the Orthodox Church."
The church attributed to the colonists the strong development of the

nineteenth-century sect movement, allegedly liberally bankrolled by Bismarck, which "already has seized many children of the Orthodox Church." According to an Orthodox priest and Duma deputy, Father Stanislavskii, the German government paid colonists 200 to 300 rubles for every Slavic peasant convert.[34] Not all the Russian press condemned the colonists, however. In particular, *Rech* and *Russkiia vedomosti* were concerned about the possible consequences of liquidation on agriculture and about the social injustice to the colonists whose loyalty was beyond doubt. Alexander Kerensky defended the loyalty and devotion of the colonists on the floor of the Duma and rebuked the government for finding it expedient to divert the masses' disgust and disdain of the government's handling of the war by throwing the colonists "to the wrath of the mob."[35]

Organized opposition to the foreign settlers was also new. In 1915 the Society of 1914, whose ultimate goal was the destruction of German economic power, held numerous meeting in the capital cities, warning people of the threat of German influence which would achieve what the Kaiser's armies could not. Convinced that the Russian armies would ultimately triumph on the battlefields, members of the society feared that, although Russia would win the war, it would lose the peace to German economic infiltration. Portraying the two million Germans in the empire as greedy but crafty capitalists, the Society of 1914 warned of the Germans' possible postwar economic takeover of the Russian economy. Ironically, the society's grossly exaggerated claims of German landholding would damage most the least threatening element of the enemy within, the smallholders of the Lower Volga.[36]

The last tortuous chapter in the history of the Volga German land question began with the enactment of the law of February 2, 1915, which would be repeatedly broadened and amended to encompass the dispossession and deportation of the Volga colonists in favor of the Russian peasants.[37] Using its emergency power as contained in article 87 of the Fundamental Laws, the Russian government on February 2 announced its intention to expropriate all German nationals' landholdings including the liquidation of colonist holdings all along Russia's western borders. The momentous transfer of foreign settlers' property was originally limited to the western frontier, and was intended to placate peasant land hunger, inasmuch as the government designated the Peasant Land Bank as the purchaser of the alienated lands. However, subsequent supplemental legislation, alterations, and interpretations of the original legislation resulted in its being broadened to include most of Russia and all Russian residents with German antecedents. Although much of the western frontier fell quickly into the hands of the advancing German armies, and provincial officials were too busy with other matters to implement such a law, unforeseen reactions caused the government not to carry out its land revolution.

The land program was intended to conciliate the irascible Russian peasantry, but the actual effect was that it agitated them. The warning of Kadet Leader Paul Miliukov in the Duma was prophetic: "But gentlemen, you delude yourselves; the land of the colonists is insufficient, and whoever begins with their land will surely have to finish with yours."[38] The police informed the Ministry of the Interior that reports of alienation of colonist lands had alarmingly aroused peasant expectations of a general alienation of all large estates; therefore, execution of the liquidation of the colonies threatened to snowball into a peasant land revolution that would destroy the social and economic foundations of the regime. As one Soviet historian has noted, "The liquidation policy not only lost its significance for tsarism, but even became dangerous."[39] Finally, the colonists, stunned by the news that they were about to be deprived of their livelihood, refused to sow crops and sold off their movable property (even dairy cattle were sold for slaughter), exacerbating the country's already precarious food situation. These events, as well as reports of reduced tax collections and declining land prices, forced the Council of Ministers in the spring of 1916 to review, and therefore delay, the implementation of the land expropriation. In the fall of 1916, reports of peasant agitation for general alienation of landed property increased so dramatically that in January 1917, Minister of Justice N. A. Dobrovolskii received Nicholas II's permission to reconsider the entire question of liquidation of colonist property.[40]

Perhaps the peasantry was not deceived about the true purpose of the land expropriation, which was to avoid expropriation of large landowners and thereby preserve the socioeconomic power of the gentry class, considered to be the political bedrock of the Russian political system. The government also wished to expropriate the foreign settlers to save gentry lands from becoming targets of peasant unrest by offering peasants instead the confiscated holdings of the small German peasant landholders.[41] The class nature of the 1915 legislation and amendments also becomes readily apparent, inasmuch as it applied only to settlers of German descent who were members of rural townships and villages, thereby preserving the rural lands of "German" landlords, merchants, and industrialists. Only the lands of the poorer colonists would be liquidated.

Whereas lands of the colonists would be liquidated regardless of when they became Russian subjects, German estate lands would be expropriated only if the owner had become a Russian subject after 1880, although not even then if an ancestor had served as an officer in the Russian army. Thus the legislation exempted lands of noncolonist Germans and wealthy landowners of colonist origin, such as Konstantin Grimm and others who had left their communes and lived on their own estates.

On February 6, 1917, less than three weeks before the collapse of the tsarist government, Nicholas II decreed a much more drastic policy, which completely altered the original stated purpose of the land liquidation policy, which was to protect national security by expropriating the extensive German landholdings along Russia's western border. Besides ordering officials to proceed with land alienation, Nicholas sanctioned the extension of the expropriation of German-Russian lands to the twenty-eight interior provinces of Russia, which included Saratov and Samara.[42] The vindictive new policy proposed to injure innocent Russian subjects of German ancestry by compelling them to sell their lands. The Volga Germans were given one year to negotiate the sale of their lands to the Peasant Land Bank, which would then use the lands for Russian resettlement. Fortunately for the colonists, revolution erupted in Petrograd in late February, giving them another quarter century to cultivate their lands before Stalin completed the chapter and ruthlessly expelled them from the entire region in 1941. The collapse of the old regime removed at least momentarily the threat of expropriation. However, the objective of the anti-German forces, the eradication from Russia of all traces of German influence in the countryside, almost became a reality.

The Volga Germans greeted the fall of the old order in March 1917 with jubilation. Like most inhabitants of the empire, they were surprised by the suddenness of the event, for the tight censorship meant that nothing could be learned from the newspapers. They could not but cheer the demise of a regime that attempted to dispossess them economically and culturally by stripping them of their lands and ruthlessly enforcing Russification. Others felt bitterly about the conduct of the war and complained of the utter indifference of the old regime toward the deplorable conditions suffered by the civilian sector, especially the widespread food shortages. Newspapers reported that in the German settlements the overthrow of the government evoked "joyous demonstrations and efforts to offer assistance to the new government."[43] Many Volga German communes had voluntarily offered monetary gifts and gifts in kind amounting to 12,000 rubles and 250 tons of grain. Two settlements took up collections to aid the families of workers and soldiers who died in the revolution.

The intoxication of the February Revolution quickly wore off with the formation of a new government. Other than vague aspirations, the Provisional Government had no clear plan of action to resolve the popular cry for "Peace, Bread, and Land." Its indecisiveness eventually cost the support of the ethnic minorities, whose patience was exhausted waiting for the chimerical Constituent Assembly. But above all, failure to address the persistent land problem most aggrieved the Volga Germans as well as the Russian peasantry. In the eyes of the Volga Germans, the Provisional Government began inauspiciously by lamely declaring on March 11 that the February 6 decree, extending the laws that restricted foreign settlers' landholding to the whole territory of Russia, would be suspended, not revoked as the colonists hoped, until their revision or abolition by a democratically elected Constituent Assembly. The Volga Germans were not impressed with these legal niceties, because it meant that their deportation from the Volga Valley was only postponed, not abrogated. Thus, even though the imperial government's land transfer operation had barely begun and the Provisional Government quickly ordered a halt to all liquidation proceedings of foreign settlers' property, the Volga Germans remained in a precarious and tenuous situation. As the summer passed and the Provisional Government implemented no land reform, the exasperation of the colonists increased; several settlements that had converted to individual tenure reverted to communal landholding and executed a land redistribution.[44] For this reason, Volga Germans never enthusiastically embraced the pusillanimous Provisional Government, and even the most apathetic colonists recognized the urgency of political action, realizing that the critical issues of 1917 were not the same as those of 1905, when the colonists became embattled to retain control of their schools and local government. In 1917, they would have to struggle with all the resources at their disposal to retain possession of their homes.

Once the cheering had stopped, the Volga Germans found that their political hopes and visions, although more radical and pressing than those held in 1905, were as diverse as those of the other peoples in the empire. The political naïveté of the Volga Germans corresponded to that of most residents of Russia, who learned little after 1905 in the arts of political organization and methods, because the reactionary nature of the period prevented all except the most conservative organizations from gaining any type of practical political experi- ence. Censorship had stemmed the flow of political information. Radical groups had been forced to operate as secret societies rather than as political parties in the real sense. Thus, until the summer of 1917, no clear political lines had been formed in the colonies as the Volga Germans awaited news of events, but par- ticularly the programs and policies of the Provisional Government and the pre- viously inert political groups. The common feeling among the Volga Germans was that there was to be no turning back, that they must vigorously and vig- ilantly work for the establishment of a new order.

The collapse of government authority resulted in unprecedented freedom and the appearance of new bodies with no clear basis or lines of authority, but which by the summer of 1917 were broadly socialist in their composition. At the lowest level, the rural population elected township executive committees to assume direction of local government, whose primary interest became the res- olution of the land question. Executive committees sprouted up at all levels of government, but the return of demoralized soldiers, and election of military committees in garrison towns and soviets in urban areas, incredibly confused the political picture. By the summer, most district towns were controlled by soviets.

The mountain-side colonists in Kamyshin District exhibited the first political activity, committing all their efforts and hopes to the promised Constituent As- sembly and the land program of the Socialist Revolutionaries. On March 25, all settlements in Kamyshin District sent delegates to a congress in Golyi Karamysh for the purpose of uniting the population and preparing for elections to the Constituent Assembly.[45] The first piece of business was to send congratulatory greetings to the Provisional Government *and* the Petrograd Soviet of Workers' and Soldiers' Deputies, indicating the radical mood of the delegates. Out of this meeting emerged a temporary protogovernment, an executive committee in Golyi Karamysh, whose purpose was to maintain order and calm in the set- tlements working through village and township level executive committees until a districtwide assembly of all residents could convene in Kamyshin, the district administrative center. The choice of this town was to be of great signif- icance, because it had long been a stronghold of the SR party. It was the home of the most outstanding SR leader, Victor Chernov, and in the May elections the party won an absolute majority of the municipal council seats.

In early April in response to the colonists' initiative, the town of Kamyshin became the site of a general meeting of representatives from all villages and townships in the district. Out of this assembly was formed the socialist-oriented Kamyshin District Executive Committee, which was to function as a sort of shadow government and play the role of "guardian" of the revolution and the people's rights, particularly monitoring the activities of any remaining authorities and of the zemstvo, which continued to operate. The Executive Committee's composition reflected the ethnic balance of the district, with the Volga Germans having just over half its members. The most prominent colonist and dominant force on the Executive Committee was the indefatigable radical politician, Jacob Dietz. By June, the District Executive Committee was already pro-Socialist Revolutionary in its orientation, extremely dissatisfied that the Provisional Government had deferred a definitive land settlement until the meeting of the Constituent Assembly, which left the fate of the colonists in doubt. In May, the SR deputies to the Congress of Soviets of Peasant Deputies in Petrograd had demanded that all land belonging to landlords, the church, and the state be divided among the peasantry. Although Dietz did not condone all of the SRs' tactics, he acknowledged that their program powerfully attracted all rural elements in the district, including the *Bauernsozialisten* within the colonies.[46] The SR policy of national autonomy within the framework of a Russian federation also seemed alluring to the increasingly ethnic conscious Volga Germans, especially in light of the harsh Russification policies imposed during the war. Finally, there is no evidence that the SR participation in the Provisional Government coalition damaged their reputation among the rural Volga German settlers.[47]

Neither of the Social Democratic groups, the Mensheviks and the Bolsheviks, held much appeal for the Volga Germans, although the close cooperation between the SRs and Mensheviks probably would have made them less odious to the colonists. The Marxist program was directed to the urban industrial workers, whereas the colonists were still overwhelmingly peasant toilers. There is no indication that the Marxist parties even considered the Volga Germans a serious or useful political ally until after the Bolshevik seizure of power. The Bolsheviks were particularly repugnant to those colonists who had heard reports, circulated by the clergy, of the Leninists' proclaimed atheism. Although both Bolsheviks and Mensheviks were active in the city of Saratov, even there the Volga German flour mill workers showed much more interest in the Socialist Revolutionary program and speakers. During the 1905 Revolution, the SRs had planted deep roots in Saratov Province; though they remained dormant during the post-1906 reactionary period, they quickly grew again in 1917. As disgust with the Provisional Government–SR–Menshevik coalition swelled, the Bolsheviks gained support among the Volga German mill workers of Saratov, Kamyshin, and Ekaterinenstadt and began to elect delegates to the newly formed soviets in the larger towns. For example, in the September elections to the Saratov Workers' and Soldiers' Soviet, which returned a Bolshevik majority, one of the two deputies representing the Schmidt Brothers Flour Mills was a Volga German Bolshevik described in the press simply as Comrade Schaeffer; former colonists affiliated with the Social Democrats also held numerous posts on committees of factory workers, while some mill hands expressed interest in the Socialist Revolutionary program.[48] However, in terms of the total Volga German population, Social Democratic supporters remained minuscule and confined to the large towns.

The first political assembly to allegedly represent all Volga Germans gathered in the city of Saratov from April 25 to 27 to formulate petitions to present to the Provisional Government, which had sent an official representative. Initiative for the meeting had come from the flour milling magnate Fedor (Friederich) Petrovich Schmidt, chairman of the Saratov stock exchange and on the executive council of the Russian Flour Millers Congress, and a few other professional Saratov Germans, who wished to act on the promise of ethnic political autonomy made by the Provisional Government and on an appeal from former colonists convening in southern Russia. Apparently, inspiration for the meeting in southern Russia had come from Odessa, where, on March 21, German-Russians living in the Ukraine had convened an assembly of compatriots whose purpose was to advance German-Russian autonomy by organizing a political union of all German-Russians (*politicheskii soiuz vsekh russkikh nemtsev*); the Odessa gathering had circulated its plea for a German political union throughout the empire.[49] The appeal served to mobilize the Volga Germans; but the Volga settlers in 1917, as in 1905, would reject association with any pan-German political union dominated by prosperous landowners, clergy, intellectuals, and ex-deputies from the conservative Fourth Duma, with whom they had nothing in common.

The Saratov convocation came to be officially known as the Assembly of District Representatives of the Volga Colonies (*Versammlung der Kreisbevoll-mächtigen der Wolgakolonien*), although the politically disparate 326 member assembly could not claim to be representative, because its hasty and haphazard convocation precluded uniform selection procedures and equal representation, and socioeconomic class antagonisms quickly surfaced to disrupt its proceedings. Jacob Dietz, and others like him who had denounced the pan-German movement a decade earlier, refused to attend. This diverse body then represented the views of the small but prosperous, liberal, and nationalistic elements of urbanized Volga German society. Therefore, the few urban residents of Saratov, chiefly merchants, were overrepresented, and rural settlers from distant colonies on both sides of the Volga were not represented. In fact, the teacher, Adam Emich, complained that rural colonists were grossly underrepresented. He attacked the composition of the meeting for harboring too many clergy and urban Volga Germans who represented only themselves. The division of the assembly was also evident in language when some delegates, whose knowledge of German was weak, had to address the assemblage in Russian. The rancorous dispute that waged over the official language of the meeting was finally resolved by compromise: speeches and debate could be in either Russian or German, but the written record would be in German.[50] Thus the polarization of Russia, which would become strident by the summer of 1917, already was evident among the Volga Germans.

After two days of committee work, the assembly adopted several resolutions, but four in particular reflected the major Volga German concerns and priorities. First, although angered by the Provisional Government's failure to provide a land program, the assembly conditionally pledged its support of the government as long as it honored the freedoms promised: legal equality; full freedom of religion, speech, press, and association; and autonomy for ethnic minorities (except for Poland, which was under German control and declared independent). The post-1905 leftward shift of the colonists was most clearly manifested in its land resolution, which called for expropriation without compensation, thus marking the Volga Germans' rejection of the Constitutional Democrats' more conservative land policy of expropriation with compensation. The resolution did not denounce private landownership among smallholders, who farmed for themselves, but was directed primarily against the large gentry and Crown estates which relied on hired labor; the resolution stipulated compensation only for those lands acquired by individuals through their own efforts. While not acknowledging loyalty to any specific party's land program, the resolution supported the granting of land on equal terms to those who worked it with their own hands (*uravnitel'no-trudovoe pol'zovanie*), a basic plank in the SR program.[51] In this way, the Volga settlers hoped for a major cost-free land redistribution to alleviate their land hunger.

The gathering assented to the committee on education's twenty-nine-point resolution aimed at improving the deplorable state of education in the colonies, and also aimed at preserving ethnic identity while preparing Volga German youth to function productively in the Russian world in which they lived. The sole use of the Volga dialect as the language of instruction was the primary request. Russian language instruction would begin after the first grade, but would be taught as a foreign language with emphasis on spoken rather than written Russian. In this way, children would first gain knowledge of their dialect and then begin the study of the language of the larger society. An ex-soldier delegate, only recently returned from the Caucasus front, spoke movingly in favor of Russian language instruction, claiming that his military service would not have been so difficult if he had possessed a better command of Russian. Although the colonists advocated local autonomy in the administration and control of schools, they declared that the central government should bear sole fiscal responsibility for the funding of public education.[52]

As the temporary or provisional equivalent of the government in Petrograd, the assembly created a Central Committee of the Volga German Colonists to meet in Saratov (*Zentralkomitee der deutschen Wolgakolonisten*), which was supposed to guide and direct the efforts of the Volga Germans until the formal establishment of an autonomous Volga German territory. Probably the only thing certain about this amorphous body was that it would meet in Saratov. Like the Provisional Government, it lacked a legal basis, public support, financial resources, and executive power. Although a compromise was reached, a clear rift emerged between the urban Saratov Germans and the larger rural element of Volga Germans when the Saratov delegates suggested that the Central Committee be made up of an equal number of delegates from the urban and rural ranks—twelve from Saratov and twelve from the rural townships. The compromise granted twelve seats to the urban dwellers and one delegate each to the forty-six rural townships represented at the assembly. No funding was provided for the operation of the Central Committee, but the delegates agreed that a newspaper should be printed as the official organ of the group. A one-time ten kopeck assessment on each settler was passed to support the *Saratower deutsche Volkszeitung*, although the Central Committee had no way to enforce collection of the fee.

The swift and wild fluctuations of political opinion brought on by the fast-paced events of 1917 make it difficult to ascertain the political mood of the Volga Germans at any one moment. Commenting on the unsettled mood in the city of Saratov, one local correspondent wrote: "The devil only knows what the Saratov citizen is doing. In the spring he declared himself a republican, in July, a socialist, but as the Constituent Assembly approached another reversal began: Saratov became Bolshevik."[53]

One thing had become clear by the summer of 1917: the lack of political consensus among the Volga Germans was comparable to the proliferation of views and political groups that characterized all of Russia. Everyone agreed that reforms were needed, but what needed to be reformed and the methods or instruments to be used were by no means clear. The Volga Germans formed no well-defined and broad-based political parties of their own, and often subscribed to the ideas of the national political groupings. Thus, even though the Volga Germans generally espoused non-Marxian or peasant socialist viewpoints directed at radical land and social reforms, there were some who held moderate and reformist opinions more narrowly focused on political change.[54] The divided political opinion could be clearly seen in the two new Volga German newspapers that appeared in the summer of 1917. The *Saratower deutsche Zeitung*, which resumed publication in Saratov on July 1 under the editorship of Johannes Schleuning, mirrored the views of the Central Committee and those who desired Volga German political autonomy above all else.[55] A variation of the socialist position also emerged in July and was presented in the Ekaterinenstadt-based newspaper, *Der Kolonist*, published by Adam Emich; in time, this large colony became the meeting place of most Volga German socialists.

To describe the socialists' position is difficult because they never developed a coherent program or strong unified organization. On July 8, the organizational meeting of the Union of Volga German Socialists (known as the *Soiuz Nemtsev-Sotsialistov Povolzh'ia* and the *Bund der deutschen Sozialisten an der Wolga* but hereafter cited as UVGS) convened at the ecclesiastical seminary in Saratov.

Delegates claimed to be the representatives of German workers and peasants living in the Lower Volga region. While organized chiefly to carry out propaganda and agitation for the Constituent Assembly elections, particularly to condemn the Provisional Government's inaction on land reform and articulate the dire economic straits of the working classes, the body also voted to back the Bolshevik slate of candidates in the elections to the Saratov City Duma.[56] The UVGS never developed beyond a very loose federation of socialists, which drew its main supporters from such disparate ranks as urban workers, poor peasants, and teachers.

Unlike the Saratov-based Central Committee, which pondered and fussed over political questions and cultural autonomy, Emich and his followers argued that such issues were not nearly as important as economic and social reform. The socialists were critical of the do-nothing policies of the Provisional Government and sympathetic to the growing revolutionary mood in the empire. The socialists argued that the chief goal of the Volga Germans, most of whom were backward, poor, and short of land, should be social and economic liberation, not political liberation, for they were too few and politically naive. "The stomach comes first" might have been their slogan, or the Bolshevik one of "Bread, Land, and Peace." The socialists stressed economic issues, such as land expropriation, lower taxes, and workers' rights, rather than political autonomy. They argued that the political disappearance of the emperor and weakening of the Russian Empire would not necessarily lead to social and economic justice. Only after the healthy economic development of the settlers would political emancipation follow.

Radical reform of the Russian state, not Volga German political autonomy, formed the major concern of another vocal and influential element that had also come under the influence of the Socialist Revolutionaries. During the revolutionary heyday of 1905, many Volga German teachers had sought to form unions to affiliate with the national Teachers' Union, which was dominated by the SRs. Remembering the lessons learned in 1906, colony teachers became the first group to organize in the Volga settlements after the March overthrow of the tsarist regime, but this time for the purpose of political work. In April 1917, colony teachers organized unions in Kamyshin and Ekaterinenstadt, whose purpose was to enhance colonists' political awareness by holding village meetings and encouraging them to support the establishment of a democratic republic with a one-chamber legislative body and the speedy convocation of a constituent assembly.[57] Thus teachers stood in the forefront of the twentieth-century political awakening in the Volga colonies and became excellent conveyors of political propaganda.

The impotent Central Committee hobbled along for much of the summer and tried but failed to smooth relations among discontented factions. The second, and what was to be the last, convocation of the Volga German assembly lasted for three days in late August in the port colony of Schilling, a concession to those who distrusted the urban setting and feared the radical influence of events in Saratov. Unlike the first meeting, nothing productive resulted from this assembly. Heated discussion and debate centered on the forthcoming elections to the Constituent Assembly, with both groups jockeying for influence. Quarrels between socialists and political unionists became acrimonious. Although the assembly elected two candidates to stand for election to the Constituent Assembly, immediately after the closing of the assembly the socialist delegates adjourned to Ekaterinenstadt where the UVGS gathered and selected two of their own candidates to run in the elections for the Constituent Assembly.[58]

The Socialist Revolutionaries waged a vigorous campaign to win Volga German votes for the forthcoming elections to the Constituent Assembly. They directed their campaign to the poor through the colony intelligentsia, particularly teachers and employees of the zemstvos, and struggled vigorously to overcome the obstruction and interference of conservative colony authorities. In September, the 400-delegate Peasant Congress of Saratov province, called by the SR party, heard reports from Kamyshin agitators that the colonists had not yet come over to the side of the party because of the hostility of the kulaks and village elders. In some colonies, these two groups had attempted to prevent the circulation of SR literature, but they had failed: "The German poor asked us to have our literature published in German."[59]

The leftward shift in Russian public opinion that occurred during the fall of 1917—especially after the Kornilov affair resulted in a surge of Bolshevik popularity and the victories of the revolutionary parties in the Constituent Assembly elections—also touched the Volga Germans, who never seriously considered any type of reconciliation with their former, if only temporary, 1905–6 political allies, the Constitutional Democrats. Whereas the Volga towns often voted for the Bolshevik slate, the rural areas voted overwhelmingly for the SRs. In assembly elections, the Volga Germans appear to have scattered their votes among three groups: The Union of Volga German Socialists, the nonsocialist German political unionists (who took the name of Organizational Council of the Volga Germans, hereafter OCVG; *Organisationsausschuss der Wolgadeutschen*), and the SRs. The first two of these were not really political parties in the strict sense of the word, but loosely formed interest groups that had hastily decided to run a slate of candidates.

The political and electoral divisions of the Volga Germans preordained their weak showing in the Constituent Assembly elections and their failure to elect a Volga German to the assembly, yet their voting unequivocally records that on issues they voted overwhelmingly for self-government and expropriation of land without compensation. Voting by provinces effectively dispersed the Volga German votes within Samara and Saratov provinces. Division along political lines further diluted the Volga German vote. Although election returns are lacking for the mountain-side Volga Germans, fortunately complete results are available from Samara Province, and the tallies show a close race between the two colonist delegate slates, the OCVG national or political unionists' list receiving 47,405 votes (53 percent) and the socialist UVGS slate 42,156 votes (47 percent) of the votes cast for the two German slates.[60] There is no way of knowing how many Volga Germans voted the SR ticket; if there was no vigorous and concerted anti-SR village intimidation, then based on the intensive SR campaign in the colonies and their big electoral victories in Saratov Province (59 percent of the total vote) and Samara Province (57 percent), indubitably they ran a respectable third. The narrow ethnic focus of the Volga German candidates, as well as their long-standing linguistic and physical isolation, contributed to their failure to attract any political support beyond their settlements. In Saratov District where Volga Germans resided, the Volga German slates collected only 177 votes from the noncolonist townships.[61]

To contend that the Volga Germans clamored for political autonomy would be a historical distortion, for this idea only took concrete form in April 1918, apparently as a result of the Land Decree's curbing the threat of Volga German expropriation and the Bolsheviks' advancement of a Soviet federation of republics. As late as the summer of 1919, political autonomy failed to arouse Volga Germans, who reportedly focused their lively debates and discussions on the perennial, controversial issues: land, economy, and education.[62] In 1917, issues rather than a well-thought-out political ideology motivated the colonists to action, and the two most obvious, urgent, and portentous were expropriation of Volga German lands and banishment. Even those moderate leaders, such as businessman Fedor Schmidt, who convened the Saratov assembly, sought political union not as an end but as a means for Volga Germans to present a united front to combat the government's draconian land and resettlement plans. He and others chiefly sought a political instrument or vehicle to express and represent Volga German opinion, not independence or autonomy. Perhaps administrative consolidation or amalgamation, in addition to local self-government, would best describe the principal political concerns of the colonists in 1917. Because of their modest population and checkered geographic configuration of dispersed settlements, few Volga Germans could conceive of a distinct, physical political existence in 1917. The tsarist administrative structure, however, had blocked any type of political dialogue among all Volga Germans, who were scattered among four separate districts and two provinces.

Comparing the colonists' response to the events of 1917 with their reaction to those of 1905 provides some interesting insights. The Volga Germans constituted a part of the general socialist orientation so typical of the 1917 radical political culture of the Lower Volga region. This is reflected in their land policies and rejection of the liberal Kadet party, with which they had a political flirtation in 1905. The Volga Germans again rejected all efforts to link up with other German citizens of the empire, the majority of whom were moderates and liberals adhering to a nonsocialist program, indicating that the colonists had no strong nationalist affinities with these groups. On the other hand, their own bonds of ethnic identity proved stronger than their class loyalties; they manifested this by forming quasi-political parties rather than joining established national parties. The one lesson they had learned from 1905 was that this time the reactionaries should not again rob them of the fruits of revolution, for a return of the old regime would again threaten their economic and social survival; this, perhaps, is the best explanation of their radical leftward political shift in 1917. By the fall of 1917, the Volga Germans, like most of the peoples of the Lower Volga, associated the Provisional Government with an unpopular land policy, political inaction, an unpopular war, and economic ineptitude.

On the other hand, 1917 also revealed how shattered and divided the Volga Germans remained. Divisions along class lines fractured them: the vast majority could be labeled peasant socialists, others were Marxian socialists, and a wealthy elite were moderate liberals. Centripetal regional centers haphazardly emerged in Saratov, Kamyshin, Golyi Karamysh, Ekaterinenstadt, and

Novouzensk, which competed for Volga German political allegiance and pulled them in opposite directions. Disparate bodies, such as zemstvo executive committees, soviets, township committees, and factory committees, hopelessly complicated and confused the fluid political situation. Although less important a concern, baleful religious differences still lingered and bred suspicion. The rainbow political spectrum clearly disproved the long-held conception of Volga German homogeneity. They were as politically disparate as other subjects of the Russian state.

The Volga German reaction to the November revolution falls beyond the scope of this book, because the revolution was part of a broader socioeconomic and political process that did not become stabilized until the early 1920s. Because of the chaotic conditions of the time and collapse of governmental authority, Bolshevik power would take months to effectively penetrate peasant villages and Volga German settlements. Initially, the Bolshevik revolutionary Decree on Land gave the peasants and Volga Germans what they wanted—confiscation of all but ordinary peasant and Cossack lands, egalitarian land use and redistribution, abolition of private property with land no longer to be bought, sold, or mortgaged, and possession by tillers of the soil—and momentarily assuaged the greatest fears of the Volga Germans, because none could foresee the disaster that lay ahead.[63] That Volga German antipathy toward the new Bolshevik government did not arise until much later is evident from the remark of an eyewitness: "Most people who had come to America before WW I felt a greater animosity toward the new regime . . . than did those of us who stayed to watch the waste transpire [during the Civil War]."[64] The decrees on peace and minorities' self-determination also placated the Volga German communities. The radicalized soldiers, thousands of whom were Volga Germans who made their presence felt after the summer of 1917, were quite sympathetic and receptive to Bolshevik propaganda. A long-held aspiration of the Volga Germans was realized July 1, 1918, with the Bolsheviks officially granting self-government to the former colonists. Yet other signs indicate growing Volga German opposition and tenuous attachment to the ideology of the new government, especially as civil war spread and the urban food crisis moved the government to put pressure on the peasantry, particularly in the form of food requisitioning.[65] The dearth of Volga German Bolsheviks is best attested to by the almost total absence of Volga Germans in the government of the Volga German autonomous republic formed in 1924. The highest officials were generally foreign communists from either Germany or Austria, and the capital of the new republic was a Russian town, Pokrovsk.[66] However, the combined human and natural disaster that soon struck the Lower Volga made impossible any kind of compromising political discussion. The Civil War embroiled the Volga Germans in a political maelstrom, with their homes and villages becoming the front line of the battle zone; violence, famine, and ruin long attended the Volga Germans. They became weak pawns in the hands of ruthless groups that spared no violence in quest of their goal, the political mastery of the Russian Empire.

pilogue

During the last sixty years of tsarist rule, the Volga Germans braved a tumultuous phase of their history as they entered the modern era. The tempo of change accelerated so rapidly that the preceding century of their Russian existence appeared to be almost static, or frozen, in time. People do not make history, but are shaped by it, and the Volga Germans were carried along in the Russian stream and the European river of history. Bearing little resemblance to other foreign settlers in Russia, they lived much as their Slavic neighbors did and endured similar problems, except that they also had to fear the government's efforts to erase their ethnic identity. Increasingly, they became victims of circumstances and forces beyond their control. They were victims of most of the "isms" commonly associated with modern Europe: capitalism, industrialization, nationalism, secularism, and modern state building. The economic transition from subsistence agriculture to commercial farming had been completed as economic isolation succumbed to interdependence. The industrial age had significant societal implications, altering class relations, offering new individual economic opportunities, and breaking down the physical isolation of the Lower Volga region. Until the post-1905 revolutionary and military conflagrations afflicted Russia, each day and month might have seemed uncertain and temporary, but collectively those years constituted the longest period of tranquility that the colonies had ever experienced. Considerable material progress, accompanied by mobility, technology, and the cheap products of industrialization, fostered a nascent spirit of secularism. Yet the transition from an agrarian to an urbanized, industrialized, and technocratic society remained incomplete by 1917, when a political era came to an abrupt end.

In less than half a century, the Volga Germans had been transformed from privileged to despised, from loyal frontier settlers to seditious pariahs. The Volga Germans endured severe shocks and upheavals resulting from the Alexandrian reforms and the general deterioration of political and socioeconomic relations within Russia, as well as government-initiated policies directed solely at them. The troublous days of conscription quickly passed, but attempts at political centralization and integration persistently disrupted and agitated Volga German communities. The imperial government relentlessly, if not successfully, sought to reshape the Volga German people and communities. Direct government intervention became a common but irksome, and sometimes truly disruptive, fact of life. Rules, regulations, and decrees—many part of elaborate reforms and others dealing specifically with the foreign settlers—violated the previous tranquility and anonymity of the colonies. The greatest political threat occurred during World War I when the government contrived to dispossess them of their livelihood—land.

The process of modernization occurred in conjunction with the complicated and ambiguous process of education being forced on the Volga Germans. On one level, the state served as the compelling agent that attacked colonist localism and insularity in order to shape the lower classes into obedient, productive subjects sharing a common loyalty to the Russian state and society. At another level, the Volga Germans themselves gradually, but often reluctantly, developed a new interest in education in response to broad structural pressures around them, such as administrative integration, the rise of market agriculture, and obligatory military service. Although the level of learning was not high in the rural schools, and the pupils did not retain all they learned, the more secularized educational environment could hardly avoid challenging and eroding traditional values.

These were years of apparent prosperity, yet mother nature treated the colonists the harshest of all. Their material life did in fact change, but with no marked consistency. It is no exaggeration that the Volga Germans suffered more from the vagaries of weather and climate than from government-initiated policies. Whereas historians recall the reactionary policies of Alexander III, the colonists had seared in their collective memories the crop failures and famines of the 1880s and 1890s, and reckoned time in terms of the last good harvest. The threat of famine lingered much longer than elsewhere; the worst Lower Volga crop disasters occurred between 1881 and 1906, whereas in parts of Western Europe the fear of famine had vanished by the mid-eighteenth century. The only parallels to the 1891 famine occurred in Ireland in 1846, in India in 1866 and 1877, and in China in 1878.

Although the harsh physical environment and concomitant food shortages caused frequent human suffering and torment, reaching disastrous proportions in 1891, the population growth of the Volga Germans corresponded closely to that of the rest of Europe, where population, by more than doubling in the nineteenth century, expanded more rapidly than in any previous period. Similarly, population growth was accompanied by population movement on a considerable scale. A small group of Volga Germans joined the European exodus to North and South America, and migration within the Russian Empire quickened in the 1890s as settlers sought employment as temporary field workers or permanent employees in towns, particularly along the Volga, in Siberia, and the Caucasus. While migration might be only temporary, emigration, because of the long distances involved, was usually permanent.

By 1917, the Volga Germans had become fully cognizant of the effects of Europe's first industrial revolution, often called the "revolution of coal and iron," but had only scant knowledge of the post-1870 second industrial revolution, sometimes labeled the "revolution of steel and electricity." The coal and iron age had brought railroads which opened new industrial markets, such as the Donets basin, with more workers to feed and clothe; cheap iron became available for use in the manufacture of simple agricultural equipment made in the colonists' workshops; and the steam engine quickened transportation and provided an efficient power source for mills and plants. The Volga Germans benefited from the striking expansion of Russian textile industries between 1870 and 1914, when their small domestic workshops competed well with modern plants and factories.

The Volga Germans had not felt the full impact of the second industrial revolution. Most of the inventions of the steel and electric revolution, such as the internal combustion engine, Edison's incandescent filament lamp, the telephone, and the automobile, remained rarities within their settlements, although stores in the largest trading colonies and major Russian towns offered Gillette safety razors, Singer sewing machines, cameras, typewriters, and even

American shoes. The threshing machine, the largest piece of machinery familiar to the rural settlers, was still powered by a coal or wood-fueled steam engine rather than a gasoline-powered internal combustion engine. Although pig iron remained the primary material, the cheaper production of steel ensured its more frequent use in machinery production. Electricity became a new source of energy increasingly used in the flour milling industry, for street lighting, and driving trolleys, but had not yet made its way into villages and homes. The burgeoning new petroleum industry around Baku and Grozny attracted Volga Germans to these thriving industrial towns. The expansion of German chemical industries enabled colonist sarpinka manufacturers to switch from natural chemical dye substances to improved synthetic dyes made from coal tar. However, chemical fertilizers and insecticides had not yet been applied to the Volga valley fields.

Even with the revolutionary impact of the two industrial revolutions, in 1917 most Volga Germans still engaged in agriculture, although they were not as predominantly agrarian as the Russian peasantry as a whole, with the notable exception of the trans-Volga settlers. The mixed cottage industry and farm economy of the Volga Germans of Saratov Province made them unique and better able to overcome the vicissitudes of nature and higher government exactions. The remoteness of the settlements, the strong influence of custom and tradition, and the complications of land tenure hampered the adoption of scientific agricultural methods as practiced in Western Europe. Elaborate rotation of crops—especially the cultivation of turnips, peas, beans, and clovers, which restored nitrogen to the soil—had not gained a foothold in the colonies by 1917. While the sobriquet of "model farmers" cannot, therefore, be accurately applied to the Volga Germans, historians have consistently overlooked their significant contributions in the manufacture of textiles and agricultural machinery, and, above all, as middlemen in the grain trade and entrepreneurs in the flour milling industry.

The consequences of the great nineteenth-century political revolution, catalyzed by the post-1789 events in France, seem to have been of less importance to the Volga Germans than the two industrial revolutions. The revolutionary armies of France, bringing with them the slogan "Liberty, Equality, and Fraternity"—later evolving into the ideas of liberalism, self-government, and nationalism—advanced far into Central Europe, the Balkans, and even Russia, but they never reached as far as the Volga, and the imperial autocrats ruthlessly eliminated all radical political thought. These momentous ideas germinated and fructified primarily in the minds of intellectuals, attracted the middle class, but rarely penetrated the less educated peasant masses.

Patriotism—meaning love of one's country—and loyalty to their adopted Russian homeland remained constants of Volga German history, even in the face of hostile government policies and growing xenophobia. They long perceived themselves primarily as subjects of a dynastic patrimony to which they owed allegiance and service, rather than as a distinct national group of free and equal citizens. They had no proud memories of an independent past. They rejected political autonomy and appeals for a political union of all German-speaking subjects, and only in the twentieth century did they belatedly but not clearly conceive of the modest hope for self-government and cultural autonomy within the Russian Empire. The difficulty of drawing boundaries creating a bona fide Volga German "republic" in the Soviet period seems to validate the unfeasibility of political autonomy. Whereas many Europeans, but especially Germans and Italians, long remained more attached to their provincial rulers and cultures than to the ideal of national unity, so too did the Volga Germans attribute their uniqueness not only to ethnic factors but also to their Volga domicile; many emphatically stated that they were "Wolga Deutsch," not "Schwarzen Deutsch" or Black Sea Germans. A century and a half after leaving Western Europe, they had lost, modified, or forgotten much of their "Germanness," however that may be defined; they had become the hybrid "Volga German-Russian," chiefly through involvement in military and government service and more frequent contact with the Russian economic and social milieu, whether by negotiating grain prices or purchasing incidental domestic articles. Russian could now be heard more frequently in the colonies, and Russian words freely entered the vocabulary of the dialect. Ironically, the government's Russification policies heightened Volga German ethnicity, because, by stressing uniformity, they magnified cultural diversity.

Nevertheless, the Volga Germans scrutinized Soviet policies from the standpoint of disaffected peasants, not fervent nationalists, and, until the late spring of 1918, were prepared to accept the new regime. The short-lived peasant-Bolshevik honeymoon began to lose ardor in May 1918, when the Soviet government implemented grain requisitioning to address the urban food crisis and bolster the faltering economy; in a stroke of the pen, the Bolsheviks voided the political advantages their land program had earned among the peasantry. Thousands of Committees of Poor Peasants (*Kombedy*), accompanied by armed detachments of urban workers, terrorized the countryside and alienated the peasantry in the battle for food. Like peasants elsewhere, the Volga Germans resisted, resorting to force, then later, when cowed, passively left their fields unplanted. Grain exactions eventually became so high that no seed was available for planting. The food policy of the new government proved politically expensive, alienating the better-off peasantry and generating class warfare in villages. Designed to heal the festering wound caused by grain requisitioning, the New Economic Policy announced in March 1921 offered the peasantry a fixed tax in kind.

Although Soviet control of the Lower Volga remained tenuous throughout the Civil War, the fledgling government reversed the tsarist policy that manipulated the Volga Germans as scapegoats, instead favoring the Volga Germans with political concessions and actually encouraging use of the dialect in administration and education (although banning religious instruction in schools). The communist regime granted the Volga Germans the appearance of self-determination by the October 19, 1918, recognition of the Volga German Workers' Commune and by the establishment of the Autonomous Soviet Socialist Republic of Volga Germans on January 6, 1924.[1] However, Soviet policy vis-à-vis the Volga Germans was predicated on international events, particularly those in Germany, not on conditions in the Lower Volga. The survival of the new socialist experiment depended on revolution abroad; it was widely held that Germany was the most susceptible. It was no simple happenstance that the creation of these two political institutions coincided with revolutionary situations in Germany; unable to lend matériel or military assistance, the Bolsheviks offered political propaganda. Thus Bolshevik authorities eagerly advanced Volga German autonomy as a model to inspire the German proletariat to topple the bourgeois-dominated government of imperial Germany. At the time, all other German-inhabited areas of the Russian state were under German occupation, so that the Volga region was the only area available for this Soviet experiment. In the mid-1920s, the Soviet government used the Volga German ASSR as a conduit for much-needed Western capital. Until Stalin's ascendancy, the Bolshevik government pressed for Volga German autonomy out of political expediency.

The years under Soviet rule were disastrous, as ultimately, under Stalin, the government brutally executed the policy launched by the tsarist regime and accomplished the diaspora of the Volga Germans. The effects of the Civil War and the famine of 1921–22 seriously disrupted life in the Volga German communities, culminating in a considerable socioeconomic leveling of the inhabitants. Commenting in 1927 about farming households, one observer remarked about the "almost complete elimination of stratification."[2] Preceded by several years of poor harvests, the 1921 famine decimated the population; by the summer of 1922, about 50,000 had perished and 70,000 had fled their homesteads. By 1923, the sown area had dropped dramatically, amounting to no more than 43 percent of the 1914 area sown, primarily the result of a weakened population stripped of horses, equipment, and seed during the Civil War. The church became a particular target of persecution, so that by 1925 only fourteen of forty Lutheran ministers remained in their pulpits.[3] The only period of relative tranquility and economic recovery for the Volga Germans in the Soviet period occurred between 1924 and 1928, in the epoch of the New Economic Policy, although serious flooding in 1925 inundated many riverine settlements.[4] By 1926, sizable quantities of grain again were marketed, and the area under cultivation amounted to about two-thirds of the prewar figure; but the Stalin revolution would make this short-lived.

The mass, forced collectivization of agriculture in 1929–30 set into motion the diaspora, which was completed in 1941. Zealous armed detachments deported thousands of Volga German families to Siberia, leaving villages in turmoil and the remaining, recently converted collective farmers shocked and dispirited. Stalin's purges and reign of terror also led to the forcible transplantation of countless settlers, particularly the religious faithful, from the Volga region to the dictator's gulag archipelago.[5] The final catastrophe struck August 28, 1941, when the Presidium of the Supreme Court of the Soviet Union announced that Soviet military organs had unmasked thousands of spies and saboteurs among the Volga Germans, allegedly preparing to assist the invading Nazi forces. The government ordered the approximately 380,000 remaining Volga Germans deported and dispersed to such remote areas as the Altai region, Kazakhstan, and various parts of Siberia, where most were forced to serve in labor detachments under quite harsh conditions. In effect, Stalin erased the Volga Germans from history.

In 1956, the history of the nationalities suppressed and dispersed during World War II slowly began to unfold. In his secret report to the Twentieth Party Congress, Nikita Khrushchev denounced Stalin's forced deportation of the Muslim Karachais, Chechens, Ingushi, Balkars, and the Buddhist Kalmyks, and allowed them to return to their original homes. However, Khrushchev notably omitted any reference to the deported Germans and Crimean Tatars. In 1964, the party initiated a partial, inconsistent rehabilitation of all Soviet Germans, but like the tsarist government, the Soviets failed to distinguish between the various German elements residing in the empire. Their experiences during World War II were quite dissimilar; the Volga Germans, for example, never fell under Nazi occupation and could bear no stigma of collaboration. In its decree of August 29, 1964, the Presidium of the USSR Supreme Soviet stated that the previous blanket accusations leveled at the Soviet Germans had been unfounded, a manifestation of the Stalin personality cult. The decree did not address resettlement of the Germans to their former homes, ostensibly because the regions of their prewar domicile had already become occupied by other Soviet citizens. Apparently the real reason Volga Germans have not been allowed to return to their original homes is that Soviet authorities consider them essential for the continued economic development of those regions where they are now residing. The dissident Medvedev twins asserted that the Volga Germans deported to Kazakhstan in 1941 comprised the basic, permanent work force that implemented Khrushchev's "virgin lands" program, and therefore it was economically inexpedient to allow them to return to their homes along the Volga.[6]

The Soviets have succeeded much better than the tsarist regime in forcing the assimilation of the Volga Germans, with about one-third of them reporting in 1970 that Russian was their mother tongue. Today there are no Volga German settlements or institutions. Knowledge of the Volga German dialect and heritage has faded significantly, primarily the result of their dispersal all over the Soviet Union, the absence of any Volga German communities, the high degree of urban residents (39 percent in 1959), the lack of any schools offering instruction in the dialect, marriage outside the ethnic group, and, at least among the career-minded, the conscious decision to deny or conceal any German heritage.[7] Finally, Volga Germans make up only a small part of the 93,000 Soviet Germans who have been allowed to emigrate during the post-Stalin period, because the Soviet government generally has recognized only family reunification as grounds for emigration. This means that most of those emigrating to West Germany are related to former Soviet Germans who lived in the occupied western areas of the Soviet Union and fled with the retreating German armies in 1944. The future does not look propitious for the continued survival of Volga German ethnicity.

𝕹otes

Introduction

1. This view was most recently presented in Kyril Fitzlyon and Tatiana Browning, *Before the Revolution* (Woodstock, N.Y., 1978), p. 52.

2. Both Soviet and Western scholars have stressed the need for a study of the post-1860 period. See, for example, A. G. Karevskaia, "O gosudarstvennykh krest'ianskikh Samarskoi Gubernii vo vtoroi polovine XIX veka (kratkii obzor istochnikov i literatury)," in S. G. Basin (ed.), *Revoliutsionnoe dvizhenie v srednem Povolzh'e i Priural'e*, in *Nauchnye trudy Kuibyshevskogo Ped. Instituta* 183 (1977): 3–13. Adam Giesinger, former editor of the *Journal of the American Historical Society of Germans from Russia*, stated on the editor's page of the Winter 1984 edition: "Because the great majority of the forebears of the members of our society came to America during the latter period [1885 to 1914], research on conditions in the German colonies in Russia during those years would provide information of great interest to us. Very little has been done as yet in that field." For the immigration history, see Roger P. Bartlett, *Human Capital: The Settlement of Foreigners in Russia 1762–1804* (Cambridge, 1979). Three general accounts based on non-Russian sources are Adam Giesinger, *From Catherine to Khrushchev: The Story of Russia's Germans* (Battleford, Sask. 1974); Fred Koch, *The Volga Germans in Russia and the Americas, from 1763 to the Present* (University Park, Pa., 1977); and Hattie Plum Williams, *The Czar's Germans: With Particular Reference to the Volga Germans*, ed. Emma S. Haynes, Phillip B. Legler, and Gerda S. Walker (Denver, 1975). The most recent account is Ingeborg Fleischhauer's *Die Deutschen im Zarenreich* (Stuttgart, 1986), which deals with all Germans in the Russian Empire. The author's thesis is to portray Germans as a positive force in Russian history; she does not always interpret Volga German history and society correctly.

3. Marc Raeff, *Understanding Imperial Russia*, trans. Arthur Goldhammer (New York, 1984), p. 173.

4. Edward Thaden, *Russia's Western Borderlands, 1710–1870* (Princeton, 1984), p. 167.

5. Richard Lingeman, *Small Town America* (New York, 1980), p. 253.

6. George Rudé, *Europe in the Eighteenth Century: Aristocracy and the Bourgeois Challenge* (London and New York, 1972), p. 19.

7. Bartlett, *Human Capital*, p. 59.

8. Katharina Drotleff, *Lasst sie selber sprechen: Berichte russlanddeutscher Aussiedler* (Hannover, 1980), pp. 9–10.

9. The dean of German-Russian studies, Karl Stumpp, propounded this historical interpretation in his numerous writings, chief of which is *The German-Russians: Two Centuries of Pioneering*, trans. Joseph Height (New York, 1971), and it is clearly stated in the title of his German-language bibliography of German-Russian literature, *Das Schrifttum über das Deutschtum in Russland* (Tübingen, 1970). A great many, but by no means all, of the publications of the Stuttgart-based Landsmannschaft der Deutschen aus Russland bear the imprint of Stumpp's influence. Ingeborg Fleischhauer's *Die Deutschen im Zarenreich* and *The Soviet Germans: Past and Present* (New York, 1986), co-authored with Benjamin Pinkus, carry on this historical tradition.

Chapter One

1. "Vospominaniia A. M. Fadeeva," *Russkii arkhiv*, no. 5, 1891, p. 43. The best accounts of the conditions of the original settlement are Roger Bartlett's *Human Capital* and Grigorii G. Pisarevskii, "Nizhnee Povolzh'e v tret'ei chetverti XVIII veka," *Izvestiia pedagogicheskogo fakul'teta: Obshchestvennye nauki* (Azerbaidzhanskii gosudarstvennyi universitet imeni V. I. Lenina) 14 (1929): 221–29. See also Samarskoe gubernskoe zemstvo, *Sbornik statisticheskikh svedenii po Samarskoi Gubernii*, vol. 7 (Samara, 1890), pp. 12–15; and Flegont V. Dukhovnikov, "Nemtsy, drugie inostrantsy i prishlye liudi v Saratove," *Saratovskii krai: Istoricheskie ocherki, vospominaniia, materialy* 1 (1893): 237–64. A description of the region before the arrival of the colonists is in Georgii I. Peretiatkovich, *Povolzh'e v XVII i nachale XVIII veka* (Odessa, 1882), pp. 3–26.

2. N. F. Khovanskii, "K istorii nemetskikh kolonii Saratovskoi Gubernii (iz del senatskago arkhiva)," *Trudy saratovskoi uchenoi arkhivnoi komissii* 31 (1914): 51.

3. Georg Löbsack, *Einsam Kampft das Wolgaland* (Leipzig, 1936), pp. 60–61. Nikolai M. Druzhinin, *Gosudarstvennye krest'iane i reforma P. D. Kiseleva* (Leningrad, 1958), 2:373.

4. Frederick Merk, *History of the Westward Movement* (New York, 1980), p. 247.

5. Carl Lehmann and Parvus [Alexander Helphand], *Das hungernde Russland* (Stuttgart, 1900), p. 262.

6. Saratovskoe gubernskoe zemstvo, *Sbornik statisticheskikh svedenii po Saratovskoi Gubernii*, vol. 11 (Saratov, 1891), pt. 3:1–9. Samarskoe gubernskoe zemstvo, *Sbornik statisticheskikh svedenii*, 7:1–7.

7. "Istoriia i statistika kolonii inostrannykh poselentsev v Rossii," *Zhurnal ministerstva gosudarstvennykh imushchestv* 55, pt. 1 (1885): 60. A. L., "Opisanie kolonii inostrannykh poselentsev v Samarskoi Gubernii," *Samarskiia gubernskiia vedomosti*, Mar. 7, 1853, p. 56.

8. "Soll man Wälder pflegen, oder nicht?" *Saratowsche deutsche Zeitung*, Aug. 23, 1866, p. 513.

9. Saratovskoe gubernskoe zemstvo, *Sbornik statisticheskikh svedenii po Saratovskoi*

Gubernii, vol. 6 (Saratov, 1887), p. 44. The problems and delays in the survey of the Russian Empire, which was not even begun until 1766 and continued until the mid-nineteenth century, are well documented in Ivan E. German, *Istoriia russkago mezhevaniia,* 2d ed. (Moscow, 1910). *Polnoe sobranie zakonov Rossiiskoi Imperii,* first series, art. 12,095 (original landholding law), Mar. 19, 1764, pp. 648–54; art. 23,408 (minister of interior report on colony land conditions), Dec. 18, 1808, p. 729. Pisarevskii, "Nizhnee Povolzh'se," pp. 223–29. Khovanskii, "K istorii nemetskikh kolonii," p. 58.

10. A. A. Klaus asserts that only poor and shiftless colonists accepted such favorable conditions as a way of getting out of debt and starting life anew. He contrasted this resettlement with that of the colonies in southern Russia, where requests to relocate were so numerous that a careful selection process was established. A. A. Klaus, "Obshchina-sobstvennik i eia iuridicheskaia organizatsiia," *Vestnik Evropy,* March 1870, p. 79. The best account of Kiselev's program is in Nikolai M. Druzhinin, *Gosudarstvennye krest'iane i reforma P. D. Kiseleva,* 2 vols. (Moscow and Leningrad, 1946 and 1958). For information on the colonies in particular, there is A. A. Klaus, *Nashi kolonii* (St. Petersburg, 1869), appendix 2, p. 44. "Istoriia i statistika kolonii inostrannykh poselentsev v Rossii," *Zhurnal ministerstva gosudarstvennykh imushchestv* 54, pt. 1 (1855): 71–88.

11. Walter Prescott Webb, *The Great Plains* (Boston, 1931), p. 506.

12. Druzhinin, *Gosudarstvennye krest'ian,* 2:192. *Polnoe sobranie zakonov Rossiiskoi Imperii,* second series, art. 8,146 (law delaying implementation of colonist supplemental land legislation), May 21, 1835, pp.

436–38; art. 13,255 (law granting colonists vacant state lands in trans-Volga region), Mar. 12, 1840, pp. 138–40.

13. Pastor Wilhelm Stärkel, "A Voice from the Old Country: The Stärkel Letters," trans. Paul Reitzer, *Journal of the American Historical Society of Germans from Russia* 2, no. 1 (Spring 1979): 63. See also Peter Haller, *Vospominaniia P. K. Gallera* (Saratov, 1927), pp. 13–14.

14. "Istoriia i statistika kolonii inostrannykh poselentsev v Rossii," *Zhurnal ministerstva gosudarstvennykh imushchestv* 55, pt. 1 (1855): 66–67.

15. A. N. Minkh, *Narodnye obychai, sueveriia, predrassudki i obriady krest'ian Saratovskoi Gubernii* (St. Petersburg, 1890), p. 11.

16. The following sources were used to compile these data: "Istoriia i statistika kolonii inostrannykh poselentsev v Rossii," *Zhurnal ministerstva gosudarstvennykh imushchestv* 55, pt. 1 (1855): 65; Ministerstvo gosudarstvennykh imushchestv, *Statisticheskii obzor gosudarstvennykh imushchestv za 1858 god* (St. Petersburg, 1861), pp. 646–47; Klaus, *Nashi kolonii,* appendix 4, pp. 46–59; *Saratowsche deutsche Zeitung,* May 28, 1865, p. 467; "Svedeniia o sostoianii kolonii v Saratovskoi Gubernii," *Saratovskiia gubernskiia vedomosti,* no. 81 (1871), n.p.; Tsentral'nyi statisticheskii komitet, *Pervaia vseobshchaia perepis' naseleniia Rossiiskoi Imperii, 1897 g.* (St. Petersburg, 1899–1900), 36:72–74 and 38:3,225; Statisticheskii komitet Oblastnogo Voiska Donskogo, *Spisok naselennykh mest Oblasti Voiska Donskogo po pervoi vseobshchei perepisi naseleniia Rossiiskoi Imperii, 1897 goda* (Novocherkassk, 1905), p. xxiii; Gottlieb Beratz, *Die deutschen Kolonien an der unteren Wolga* (Saratov, 1915), pp. 304–11.

This picture of record population increase held true only through the halcyon years preceding World War I, with the colonies suffering a demographic disaster in the 1920s. The prewar years witnessed an exodus of emigration to America and a smaller but still notable internal migration to the frontiers of the Russian Empire. World War I, the Civil War, the 1921 famine, and several consecutive poor harvests decimated the population of the colonies. Under normal conditions, Soviet demographers speculated, the Volga German population would have increased 50 to 60 percent between 1897 and 1926; yet in fact it had grown by only 14.8 percent, whereas the non-German increase in the neighboring areas was 24 percent. From another perspective, between 1897 and 1914 the colonists' population growth was 30.4 percent; between 1914 and 1920 population remained stable with no increase; and between 1920 and 1926 population declined precipitously, the result of severe famines taking the lives of tens of thousands. The unparalleled 1921 famine struck the meadow-side colonists hardest when population dropped by 18.6 percent between 1920 and 1926, forcing many of them to flee to Saratov Province, where there was more food. The population of the colonists of Saratov Province dropped less precipitously, only 8.4 percent! In 1926 the Volga German population was 12 percent lower than it had been in 1914, with some colonies having lost over one-third of their residents. Only in 1925–26, with the return of good harvests, did the German-speaking population begin to grow again. ASSR Nemtsev Povolzh'ia, Statisticheskoe upravlenie, *Predvaritel'nye vsesoiuznoi perepisi naseleniia 1926 goda po Avton. Sots. Sov.*

Respublike Nemtsev Povolzh'ia (Pokrovsk, 1927), pp. 9–11.

17. Haller, *Vospominaniia*, pp. 16–21.

Chapter Two

1. A. Klaus, "O zaniatiiakh komissii," *Pravitel'stvennyi vestnik*, Jan. 20, 1870, pp. 1–4.

2. *Polnoe sobranie zakonov Rossiiskoi Imperii*, second series, art. 6,298 (July 1, 1833); "Istoriia i statistika kolonii inostrannykh," *Zhurnal ministerstva gosudarstvennykh imushchestv* 55, pt. 1 (1855): 78.

3. Novouzenskoe uezdnoe zemstvo, *Zhurnaly novouzenskago uezdnago zemskago sobraniia*, 1886, pp. 252–53.

4. Haller, *Vospominaniia*, pp. 69–70.

5. Dukhovnikov, "Nemtsy," *Saratovskii krai* 1 (1893): 243–44; Khovanskii, "K istorii nemetskikh kolonii," p. 52.

6. Filip F. Vigel', *Vospominaniia F. F. Vigelia* (Moscow, 1864), 1:24; Konstantin I. Popov, "Zapiski o Saratove K. I. Popova," *Saratovskii krai* 1 (1893): 168.

7. Gerhard Bonwetsch, *Geschichte der deutschen Kolonien* (Stuttgart, 1919), p. 49. Gottlieb Beratz did not share this enthusiasm for the Kontora in his *Die deutschen Kolonien*, p. 114; in fact, he castigated it for arbitrariness.

8. "Istoriia i statistika kolonii inostrannykh," *Zhurnal ministerstva gosudarstvennykh imushchestv* 55, pt. 1 (1855): 84.

9. *Saratovskiia gubernskiia vedomosti*, nos. 85 and 231, 1871, p. 2.

10. Klaus, "Obshchina-sobstvennik," p. 87.

11. Details of this reform are found in *Polnoe sobranie zakonov Rossiiskoi Imperii*,

second series, art. 49,705 (June 4–16, 1871), pp. 818–19, most of which were based on the General Regulations of the Peasantry, emancipating the serfs, issued February 19, 1861.

12. Bonwetsch, *Geschichte*, p. 189.

13. See Moshe Lewin, *The Making of the Soviet System* (New York, 1985), pp. 72–87, for an interesting discussion of peasant law in the post-1860 period.

14. Saratovskii gubernskii statisticheskii komitet, *Pamiatnaia knizhka Saratovskoi Gubernii na 1872 god* (Saratov, 1873), 2, pt. 2: 154–55.

15. Bonwetsch, *Geschichte*, p. 119.

16. Thomas S. Pearson, "The Origins of Alexander III's Land Captains: A Reinterpretation," *Slavic Review* 40 (Fall 1981): 384–403; George L. Yaney, *The Systematization of Russian Government* (Urbana, Ill., 1973), pp. 368–71; George L. Yaney, *The Urge to Mobilize* (Urbana, Ill., 1982), pp. 68–85. The traditional view of the land captains as a gentry-initiated reactionary measure is ably presented in P.A. Zaionchkovskii, *Rossiiskoe samoderzhavie v kontse XIX stoletiia* (Moscow, 1970), pp. 398–405.

17. *Privolzhskii krai*, Mar. 15, 1906, p. 2.

18. Ia. Ditts, "Otnoshenii nashikh Nemtsev k Gosudarstvennoi Dume," *Privolzhskaia gazeta*, Mar. 14, 1906, p. 2.

19. Max Praetorius, *Galka eine deutsche Ansiedlung an der Wolga* (Leipzig, 1912), pp. 44–61.

20. *Saratovskii dnevnik*, Sept. 23, 1905, p. 3; *Privolzhskaia gazeta*, June 3, 1906, p. 3; and *Saratovskii vestnik*, May 21, 1917, p. 5.

21. *Privolzhskii krai*, Oct. 12, 1904, p. 2.

22. *Saratovskii dnevnik*, Dec. 21, 1906, p. 4.

23. *Saratower deutsche Zeitung*, Sept. 13, 1906, p. 3.

24. Maria Bock, *Vospominaniia o moem ottse P. A. Stolypina* (New York, 1953), p. 137.

25. *Saratovskii dnevnik*, Aug. 25, 1905, p. 3.

26. Ia. Ditts, "Putevyia zametki," *Privolzhskaia gazeta*. Feb. 25, 1906, p. 2.

27. *Polnoe sobranie zakonov Rossiiskoi Imperii, first series*, art. 23,408 (Dec. 18, 1808), pp. 727–31.

28. P. A. Golubev, *Istoriko-statisticheskiia tablitsy po Saratovskoi Gubernii za period 1862–92 g.* (n.p., n. d.), pp. 25–33.

29. "Svedeniia o sostoianii kolonii v Saratovskoi Gubernii," *Saratovskiia gubernskiia vedomosti*, no. 83, 1871, p. 2. M. I. Semenov, "Krest'ianskie platezhi i nalogi v Saratovskoi Gubernii," in *Materialy k voprosu o nuzhdakh sel'sko-khoziaistvennoi promyshlennosti v Saratovskoi Gubernii* (Saratov, 1903), pp. 44–47.

30. Saratovskoe gubernskoe zemstvo, *Sbornik statisticheskikh svedenii*, 6:160–62; Praetorius, *Galka*, pp. 38–41.

31. Jerry Henry, "Adam Franzovich Ebel" (unpublished manuscript, Special Collections, Colorado State University Library), p. 17.

32. A. M. Anfimov, *Rossiiskaia derevnia v gody pervoi mirovoi voiny* (Moscow, 1962), pp. 76–79. *Prilozhenie k vsepoddaneishemu otchetu Samarskago Gubernatora za 1881 god* (Samara, 1882), vedomost' no. 4, p. 6.

33. Terence Emmons and Wayne Vucinich (eds), *The Zemstvo in Russia* (Cambridge, 1982), p. 11.

34. Semenov, "Krest'ianskie platezhi i nalogi," pp. 10–14.

35. A. Leopol'dov, "O saratovskikh i samarskikh kolonistakh," *Severnaia pchela*, Mar. 7, 1860, p. 212. In 1863, Leopol'dov expressed essentially the same ideas in

"Neskol'ko slov o kolonistakh," *Volga,* Dec. 18, 1863, p. 554. Aleksandr Leongard, "Golos iz Saksonii za saratovskikh i samarskikh kolonistov," *Severnaia pchela,* May 2, 1860, p. 395.

36. Norman Stone, *The Eastern Front, 1914–1917* (New York, 1975), p. 213.

37. Nicholas Golovine, *The Russian Army in the World War* (New Haven, 1931), pp. 17–23.

38. *Saratovskiia gubernskiia vedomosti,* Dec. 8, 1874, pp. 2–3, and Dec. 14, 1874, p. 2.

39. Ib. d., Nov. 17, 1874, p. 2. By concentrating on the Mennonite experience, Fleischhauer's discussion of military conscription misrepresents the Volga German reaction. *Die Deutschen im Zarenreich,* pp. 309–16.

50. "K voprosu o nemetskikh shkolakh," *Privolzhskaia zhizn',* Oct. 14, 1910, p. 1. Another colonist in his memoirs also stated that military conscription was the greatest stimulus to learn Russian. Haller, *Vospominaniia,* p. 65. As late as the turn of the century in the more backward and poor colonies, the few individuals literate in Russian usually had learned it while in the army. See the autobiography of Peter Sinner, U.S. National Archives, Captured German Records, Microfilm T–81, roll 436.

41. Transcript of the oral history interview of Gus Lebsack (Special Collections, Colorado State University Library), p. 1.

42. Eduard Seib, "Der Wolgadeutsche im Spiegel seines Brauchtums," *Heimatbuch der Deutschen aus Russland* (1967–68), p. 153.

43. John Bushnell, "Peasants in Uniform: The Tsarist Army as a Peasant Society," *Journal of Social History* 13, no. 4 (1981): 565–66. Ben Eklof, *Russian Peasant Schools* (Berkeley, 1986), p. 125.

44. Löbsack, *Einsam Kampft das Wolgaland,* p. 116.

45. Saratovskoe gubernskoe zemstvo, *Sbornik statisticheskikh svedenii,* 11:5.

46. Francis S. Laing, "German-Russian Settlements in Ellis County, Kansas," *Collec tions of the Kansas State Historical Society, 1909–1910* 11 (1910): 502. Other reports, that the initial glowing accounts of America in the Volga German settlements had been replaced by more realistic accounts of hard times and rough frontier life in an alien land, can be found in Saratovskoe gubernskoe zemstvo, *Sbornik statisticheskikh svedenii,* 11:58.

47. A. N. Pavlov, "Pochemu nashi nemtsy pereseliaiutsia v Ameriku," *Saratovskii spravochnyi listok,* Dec. 23, 1877, p. 2.

48. Data on Volga German military service have been drawn from many diverse sources, but the following two published annual statistics were most useful: Ministerstvo vnutrennikh del, *Sbornik pravitel'stvennykh rasporiazhenii po voinskoi povinnosti,* vols. 3 and 4 (1874–77), p. 52 in the appendix of each volume; Saratovskii gubernskii statisticheskii komitet, *Statisticheskii obzor Saratovskoi Gubernii za* [1895–1911], list 10, pp. 7 and 8 of each volume.

49. Although we have no reliable statistics on this emigration, oral history interviewees repeatedly mentioned the fear of mobilization, not conscription, as the main reason for leaving Russia. See, for example, the transcript of the oral history interview of Philip Legler (Special Collections, Colorado State University Library), p. 5. For a more general discussion of the inequities and social impact of the mobilization during the Russo-Japanese War, see Allan Wildman, *The End of the Russian Imperial Army* (Princeton, 1980), pp. 27–45.

50. Otsenochno-statisticheskoe otdelenie saratovskoi gubernskoi zemskoi upravy, *Sbornik svedenii po Saratovskoi Gubernii za 1905 god* (Saratov, 1906), 2, pt. 2:75.

51. Ibid., p. 79.

52. Ibid., p. 86.

53. Ibid., pp 108–10; *Privolzhskii krai,* July 29, 1905, p. 2.

54. Golovine, *The Russian Army in the World War,* p. 8.

55. Transcript of the oral history interview of Amalie Klein (Special Collections, Colorado State University Library), p. 33.

56. Transcript of the oral history interview of Fred Ostwald (Special Collections, Colorado State University Library), p. 8.

Chapter Three

1. Henry, "Adam Ebel," p. 16.

2. Edward Thaden (ed.), *Russification in the Baltic Provinces and Finland, 1855–1914* (Princeton, 1981), p. 122.

3. Beratz, *Die deutschen Kolonien,* p. 230; Giesinger, *From Catherine to Khrushchev,* p. 173; and E. Gross, *Avt. Sots. Sov. Resp. Nemtsev Povolzh'ia* (Pokrovsk, 1926), p. 98.

4. Transcript of the oral history interview of Fred Ostwald, p. 5. Parents even invoked the name of the village priest to frighten children to sleep: "Or the parents may scare the child to sleep by mentioning such fearsom figures as *der Pastor, der Kirgise,* or *der Belznickel."* The latter was a masked character who traditionally visited Volga German children during the Christmas season. It is amazing that the colonists categorized the cleargy with the dreaded Kirghiz! Timothy Kloberdanz, "The Volga German Catholic Life Cycle" (master's thesis, Department

of Sociology, Colorado State University, 1974) p. 46.

5. *Privolzhskii krai,* Oct. 7, 1905, p. 3. See Karl Cramer, "Das kirchliche leben an der Wolga," in *Die Kirchen und das religiöse Leben der Russlanddeutschen,* ed. Joseph Schnurr (Stuttgart, 1972), p. 413, for some of the native son priests who graduated from the Saratov seminary. Consequently, beginning in the 1880s, the Catholic colonies fared better when dialect-speaking graduates of the seminary returned home to preach and teach.

6. Klaus, *Nashi kolonii,* pp. 394–96. Bonwetsch, *Geschichte,* p. 124.

7. Emma S. Haynes, "Researching in the National Archives," *Journal of the American Historical Society of Germans from Russia* 2 (Spring 1979): 4.

8. Hans Brandenburg, *The Meek and the Mighty* (New York, 1977), p. 123.

9. L. Rozenberg, "Nemetskaia koloniia Semenovka, Kubanskoi Oblasti, Kavkazskago Otdela," *Sbornik materialov dlia opisaniia mestnostei i plemen Kavkaza* 27:162–85.

10. See the relevant section in the chapter on the political awakening of 1905.

11. Klaus, *Nashi kolonii,* p. 419. "Istoriia i statistika kolonii inostrannykh poselentsev v Rossii," *Zhurnal ministerstva gosudarstvennykh imushchestv* 54, pt. 1 (1855): 74. Peter Sinner, *Nemtsy Nizhnego Povolzh'ia* (Saratov, 1925), p. 12. As early as 1809, the Saratov Kontora proposed that some colonists be sent to the Saratov public school to study Russian; assuming its tutelage to be temporary, it foresaw the necessity of a Russian-trained cadre of officials. The Ministry of the Interior disapproved and suggested that families wishing to teach children Russian should send them to study in Russian schools in

neighboring towns. Russkii, "O narodnom obrazovanii v nemetskikh poseleniiakh Povolzh'ia," *Russkii vestnik*, August 1897, pp. 50–52.

12. *Polnoe sobranie zakonov Rossiiskoi Imperii*, second series, art 6,551 (Nov. 7, 1833), p. 643.

13. Russkii, "O narodnom obrazovanii v nemetskikh koloniiakh Povolzh'ia," *Russkii vestnik*, September 1897, pp. 130–34. "O nemetskikh shkolakh v Kamyshinskom Uezde," *Saratovskii dnevnik*, no. 144, 1888, p. 2, and no. 153, 1888, p. 2.

14. Margeret Woltner, "Wolgadeutsche Schulprobleme," *Osteuropa* 10 (1934–35): 621.

15. *Saratowsche deutsche Zeitung*, July 13, 1865, p. 576. *Otzyvy korrespondentov tekushchei statistiki po nekotorym voprosam sel'skoi zhizni Saratovskoi Gubernii*, vol. 1 (Saratov, 1902), p. 25. *Sel'skokhoziaistvennyi listok Kamyshinskago Uezdnago Zemstva*, March 1909, pp. 12–14.

16. Sinner, *Nemtsy Nizhnego Povolzh'ia*, p. 18.

17. V. O. Zherebtsov, *Vospominaniia o saratovskoi pervoi muzhskoi gimnazii* (Saratov, 1912), pp. 53–54. For information on the Ekaterinenstadt gymnasium, see *Saratowsche deutsche Zeitung*, Jan. 4, 1866, pp. 3–4.

18. G. Dinges, "K izucheniiu govorov povolzhskikh Nemtsev," *Uchenye Zapiski Saratovskogo Gosudarstvennogo Universiteta imeni N. G. Chernyshevskogo* 4, no. 3 (1925): 12–20. Bonwetsch, *Geschichte*, p. 84.

19 . D. Mordovtsev, "Neskol'ko slov o narodnosti nemetskikh kolonistov Saratovskoi Gubernii," *Saratovskiia gubernskiia vedomosti*, no. 19, 1858, pp. 94–95.

20. V. M. Zhirmunskii, "Problemy kolonial'nyi dialektologii," *Iazyk i literature*, no. 3, 1929, pp. 180–81.

21. Dinges, "K izucheniiu govorov povolzhskikh Nemtsev," p. 14.

22. Georg Cleinow, "Die deutsche Wolga-Republik," *Osteuropa* 2 (1926–27): 130–32. Oswald Zienau, "Kultureller und wirtschaftlicher Wiederaufbau in der deutschen Wolgarepublik," *Osteuropa* 3 (1927–28): 46.

23. For a fuller discussion of this from a linguist's perspective see Paul Schach, "Facts and Fallacies about Russian-German Dialects," *Journal of the American Historical Society of Germans from Russia* 7 (Spring 1984): 21–25.

24. Praetorius, *Galka*, p. 35. *Otzyvy korrespondentov tekushchei statistiki*, 1:32.

25. Tsentral'nyi statisticheskii komitet, *Pervaia vseobshchaia perepis' naseleniia Rossiiskoi Imperii, 1897 g.*, 36:90–95. How literate the colonists were in either language is impossible to ascertain — that is, whether they were functionally literate (able to read and understand an unfamiliar text) or nonfunctionally literate (able to read only a familiar text).

26. Therefore, statements by scholars such as Adam Giesinger that the Volga Germans preserved an eighteenth-century cultural *Deutschtum* "almost unaffected by their Russian environment" are untenable. The statement was made by Giesinger in his review of Aleksander Mrdjenovic's master's thesis in the *Journal of the American Historical Society of Germans from Russia* 1 (Spring 1978): 71.

27. Eduard Seib, "Der Wolgadeutsche im Spiegel seines Brauchtums," p. 181. *Otzyvy korrespondentov tekushchei*, 1:42.

28. Kamyshinskoe uezdnoe zemstvo, *Postanovleniia kamyshinskogo uezdnogo zemskogo sobraniia*, Oct. 9–11, 1879, pp.

252–53. See also A. Ia. Maizul's, *Putevoditel' pog. Saratovu* (Saratov, 1917), p. 13.

29. See Henry, "Adam Ebel," p. 13.

30. Kloberdanz, "The Volga German Catholic Life Cycle," p. 190. The Soviet government's brutal physical dispersal of the Volga Germans during World War II rapidly accelerated their assimilation: "Since their dispersal, most Germans live in small farming villages where the dominant language is Russian. Soviet statistics show that the Germans are being assimilated faster than any other minority. In 1959, 75 per cent of the ethnic Germans gave German as their first language. By 1970, it was 66.8 per cent, and the 1979 census reported only 56 per cent." *New York Times*, Nov. 8, 1981, p. 6.

31. Athanasius Karlin, "The Coming of the First Volga German Catholics to America," trans. Emma S. Haynes, *Journal of the American Historical Society of Germans from Russia* 1 (Winter 1978): 62. Kloberdanz, "The Volga German Catholic Life Cycle," p. 9.

32. W. H. Bruford, *Germany in the Eighteenth Century: The Social Background of the Literary Revival* (Cambridge, 1952), pp. 297–98.

33. "Probably German disunity is the basic reason that Eastern European German minorities were rarely distrusted by dominant elites (although often denounced for their overbearing manner by lesser figures) until the formation of the Second Reich. After that, for understandable reasons, it was all downhill for the diaspora Germans until the expulsions at the end of World War II." John A. Armstrong, "Mobilized and Proletarian Diasporas," *American Political Science Review* 70 (1976): 401.

34. Klaus, *Nashi kolonii,* p. 447.

35. M., "Nemtsy na Povolzh'e," *Russkii mir,* Nov. 9, 1872, p. 1; Nov. 10, 1872, p. 1; Nov. 13, 1872, p. 2.

36. S. M., "Chto nemtsy zdorovo, to russkomu smert'," *Otechestvennyia zapiski,* September 1873, pp. 311–74. *Russkii mir* summarized this article on the front page of its no. 263 (October 6), 1873 edition.

37. For a detailed study of Russian foreign policy for this period and the growing anti-German feeling in Russia, one should consult George F. Kennan. *The Decline of Bismarck's European Order* (Princeton, 1979), p. 399.

38. A. A. Velitsyn, "Dukhovnaia zhizn' nashikh nemetskikh kolonii," *Russkii vestnik,* March 1890, p. 238.

39. Their articles no longer simply addressed the foreign settlers as colonists or foreign settlers, but stressed their ethnic roots by referring to them as Germans or German colonists. "Saratovskie nemtsy," *Moskovskiia vedomosti,* Oct. 26, 1891, p. 5; "Nemetskiia zavoevaniia v iugo-zapadnom krae," *Moskovskiia vedomosti,* Oct. 1, 1891, p. 4. For other articles see *Moskovskiia vedomosti,* May 3, 1891, p. 3; May 21, 1891, p. 4; May 29, 1891, p. 2; Aug. 23, 1891, p. 2; Feb. 12, 1892, p. 2; and Mar. 20 1892, p. 3.

40. A. A. Velitsyn, "Nemtsy na Volge," *Russkii vestnik,* April 1893, p. 182. See also "Dukhovnaia zhizn' nashikh nemetskikh kolonii," *Russkii vestnik,* March 1890, pp. 236–60; May 1890, pp. 212–34; September 1890, pp. 47–80. Velitsyn's serialized articles, including others on the Black Sea Germans, were republished in the book *Nemtsy v Rossii* (St. Petersburg, 1893).

41. Petr P. Semenov-Tian-Shanskii (ed.), *Rossiia: Polnoe geograficheskoe opisanie nashego otechestva,* vol. 6: *Srednee i nizhnee Povolzh'e i Zavolzh'e* (St. Petersburg, 1901), p. 161. A. Isaev defended the southern Germans living in the Ukraine, but none rose to the defense of the Volga Germans. A. Isaev,

"Zametki o nemetskikh koloniiakh v Rossii, *Russkaia mysl'* December 1894, pp. 87–112.

42. This question is examined in Winfred Kohls's article "Beitrag zur Geschichte der deutschen Kolonisten in Russland, eine Untersuchung russische Pressepolemik und der deutschen diplomatischen Berichte aus der St. Petersburger Amtszeit des Botschafters von Schweinitz," in *Archivalische Fundstucke zu den russisch-deutschen Beziehungen,* ed. Erich Amburger (Berlin, 1973), pp. 152–57.

43. Goniasinskii, "Selo Iagodnaia Poliana," *Saratovskiia gubernskiia vedomosti,* Apr. 28, 1894, p. 2. B. H. Sumner was one of the few scholars to mention the few connections the Volga Germans had either with Germany or the Baltic German landowners; see his *A Short History of Russia,* 2d ed. rev. (New York, 1949), p. 33.

44. S. Shcheglov, "Ocherki goroda Kamyshina i ego uezda" *Saratovskiia gubernskiia vedomosti,* Feb. 18, 1890, p. 106.

45. Stephen Steinberg, *The Ethnic Myth* (New York, 1981), p. 170. A Volga German writing in 1906 expressed almost exactly these points in refuting official statements aimed at instigating Russian peasant-Volga German ill will; he argued to the contrary that their common problems and interests made them natural allies if not close friends. Held, "Feindseligkeit," *Unsere Zeit,* Apr. 12, 1906, p. 3.

46. The clothes of peasants and colonists were quite similar. As early as 1816 the Saratov Kontora reported that even the cut of the male colonists' clothing was like the Russian peasantry's. Grigorii Pisarevskii, *Khoziaistvo i forma zemlevladeniia v koloniiakh Povolzh'ia v XVIII-m i v pervoi chetverti XIX-go veka* (Rostov-on-Don, 1916), p. 67. Males wore a plain, loose shirt belted at the waist over trousers. It was not customary to wear the shirt tucked in; only some urban residents did this. If necessary, a caftan or long coat would be worn over the shirt. In winter, a sheepskin coat became the outer garment. In the summer, the men wore a billed cap, which was replaced by a fur cap with earflaps in winter. Calf-high felt boots *(valenki)* were common in winter, but durring the summer men often went barefoot. Women wore the ubiquitous scarf and a loose fitting smock, which might also have a sleeveless jumper *(sarafan)* worn over it. Few cottages were without their samovar.

47. P. Dvornikov and S. Sokolov, *Geografiia Rossiiskoi Imperii,* 2d ed. (Moscow, 1913), p. 218; Maria Bock, *Vospominaniia o moem ottse P. A. Stolypina* (New York, 1953), pp. 119–24. The Russian government's impression — or one might more accurately say obsession — with the neatness of the colonies can be seen in most reports, even those of the military. See for example, *Voenno-statisticheskoe obozrenie Rossiiskoi Imperii* (St. Petersburg, 1853), 5, pt. 3: 100.

48. Goniasinskii, "Selo Iagodnaia Poliana," *Saratovskiia gubernskiia vedomosti,* Apr. 28, 1894, pp. 2–3.

49. Saratovskii gubernskii statisticheskii komitet, *Saratovskii sbornik,* vol. 2 (Saratov, 1882), p. 244.

50. A. N. Minkh, *Narodnye obychai, sueveriia, predrassudki i obriady krest'ian Saratovskoi Gubernii* (St. Petersburg, 1890), pp. 3–11. This survey of peasant life conducted between 1861 and 1881 favorably contrasted the colonists' life-style with that of the other peasants residing in the province.

51. "Khoziaistvo i zhizn' u nemtsev kolonistov i russkikh," *Saratovskiia gubernskiia*

vedomosti, Oct. 29, 1895, p. 3; Haller, *Vospominaniia,* p. 44.

52. "Nemetskiia kolonii Nikolaevskago U., Samarskoi Gubernii," *Saratovskiia gubernskiia vedomosti,* Apr. 12, 1890, p. 203.

53. Transcript of the oral interview of Amalie Klein, p. 58. In 1985, a Volga German emigrant still living in the United States wrote, "From discussions with the younger people and the articles that have been printed in earlier issues of the *Journal [of the American Historical Society of Germans from Russia],* [I feel that] many people get the idea that we were a united village of Germans who were all being repressed by the Russian folk, but that is far from actuality." Conrad Brill, "Farewell to Norka," *Journal of the American Historical Society of Germans from Russia* 8 (Winter 1985): 57.

54. Samarskoe gubernskoe zemstvo, *Sbornik statisticheskikh svedenii po Samarskoi Gubernii,* vol. 6 (Samara, 1889), p. 230.

55. Richard G. Robbins, Jr., "Russia's System of Food Supply Relief on the Eve of the Famine of 1891–92," *Agricultural History* 45, no. 4 (October 1971); 265.

56. Samarskoe gubernskoe zemstvo, *Sbornik statisticheskikh svedenii,* 7:54. Inclusion of the tiny number of Mennonite households in the German category will somewhat skew these figures. The Mennonites had much larger land and livestock holdings than those of the Volga Germans and belonged in the large land and livestock-holding categories.

57. Novouzenskoe uezdnoe zemstvo, *Novouzenskii uezd v estestvenno-istoricheskom i khoziaistvennom otnoshenii; Po dannym obsledovaniia 1908 g.,* 2 vols. (Novouzensk, 1912–13), 1:138–228.

58. "Sel. Talovka, Sosnovskoi Vol.," *Privolzhskaia gazeta,* Feb. 23, 1906, p. 3. Saratovskoe gubernskoe zemstvo, *Sbornik statisticheskikh svedenii,* 11:215.

59. Saratovskoe gubernskoe zemstvo, *Sbornik statisticheskikh svedenii,* 11:32. *Saratovskii listok,* Aug. 8, 1891, p. 2.

Chapter Four

1. "Istoriia i statistika kolonii inostrannykh poselentsev v Rossii," *Zhurnal ministerstva gosudarstvennykh imushchestv* 55, pt. 1 (1855): 88. The difficulty of maintaining livestock is discussed in S. B., "Luga po Volge i neobkhodimost' ikh uluchsheniia," *Sbornik sel'sko-khoziaistvennykh svedenii,* no. 4, 1909, pp. 28–37.

2. *Saratowsche deutsche Zeitung,* Sept. 28, 1865, p. 757; Sinner, *Nemtsy Nizhnego Povolzh'ia,* p. 7; *Unsere Zeit,* Mar. 22, 1906, p. 1; see also Apr. 12, 1906, p. 1. P. Shlegel', "Zemskaia agronomiia i naselenie," *Sbornik sel'sko-khoziaistvennykh svedenii,* no. 3, 1909 p. 13. See also Kolonist J. St., "Aufruf an meine Mitkolonisten," *Saratowsche deutsche Zeitung,* Nov. 5, 1865, pp. 845–46.

3. Saratovskoe gubernskoe zemstvo, *Sbornik statisticheskikh svedenii,* 11:204.

4. Ibid., 3:4–12. Praetorius, *Galka,* p. 47.

5. "Nemetskiia kolonii Nikolaevskago U.," *Saratovskiia gubernskiia vedomosti,* Apr. 12, 1890, p. 202; Saratovskoe gubernskoe zemstvo, *Sbornik statisticheskikh svedenii,* 6:130.

6. K. V. Zalezskii, *Sel'sko-khoziaistvennaia statistika Saratovskoi Gubernii* (St. Petersburg, 1859), pp. 122–23.

7. Otsenochno-statisticheskoe otdelenie saratovskago gubernskago zemstva, *Materialy dlia otsenki zemel' Saratovskoi Gubernii*, 3 vols. (Saratov, 1905–10), 3, pt. 1:65; E. Panfilov, "Vozmozhnyia izmeneniia v sistemakh polevodstva i sevooborotakh v Novouzenskom Uezde," *Sbornik sel'sko-khoziaistvennykh svedenii*, no. 5, 1909, pp. 54–55; Samarskoe gubernskoe zemstvo, *Sbornik statisticheskikh svedenii*, 6:217–19; Lehmann and Parvus, *Das hungernde Russland*, p. 257.

8. *Saratovskaia sel'sko-khoziaistvennaia i torgovo-promyshlennaia zemskaia nedelia*, Mar. 4, 1895, p. 183.

9. G. I. Kolesnikov, *Kul'turnoe khoziaistvo v nekul'turnom krae* (Saratov, 1908), p. 24. A. A. Klopov, *Ocherk mukomol'no-krupchatnoi promyshlennosti v Povolzh'e v 1892/3 g.* (Tver, 1894), p. 12. In *Die Deutschen im Zarenreich*, Fleischhauer erred seriously by including the Mennonites with the colonists, which is somewhat like comparing apples and oranges.

10. The physical environment, in addition to the different circumstances of settlement, exercised a strong influence on the development of diverse life-styles between the Volga and Black Sea foreign settlements. "Statisticheskiia svedeniia ob inostrannykh poseleniiakh v Rossii," *Zhurnal ministerstva vnutrennikh del* 28, no. 4 (1838): 23.

11. Numerous works discuss the colonists' farming techniques. E. Gross, *Avt. Sots. Sov. Resp. Nemtsev Povolzh'ia* (Pokrovsk, 1926), p. 52; Novouzenskoe uezdnoe zemstvo, *Novouzenskii uezd v estestvenno-istoriche skom i khoziaistvennom otnoshenii*, 2 vols. (Novouzensk, 1912–13), 1:120–27; Samarskoe gubernskoe zemstvo, *Sbornik statisticheskikh svedenii*, 6:225–27; Saratovskoe gubernskoe zemstvo, *Sbornik statisticheskikh svedenii*, 11:202–4; Praetorius, *Galka*, pp. 50–59. Transcript of the oral history interview of Anna Burkhard (Special Collections, Colorado State University Library), p. 19.

12. Klaus, "Obshchina-sobstvennik," pp. 73–74.

13. "Saratovskaia letopis'," *Saratovskii krai*, no. 1 (1893): 94. William Dando differentiated five famine zones in Russia, with Saratov being the focal point of one famine zone in which drought was a major factor. He reported nineteen famine years in the Saratov zone between 1871 and 1925; drought was the primary contributing factor in two out of three famines. W. A. Dando, "Man-Made Famines: Some Geographical Insights from an Exploratory of a Millennium of Russian Famines," *Ecology of Food and Nutrition* (London) 4 (1976): 227.

14. A graphic depiction of the suffering in the colonies is found in Rudolph Blankenburg, *Philadelphia and the Russian Famine of 1891 and 1892* (Philadelphia, 1892), pp. 37–47. The records of one colony, Galka, reveal the seriousness of agricultural depression of the 1880s and 1890s. Reports show that *each* of the preceding three decades (1850–80) had seen at least two bumper harvests; however, the last two decades of the nineteenth century yielded only *one* bumper harvest, in 1896, in that colony. Praetorius, *Galka*, p. 55.

15. Klopov, *Ocherk*, p. 22.

16. Klaus, "Obshchina-sobstvennik," p. 75; Gerhard Bonwetsch, *Geschichte*, p. 110.

17. Blankenburg, *Philadelphia and the Russian Famine*, pp. 41–42. See also the transcript of the oral history interview of Fred Ostwald, p. 1.

18. *Saratovskii listok*, Aug. 8, 1891, p. 2.

19. *Novoe vremia,* Aug. 5–17, 1898, p. 3.

20. This and the following quotations are from Statisticheskoe otdelenie pri samarskoi gubernskoi zemskoi uprave, *Sel'sko-khoziaistvennyi obzor Samarskoi Gubernii za 1898–1899 god,* vol. 2 (Samara, 1900), p. 68.

21. Dorothy Atkinson, *The End of the Russian Land Commune: 1905–1930* (Stanford, 1983), pp. 102–4.

22. Novouzenskoe uezdnoe zemstvo, *Novouzenskii uezd,* 1:127.

23. The crop failures of 1905–6 and their effects on the colonies are discussed in detail in Otsenochno-statisticheskoe otdelenie saratovskoi gubernskoi zemskoi upravy, *Sbornik svedenii po Saratovskoi Gubernii za 1906 god* (Saratov, 1906), 1:49–118 and 207–11; 2:186–87. See also *Saratowsche deutsche Zeitung,* July 5, 1906, p. 3; *Privolzhskaia gazeta,* Dec. 24, 1906, p. 3.

24. Alexis N. Antsiferov et al., *Russian Agriculture during the War* (New Haven, 1930), p. 57; Vladimir P. Timoshenko, *Agricultural Russia and the Wheat Problem* (Stanford, 1932), pp. 273–78. D. Slobodchikov (ed.), *Podvornoe i khutorskoe khoziaistvo v Samarskoi Gubernii,* vol. 1 (Samara, 1909), pp. 156–57. Annual fluctuations still plague this region, as indicated in 1984 when the Soviet government reported that hot, dry weather in the Lower Volga resulted in harvests on only 61 million acres compared with more than 80 million in 1983.

25. *Saratovskii vestnik,* Feb. 8, 1912, p. 3. E. K. Antipin, "Deiatel'nost' agronomov," *Sel'skokhoziaistvennyi listok Kamyshinskago Uezdnago Zemstva,* January 1915, p. 7.

26. S. Sinel'shchikov, "Kak mogut krest'iane obezpechit' urozhai na svoikh poliak i gde mozhno dostat' korm?" *Sbornik sel'sko-khoziaistvennykh svedenii,* no. 2, 1909, p. 9.

27. Saratovskoe gubernskoe zemstvo, *Sbornik statisticheskikh svedenii,* 11:229; Ministerstvo zemledeliia i gosudarstvennykh imushchestv, *Svod statisticheskikh svedenii po sel'skomu khoziaistvu Rossii k kontsu XIX veka,* 2 vols. (St. Petersburg, 1902), 1, pt. 3, table 7, p. 68; Saratovskoe gubernskoe zemstvo, *Sbornik svedenii po Saratovskoi Gubernii za 1902 god* (Saratov, 1904), p. 4; *Predvaritel'nye itogi vserossiiskoi sel'sko-khoziaistvennoi perepisi 1916 goda* (St. Petersburg, 1916), p. 126. Because of space limitations, only the major regional differences in colony agriculture will be discussed here. However, it should be mentioned that travelers frequently noted differences between the Protestant and Catholic settlements; no satisfactory explanation can be offered for these differences, because of the many variables. A government official sophomorically attributed it to Jesuit influence: "During church holidays, of which there are very many, the priests compel colonists to attend church and, what is more important, divert them from their agricultural work." Quoted in Grigorii G. Pisarevskii, *K istorii iezuitov v Rossii (veroispovednyi vopros v koloniiakh Povolzh'ia sto let tomu nazad)* (Warsaw, 1912), p. 11.

28. "Istoriia i statistika kolonii", p. 130; *Samarskiia gubernskiia vedomosti,* no. 11, 1853, p. 61; Semenov-Tian-Shanskii, *Rossiia,* 6:216.

29. The government's introduction of the potato in Saratov Province is discussed in Zalezskii, *Sel'sko-khoziaistvennaia statistika,* p. 172.

30. V. Shvetsov, "Sostoianie sadovodstva i ogorodnichestva v Kamyshinskom

Uezde," *Sel'sskokhoziaistvennyi listok Ka-myshinskago Uezdmago Zemstva*, July 1914, p. 194. "Saratovskiia kolonii," *Severnaia pchela*, Aug. 22, 1838, p. 751; "Istoriia i statistika kolonii" pp. 129–31; Praetorius, *Galka*, p. 53.

31. Saratovskoe gubernskoe zemstvo, *Sbornik statisticheskikh svedenii*, 11:167.

32. Ibid., 3:7–8. Saratovskii gubernskii statisticheskii komitet, *Materialy k opisaniiu Saratovskoi Gubernii* (Saratov, 1875), p. 23. The best study on this topic, providing the number of workers leaving each township for the 1899–1901 period, is by N. I. Teziakov, *Otkhozhie promysly i rynki naima sel'sko-khoziaistvennykh rabochikh v Saratovskoi Gubernii* (Voronezh, 1903).

33. Arguments for both positions can be found in Otsenochno-statisticheskoe otdelenie saratovskoi gubernskoi zemskoi upravy, *Sbornik svedenii po Saratovskoi Gubernii za 1905 god*, 3:72 and 222–25.

34. Ibid., p. 224.

35. For a more detailed examination of Volga German agriculture in this region, see my article, "Agricultural Conditions in the German Colonies of Novouzensk District, Samara Province, 1861–1914," *Slavonic and East European Review* 57 (October 1979): 531–55. Konstantin I. Popov, "Zapiski o Saratove K. I. Popova," *Saratovskii krai* 1 (1893): 222. The best study of this peasant resettlement is Nikolai M. Druzhinin, *Gosudarstvennye krest'iane i reforma P. D. Kiseleva*, 2 vols. (Moscow and Leningrad, 1946 and 1958).

36. "Putevyia zametki ot Saratova do Samary," *Samarskiia gubernskiia vedomosti*, July 5, 1852, p. 421.

37. Ministerstvo zemledeliia i gosudarstvennykh imushchestv, *Svod statisticheskikh svedenii*, 1, pt. 3, table 7, p. 68.

38. A. M. Fadeev, "Vospominaniia A. M. Fadeeva," *Russkii arkhiv*, no. 4, 1891, p. 482.

39. Beratz, *Die deutschen Kolonien*, p. 168.

40. S. Loshkarev, *Obozrenie Samarskoi Gubernii v khoziaistvennom otnoshenii* (Moscow, 1854), p. 53. Similar warnings about exploitative colony farming were printed in "Ocherk sel'skago khoziaistva samarskikh inostrannykh poselentsev v 1855 g.," *Samarskiia gubernskiia vedomosti*, no. 34 (1856), p. 151.

41. Jacob Wagele, no title, *Saratowsche deutsche Zeitung*, July 16, 1865, p. 581; Bonwetsch, *Geschichte*, p. 113.

42. Novouzenskoe uezdnoe zemstvo, *Novouzenskii uezd*, 1:127.

43. Ibid., 2:22. G. P. Sazonov, *Obzor deiatel'nosti zemstv po narodnomu prodovol'stviiu (1865–1892 gg.)*, vol. 2 (St. Petersburg, 1893), pp. 482–83.

44. Transcript of the oral history interview of Mrs. John Geringer (Special Collections, Colorado State University Library), pp. 20–21.

45. "Opisanie kolonii v Saratovskoi Gubernii poselennykh," *Sanktpeterburgskii zhurnal*, no. 7, 1805, p. 121.

46. Bauer and Sprenger, "O razvedenii tabaku v nemetskikh koloniiakh," *Samarskiia gubernskiia vedomosti*, July 20, 1863, p. 187; J. Kufeld, "Der Tabakbau in den Wolga-Kolonien: Seine Geschichte und sein trauriger Rückgang in den letzten Jahrzehnten," *Wolgadeutsche Monatshefte*, August 1923, pp. 210–11.

47. "Istoriia i statistika kolonii," p. 128. Statistics on colony tobacco production can be found in the following: A. D. Gorbunov, "O tabachnoi promyshlennosti v privolzhskom krae," *Saratovskiia gubernskiia vedomosti*, no. 45 (1858), pp. 269–70; no. 46,

pp. 274–75; no. 47, pp. 280–81;Bauer and Sprenger, "O razvedenii tabaku," pp. 187–89; "Vozdelyvanie tabaka v privol-zhskikh nemetskikh koloniiakh," *Narodnoe bogatstvo,* Nov. 5, 1863, p. 1050; *Saratowsche deutsche Zeitung,* Dec. 13, 1866, p. 775; Ivan Lishin, *Ocherk Nikolaevskago Uezda (Samarskoi Gubernii) v statisticheskom i sel'sko-khoziaistvennom otnosheniiakh* (St. Petersburg, 1880), p. 11.

48. I. Beletskii, "Sel'skokhoziaistvennyi ocherk Novouzenskago Uezda Samarskoi Gubernii," *Izvestiia Petrovskoi Zemledel'che-skoi i Lesnoi Akademii,* no. 2, 1888, pp. 127–28.

49. "Nemetskiia kolonii Nikolaevskago U.," *Saratovskiia gubernskiia vedomosti,* Apr. 12, 1890, p. 204.

50. Gobunov, "O tabachnoi promysh-lennosti," p. 270. For another view of the impact of the tax change, see Jacob and Irma Eichhorn, "Orlovskaia on the Volga," *Jour-nal of the American Historical Society of Germans from Russia* 3 (Spring 1980): 29.

51. A. M., "Obzor deiatel'nosti agro-nomov Novouzenskago Uezda," *Sbornik sel'sko-khoziaistvennykh svedenii* [Novou-zensk], no. 11–12, 1911, p. 562; G. Saar, "Saratovskaia promyshlennost' v 90-kh i v nach. 900-kh gg.," *Nizhne-volzhskoe oblastnoe nauchnoe obshchestvo kraevedeniia* 35, pt. 3 (1928): 14–15. A colonist also reported that tobacco made a recovery after the depres-sion and onerous tax legislation. See Bonwetsch, *Geschichte,* p. 119.

52. A. L., "O pol'ze torgovykh raste-nii," *Samarskiia gubernskiia vedomosti,* Nov. 28, 1853, p. 304.

53. "Istoriia i statistika kolonii," p. 129.

54. "Nemetskiia kolonii Nikolaevskago U.," p. 203.

55. Fourteen colonies in Paninskaia township accumulated debts totaling 156,500 rubles to individual lenders and 173,700 rubles to banks, amounting to an indebtedness of 28 rubles per worker or 51 rubles per household. Samarskoe gubern-skoe zemstvo, *Sbornik statisticheskikh svedenii* 6:230–37; Eichhorn, "Orlovskaia," p. 29.

56. A. S. Nifontov, *Zernovoe proiz-vodstvo Rossii vo vtoroi polovine XIX veka* (Mos-cow, 1974), pp. 315–16.

57. G. E. Fussell, *Farming Technique from Prehistoric to Modern Times* (London, 1965), p. 171.

58. Lingeman, *Small Town America,* p. 322.

59. Peter Lyashchenko, *History of the National Economy of Russia,* trans. L. M. Herman (New York, 1949), p. 468. Detailed grain price records for the Lower Volga re-gion during the 1870–1920 period were kept by John Abraham Bergman, a Mennonite settler. See V. Ziuriukin, "Prodazhnye tseny za period s 1870 po 1920 god na rynakh Nemrespubliki," *Sbornik statei i materialov* (Gosplan ASSR Nemtsev Povolzh'ia) 3 (1928): 139–64.

60. T. M. Kitanina, *Khlebnaia torgovlia Rossii v 1875–1914 gg.* (Leningrad, 1978), p. 24.

61. L. Martov, P. Maslov, and A. Potresov (eds.), *Obshchestvennoe dvizhenie v Rossii v nachale XX-go veka,* 4 vols. (St. Petersburg, 1909–11), 1:89–100.

62. A. A. Klopov, *Otchet po izsledovaniiu volzhskoi khlebnoi torgovli v 1886* (St. Petersburg, 1887), pp. 54–55. See also P. G. Ryndziunskii, *Utverzhdenie kapitalizma v Ros-sii 1850–1880 gg.* (Moscow, 1978), p. 110.

63. A. A. Klopov, *Materialy dlia izucheniia khlebnoi torgovli na Volge* (Moscow, 1886), pp. 69–70 and 104.

64. Klopov, *Otchet*, p. 6. Timoshenko, *Agricultural Russia*, pp. 296–97.

65. Klopov, *Otchet*, p. 15.

66. Detailed descriptions of Ekaterinenstadt can be found in these works: Klaus, "Obshchina-sobstvennik," pp. 76–77; Semenov-Tian-Shanskii, *Rossiia, 6:473;*, and V. Bekker, *Vospominaniia o Saratovskoi Gubernii* (Moscow, 1852), pp. 22–24.

67. Klopov, pp. 86–87.

68. Klopov, *Materialy*, pp. 35–36.

69. Semenov-Tian-Shanskii, *Rossiia*, 6:499–500.

70. Haller, *Vospominaniia*, pp. 25–27.

71. Klopov, *Materialy*, pp. 42–45 and 238.

72. Ibid., p. 44; Klopov, *Otchet*, pp. 37–42 and 142–44. See also Klopov, *Ocherk*, p. 87.

73. Klopov, *Otchet*, pp. 28–30. The southerly location of Rovnoe meant that most of its grain could be harvested earlier and shipped before the Volga closed in October, thus fewer granaries were required.

74. Saratovskii gubernskii statisticheskii komitet, *Saratovskii sbornik*, vol. 1 (Saratov, 1881), pp. 294–95, and *Materialy k opisaniiu Saratovskoi Gubernii*, p. 23.

75. Transcript of the oral history interview of Anna Burkard (Special Collections, Colorado State University Library), p. 3.

76. As recently as 1979, agricultural specialists complained of inadequate roads in Saratov Province, which caused collective farms to incur significant losses; six district centers still had no asphalt road connecting them to the provincial capital, Saratov. A. Vorotnikov, "Khlebnye marshruty," *Pravda*, Aug. 1, 1979, pp. 1–2.

77. Although aware of the railroad, a former colonist who emigrated in 1913 stated that he had never seen a railroad until he came to the United States. Untranscribed oral history interview of Peter Stoll (Special Collections, Colorado State University Library).

78. A. M. Solov'eva, *Zheleznodorozhnyi transport Rossii vo vtoroi polovine XIX v.* (Moscow, 1975), p. 165. The declining freight rates are credited with the expansion of the Saratov flour milling industry in the 1890s. Klopov, *Ocherk*, p. 138; Colin White, "The Impact of Russian Railway Construction on the Market for Grain in the 1860s and 1870s," in *Russian Transport*, eds. Leslie Symons and Colin White (London, 1975), pp. 40–42.

79. In the United States, railroad building in the Midwest boomed in the 1850s, so that by 1860 the American Western frontier was joined to the big cities of the Atlantic seaboard. In the 1860s, the abundant agricultural produce from the fertile soils of the Midwest flowed to the American Northeast and to Europe, especially to industrial Great Britain. As this railroad boom continued, it would entice many foreigners, including Volga Germans, with generous land grants.

80. Klopov, *Ocherk*, p. 159.

81. Timoshenko, *Agricultural Russia*, pp. 352–56.

82. Conrad Brill, "Farewell to Norka," *Journal of the American Historical Society of Germans from Russia* 8 (Summer 1985): 8.

83. Klopov, *Ocherk*, p. 159. Klopov, *Materialy*, pp. 170–171.

84. Saar, "Saratovskaia promyshlennost'" pp. 13–29.

85. Gubotdel VOC, *Ukazatel' torgovopromyshlennykh, kooperativnykh i dr. predpriiatiia po A.S.S.R.N.P. i Saratovskoi Gub. na 1927–28* (Saratov, 1927), p. 16.

86. P. I. Liashchenko, *Mukomol'naia promyshlennost' Rossii i inostrannye potrebitel'nye rynki* (St. Petersburg, 1909), p. 16. The details of Emanuel Borel's career can be found in *Friedensbote* 6 (June 1905): 238–42.

87. *Svod statisticheskikh dannykh o deistvuiushchikh mel'nitsakh v evropeiskoi Rossii* (St. Petersburg, 1895), pp. 10–12; Ministerstvo torgovli i promyshlennosti, *Sbornik svedenii o deistvuiushchikh v Rossii torgovykh domakh* (St. Petersburg, 1912), pp. 16–18.

88. *Mukomol'noe delo v Rossii,* 2d ed. rev. (Odessa, 1912), pp. 414–35.

89. Liashchenko, *Mukomol'naia promyshlennost' Rossii,* p. 16; *Sputnik po gorodu Saratovu* (Saratov, 1898), p. 3.

90. Löbsack, *Einsam Kampft das Wolgaland,* p. 72.

91. "Istoriia i statistika kolonii," p. 124.

92. Ministerstvo finansov, *Spisok mukomol'nykh mel'nits Rossii v 1908 godu* (St. Petersburg, 1909), pp. 41–44; Saratovskii gubernskii statisticheskii komitet, *Pamiatnaia knizhka Saratovskoi Gubernii na 1872 god* (Saratov, 1873), 2, pt. 2: 249.

93. Ch. D. S., "Landwirthschaftlichen Zustände auf den Wolga-Kolonien," *Saratowsche deutsche Zeitung,* Apr. 5, 1866, p. 199.

94. Löbsack, *Einsam Kampft das Wolgaland,* p. 14.

95. Kamyshinskoe uezdnoe zemstvo, *Postanovleniia,* Oct. 10–12, 1890, pp. 229–31.

96. Klopov, *Ocherk,* p. 158; *Saratowsche deutsche Zeitung,* May 20, 1866, p. 297.

97. *Mukomol'noe delo v Rossiia,* pp. 392–404.

98. Saratovskoe gubernskoe zemstvo, *Sbornik statisticheskikh svedenii,* 11:193–94.

Chapter Five

1. For further details regarding the original land legislation, see Bartlett, *Human Capital,* pp. 72–73. The topic is also thoroughlt discussed in Klaus, *Nashi kolonii,* p. 234. George Yaney's *The Urge to Mobilize* is a superb discussion of peasant agriculture and the Stolypin land reform, but in a passing reference he equates Volga German farming with that of the Mennonites and south Russian colonists (p. 167).

2. The best study of colony land tenure is Grigorii G. Pisarevskii, *Khoziaistvo i forma zemlevladeniia v koloniiakh Povolzh'ia v XVIII-m i v pervoi chetverti XIX-go veka* (Rostov-on-Don, 1916), p. 3.

3. Ibid.

4. Saratovskoe gubernskoe zemstvo, *Sbornik statisticheskikh svedenii,* 11:147. Although these were the reasons the colonists gave for the adoption of the new system, perhaps what lay implicitly behind their reasoning was the land reform of 1871, which assessed a land rent on each colony calculated on the total amount of land the colony held. Since the colony was collectively responsible for this rent, it would seem only proper that each family have a fair share of the land. Not all remained content with this backward system. Consolidation of land into one large allotment began to stir some colonists, who spoke out against the periodic division and reallocation of the scattered strips of land to each household. See, for example, G., "Erwiederung auf den Artikel 'Landwirthschaftliche Zustände in den Wolga Kolonien,'" *Saratowsche deutsche Zeitung,* May 24, 1866, p. 303; May 27, 1866, pp. 309–11; May 31, 1866, pp. 317–19; and June 3, 1866, p. 328.

5. Saratovskoe gubernskoe zemstvo, *Sbornik statisticheskikh svedenii, 11:147.*

6. *Saratovskaia sel'sko-khoziaistvennaia i torgovo-promyshlennaia zemskaia nedelia,* Mar. 4, 1895, p. 183.

7. *Polnoe sobranie zakonov Rossiiskoi Imperii,* first series, vol. 30, art. 23, 408 (Dec. 18, 1808), p. 729.

8. *Saratowsche deutsche Zeitung,* Feb. 23, 1865, p. 266; Ch. D. S., "Landwirthschaftliche Zustände auf den Wolga-Kolonien," *Saratowsche deutsche Zeitung,* Apr. 1, 1866, p. 191; Obervorsteher C. Schneider, "Schreiben des Obervorstehers des Ustkulalinschen Kreises Schneider an das Ustkulalinsche Kreisamt und den Landwirthschaftlichen Verein dieses Kreises," *Saratowsche deutsche Zeitung,* Aug. 10, 1865, p. 641.

9. A. A. Klaus, "O zaniatiiakh komissii," *Pravitel'stvennyi vestnik,* Jan. 20, 1870, pp. 1–4. The law of June 4, 1871, is found in *Polnoe sobranie zakonov Rossiiskoi Imperii,* second series, vol. 46, art. 49,705, pp. 818–19. The goal of rural private landownership was in essence abandoned in the 1890s, as legislation strengthened the commune and made private ownership more difficult. A law of December 1893 prohibited the sale of village lands by the commune without the approval of administrative officials, forbade the mortgage of peasant land, and decreed that such land could only be sold to peasants.

10. Saratovskii gubernskii statisticheskii komitet, *Pamiatnaia knizhka Saratovskoi Gubernii na 1872 god* (Saratov, 1873), 2, pt. 2:154–55.

11. Ibid. Saratovskoe gubernskoe zemstvo, *Sbornik statisticheskikh svedenii,* 11:71 and 248.

12. Semenov, "Krest'ianskie platezhi," p. 28.

13. As stated in the preceding chapter, redemption payments were so resented and despised that one cannot rule out that colonists were unwilling to pay them. Also, there is some indication that many hoped and believed the government would reduce redemption payments and cancel or reduce arrears, as it had done in 1881 when some former serfs had gotten so behind in payments; the former serfs of Kamyshin District had their annual redemption payments reduced by 8,000 rubles. In 1905, the government did in fact abolish redemption payments. See H. J. Habakkuk and M. Postan (eds.). *The Cambridge Economic History of Europe* (Cambridge, 1965), 6, pt. 2: 769.

14. Otsenochno-statisticheskoe otdelenie saratovskago gubernskago zemstva, *Materialy,* 1:144; Samarskoe gubernskoe zemstvo, *Sbornik statistcheskikh svedenii,* 7:266–77.

15. Saratovskoe gubernskoe zemstvo, *Sbornik statisticheskikh svedenii,* 11:222.

16. Immigration to America was an alternative only for the wealthier and nonindebted. The Volga German who emigrated had to pay his own expenses, as well as having all debts and taxes paid before the village assembly would release him. Households relinquished their allotments to the community without payment; therefore, the only way to raise capital was through the sale of personal possessions.

17. Frederick Merk, *History of the Westward Movement* (New York, 1979), pp. 439 and 472.

18. Ibid.

19. Richard Overton, *Burlington Route* (New York, 1965), pp. 184 and 283.

20. Merk, *History of the Westward Movement,* p. 472.

21. Saratovskoe gubernskoe zemstvo, *Sbornik statisticheskikh svedenii*, 11:222.

22. Ibid., p. 32.

23. Ibid., pp. 258–60.

24. Anfimov, *Rossiiskaia derevnia*, pp. 49–54.

25. Zalezskii, *Sel'sko-khoziaistvennaia statistika*, p. 19. Otsenochno-statisticheskoe otdelenie saratovskoi gubernskoi zemskoi upravy, *Sbornik svedenii po Saratovskoi Gubernii za 1899* (Saratov, 1900), 1:136.

26. Golubev, *Istoriko-statisticheskiia tablitsy*, p. 19.

27. Semenov, "Krest'ianskie platezhi," p. 47.

28. Individual Volga German household acquisition of land never amounted to much, and it was argued that the system of repartitional tenure militated against purchase. Among the Black Sea colonies, which practiced hereditary, nonrepartitional tenure and where there were extensive land purchases, each family had to look out for its own needs, knowing the commune would not be redividing the lands to take care of their sons' land needs. It followed from this argument that Volga German families, rather than purchase outside lands, depended on the commune to care for land needs by constantly redividing allotments among male members. Statisticheskii komitet Oblastnago Voiska Donskogo, *Sbornik Oblastnago Voiska Donskogo* (Novocherkassk, 1901), 1:99.

29. V. Vdovin, *Krest'ianskii pozemel'nyi bank, 1883–95 gg.* (Moscow, 1959), pp. 20–21.

30. P. N. Pershin, *Agrarnaia revoliutsiia v Rossii* (Moscow, 1966), 1:81. Golubev, *Istorik-statisticheskiia tablitsy*, p. 18.

31. Vdovin, *Krest'ianskii pozemel'nyi bank*, pp. 42–47. V. Obukhov, "Deiatel'-nost' krest'ianskago banka v Saratovskoi Gubernii," *Materialy k vorposu o nuzhdakh sel'sko-khoziaistvennoi promyshlennosti v Saratovskoi Gubernii* (Saratov, 1903), p. 16. Throughout the empire between 1906 and 1915, the Bank assisted peasants in the purchase of over 4.3 million dessiatinas of land. Thus, although as much in need of land as other peasants in the region, the Volga colonists remained at a serious disadvantage in obtaining land.

32. Nikolaevskoe uezdnoe zemskoe sobranie, *Postanovleniia nikolaevskogo uezdnogo zemskogo sobraniia*, 1906, p. 147. The letter is also recorded in the journal of the Novouzensk District Zemstvo, *Zhurnal novouzenskogo uezdnogo zemskogo sobraniia*, 1905, pp. 42–43. The government never deviated from this policy in regard to state lands, and made only a single exception in the sale of private lands in order to profit a court favorite. In 1902, the Bank granted the colony of Iagodnaia Poliana special permission to use the Peasant Land Bank to purchase 2,773 dessiatinas from Count Nesselrode for 300,576 rubles, or 108 rubles per dessiatina, a highly inflated price (a dessiatina of land sold for 61 rubles in neighboring Kamyshin District). The Bank acquiesced in this sale because Iagodnaia Poliana was the only prospective buyer bordering the Nesselrode property. For details, see *Saratower deutsche Zeitung*, Sept. 20, 1906, p. 2.

33. Antsiferov, *Russian Agriculture during the War*, p. 309. Atkinson, *The End of the Russian Land Commune*, p. 68.

34. Kolesnikov, *Kul'turnoe khoziaistvo*, p. 23.

35. *Saratower deutsche Zeitung*, Sept. 20, 1906, p. 1.

36. Samarskoe gubernskoe zemstvo, *Sbornik statisticheskikh svedenii*, 6:26 and 7:27.

This view is supported in *Statistiche skii komitet Oblastnago Voiska Donskogo, Sbornik Oblastnago Voiska Donskogo,* p. 99.

37. Novouzenskoe uezdnoe zemstvo, *Novouzenskii uezd,* 1:217. Tsentral'nyi statisticheskii komitet MVD, *Statistika zemlevladeniia 1905 g.* (St. Petersburg, 1906), 28:26. Adjustments had to be made to exclude Mennonite colonies listed in the Novouzensk District figure. In 1908, Kolesnikov gave the following size of household allotments in Novouzensk District: Mennonites (93 dessiatinas), state peasants (29.7), colonists (27.3), and former Crown peasants (19). See Kolesnikov, *Kul'turnoe khoziaistvo,* p. 48.

38. Tsentral'nyi statisticheskii komitet MVD, *Statistika zemlevladeniia 1905 g.,* 42:43.

39. Kolesnikov, *Kul'turnoe khoziaistvo,* pp. 11–13.

40. Klaus, *Nashi kolonii,* appendix 2, pp. 10–18. Tsentral'nyi statisticheskii komitet MVD, *Statistika zemlevladeniia 1905 g.,* 28:26.

41. Otsenochno-statisticheskoe otdelenie saratovskago gubernskago zemstva, *Materialy,* 1, pt. 2:418–19. *Privolzhskaia gazeta,* June 6, 1906, p. 3. A former settler succinctly described the dismal land situation by the turn of the century: "Yeah, and it [land] was divided every twelve years. And it got less. Every time they divided it, it got less. More people." Transcript of the oral history interview of Peter Stoll (Special Collections, Colorado State University Library), p. 8.

42. Tsentral'nyi statisticheskii komitet MVD, *Statistika zemlevladeniia 1906 g.,* 2:46–47.

43. *Saratovskii listok,* Aug. 11, 1905, p. 3; Aug. 17, p. 3.

44. Atkinson, *The End of the Russian Land Commune,* p. 70. Fleischhauer fails to note the credit problem and barely mentions the Stolypin land reform. *Die Deutschen im Zarenreich,* pp. 411–14.

45. Numerous colonists evidently adopted this course. Praetorius reported that in the colony of Galka and surrounding environs in southern Saratov Province several households, believing they could not make a satisfactory livelihood off the scattered strips they received, sold them and used the money to emigrate to America. Praetorius, *Galka,* p. 48; see also Sinner, *Nemtsy Nizhnego Povolzh'ia,* p. 7. Dorothy Atkinson's *The End of the Russian Land Commune* and George Yaney's *The Urge to Mobilize* provide details of the Stolypin reform.

46. Several authors present these colonist concerns: Praetorius, *Galka,* pp. 18–19; Sinner, *Nemtsy Nizhnego Povolzh'ia,* p. 7; and Bonwetsch, *Geschichte,* pp. 126–27.

47. Despite the pressure of the land captain, colony elders resisted swift conversion and often took a deliberate wait-and-see attitude before introducing the discussion of private landownership in the colony assembly. Praetorius, *Galka,* p. 19.

48. Praetorius stated that the meadowside colonies were the first to accept the reform, and that reports of their fair and satisfactory conversion to private landholding more than anything else helped to allay the colonists' worst fears of the reform. Ibid., p. 19. Atkinson, *The End of the Russian Land Commune,* pp. 79–83.

49. *Kamyshinskiia vesti,* Feb. 14, 1910, p. 1. See also "Perekhod k otrubnomu khoziaistvu," *Sel'skokhoziaistvennyi listok Kamyshinskago Uezdnago Zemstva,* May 1909, p. 14.

50. Samarskii gubernskii statisticheskii komitet, *Pamiatnaia knizhka Samarskoi Gubernii za 1912 god* (Samara, 1913), pp. 7–9. "Zemleustroistvo i pereselenie," *Sbornik*

sel'sko-khoziaistvennykh svedenii, no. 7, 1909, p. 30.

51. Shtentsel', "Stranichka iz proshlago (k istorii nemetskikh kolonii)," *Vestnik novouzenskago zemstva*, September–December 1913, p. 187.

52. Lyashchenko, a critic of the reform, derived the 25 percent figure, which many other respected scholars have accepted; however, Lyashchenko also pointed out that the Lower Volga was not one of the regions most attracted to the Stolypin reforms. There by 1915, 21.7 percent of households had actually separated from the community; however, this amounted to only 12.2 percent of the total former communally held allotment lands. Peter Lyashchenko, *History of the National Economy of Russia*, trans. L. M. Herman (New York, 1949), p. 748.

53. "Khutorskoe i otrubnoe khoziaistvo," *Privolzhskaia zhizn'*, Mar. 27, 1911, p. 2. The reluctance of rural elements in Saratov Province to change is also corroborated by Pershin, who showed that by 1917 only 16 percent of the households had adopted private ownership, while Dubrovskii cited a figure of 18.6 percent. P. N. Pershin, *Uchastkovoe zemlepol'zovanie v Rossii* (Moscow, 1922), p. 8; S. M. Dubrovskii, *Stolypinskaia zemel'naia reforma* (Moscow, 1963), p. 201. Opposition was so strong in some colonies that the elders tried to thwart the efforts of colonists requesting private consolidated plots. In Sevastianovka, the village elder tried to discredit the few reform advocates by informing the minister that the would-be separators belonged to a religious sect and by sending a scatching letter to the public school inspector, which accused the teacher of agitating the colonists. "Korrespondentsiia," *Privolzhskaia zhizn'*, July 8, 1910, p. 3.

54. Samarskii gubernskii statisticheskii komitet, *Pamiatnaia knizhka Samarskoi Gubernii za 1912 god*, pp. 3–4.

55. I. V. Chernyshev, *Obshchina posle 9 noiabria 1906 g.* (Petrograd, 1917), 2:10 and 2:121. The larger the settlement or colony, the more complex and difficult the implementation of the land reform, at least fairly, inexpensively, expeditiously, and efficiently. Costs appeared to be uppermost in the minds of many householders, who expressed concern that the community would be burdened with too many expenses, such as survey costs, litigation fees, and other assessments, and that the result would not substantially improve the economic condition of the community. While two Soviet sources indicate that considerable Volga German opposition arose against the Stolypin reforms, there is no indication, as they claim, that support and opposition divided along class lines, the kulaks versus the landless. Sinner, *Nemtsy Nizhnego Povolzh'ia*, p. 7; *Izvestiia*, June 2, 1918, p. 3, and July 9, 1918, p. 3.

56. Samarskii gubernskii statisticheskii komitet, *Pamiatnaia knizhka Samarskoi Gubernii na 1912 god*, p. 2. Chernyshev, *Obshchina posle 9 noiabria 1906 g.* 2:123.

Chapter Six

1. Otsenochno-statisticheskoe otdelenie saratovskoi gubernskoi zemskoi upravy, *Sbornik svedenii po Saratovskoi Gubernii za 1905 god*, 2, pt. 2:19.

2. Olga Crisp, *Studies in the Russian Economy before 1914* (London, 1976), p. 49. See also Mikhail I. Tugan-Baranovsky, *The Russian Factory in the Nineteenth Century*, trans. Arthur and Claora Levin (Homewood, Ill., 1970), pp. 171–215, 363–413.

3. Ministerstvo gosudarstvennykh imushchestv, *Otchety i izsledovaniia po kustarnoi promyshlennosti v Rossii* (St. Petersburg, 1892), 1:7–11. A similar conclusion was reached by the colonist Gottlieb Bauer, *Geschichte der deutschen Ansiedler an der Wolga, seit ihrer Einwanderung nach Russland bis zur Einfuhrung der allgemeinen Wehrpflicht (1762–1874)* (Saratov, 1908), pp. 56–58. Fleischhauer, in *Die Deutschen im Zarenreich* (pp. 316–29), lauds the industry of the Mennonites and south Russian colonies, but ignores the contributions of the Volga Germans.

4. The colony of Norka was located on the important Saratov to Don trade route (torgovyi trakt), which greatly facilitated Norka's becoming one of the most prosperous and largest trading colonies.

5. There has been much dispute over the character and occupations of the original colonists, especially over whether they were "fit" or "unfit" for agriculture. More to the point is that many of the settlers *did not wish to be peasants*. Most sources indicate that among the original settlers there were a large number of artisans and craftsmen, shoemakers, coopers, wagonmakers, blacksmiths, masons, potters, locksmiths, and tailors, to name just a few. Even Falk, who says that many of the settlers were "lazy and mischievous," indicated that there were artisans and craftsmen among them. J. P. Falk, "Zapiski puteshestviia Akademika Fal'ka," in *Polnoe sobranie uchenykh puteshestvii po Rossii* (St. Petersburg, 1824), 6:114. If Falk's remarks are correct, these people could have done peasant work, and in fact most of their recent ancestors had probably been peasants; but they would not have chosen peasant life, which they considered socially and economically backward. To go back to farming

would have been going backward, not forward, for these people. Therefore, if many of these individuals were forced to live as peasants, they must have done so grudgingly and with little enthusiasm for farming.

6. Flegont F. Dukhovnikov, "Nemtsy, drugie inostrantsy i prishlye liudi v Saratove," *Saratovskii krai* 1 (1893): 259. For further information about other Sarepta influences on the Volga colonies, see Bartlett, *Human Capital,* p. 104.

7. Tugan-Baranovsky, *The Russian Factory,* p. 178.

8. Ibid., p. 188.

9. "Statisticheskiia svedenii ob inostrannykh poseleniiakh v Rossii," *Zhurnal ministerstva vnutrennikh del* 28, no. 4 (1838): 58–59.

10. M. V., "Sarpinochnoe proizvodstvo v saratovskikh koloniiakh," *Trudy imperatorskago vol'nago ekonomicheskago obshchestva,* May 1874, p. 295.

11. Guch, "Fabrikatsiia sarpinki v nemetskikh koloniiakh," *Saratovskiia gubernskiia vedomosti,* Dec. 5, 1870, p. 2.

12. *Tekstil'noe delo v Rossii* (Odessa, 1910–11), pp. 465–68.

13. Ministerstvo gosudarstvennykh imushchestv, *Otchety i izsledovaniia,* 1:10.

14. P. N. Stepanov, *Saratovskaia sarpinka* (Marxstadt, 1920), p. 4.

15. *Tekstil'noe delo,* pp. 465–68.

16. Stepanov, *Saratovskaia sarpinka,* p. 6.

17. M. V., "Sarpinochnoe proizvodstvo," p. 301.

18. "Saratovskaia sarpinka na kazanskoi vystavke," *Saratovskiia gubernskiia vedomosti,* July 1, 1890, p. 390.

19. Brandenburg, *The Meek and the Mighty,* p. 24.

20. Semenov-Tian-Shanskii, *Rossiia,* 6:498.

21. *Obzor kustarnykh promyslov Rossii*, eds. D. A. Timiriazev and N. V. Ponomarev (St. Petersburg, 1902), p. 38.

22. Ministerstvo torgovli i promyshlennosti, *Svod otchetov fabrichnykh inspektorov za 1905 god* (St. Petersburg, 1908), p. 25.

23. *Tekstil'noe delo*, pp. 465–68.

24. Ministerstvo gosudarstvennykh imushchestv, *Otchety i izsledovaniia*, 1:19.

25. V. Gusev, "Sarpinochnoe proizvodstvo v russkikh seleniiakh Kamyshinskago Uezda," *Saratovskaia zemskaia nedelia*, February 1902, p. 124. *Sputnik po gorodu Saratovu* (Saratov, 1898), p. 133.

26. Gusev, "Sarpinochnoe proizvodstvo," pp. 125–29.

27. N. Bogdanov, "Materialy po obsledovaniiu sarpinochno-tkatskogo proisvodstva kooperativnykh tovarishchestv i trudovykh artelei Kamyshinskogo Kraia, Saratovskoi Gubernii," *Vestnik kustarnoi promyshlennosti*, December 1918, p. 20.

28. Numerous sources present rate and wage studies. The most reliable ones cited here are M. V., "Sarpinochnoe proizvodstvo," pp. 296–98; Semenov-Tian-Shanskii, *Rossiia*, 6:250–52; and Ministerstvo gosudarstvennykh imushchestv, *Otchety i izsledovaniia*, 1:11–15.

29. Kamyshinskoe uezdnoe zemskoe sobranie, "Doklad A. M. Loginova," *Postanovleniia kamyshinskogo uezdnogo zemskogo sobraniia*, Feb. 28, 1903, p. 2. For example, Eduard Seib indicated that weaving was commonly done among Saratov Province colonists, but he does not develop its economic importance. See Eduard Seib, "Der Wolgadeutsche im Spiegel seines Brauchtums," *Heimatbuch der Deutschen aus Russland* (1967–68), pp. 145–209.

30. M. V., "Sarpinochnoe proizvodstvo," p. 299.

31. Saratovskoe gubernskoe zemstvo, *Sbornik svedenii po Saratovskoi Gubernii za 1899* (Saratov, 1901), 2:8–30.

32. Saratovskoe gubernskoe zemstvo, *Sbornik statisticheskikh svedenii*, 11:17.

33. Transcript of the oral history interview of Lydia Miller (Special Collections, Colorado State University Library), p. 8.

34. Bogdanov, "Materialy," p. 21.

35. Semenov-Tian-Shanskii, *Rossiia*, 6:248.

36. M. Hagin, "Dehler eine Wolgadeutsche Siedlung," *Heimatbuch der Deutschen aus Russland* (1966), p. 85. Haller, *Vospominaniia*, pp. 25–27.

37. Saratovskoe gubernskoe zemstvo, *Sbornik statisticheskikh svedenii*, 11:202.

38. E. A. Iseev, "O merakh zemstva k uluchsheniiu zemledel'cheskago khoziaistva v gubernii," *Sbornik saratovskago zemstva*, Feburary 1893, p. 4.

39. M. A. Shevchenko, *Nizhnee Povolzh'e* (Moscow and Leningrad, 1929), pp. 89–90. Anfimov, *Rossiiskaia derevnia*, p. 64.

40. Ministerstvo gosudarstvennykh imushchestv, *Otchety i izsledovaniia*, 1:24–25.

41. *Mukomol'noe delo v Rossii*, 2d ed. rev. (Odessa, 1912), p. 409.

42. Shevchenko, *Nizhnee Povolzh'e*, p. 90. Semenov-Tian-Shanski, *Rossiia*, 6:248; Praetorius, *Galka*, p. 52.

43. Kamyshinskoe uezdnoe zemstvo, *Postanovleniia*, Feb. 28, 1903, pp. 1–3. Saratovskoe gubernskoe zemstvo, *Sbornik statisticheskikh svedenii*, 11, pt. 3:28.

44. E. Gross, *Avt. Sots. Sov. Resp. Nemtsev Povolzh'ia*, p. 80.

45. Kamyshinskoe uezdnoe zemstvo, *Postanovleniia*, Feb. 28, 1903, pp. 3–20.

46. Ibid., p. 29. Gross, *Avt. Sots. Sov. Resp. Nemtsev Povolzh'ia*, p. 80.

47. See the section in the chapter on the zemstvos.

48. Gubotdel VOC, *Ukazatel' torgovopromyshlennykh, kooperativnykh i dr. predpriiatiia po A.S.S.R.N.P. i Saratovskoi Gub. na 1927–28* (Saratov, 1927), p. 137.

49. Saratovskoe gubernskoe zemstvo, *Sbornik statisticheskikh svedenii*, 11:220.

50. Ibid., p. 355; Praetorius, *Galka*, p. 51.

51. Saratovskoe gubernskoe zemstvo, *Doklady saratovskoi gubernskoi zemskoi upravy ocherednomu saratovskomu gubernskomu zemskomu sobranniiu 2* (1892): 83–85. M. I. Semenov, "K kharakteristike kustarnoi promyshlennosti v Saratovskoi Gubernii," *Saratovskaia zemskaia nedelia,* May 23, 1891, appendix, p. 4.

52. M. I. Semenov, "K kharakteristike kustarnoi promyshlennosti v Saratovskoi Gubernii," *Saratovskaia zemskaia nedelia,* June 6, 1898, appendix, pp. 35–36. Semenov-Tian-Shanskii, *Rossiia,* 6:250.

53. Ministerstvo gosudarstvennykh imushchestv, *Otchety i izsledovaniia,* 1:26.

54. Ibid., pp. 21–23; Saratovskoe gubernskoe zemstvo, *Sbornik statisticheskikh svedenii,* 11:26–27.

55. Semenov-Tian-Shanskii, *Rossiia,* 6:247.

56. Ministerstvo gosudarstvennykh imushchestv, *Otchety i izsledovaniia,* 1:22.

57. Ibid., pp. 21–22; M. V., "O sel'skikh tekhnicheskikh proizvodstvakh v saratovskikh koloniiakh," *Trudy imperatorskago vol'nago ekonomicheskago obshchestva,* May 1873, pp. 525–26; and Semenov-Tian-Shanskii, *Rossiia,* 6:247.

58. Otsenochno-statisticheskoe otdelenie saratovskoi gubernskoi zemskoi upravy, *Sbornik svedenii po Saratovskoi Gubernii za 1905 god* (Saratov, 1906), 3:220.

Olga Crisp also found that the cost of raw materials and poor harvests, rather than factory competition, posed the greatest threat to cottage industry in Russia. Crisp, *Studies in the Russian Economy,* p. 49.

59. "Saratovskiia kolonii," *Severnaia pchela,* Aug. 22, 1838, p. 751. M. V., "O sel'skikh tekhnicheskikh proizvodstvakh," p. 525.

60. Otsenochno-statisticheskoe otdelenie saratovskago gubernskago zemstva, *Materialy,* 1:137. See also the letter of the editor in *Saratovskiia gubernskiia vedomosti,* Sept. 4, 1894, pp. 1–2.

61. Kamyshinskoe uezdnoe zemstvo, *Postanovleniia,* Sept. 24–28, 1868, pp. 144–49; Sept. 24–29, 1872, p. 63; Oct. 24–27, 1886, pp. 207–8.

62. Saratovskoe gubernskoe zemstvo, *Sbornik statisticheskikh svedenii,* 11:235–37.

63. V. I. Lenin, *Sochineniia,* 4th ed. (Moscow, 1950), 3:340. Lenin erred by asserting that this capitalist manufacturing "tore away the workers from the land." To the contrary, the colonists were "pushed" or "attracted" to weaving because of growing land scarcity and small and unreliable farm earnings. Likewise, the weavers of the colonies never left the village and land; only a few, those in the dye works and warping mills, became anything like factory laborers.

64. These figures came from the appendix in Beratz, *Die deutschen Kolonien,* pp. 304–11. V. I. Kovalevskii (ed.), *Rossiia v kontse XIX veka* (St. Petersburg, 1900), pp. 60–67. A description of Golyi Karamysh in 1900 is found in Semenov-Tian-Shanskii, *Rossiia,* 6:498.

65. Saratovskoe gubernskoe zemstvo, *Sbornik statisticheskikh svedenii,* 3:7–8. The colonies in Saratov Province rarely sent out more than 5 percent of their members as

seasonal laborers, whereas some neighboring peasant communes had as much as 30 to 40 percent of their population serving as seasonal laborers.

66 Kamyshinskoe uezdnoe zemstvo, *Postanovleniia*, 1895, p. 124.

67. According to 1865 grain trade information, the Reinach family was listed as being in the top twenty grain dealers at the Nizhnii Novgorod fair. See N. N. Ovsiannikov, *O torgovle na nizhegorodskoi iarmarke* (Nizhnii Novgorod, 1867), p. 85. In 1897, Emanuel Ivanovich Borel sold 6,476 dessiatinas of land near Kamyshin to former state peasants for 545,750 rubles. *Privolzhskaia gazeta*, June 7, 1906, p. 3.

68. *Unsere Zeit*, Mar. 26, 1906, p. 2. Several other Golyi Karamysh *fabrikanty* families each donated hundreds of rubles to the school. Andrew A. Bender, who had his factory and residence in Saratov, nevertheless was buried in Golyi Karamysh, his native settlement, and bequeathed it part of his fortune. *Saratovskii vestnik*, Nov. 14, 1917, p. 1.

Chapter Seven

1. This chapter supplements the excellent recent reassessment of the zemstvos which considerably altered the traditional view of the zemstvo as a liberal, progressive organ constantly struggling with an entrenched reactionary bureaucracy to defend and advance peasant interests. However, that study does not adequately treat the peasant zemstvos and provide a case study of a district zemstvo such as is undertaken in this chapter. Terence Emmons and Wayne Vucinich (eds.), *The Zemstvo in Russia* (Cambridge, 1982).

2. The zemstvo study confirmed that although the 1890 legislation modified the franchise, size, and composition of the zemstvo, such laws formed no watershed regarding zemstvo activities and programs. Ibid., p. 37.

3. Boris Veselovskii, *Istoriia zemstva za sorok let* (St. Petersburg, 1911), 4:214.

4. During the 1865–90 period, the colonists usually had only three deputies out of forty-six; after the 1890 "reform," they elected two of twenty-seven deputies. Rarely did a Nikolaevsk colonist get elected to the important executive board. However, the record of the Nikolaevsk District zemstvo paled compared with those of Kamyshin and Novouzensk, and was even labeled a "disgrace" (*pozor*). See *Privolzhskii krai*, May 21, 1906, p. 2.

5. Novouzenskoe uezdnoe zemstvo, *Novouzenskii uezd*, 1:134–38.

6. Saratovskii gubernskii statisticheskii komitet, *Materialy k opisaniiu Saratovskoi Gubernii*, p. 4.

7. Veselovskii cursorily discusses the peasant zemstvos, and although he admits that they differed significantly from gentry-dominated zemstvos, he remains skeptical of their "progressiveness," preferring to view peasants as being under direct or indirect gentry influence. See his *Istoriia zemstva*, 4:187–201.

8. Veselovskii's Marxist perspective caused him to commit some serious historical fallacies, one such being what he labeled the attempts in the 1880s of the Russian "bourgeoisie" to seize control of some district zemstvos. He asserts that the "middle class," initially indifferent to the zemstvos because of the zemstvos' limited taxing power over their enterprises, sought to take control of the zemstvos in the 1880s when the

zemstvos raised the valuation of their enterprises and thus their taxes. He cited the alleged "takeover" in 1884 by the sarpinka *fabrikanty* (weaving entrepreneurs) of the Kamyshin District zemstvo as an example. See Veselovskii, *Istoriia zemstva,* 3:312 and 4:201. In fact, the sarpinka "middle class" had voted in and controlled the first curia elections since the first election in 1866, primarily because there were so few gentry in the district and they rarely participated in the zemstvo. What brought the 1884 election notoriety was the low voter turnout, not a bourgeois conspiracy. Because of a low turnout of only eighteen landowners and an unusually high turnout of fifty-six *fabrikanty,* the wealthy colonists won seventeen of the twenty-three seats from the landowner curia. The provincial governor challenged the election results, alleging that the *fabrikanty* failed to meet the high property qualifications. The district zemstvo, however, verified both the property qualifications and the election results. See S. A. Priklonskii, *Ocherki samoupravleniia* (St. Petersburg, 1886), pp. 71–73.

9. Kamyshinskoe uezdnoe zemstvo (hereafter KUZ), *Postanovleniia,* Sept. 24–27, 1874, pp. 20–22; Oct. 24–27, 1886, pp. 62–63.

10. This information was obtained from the Kamyshin and Novouzensk zemstvo publications deposited in the Saltykov-Shchedrin Library in Leningrad, especially the *Postanovleniia* and *Zhurnaly* of these zemstvos.

11. *Privolzhskii krai,* Mar. 15, 1906, p. 2.

12. -yi, "Zemstvo posledniago vremeni," *Zemskoe delo,* July 5, 1910, p. 1051.

13. P. N. Stepanov, *Saratovskaia sarpinka* (Marxstadt, 1920), p. 7.

14. Novouzenskoe uezdnoe zemstvo, *Zhurnaly novouzenskago uezdnago zemskago sobraniia* (hereafter cited as NUZ, *ZNUZS*), 1906, p. 1.

15. KUZ, *Sbornik dokladov po ekonomicheskim voprosam* (Kamyshin, 1910), p. 118.

16. Otsenochno-statisticheskoe otdelenie saratovskoi gubernskoi zemskoi upravy, *Sbornik svedenii po Saratovskoi Gubernii za 1905* (Saratov, 1905), 2, pt. 2:26.

17. Praetorius, *Galka,* p. 60.

18. Otsenochno-statisticheskoe otdelenie saratovskoi gubernskoi zemskoi upravy, *Sbornik za 1905,* 2, pt. 2:50–51.

19. *Saratovskiia gubernskiia vedomosti,* Nov. 16, 1895, p. 1.

20. Veselovskii, *Istoriia zemstva,* 1:633–39 and 2:136.

21. Klaus, *Nashi kolonii,* p. 442; J., "Welchen Zweck hat die Centralschule?" *Saratowsche deutsche Zeitung,* Aug. 26, 1866, pp. 520–21. Ben Eklof's recent study challenges the view that the government and elites acted as the agents and promoters of peasant literacy. He shows that even before the expansion of schools in the late nineteenth century, peasants had achieved considerable literacy outside of official schools through such noninstitutional sources as tutors, unregistered schools, and cooperatives, noting that this was especially the case in Saratov Province. Ben Eklof, *Russian Peasant Schools* (Berkeley, 1986), pp. 471–82.

22. N. Kazanskii, "Narodnoe obrazovanie v Saratovskoi Gubernii," *Russkaia mysl',* August 1896, p. 42.

23. Veselovskii, *Istoriia zemstva,* 1:723.

24. Ibid.

25. NUZ, *ZNUZS,* 1869, p. 199.

26. KUZ, *Postanovleniia,* Oct. 24–27, 1886, pp. 47–48.

27. Russkii, "O narodnom obrazovanii v nemetskikh poseleniiakh Povolzh'ia," *Russkii vestnik,* August 1897, pp. 51–58.

28. Ibid., p. 143.

29. Eklof, *Russian Peasant Schools,* p. 84.

30. See Haller, *Vospominaniia,* pp. 63–64. Peter Sinner stated he learned little until leaving the parish school for the zemstvo-supported cooperative school in Schilling, which trained him in the fundamentals of reading, writing, and arithmetic. U.S. National Archives, Captured German Records, Microfilm T-38, roll 436.

31. D. I. Tikhomirov, *Obshchiia svedeniia o zemskikh shkolakh Saratovskoi Gubernii* (Saratov, 1899), p. 31.

32. The zemstvo schools spread rapidly throughout Russia; in 1880, of the 22,770 primary schools in Russia, 17,782 were maintained either entirely by a zemstvo or supported by the peasant communities with its help. Paul Miliukov, *History of Russia,* trans. Charles Markmann (New York, 1969), 3:43.

33. NUZ, *ZNUZS,* 1872, p. 107; 1886, p. 98.

34. Ibid., 1891, pp. 60–61.

35. Ibid., 1906, pp. 534–39. Although reliable statistics are unavailable, the trend in the Volga colonies was toward the expansion of zemstvo and public schools, and the contraction and demise of the church schools. By 1909, about 44 percent of all colony schools were zemstvo schools. In 1915, the Ministry of Public Education ordered the closure of the remaining church schools, alleging that they had inadequately and poorly trained teachers, and causing them to be converted into zemstvo schools. See NUZ, *ZNUZS,* 1915, p. 428; KUZ, *Postanovleniia,* 1915, pp. 20–21; Bonwetsch,

Geschichte, p, 125; and J. Müller, "Kurzer historischer Bericht über den Zuständ der Volksaufklärung im Gebiete der Wolgadeutschen," *Beitrage zur Heimatkunde des deutschen Wolgagebiets,* ed. Georgii G. Dinges (Pokrovsk, 1923), pp. 53–54.

36. G. U., *Nemetskiia tserkovnoprikhodskiia uchilishcha v Kamyshinskom Uezde* (Saratov, n.d.), p. 3.

37. J., "Welchen Zweck hat die Centralschule?" *Saratowsche deutsche Zeitung,* Aug. 26, 1866, p. 520.

38. KUZ, *Postanovleniia,* Oct. 24–27, 1886, p. 63.

39. Saraqtovskoe gubernskoe zemstvo, *Sbornik statisticheskikh svendenii,* 11:89.

40. "K voprosu o nemetskikh shkolakh," *Privolzhskaia zhizn',* Oct. 14, 1910, p. 1.

41. *Saratovskiia gubernskiia vedomosti,* Sept. 20, 1874, p. 2.

42. KUZ, *Postanovleniia,* Oct. 7–12, 1887, pp. 122–23.

43. J. Schäfer, "Eine neu zu errichtende Privatschule für Knaden zu Goloikaramysch," *Saratowsche deutsche Zeitung,* Feb. 26, 1865, p. 273.

44. The zemstvo refused one request for a zemstvo school because backing of the entire colony was absent. Colonist Andrew Miller ofGololobovka had agreed to assume all costs of a zemstvo school if the zemstvo would pay the 300-ruble teacher's salary. Since the colony assembly had not approved the petition for the zemstvo school, the district zemsto rejected Miller's offer. See KUZ, *Postanovleniia,* Sept. 29 – Oct. 5, 1871, p. 9.

45. Kazanskii, "Narodnoe obrazovanie," p. 52.

46. There is no satisfactory English equivalent for *real'noe uchilishche.* Although its

curriculum corresponded closely to the gymnasium's, the *real'noe uchilishche* did not prepare students for university education (offering no classical languages), but offered instead technical and professional training designed for careers in business, trades, commerce, agriculture, and industry.

47. KUZ, *Postanovleniia*, Nov. 1–2, 1873, pp. 8–13.

48. Ibid., Oct. 14–17, 1885, pp. 134–35.

49. KUZ, "Doklad zemskoi upravy kamyshinskomu ocherednomu uezdnomu zemskomu sobraniiu 1908," *Doklady i zhurnaly kamyshinskago ocherednago i ekstrennago zemskikh sobranii 1908 goda*, p. 5.

50. *Saratovskii vestnik*, Feb. 14, 1912, p. 5.

51. Haller, *Vospominaniia*, p. 68.

52. Veselovskii, *Istoriia zemstva*, 4:232.

53. G. I. Kolesnikov, "Novouzenskii Uezd (v ego proshlom i nastoiashchem)," *Vestnik novouzenskago zemstva*, March-April 1912, p. 35.

54. See Haller, *Vospominaniia*, p. 67. The name P. K. Haller was widely known in the Russian medical profession. Details of his medical career can be found in G. A. Shchetov, "Vrach P. K. Galler-vospitannik Tartuskogo Universiteta," *Tartu ulikooli ajaloo Kusimusi* 6 (1977): 70–79.

55. KUZ, *Postanovleniia*, Oct. 4–7, 1888, pp. 58–59.

56. *Privolzhskaia gazeta*, June 29, 1906, p. 3.

57. NUZ, *ZNUZS*, 1867, p. 51.

58. Saratovskaia uchenaia arkhivnaia komissiia, *K piatidesiatiletiiu zemskikh uchrezhdenii* (Saratov, 1913), p. 58.

59. KUZ, *Postanovleniia*, 1913, p. 6.

60. *Sanktpeterburgskiia vedomosti*, Jan. 27, 1866, p. 1.

61. *Pravitel'stvennyi vestnik*, Apr. 2, 1869, p. 3.

62. KUZ, *Sbornik dokladov po ekonomicheskim voprosam*, pp. 114–15.

63. E. K. Antipin, "Ob ekonomicheskikh meropriiatiiakh kamyshinskago zemstva v 1914 godu," *Sel'skokhoziaistvennyi listok Kamyshinskago Uezdnago Zemstva*, February 1915, p. 25.

64. Praetorius, *Galka*, p. 50.

65. Antipin, "Ob ekonomicheskikh meropriiatiiakh," p. 25.

66. Kolonist J. St., "Aufruf an meine Mitkolonisten," *Saratowsche deutsche Zeitung*, Nov. 5, 1865, p. 846. Saratovskoe gubernskoe zemstvo, *Sbornik statisticheskikh svedenii*, 11:204.

67. Veselovskii, *Istoriia zemstva*, 2:136, 396–97, and 404.

68. "Agronomicheskoe i gidrotekhnicheskoe biuro pri novouzenskoi uezdnoi zemskoi uprave," *Vestnik novouzenskago zemstva*, January–February 1912, pp. 174–78.

69. Eduard Seib, "Der Wolgadeutsche im Spiegel seines Brauchtums," *Heimatbuch der Deutschen aus Russland* (1967–68), p. 181.

70. Antipin, "Ob ekonomicheskikh meropriiatiiakh," p. 24.

71. Praetorius, *Galka*, p. 60.

72. The *Vestnik novouzenskago zemstva* and *Sel'skokhoziaistvennyi listok Kamyshinskago Uezdnago Zemstva* continued publication in side-by-side Russian and German until 1915, when the government's anti-German policies prohibited continued publication in German.

73. Antipin, "Ob ekonomicheskikh meropriiatiiakh," p. 25.

74. KUZ, *Postanovleniia*, Feb. 28, 1903, p. 20.

75. KUZ, *Sbornik dokladov po ekonomic-heskim voprosam*, pp. 308–10.

76. Ibid., pp. 143–46.

77. Veselovskii, *Istoriia zemstva*, 2:257.

78. Novouzenskoe uezdnoe zemstvo, *Proizvodstvo masterskikh novouzenskago uezdnago zemstva* (Saratov, 1913), pp. 1–34. NUZ, *ZNUZS*, 1905, pp. 1287–88.

79. Novouzenskoe uezdnoe zemstvo, *Proizvodstvo masterskikh*, pp. 36–39.

80. For a fuller discussion of the zemstvos and food provisioning, see the excellent account given in Veselovskii, *Istoriia zemstva*, 2:295–358.

81. *Polnoe sobranie zakonov Rossiiskoi Imperii*, first series, vol. 26 (1800), p. 307.

82. Veselovskii, *Istoriia zemstva*, 2:223.

83. KUZ, *Postanovleniia*, Aug. 18–19, 1880, pp. 3–4.

84. Another indicator of the growth of the "third element" is a comparison of zemstvo expenditures, much of which went to salaries. The decade of the 1890s, despite a number of bad harvest years, witnessed a significant growth in zemstvo expenditures. See figures in Veselovskii, *Istoriia zemstva*, 1:633–34.

85. Praetorius, *Galka*, pp. 44–60.

86. In 1915 the Novouzensk zemstvo awarded one-third of postprimary education stipends to Volga German children, with German girls receiving one-third of them. The origins of these Volga German students are also interesting; most of their parents were zemstvo teachers or village clerks. NUZ, *ZNUZS*, 1915, pp. 146–47. Early on, the colonists' children competed for zemstvo stipends; 80 percent of applicants for Novouzensk zemstvo stipends to teacher-training schools were Volga German youth. NUZ, *ZNUZS*, 1872, pp. 62–63.

87. See KUZ, *Postanovleniia*, 1881, p. 133, and 1882, p. 95.

Chapter Eight

1. For greater detail, see Thomas Fallows, "Forging the Zemstvo Movement: Liberalism and Radicalism on the Volga, 1890–1905" (Ph.D. dissertation, Harvard University, 1981).

2. These points have been discussed in detail in the "Society" and "Land Question" chapters. See also Martov, Maslov, and Potresov, *Obshchestvennoe dvizhenie*, 1:250.

3. *Saratovskii dnevnik*, May 9, 1905, p. 2.

4. Otsenochno-statisticheskoe otdelenie saratovskoi gubernskoi zemskoi upravy, *Sbornik svedenii po Saratovskoi Gubernii za 1905 god*, 2:41–42.

5. *Saratower deutsche Zeitung*, Aug. 30, 1906, p. 2.

6. See Thaden's *Russification in the Baltic Provinces and Finland*, pp. 72–73, for a discussion of the Baltic Province protests against the government's attempts to Russify schools there.

7. Details about the administrative implementation of this policy are included in the zemstvo chapter.

8. P. Luppov, *Nemetskiia nachal'nyia shkoly v Rossii* (Petrograd, 1916), pp. 10–33; A. Gorodetskii, "Nemetskiia shkoly," *Kamyshinskii ezhenedel'nik*, Feb. 5, 1906, p. 2; and G. U., *Nemetskiia tserkovno-prikhodskiia uchilishcha*, pp. 2–4. The struggle between the supporters of secular and religious education was not confined to the colonies, but became acute throughout Russia during the last two decades of the nineteenth century. Scott Seregny discusses this

conflict in Saratov Province in his article, "Politics and the Rural Intelligentsia in Russia: A Biographical Sketch of Stepan Anikin, 1869–1919," *Russian History* 7, pts. 1–2 (1980): 169–200.

9. To worship in another language was considered a sacrilege, and in the American congregations of Volga German immigrants many acrimonious disputes arose when pressure built to offer services in English.

10. Sinner, *Nemtsy Nizhnego Povolzh'ia*, p. 12.

11. G. U., *Nemetskiia tserkovnoprikhodskiia uchilishcha*, p. 1.

12. *Kamyshinkii vestnik*, Jan. 18, 1906, p. 3; Seregny, "Politics and the Rural Intelligentsia," pp. 175–76.

13. Ia. Ditts, "Putevyia zametki," *Kamyshinskii vestnik*, Jan. 1, 1906, p. 3.

14. KUZ, *Postanovleniia*, 1907, 4:2–3; and K. Dumler, "O nemetskikh shkolakh," *Saratovskii listok*, Aug. 13, 1905, p. 3. The complexity and divisiveness of the school issue in the colonies was cogently expressed by Pastor Seib in two lead newspaper articles. See *Unsere Zeit*, Mar. 16, 1906, p. 1, and Mar. 22, 1906, p. 2.

15. N. Speranskii (ed.), *1905 god v Samarskom Krae* (Samara, 1925), p. 402.

16. Ibid., p. 107, and Imperatorskoe vol'nago ekonomicheskago obshchestvo, *Agrarnoe dvizhenie v Rossii v 1905–1906 gg.* (St. Petersburg, 1908), 1:162.

17. Speranskii, *1905 god v Samarskom Krae*, p. 484.

18. *Saratovskii listok*, Apr. 29, 1906, p. 3.

19. In December 1905, conservative gentry landowners active in the provincial zemstvo formed the Party of Legal Order, which later became part of the Right Bloc and Octobrist coalition. Konstantin N. Grimm was one of its charter members, the only Volga German prominent in rightist politics. *Saratovskii listok*, Jan. 6, 1906, p. 2, and Jan. 15, 1906, p. 2.

20. U. S. National Archives, Captured German Records, Microfilm T-81, roll 436. Sinner's handwritten life story was translated and published by Adam Giesinger in the *Journal of the American Historical Society of Germans from Russia* 7 (Spring 1984): 17–20; 7 (Summer 1984): 25–31; and 7 (Fall 1984): 26–32.

21. Beginning with issue number 7, it was officially called *Saratower deutsche Zeitung*. Several Volga German newspapers bore the same title or a similar one. The first Volga German newspaper, *Saratower deutsche Zeitung*, appeared twice a week in Saratov between October 13, 1864, and December 30, 1866. Although intended to be a paper for the Volga Germans, it carried very little local colony news, but rather printed foreign and Russian news items, as well as news of the Saratov German community. Its editor, E. Ecke, intended to enlighten the bucolic, traditional Volga German farmers. The newspaper proved to be a financial failure because it had few subscribers and high printing costs. Between 1907 and 1915, the newspaper resurrected itself in several forms; its successive titles were *Deutsche Volkszeitung, Saratower deutsche Volkszeitung*, and *Volkszeitung*. However, these offshoots were more tightly censored and never enjoyed the freedom of the short-lived 1906 publication.

22. *Unsere Zeit*, Mar. 5, 1906, p. 1. According to Jeffrey Brooks, newspaper reading became quite common throughout the empire during the Russo-Japanese War among all peasants and lower-class urban residents as they earnestly sought war news. Jeffrey Brooks, *When Russia Learned to Read* (Princeton, 1985), p. 28.

23. *Saratower deutsche Zeitung,* Sept. 13, 1906, p. 2.

24. Sinner, *Nemtsy Nizhnego Povolzh'ia,* p. 13. A similar weekly, *Klemens,* was published by the Catholic diocese of Tiraspol in Saratov between 1897 and 1907.

25. *Privolzhskii krai,* Jan. 13, 1906, p. 2.

26. *Saratovskii dnevnik,* July 12, 1905, p. 3, and Dec. 24, 1905, p. 4.

27. Ditts, "Putevyia zametki," *Kamyshinskii vestnik,* Jan. 18, 1906, p. 2. Other examples of Dietz's anticlerical findings can be found in *Privolzhskii krai,* Oct. 7, 1905, p. 3; and *Saratower deutsche Zeitung,* May 24, 1906, p. 1, and June 14, 1906, p. 3.

28. As late as 1915, Karl Lindemann inaccurately described the political views of the Volga Germans by assuming political homogeneity among the colonists in Russia. See his *Zakony 2 fevralia i 13 dekabria 1915 g.* (Moscow, 1916), p. 177.

29. *Privolzhskaia gazeta,* Apr. 19, 1906, pp. 3–4.

30. "Deputat Ia. E. Ditts v roli obviniaemago i ego ob'iasnenie," *Privolzhskaia gazeta,* June 6, 1906, p. 3.

31. *Saratower deutsche Zeitung,* Feb. 8, 1906, p. 1.

32. *Privolzhskaia gazeta,* June 6, 1906, p. 3.

33. Ditts, "Putevyia zametki," *Kamyshinskii vestnik,* Feb. 2, 1906, p. 2.

34. Ia. Ditts, "Otnoshenii nashikh Nemtsev k Gos. Dume," *Privolzhskaia gazeta,* Mar. 14, 1906, pp. 2–3.

35. "Der Wahlkampf," *Saratower deutsche Zeitung,* Mar. 29, 1906, p. 1.

36. *Unsere Zeit,* Apr. 9, 1906, p. 1.

37. *Privolzhskii krai,* Feb. 7, 1906, p. 2.

38. S., "Golos uezda," *Privolzhskaia gazeta,* Apr. 12, 1906, p. 2; *Ibid.,* Apr. 9, 1906, p. 3; *Privolzhskii krai,* Apr. 11, 1906, p. 2.

39. *Privolzhskaia gazeta,* Apr. 16, 1906, p. 3, and June 4, 1906, p. 3. For information on the Samara delegates, see *Saratower deutsche Zeitung,* Mar. 15, 1906, p. 2.

40. *Privolzhskaia gazeta,* Apr. 19, 1906, p. 1.

41. M. M. Boiuovich, *Chleny Gosudarstvennoi Dumy: Pervyi sozyv* (Moscow, 1906), p. 294.

42. *Privolzhskaia gazeta,* Mar. 9, 1906, p. 3, and Apr. 19, 1906, pp. 3–4.

43. "Einkommensteuer," *Saratower deutsche Zeitung,* Mar. 29, 1906, p. 1, and June 14, 1906, p. 3.

44. Ditts, "Putevyia zametki," *Kamyshinskii vestnik,* Jan. 18, 1906, p. 2.

45. *Vestnik partii narodnoi svobody,* Aug. 30, 1906, p. 3.

46. *Samarskiia gubernskiia vedomosti,* Mar. 25, 1906, pp. 1–3. Ivan Fedorovich Schwab, who taught in a zemstvo school in Novouzensk District from 1908 to 1914, was one of the few to join the Bolshevik branch of the Russian Social Democratic Party; in January 1924 he became the chairman of the Central Executive Committee of the Volga German autonomous republic. Sinner, *Nemtsy Nizhnego Povolzh'ia,* p. 20.

47. Toivo U. Raun, "The Revolution of 1905 in the Baltic Provinces and Finland," *Slavic Review* 43, no. 3 (Fall 1984): 451–67.

48. Robert Daniels, *Russia* (Cambridge, Mass., 1985), p. 94.

Chapter Nine

1. "K bezporiadkam v Kamyshine," *Saratovskii listok,* Sept. 1, 1906, p. 3.

2. *Privolzhskii krai,* Jan. 18, 1907, p. 2; Feb. 1, 1907, p. 2.

3. *Privolzhskii krai,* Jan. 25, 1907, p. 2.

4. M. M. Boiuovich, *Chleny Gosudarstvennoi Dumy: Vtoroi sozyv* (Moscow, 1907), p. 289.

5. Irma and Jacob Eichhorn, "Orlovskaia on the Volga," *Journal of the American Historical Society of Germans from Russia* 3 (Spring 1980): 35; -yi, "Zemstvo posledniago vremeni," *Zemskoe delo,* July 5, 1910, p. 1051; M. M. Boiuovich, *Chleny Gosudarstvennoi Dumy: Tretii sozyv* (Moscow, 1907), pp. 285 and 298.

6. Scott Seregny addresses this point in a forthcoming article "Professional and Political Activism: The Teachers' Movement in Saratov Province, 1890–1914," which will appear in a monograph on Saratov Province coedited with Rex Wade.

7. Ibid.

8. *Privolzhskii krai,* Nov. 2, 1906, p. 3.

9. A. E. Chuev, "Doklad po narodnomu obrazovaniiu," *Doklady i zhurnaly Kam. ocherednogo i ekstrennago zemskikh sobranii 1908 goda,* n.d., pp. 1–8.

10. "Doklad o vseobshchem obuchenii detei v Kamyshinskom Uezde," *Doklady i zhurnaly Kam. ocherednogo i ekstrennago zemskikh sobranii 1908 goda,* Jan. 9, 1908, p. 6.

11. Ibid., pp. 2–8.

12. *Volkszeitung,* July 31, 1914, p. 2.

13. Anfimov, *Rossiiskaia derevnia;* Antsiferov, *Russian Agriculture during the War.*

14. An excellent discussion of the difficulty and problems of arriving at accurate mobilization and conscription figures for World War I is found in L. M. Gavrilov and V. V. Kutuzov, "Istoshchenie liudskikh reservov russkoi armii v 1917 g.," in *Pervaia mirovaia voina,* ed. A. L. Sidorov (Moscow, 1968), pp. 145–57.

15. Between the ages of twenty-one and forty-three, Russian males were liable for some form of military service. If drafted, they had a combined obligation of twenty-one years broken down as follows: three years on active duty, seven years in the first class reserve, eight years in the second class reserve, and three in the first class of the militia, or *opolchenie.* Those young males not conscripted were enrolled as members of the militia, which had two classes, the first of which could be mobilized during wartime, while the second performed auxiliary work in the rear. Those twenty-one year olds unconditionally exempted from conscription, the sole son or worker or married man, were put in the second class of the militia, which meant that they never had to face call-up and therefore sat out the war, because only the first class was mobilized during World War I. Golovine, *The Russian Army in the World War,* p. 52.

16. Löbsack, *Einsam Kampft das Wolgaland,* p. 145.

17. Tsentral'noe statisticheskoe upravlenie, Otdel voennoi statistiki, *Rossiia v mirovoi voine 1914–18 goda* (Moscow, 1925), p. 21.

18. Anfimov, *Rossiiskaia derevnia,* p. 192.

19. Ibid., pp. 200–204.

20. Ibid., pp. 223 and 283.

21. Ibid., p. 275.

22. Gross, *Avt. Sots. Sov. Resp. Nemtsev Povolzh'ia,* p. 10.

23. "Letters to Pauline," *Journal of the American Historical Society of Germans from Russia* 8 (Winter 1985): 29.

24. This is reference to publication of Gottlieb Beratz's *Die deutschen Kolonien,* which is discussed by M. Hagin, "Dehler eine Wolgadeutsche Siedlung," *Heimatbuch der Deutschen aus Russland* (1966), p. 87.

25. "Mestnaia khronika," *Vestnik novouzenskago zemstva,* Jan.–Feb. 1915, pp.

3, 149, and 184; *Novoe vremia*, Apr. 24–May 7, 1915, p. 7.

26. Examples of this anti-German literature are A. S., *Nemetskii vopros v russkoi publitsistike* (Moscow, 1915); A. A. Dunin', "V nemetskikh kogtiakh: Povest'," *Istoricheskii vestnik*, Jan. 1917, pp. 1–35; M. V. Murav'ev, ed., *"Nemetskoe zlo" sbornik statei posviashchennykh voprosu o bor'be s nashei "vnutrennei Germaniei"* (Moscow, 1915); A. M. Rennikov, *Zoloto Reina o Nemtsakh v Rossii* (Petrograd, 1915); Ivan Ivanovich Sergeev, *Mirnoe zavoevanie Rossii Nemtsami* (Petrograd, 1915); and Grigorii A. Yevreinov, *Rossiiskie Nemtsy* (Petrograd, 1915).

27. L. Shtrandt, *Kak vedut svoe khoziaistvo nemtsy Povolzh'ia* (Moscow, 1926), p. 4.

28. Baron Boris Nolde, *Russia in the Economic War* (New Haven, 1928), pp. 104–5.

29. See Sergei Shelukhin, *Nemetskaia kolonizatsiia na iuge Rossii* (Odessa, 1915); Kuzmin-Karavaev, "Voprosy vnutrennoi zhizni," *Vestnik Evropy*, Dec. 1914, p. 389.

30. See for example *Novoe vremia*, Jan. 4–17, 1915, p. 5; Jan. 6–19, p. 7; Jan. 7–21, p. 7; Jan. 24–Feb. 6, p. 15; July 6–19, p. 4; July 14–27, p. 6; and July 14–27, p. 6.

31. *Vechernee vremia*, Apr. 20–May 3, 1915, p. 4.

32. *Izvestiia*, June 2, 1918, p. 2.

33. A. A. Dunin', "Nemtsy v samarskikh stepiakh," *Istoricheskii vestnik*, Nov. 1915, pp. 543–58.

34. *Saratovskii listok*, Dec. 8, 1916, p. 3; P. L., "O nemetskoi kolonizatsii v Rossii," *Prikhodskii listok*, Dec. 31, 1915, pp. 2–3; David Rempel, "The Expropriation of the German Colonists in South Russia during the Great War," *Journal of Modern History* 4, no. 1 (1932): 53–55.

35. IV Gosudarstvennaia duma, *Stenograficheskie otchety* 5 (Aug. 3, 1915): 426–34.

36. See Ivan I Sergeev, *Mirnoe zavoevanie Rossii Nemtsami (doklad, prochitannyi v chrezvychainom obshchem sobranii gg. chlenov "Obshchestva 1914 goda" 13 marta 1915 goda)* (Petrograd, 1915).

37. The legislation efforts to limit German landholding in Russia is examined in Karl Eduardovich Lindeman, *Prekrashchenie zemlevladeniia i zemlepol'zovaniia poselian' sobstvennikov: Ukazy 2 fevralia i 13 dekabria 1915 goda i 10, 15 iiulia i 19 avgusta 1916 goda i ikh vliianie na ekonomicheskoe sostoianie iuzhnoi Rossii* (Moscow, 1917). The actual legislation can be found in *Sobranie uzakonenii* (1915), arts. 350 and 351.

38. Miliukov's complete speech can be found in IV Gosudarstvennaia duma, *Stenograficheskie otchety* 5 (Aug. 3, 1915): 497–508.

39. V. S. Diakin, "Pervaia mirovaia voina i meropriiatiia po likvidatsii tak nazyvaemogo nemetskogo zasil'ia," in *Pervaia mirovaia voina*, ed. A. L. Sidorov (Moscow, 1968), p. 230.

40. Ibid. According to Diakin, the emperor's assent to reconsideration indicated the danger and failure of the liquidation scheme. The Duma had studied but not approved the liquidation decree by the time of the February Revolution. See also P. K. Fomenko, *Zakon 2 fevralia 1915 goda o nemetskom zemlevladenii* (Odessa, 1915), p. 4.

41. E. D. Chermenskii, *IV Gosudarstvennaia duma i sverzhenie tsarizma v Rossii* (Moscow, 1976), pp. 165–68; Diakin, "Pervaia mirovaia voina," p. 230.

42. Lindeman, *Prekrashchenie zemlevladeniia i zemlepol'zovaniia poselian' sobstvennikov*, pp. 159–89.

43. *Saratovskii vestnik*, Mar. 18, 1917, p. 4. Donald Raleigh's recent work, *Revolution*

on the Volga: 1917 in Saratov (Ithaca, N.Y., 1986), traces the course of the revolution in the provincial capital city.

44. Pershin, *Uchastkovoe zemlepol'zovanie v Rossii*, p. 39; *Izvestiia*, July 9, 1918, p. 2.

45. *Saratovskii vestnik*, Mar. 30, 1917, p. 4.

46. *Saratovskii vestnik*, June 8, 1917, p. 4.

47. Donald Raleigh confirmed that the SRs continued to dominate local politics in Saratov Province. Raleigh, *Revolution on the Volga*, p. 213.

48. *Sotsial-demokrat*, June 27, 1917, p. 4. *Proletarii povolzh'ia*, Apr. 22, 1917, p. 4. *Saratovskii vestnik*, June 13, 1917, p. 3. Although few Volga Germans appear to have been Bolshevik party activists, strong sympathy for the party's ideas existed in the larger colonies. A former Norka resident stated, "There were many townsmen who were pro-Bolshevik and felt they had been victims of our own prosperous German merchants." Brill, "Farewell to Norka," p. 55.

49. *Russkoe slovo*, Mar. 23–Apr. 5, 1917, p. 3, and May 17–30, 1917, p. 3. The First All-Russian Congress of Russian Citizens of German Nationality opened in Odessa on May 14, and was largely controlled by the intelligentsia, deputies to the Duma, and the clergy. Although claiming to represent over three million, it did not express the views of the largest single group, the half-million Volga German farmers who sent no representatives. On June 10, when the Ukrainian Rada (national council) proclaimed separation and de facto independence from the Provisional Government, the southern Germans and Volga Germans no longer were parts of the same political structure.

50. Minutes of this assembly are found in *Verhandlung der Versammlung der*

Kreisbevollmächtigen der Wolgakolonien in Saratow am 25 bis 27 April 1917 (Saratov, 1917).

51. Ibid., p. 20. The SR land program had many appealing features, but particularly the nebulous policy of land socialization which affirmed that the land would belong neither to individuals nor to societies, neither to the state nor local government, but that "all the land should belong to all the people"—whatever that meant. Furthermore, the SR program did not insist upon collectivist production, but allowed for individual or cooperative cultivation.

52. Ibid., p. 17.

53. *Saratovskii listok*, Nov. 16, 1917, p. 2.

54. One should not be confused by statements by Löbsack, *Einsam Kampft das Wolgaland*, p. 199, and Sinner, *Nemtsy Nizhnego Povolzh'ia*, p. 20, indicating that there were few Volga German socialists. Both authors mean by this active party adherents of the major Russia socialist parties, the SRs and SDs. However, prevailing Volga German political views, particularly on the crucial issues of land use and expropriation without compensation, were most definitely socialist.

55. For Johannes Schleuning's views, see his *Aus tiefster Not: Schicksale der deutschen Kolonisten in Russland* (Berlin, 1922).

56. *Sotsial-Demokrat*, June 28, 1917, p. 4.

57. *Saratovskii vestnik*, Apr. 14, 1917, p. 4.

58. Fritz Hans Reimisch, *Die deutschen Wolga-Kolonien von ihrer Gründung bis zu den Tagen ihrer grössten Leidenzeit* (Berlin, 1922), p. 16.

59. *Proletarii Povolzh'ia*, Sept. 12, 1917, p. 4.

60. The dearth of information on these elections is discussed in Oliver Radkey's study of the Constituent Assembly. His research unearthed no election returns for Kamyshin District, where most of the Saratov Province Volga Germans resided. Oliver Radkey, *The Election to the Russian Constituent Assembly of 1917* (Cambridge, 1950), pp. 13 and 81–83; Samara election returns are in the Appendix. One article indicated a breakdown in telegraphic communications between the district and next higher level electoral commission as the problem. "Chleny uchreditelnago sobraniia Saratovskoi Gubernii" *Vestnik privolzhskago kraia*, Dec. 16, 1917, p. 2. Candidates are listed in *Saratovskii vestnik*, Oct. 15, 1917, p. 4.

61. *Saratovskii listok*, Nov. 21, 1917, p. 3. We will probably never know whether the colonists voted their individual consciences or the herd instinct, which Radkey states was strong in the villages. "But in the villages an inferior political consciousness permitted the populace to be swayed now one way and now the other, depending upon the intensity and the persistence of the pressure applied. Apparently, in numberless cases there was a herd, and it did stampede. Yet in extenuation of the showing of the village, it may be urged that a considerable element stood out from the herd and exhibited a will of its own. How large a proportion it was cannot be estimated, in view of the paucity of information." Radkey, *The Election to the Russian Constituent Assembly*, p. 70.

62. *Zhizn' natsional'nostei* no. 33 (July 6, 1919): 2. Although in no way definitive and even exaggerative of the importance of political autonomy as an issue in 1917, the best account of these 1918 events can be found

in Aleksander Mrdjenovic, "The Volga-German *Gemeindeschaft* and Political Autonomy Amidst Domestic Turmoil, 1914–1922" (master's thesis, Department of History, University of Kansas, 1976), pp. 55–67.

63. Details of and responses to the Bolshevik land decree can be found in Atkinson, *The End of the Russian Land Commune*, pp. 165–85.

64. Brill, "Farewell to Norka," p. 14.

65. In July 1918, reports of armed Volga German opposition appeared in *Izvestiia*, July 24, 1918, p. 2.

66. See Adolf Grabowsky, "The German Republic on the Volga," *Journal of the American Historical Society of Germans from Russia* 2 (Winter 1979): 19.

Epilogue

1. See Gross, *Avt. Sots. Sov. Resp. Nemtsev Povolzh'ia*, pp. 33, 84, and 118.

2. N. Libikh, "Naselenie, khoziaistva, posevnye ploshchadi i skot po Nemrespublike v 1927 godu," *Sbornik statei i materialov* [Gosplan ASSR Nemtsev Povolzh'ia], no. 3, 1928, p. 11.

3. Gross, *Avt. Sots. Sov. Resp. Nemtsev Povolzh'ia*, pp. 21–38 and 98.

4. In 1922 some suggested that Volga German agrarian recovery might quicken if the Mennonites could be enlisted as disseminators of agricultural instructions. *Zhizn' natsional'nostei*, no. 138 (March 14, 1922), p. 10.

5. In his stories about life in the Kolyma camps, Shalamov mentioned one such Volga German prisoner—Adam Frisorger, a former Lutheran pastor on the meadow side.

Varlam Shalamov, *Graphite,* trans. John Glad (New York, 1981), pp. 27–29.

6. Roy A. and Zhores A. Medvedev, *Khrushchev: The Years in Power,* trans. Andrew R. Durkin (New York, 1976), p. 122.

7. Ann Sheehy, "The Volga Germans," *AHSGR WorkPaper,* no. 13 (Dec. 1973), p. 7.

$\mathcal{B}$ibliography

Oral Interviews

Burkhard, Anna. Transcript of oral history interview. Special Collections, Colorado State University Library.

Geringer, Mrs. John. Transcript of oral history interview. Special Collections, Colorado State University Library.

Klein, Amalie. Transcript of oral history interview. Special Collections, Colorado State University Library.

Lebsack, Gus. Transcript of oral history interview. Special Collections, Colorado State University Library.

Legler, Philip. Transcript of oral history interview. Special Collections, Colorado State University Library.

Miller, Lydia. Transcript of oral history interview. Special Collections, Colorado State University Library.

Ostwald, Fred. Transcript of oral history interview. Special Collections, Colorado State University Library.

Stoll, Peter. Untranscribed oral history interview. Special Collections, Colorado State University Library.

Public Documents

Gosudarstvennaia Duma. *Stenograficheskie otchety* [Stenographic Reports of the Fourth State Duma]. Chetvertoe sozyv. Vol. 5 (Aug. 1915).

Kamyshinskoe uezdnoe zemstvo. *Postanovleniia kamyshinskogo uezdnogo zemskogo sobraniia* [Resolutions of the Kamyshin District Zemstvo Assembly]. 1868–1916.

Kamyshinskoe uezdnoe zemstvo. *Sbornik dokladov po ekonomicheskim voprosam* [Collection of Reports on Economic Questions]. Kamyshin, 1910.

Nikolaevskoe uezdnoe zemskoe sobranie. *Postanovleniia nikolaevskogo uezdnogo zemskogo sobraniia* [Resolutions of the Nikolaevsk District Zemstvo Assembly]. 1871–1917.

Novouzenskoe uezdnoe zemstvo. *Zhurnaly novouzenskogo uezdnogo zemskogo sobraniia* [Journals of the Novouensk District Zemstvo Assembly]. 1866–1917.

Polnoe sobranie zakonov Rossiiskoi Imperii [Complete Collection of the Laws of the Russian Empire]. First series

(1649–1825). 44 vols. in 51. St. Petersburg, 1830.

Polnoe sobranie zakonov Rossiiskoi Imperii [Complete Collection of the Laws of the Russian Empire]. Second series (1825–81). 40 vols. in 125. St. Petersburg, 1830–1884.

Svod zakonov Rossiiskoi Imperii [Code of Laws of the Russian Empire]. Vol. 12: "Svod uchrezhdenii i ustavov o koloniiakh inostrantsev v imperii" [Founding Code and Statutes of the Colonies of Foreigners in the Empire], St. Petersburg, 1857. Vol. 9: "Polozheniia o sel'skom sostoianii" [Statutes about Rural Affairs], St. Petersburg, 1876. Vol. IX: "Osoboe prilozhenie k zakonam o sostoianiiakh: Polozheniia o sel'skom sostoianii" [Special Supplement to the Statutes on Rural Affairs: Statutes about Rural Affairs], St. Petersburg, 1902.

U.S. Senate, Senate Documents, Reports of the Immigration Commission. *Emigration Conditions in Europe*. Vol. 12, 61st Cong., 3d Sess., 1911.

Articles

"Agronomicheskoe i gidrotekhnicheskoe biuro pri novouzenskoi uezdnoi zemskoi uprave" [The Agronomy and Hydrotechnical Bureau of the Novouzensk District Zemstvo Board]. *Vestnik novouzenskago zemstva*, January-February 1912, pp. 174–78.

A. L. "O nachale i obrazovanie kolonii" [Concerning the Origin and Formation of the Colonies]. *Samarskiia gubernskiia vedomosti*, Feb. 21, 1853, pp. 41–43; Feb. 28, 1853, pp. 48–49.

A. L. "Opisanie kolonii inostrannykh poselentsev v Samarskoi Gubernii" [Description of the Colonies of Foreign Settlers in Samara Province]. *Samarskiia gubernskiia vedomosti*, Mar. 7, 1853, pp. 55–56; Mar. 14, 1853, pp. 59–61.

A. L. "O pol'ze torgovykh rastenii" [The Benefits of Commercial Crops]. *Samarskiia gubernskiia vedomosti*, Nov. 28, 1853, pp. 304–5.

Al'man, B. D. "Vliianie trakhomy na ekonomicheskoe polozhenie poselian' nemetskikh kolonii" [The Influence of Trachoma on the Economic Condition of the Settlers of the German Colonies]. *Vestnik novouzenskago zemstva*, May-June 1912, pp. 70–80.

A. M. "Obzor deiatel'nosti agronomov Novouzenskago Uezda" [Review of the Activities of the Agronomists of Novouzensk District]. *Sbornik sel'skokhoziaistvennykh svedenii* (Novouzensk), no. 11–12, 1911, pp. 544–72.

Antipin, E. K. "Deiatel'nost' agronomov" [Activities of the Agronomists]. *Sel'skokhoziaistvennyi listok Kamyshinskago Uezdnago Zemstva*, January 1915, pp. 7–8.

Antipin, E. K. "Ob ekonomicheskikh meropriiatiiakh kamyshinskago zemstva v 1914 godu" [Concerning the Economic Measures of the Kamyshin Zemstvo in 1914]. *Sel'skokhoziaistvennyi listok Kamyshinskago Uezdnago Zemstva*, February 1915, pp. 21–25.

Armstrong, John A. "Mobilized and Proletarian Diasporas." *American Political Science Review* 70 (1976): 393–408.

Bauer and Sprenger. "O razvedenii tabaku v nemetskikh koloniiakh" [The Cultivation of Tobacco in the German

Colonies]. *Samarskiia gubernskiia vedomosti*, July 20, 1863, pp. 187–89.

Beletskii, I. "Sel'skokhoziaistvennyi ocherk Novouzenskago Uezda Samarskoi Gubernii" [An Agricultural Sketch of Novouzensk District, Samara Province]. *Izvestiia Petrovskoi Zemledel'cheskoi i Lesnoi Akademii*, no. 2, 1888, pp. 7–146.

Bogdanov, N. "Materialy po obsledovaniiu sarpinochno-tkatskogo proisvodstva kooperativnykh tovarishchestv i trudovykh artelei Kamyshinskogo Kraia, Saratovskoi Gubernii" [Materials Based on an Inspection of Sarpinka-Weaving Production in the Cooperatives and Workers' Artels of the Kamyshin Region, Saratov Province]. *Vestnik kustarnoi promyshlennosti*, December 1918, pp. 16–37.

Brill, Conrad. "Farewell to Norka." *Journal of the American Historical Society of Germans from Russia* 8 (Summer 1985): 1–16; 8 (Winter 1985): 54–66.

B., Sh. "Sem'ia nemtsev-kolonistov" [The Community of German Colonists]. *Istoricheskii vestnik*, July 1906, pp. 200–204.

"Bunt nemetskikh kolonistov (koloniia Egkeim, Novouzenskogo Uezda, Samarskoi Gubernii)" [Riot of German Colonists (the Colony of Eckheim, Novouzensk District, Samara Province)]. *Golos Moskvy*, Apr. 12, 1915, p. 2.

Bushnell, John. "Peasants in Uniform: The Tsarist Army as a Peasant Society." *Journal of Social History* 13, no. 4 (1981): 565–76.

B-v, P. "Zametki o khoziaistve krest'ian Samarskoi Gubernii" [Notes on the Peasant Economy of Samara Province]. *Trudy*

imperatorskago vol'nago ekonomicheskago obshchestva, May 1873, pp. 155–78.

Ch. D. S. "Landwirthschaftlichen Zustände auf den Wolga-Kolonien." *Saratowsche deutsche Zeitung*, Apr. 1, 1866, p. 191; Apr. 5, 1866, pp. 197–99; Apr. 8, 1866, pp. 205–7; Apr. 12, 1866, pp. 213–14.

"Chleny uchreditelnago sobraniia Saratovskoi Gubernii" [Members of the Constituent Assembly from Saratov Province]. *Vestnik privolzhskago kraia*, Dec. 16, 1917, p. 2.

Chuev, A. E. "Doklad po narodnomu obrazovaniiu" [Report on Public Education]. *Doklady i zhurnaly Kam. ocherednogo i ekstrennago zemskikh sobranii 1908 goda*, n.d., pp. 1–8.

Cleinow, Georg. "Die deutsche Wolga-Republik." *Osteuropa* 2 (1926–27): 128–40.

Dando, W. A. "Man-Made Famines: Some Geographical Insights from an Exploratory of a Millennium of Russian Famines." *Ecology of Food and Nutrition* (London) 4 (1976): 219–34.

"Deputat Ia. E. Ditts v roli obviniaemago i ego ob'iasnenie" [Deputy Jacob E. Dietz in the Role of the Accused and His Explanation]. *Privolzhskaia gazeta*, June 6, 1906, p. 3.

"Der Wahlkampf." *Saratower deutsche Zeitung*, Mar. 29, 1906, p. 1.

Diakin, V. S. "Pervaia mirovaia voina i meropriiatiia po likvidatsii tak nazyvaemogo nemetskogo zasil'ia" [The First World War and Measures Regarding the Liquidation of the So-Called German Dominance]. In A. L. Sidorov (ed.), *Pervaia mirovaia voina* (Moscow, 1968), pp. 227–38.

Dinges, G. "K izucheniiu govorov povol-zhskikh Nemtsev" [Toward a Study of the Dialects of the Volga Germans]. *Uchenye zapiski Saratovskogo Gosudarstven-nogo Universiteta imeni N. G. Chernyshe-vskogo* 4, no. 3 (1925): 12–20.

Ditts, Ia. "Iz istorii nemetskikh kolonii" [From the History of the German Colonies]. *Saratovskii listok*, June 28, 1914, p. 2; July 1, 1914, p. 2; July 2, 1914, p. 2.

Ditts, Iakov Tim. "K 150-letnemu iubileiu nemetskikh kolonii (1764–1914)" [For the 150th Anniversary of the German Colonies (1764–1914)]. *Saratovs-kii listok*, June 29, 1914, p. 2.

Ditts, Ia. "Otnoshenii nashikh Nemtsev k Gosudarstvennoi Dume" [Attitudes of Our Germans toward the State Duma]. *Privolzhskaia gazeta*, Mar. 14, 1906, pp. 2–3.

Ditts, Ia. "Pervaia nemetskaia koloniia v Povolzh'e" [The First German Colony in the Lower Volga]. *Saratovskii listok*, Mar. 11, 1914, pp. 2–3.

Ditts, Ia. "Pugachev v nemetskikh kolonii-akh" [Pugachev in the German Colonies]. *Saratovskii listok*, June 26, 1914, p. 2; June 27, 1914, p. 2.

Ditts, Ia. "Putevyia zametki" [Travel Notes]. *Privolzhskaia gazeta*, Feb. 25, 1906, pp. 2–3.

Ditts, Ia. "Putevyia zametki" [Travel Notes]. *Kamyshinskii vestnik*, Jan. 1, 1906, pp. 2–3; Jan. 4, 1906, p. 2; Jan. 18, 1906, p. 2; Feb. 2, 1906, pp. 2–3.

"Dnevnik Pastora Gubera s 6-go po 31-e avgusta 1830 g." [The Diary of Pastor Huber from the 6th to 31st of August 1830]. *Russkaia starina*, no. 8, 1878, pp. 581–90.

Dukhovnikov, Flegont V. "Nemtsy, drugie inostrantsy i prishlye liudi v Saratove" [Germans, Other Foreigners and Newly Arrived Peoples in Saratov]. *Saratovskii krai: Istoricheskie ocherki, vospominaniia, materialy* 1 (1893): 237–64.

Dukhovskii. "Kolonii na Volge" [Colonies on the Volga]. *Kazanskii vestnik* 25, pt. 1 (1829): 56–64.

Dumler, K. "O nemetskikh shkolakh" [About German Schools]. *Saratovskii listok*, Aug. 13, 1905, p. 3.

Dum-Dum. "Esche nemnogo o 'nemets-kom progresse'" [Still More about "German Progress"]. *Privolzhskaia gazeta*, Feb. 21, 1906, pp. 2–3.

Dunin', A. A. "Nemtsy v samarskikh stepiakh" [Germans in the Samara Steppe]. *Istoricheskii vestnik*, November 1915, pp. 543–58.

Dunin', A. A. "V nemetskikh kogtiakh: Povest'" [In the German Claws: A Tale]. *Istoricheskii vestnik*, January 1917, pp. 1–35.

"Dvizhenie narodonaseleniia v Saratovs-koi Gubernii (1844–1853)" [The Movement of Population in Saratov Province (1844–1853)]. *Saratovskiia gubernskiia vedomosti*, no. 47, 1854, pp. 218–20.

Eichhorn, Jacob, and Irma Eichhorn. "Orlovskaia on the Volga." *Journal of the American Historical Society of Germans from Russia* 3 (Spring 1980): 23–28.

"Einkommensteuer." *Saratower deutsche Zeitung*, Mar. 29, 1906, p. 1; June 14, 1906, p. 3.

Fadeev, A. M. "Vospominaniia A. M. Fadeeva" [Memoirs of A. M. Fadeev]. *Russkii arkhiv*, no. 4, 1891, pp. 465–94; no. 5, 1891, pp. 14–60.

Faidel, Arthur. "Kak zaselialis' nemetskiia kolonii" [How the German Colonies Were Settled]. *Saratovskii listok*, July 12, 1914, p. 2.

Falk, J. P. "Zapiski puteshestviia Akademika Fal'ka" [Notes of the Travels of Academician Falk]. In *Polnoe sobranie uchenykh puteshestvii po Rossii*, vol. 6 (St. Petersburg, 1824), pp. 109–18.

G. "Erwiederung auf den Artikel 'Landwirthschaftliche Zustände in den Wolga Kolonien." *Saratowsche deutsche Zeitung*, May 24, 1866, p. 303; May 27, 1866, pp. 309–11; May 31, 1866, pp. 317–19; and June 3, 1866, p. 328.

Gavrilov, L. M., and V. V. Kutuzov. "Istoshchenie liudskikh reservov russkoi armii v 1917 g." [Exhaustion of the Russian Army's Manpower Reserves in 1917]. In A. L. Sidorov (ed.), *Pervaia mirovaia voina* (Moscow, 1968), pp. 145–57.

Giesinger, Adam. "Villages in Which Our Fore-Fathers Lived." *AHSGR Work Paper* 16 (December 1974): 30–33.

Golubev. "Prichiny ekonomicheskago upadka Samarskoi Gub." [Causes of the Economic Decline of Samara Province]. *Sbornik saratovskago zemstva*, August 1893, pp. 88–111.

Goniasinskii. "Selo Iagodnaia Poliana" [The Village of Iagodnaia Poliana]. *Saratovskiia gubernskiia vedomosti*, Apr. 28, 1894, pp. 2–3.

Gorbunov, A. D. "O tabachnoi promyshlennosti v privolzhskom krae" [About the Tobacco Industry in the Lower Volga Region]. *Saratovskiia gubernskiia vedomosti*, no. 45, 1858, pp. 269–70; no. 46, 1858, pp. 274–75; no. 47, 1858, pp. 280–81.

Gorodetskii, A. "Nemetskiia shkoly" [German Schools]. *Kamyshinskii ezhenedel'nik*, Feb. 5, 1906, pp. 20–22.

Gorodetskii, M. "K istorii rimskago katolitsizma v Rossii (tiraspol'skaia ili saratovskaia latinskaia eparkhiia)" [Concerning the History of Roman Catholicism in Russia (the Tiraspol or Saratov Latin Diocese)]. *Istoricheskii vestnik*, October 1889, pp. 122–34.

Grabowsky, Adolf. "The German Republic on the Volga." Translated by Adam Giesinger. *Journal of the American Historical Society of Germans from Russia* 2 (Winter 1979): 19–24.

Guch von. "Fabrikatsiia sarpinki v nemetskikh koloniiakh" [The Manufacture of Sarpinka in the German Colonies]. *Saratovskiia gubernskiia vedomosti*, Dec. 5, 1870, p. 2.

Gusev, V. "Sarpinochnoe proizvodstvo v russkikh seleniiakh Kamyshinskago Uezda" [Sarpinka Production in Russian Settlements of Kamyshin District]. *Saratovskaia zemskaia nedelia*, February 1902, pp. 124–34.

Hagin, M. "Beitrag zur wirtschaftlichen und kulturellen Leistung der Wolgadeutschen." *Heimatbuch der Deutschen aus Russland* (1967–68), pp. 81–105.

Hagin, M. "Dehler eine Wolgadeutsche Siedlung." *Heimatbuch der Deutschen aus Russland* (1966), pp. 74–91.

Haynes, Emma S. "Germans from Russia in American History and Literature." *AHSGR Work Paper* 5 (September 1974): 4–20.

Haynes, Emma S. "Researching in the National Archives." *Journal of the American Historical Society of Germans from Russia* 2 (Spring 1979): 1–6.

Held. "Feindseligkeit." *Unsere Zeit*, Apr. 12, 1906, p. 3.

Isaev, A. "Zametki o nemetskikh koloniiakh v Rossii" [Notes about the German Colonies in Russia]. *Russkaia mysl'*, December 1984, pp. 87–112.

Iseev, E. A. "O merakh zemstva k uluchsheniiu zemledel'cheskago khoziaistva v gubernii" [About Zemstvo Measures to Improve the Agricultural Economy in the Province]. *Sbornik saratovskago zemstva*, February 1893, p. 4.

"Istoricheskiia i statisticheskiia svedeniia o sareptskoi kolonii" [Historical and Statistical Information about the Sarepta Colony]. *Zhurnal ministerstva vnutrennikh del* 28, no. 5 (1838): 245–60.

"Istoriia i statistika kolonii inostrannykh poselentsev v Rossii" [History and Statistics of the Colonies of Foreign Settlers in Russia]. *Zhurnal ministerstva gosudarstvennykh imushchestv* 52, pt. 2 (1854): 36–78; 53, pt. 2 (1854): 1–34; 54, pt. 1 (1855): 71–88; 55, pt. 1 (1855): 57–88 and 121–37.

Iudin, P. L. "Nemetskoe zaselenie: Povolzhskie kolonisty" [The German Settlement: The Volga Colonists]. *Russkii arkhiv*, no. 4, 1915, pp. 474–94.

Ivanenko, G. "Po povodu zakona 13 dekabria 1915 g." [On the Occasion of the December 13, 1915 Law]. *Zhurnal ministerstva iustitsii* 4 (1916): 209–19.

"Iz Kamyshinskogo Uezda: O nemetskikh koloniiakh" [From Kamyshin District: About the German Colonies]. *Saratovskii dnevnik*, no. 108, 1888, p. 2.

"Iz Sarepty" [From Sarepta]. *Vostochnye izvestiia*, no. 10, 1814, pp. 90–93.

"Izvlechenie iz otcheta ministerstva vnutrennikh del – sostoianie kolonii" [Extract from the Report of the Ministry of the Interior: Conditions of the Colonies]. *Zhurnal ministerstva vnutrennikh del* 30, no. 12 (1838): 475–84.

J. "Welchen Zweck hat die Centralschule?" *Saratowsche deutsche Zeitung*, Aug. 26, 1866, p. 520.

"K besporiadkam v Kamyshine" [About the Disorders in Kamyshin]. *Saratovskii listok*, Sept. 1, 1906, p. 3.

"K pereimenovanniiu nemetskikh nazvanii gorodov v Rossii" [Concerning the Renaming of the German-named Towns in Russia]. *Novoe vremia*, Dec. 2–15, 1915, p. 3.

"K voprosu o likvidatsii nemetskago zemlevladeniia" [Concerning the Question of the Liquidation of German Landholders]. *Novoe vremia*, Dec. 2–15, 1915, p. 3.

"K voprosu o nemetskikh shkolakh" [Concerning the Question of German Schools]. *Privolzhskaia zhizn'*, Oct. 14, 1910, pp. 1–2.

Kadykov, St. "Selo Ekaterininskoe, Samarskoi Gubernii" [The Village of Ekaterinenstadt, Samara Province]. *Samarskiia gubernskiia vedomosti*, no. 41, 1858, pp. 693–95; no. 42, 1858, pp. 710–12.

Kämmerer, A. "Zwei Hemmnisse des Unterrichts in unsern Volksschulen." *Saratower deutsche Zeitung*, Mar. 15, 1906, p. 3.

Kappes, S. "Sel'skoe khoziaistvo Nemrespubliki po dannym mestnykh statistiko-ekonomicheskikh issledovanii samarsk. i saratovsk. zemstv v 1887 g." [Agriculture in the German Republic Based upon Local Figures from Statistical-Economic Surveys of the Samara and Saratov Zemstvos in 1887].

Sbornik statei i materialov [Gosplan AS-SRNP], no. 2, 1927, pp. 133–56.

Karevskaia, A. G. "O gosudarstvennykh krest'ianskikh Samarskoi Gubernii vo vtoroi polovine XIX veka (kratkii obzor istochnikov i literatury)" [About the State Peasants of Samara Province in the Second Half of the Nineteenth Century (a Short Review of the Sources and Literature)]. In *Revoliutsionnoe dvizhenie v srednem Povolzh'e i Priural'e*, edited by S. G. Basin, in *Nauchnye trudy Kuibyshevskogo Ped. Instituta* 183 (1977): 3–13.

Karkling, A. "O melkom kredite u nemetskago naseleniia" [Concerning Petty Credit among the German Population]. *Sbornik sel'sko-khoziaistvennykh svedenii*, no. 4, 1911, pp. 205–18.

Karlin, Athanasius. "The Coming of the First Volga German Catholics to America." Translated by Emma S. Haynes. *Journal of the American Historical Society of Germans from Russia* 1 (Winter 1978): 61–69.

Kazanskii, N. "Narodnoe obrazovanie v Saratovskoi Gubernii" [Public Education in Saratov Province]. *Russkaia mysl'*, July 1896, pp. 1–18; August, 1896, pp. 41–63.

Kedrov, S. "Kratkii obzor istorii saratovskago kraia" [A Short Survey of the History of the Saratov Region]. *Saratovskii krai* 1 (1893): 3–18.

Khovanskii, N. F. "K istorii nemetskikh kolonii Saratovskoi Gubernii (iz del senatskago arkhiva)" [Concerning the History of the German Colonies of Saratov Province (from the Records of the Senate Archive)]. *Trudy saratovskoi uchenoi arkhivnoi komissii* 31 (1914): 51–58.

"Khoziaistvo i zhizn' u nemtsev kolonistov i russkikh" [Economy and Life among the German Colonists and Russians]. *Saratovskiia gubernskiia vedomosti*, Oct. 29, 1895, p. 3.

"Khronologicheskaia vedomost' o pozhertvovaniiakh, sdelannykh gosudarstvennymi krest'ianami i kolonistami v pol'zu voisk" [Chronological Record of the Donations Made by State Peasants and Colonists to Aid the Armed Forces]. *Zhurnal ministerstva gosudarstvennykh imushchestv* 51, pt. 2 (1854): 9–14.

K-ii. "Narodnoe obrazovanie v 1911 goda" [Public Education in 1911]. *Privolzhskaia zhizn'*, Jan. 12, 1912, pp. 1–2.

Kirsanov, D. I. "Besedy po sel'skomu khoziaistvu" [Conversations about Agriculture]. *Vestnik novouzenskago zemstva*, March-April 1913, pp. 7–19; May-June 1913, pp. 32–50; September-December 1913, pp. 7–19.

Klaus, A. A. "Dukhovenstvo i shkoly v nashikh nemetskikh koloniiakh" [Clergy and Schools in Our German Colonies]. *Vestnik Evropy*, January 1869, pp. 138–74; May 1869, pp. 235–74.

Klaus, A. A. "Obshchina-sobstvennik i eia iuridicheskaia organizatsiia" [Community-Proprietor and Its Legal Organization] *Vestnik Evropy*, February 1870, pp. 573–628; March 1870, pp. 72–118.

Klaus, A. A. "Sektatory-kolonisty v Rossii" [Colonist Sects in Russia]. *Vestnik Evropy*, January 1868, pp. 256–300; March 1868, pp. 277–326; June 1868, pp. 665–722; July 1868, pp. 713–66.

Kleiman, V. "Avtonomnaia Oblast' Nemtsev Povolzh'ia" [The Autonomous Region of the Volga Germans]. *Zhizn' natsional'nostei*, January 1923, pp. 62–67.

Kohls, Winfred. "Beitrag zur Geschichte der deutschen Kolonisten in Russland, eine Untersuchung russische Pressepolemik und der deutschen diplomatischen Berichte aus der St. Petersburger Amtszeit des Botschafters von Schweinitz." In *Archivalische Fundstucke zu den russisch-deutschen Beziehungen*, edited by Erich Amburger (Berlin, 1973), pp. 152–57.

Kolesnikov, G. I. "Novouzenskii Uezd (v ego proshlom i nastoiashchem)" [Novouzensk District (Its Past and Present)]. *Vestnik novouzenskago zemstva*, March-April 1912, pp. 23–50.

"Kolonii na Volge" [Colonies on the Volga]. *Russkii invalid*, no. 151, 1830, pp. 602–3; no. 153, 1830, pp. 610–11.

"Koloniia Sosnovka, Kamyshinskogo U. (o pereseleniiakh)" [The Colony of Sosnovka, Kamyshin District (about Its Migrations)]. *Saratovskii dnevnik*, no. 186, 1888, p. 2.

Kolonist J. St. "Aufruf an meine Mitkolonisten." *Saratowsche deutsche Zeitung*, Nov. 5, 1865, pp. 845–46.

Kryshtofovich, F. "Emigratsiia krest'ian' v Ameriku" [The Emigration of Peasants to America]. *Sel'skokhoziaistvennyi listok Kamyshinskago Uezdnago Zemstva*, May 1913, pp. 133–41.

Kryshtofovich, F. "Kak ekhat' v Ameriku na zarabotki" [How to Go to America in Search of a Living]. *Sel'skii khoziain*, no. 17, 1913, pp. 823–25; no. 18, 1913, pp. 899–901.

Kufeld, J. "Der Tabakbau in den Wolga-Kolonien: Seine Geschichte und sein trauriger Rückgang in den letzten Jahrzehnten." *Wolgadeutsche Monatshefte*, August 1923, pp. 210–11.

Kusheva, E. "Saratov v tret'ei chetverti XVIII-go veka" [Saratov in the Third Quarter of the Eighteenth Century]. *Trudy nizhnevolzhskogo oblastnogo nauchnogo ob-va kraevedeniia* 35, pt. 2 (1928): 1–58.

Kuzmin-Karavaev. "Voprosy vnutrennoi zhizni" [Questions of Domestic Life]. *Vestnik Evropy*, December 1914, p. 389.

Laing, Rev. Francis S. "German-Russian Settlements in Ellis County, Kansas." *Collections of the Kansas State Historical Society, 1909–1910* 11 (1910): 489–528.

Leongard, Aleksandr. "Golos iz Saksonii za saratovskikh i samarskikh kolonistov" [Voice from Saxony in Defense of the Saratov and Samara Colonists]. *Severnaia pchela*, May 2, 1860, p. 395.

Leopol'dov, A. "Neskol'ko slov o kolonistakh" [A Few Words about the Colonists]. *Volga*, Dec. 18, 1863, p. 554.

Leopol'dov, A. "O saratovskikh i samarskikh kolonistakh" [About the Saratov and Samara Colonists]. *Severnaia pchela*, Mar. 7, 1860, p. 212.

Leopol'dov, A. "Opisanie kolonial'nykh inostrannykh poselenii v Samarskoi Gubernii" [Description of the Foreign Colony Settlements in Samara Province]. *Samarskiia gubernskiia vedomosti*, no. 10, 1853, pp. 55–56; no. 11, 1853, pp. 59–61.

Leopol'dov, A. "Statisticheskaia zapiska o narodakh, naseliaiushchikh Saratovskoi Gubernii" [Statistical Note about the Peoples Who Settled Saratov Province]. *Moskovskii telegraf* 52, no. 13 (1833): 135–43.

Leopol'dov, A. "Vzgliad na Novouzenskii Okrug Saratovskoi Gubernii" [A View of Novouzensk District, Saratov Province]. *Saratovskiia gubernskiia vedomosti*, no. 8, 1845, pp. 83–86; no. 9, 1845, pp. 90–93.

Leopol'dov, Andrei. "Vzgliad na zavolzhskii krai v Saratovskoi Gubernii" [A View of the Trans-Volga Region in Saratov Province]. *Severnaia pchela*, Dec. 19, 1835, pp. 1155–56; Dec. 21, 1835, p. 1164.

"Letters to Pauline." *Journal of the American Historical Society of Germans from Russia* 8 (Winter 1985): 27–40.

Libikh, N. "Naselenie, khoziaistva, posevnye ploshchadi i skot po Nemrespublike v 1927 godu" [Population, Economy, Sown Areas, and Livestock in the German Republic in 1927]. *Sbornik statei i materialov* [Gosplan ASSR Nemtsev Povolzh'ia], no. 3, 1928, pp. 1–34.

Long, James W. "Agricultural Conditions in the German Colonies of Novouzensk District, Samara Province, 1861–1914." *Slavonic and East European Review* 57, no. 4 (October 1979): 531–55.

Long, James W. "The Volga Germans and the Zemstvos, 1865–1917." *Jahrbücher für Geschichte Osteuropas* 30 (1982): 336–61.

Loos, Johann and Merkel, Tobias. [Untitled article.] *Saratowsche deutsche Zeitung*, Nov. 9, 1865, pp. 854–55; Nov. 12, 1865, pp. 861–63.

M. "Nemtsy na Povolzh'e (pis'ma iz Saratova)" [Germans on the Lower Volga (Letters from Saratov)]. *Russkii mir*, Nov. 9, 1872, p. 1; Nov. 10, 1872, pp. 1–2; Nov. 13, 1872, pp. 1–2.

Mats'evich, K. "K voprosu o pod'eme sel'skokhoziaistvennoi kul'tury" [Concerning the Question of the Development of Agriculture]. In *Materialy k voprosu o nuzhdakh sel'sko-khoziaistvennoi promyshlennosti v Saratovskoi Gubernii* (Saratov, 1903), pp. 1–122.

"Mestnaia khronika" [Local Chronicle]. *Vestnik novouzenskago zemstva*, January–February 1915, pp. 130–201.

Mikhailov, N. "Koloniia Sarepty po vliianiiu na blizhaishiia mesta Astrakhanskoi i Saratovskoi Gub." [The Sarepta Colony and Its Influence on Neighboring Localities in Astrakhan and Saratov Provinces]. *Astrakhanskiia gubernskiia vedomosti*, no. 40, 1846, pp. 267–68.

Minkh, A. N. "Shcherbakovka nemetskaia" [German Shcherbakovka]. *Saratovskiia gubernskiia vedomosti*, Feb. 23, 1895, p. 3.

Mordovtsev, D. "Neskol'ko slov o narodnosti nemetskikh kolonistov Saratovskoi Gubernii" [A Few Words about the Nationality of the German Colonists of Saratov Province]. *Saratovskiia gubernskiia vedomosti*, no. 19, 1858, pp. 94–95.

Müller, J. "Kurzer historischer Bericht über den Zuständ der Volksaufklärung im Gebiete der Wolgadeutschen." In Georgii G. Dinges (ed.), *Beitrage zur Heimatkunde des deutschen Wolgagebiets* (Pokrovsk, 1923), pp. 53–54.

M. V. "O sel'skikh tekhnicheskikh proizvodstvakh v saratovskikh koloniiakh" [About the Agricultural Production Techniques in the Saratov Colonies]. *Trudy imperatorskago vol'nago ekonomicheskago obshchestva*, May 1873, pp. 523–27.

M. V. "Sarpinochnoe proizvodstvo v saratovskikh koloniiakh" [Sarpinka Production in the Saratov Colonies]. *Trudy imperatorskago vol'nago ekonomicheskago obshchestva*, May 1874, pp. 291–301.

Neelov, N. N. "Svedeniia o kolichestve poselivshikhsia v 1769 g. kolonistakh v Saratovskoi Gubernii" [Information about the Number of People Having Settled in the Colonies in Saratov Province in 1769]. *Trudy saratovskoi uchenoi arkhivnoi komissii* 1 (1889): 176–85.

"Nemetskiia kolonii Nikolaevskago U., Samarskoi Gubernii" [The German Colonies of Nikolaevsk District, Samara Province]. *Saratovskiia gubernskiia vedomosti*, Apr. 12, 1890, pp. 202–4.

"Nemetskiia zavoevaniia v iugo-zapadnom krae" [The German Conquest in the Southwest Region]. *Moskovskiia vedomosti*, Oct. 1, 1891, p. 4.

"Nemetskoe selenie Rozenberg, Kamyshinskogo Uezda" [The German Village of Rozenberg, Kamyshin District]. *Saratovskiia gubernskiia vedomosti*, no. 56, 1890, pp. 436–37; no. 58, 1890, pp. 451–52.

"Nemtsy-gosti" [Germans-Visitors]. *Saratovskii dnevnik*, no. 167, 1889, p. 1.

"Nemtsy-kolonisty na Povolzh'e" [Germans-Colonists on the Volga]. *Russkii mir*, Oct. 6, 1873, p. 1.

"Novouzenskie Mennonity" [Novouzensk Mennonites]. *Saratovski dnevnik*, no. 166, 1889, p. 1.

"Ob inostrannykh poselentsakh v Saratovskoi i Samarskoi Guberniiakh i v Bessarabskoi Oblasti" [About the Foreign Settlers in Saratov and Samara Provinces and in the Bessarabian Region]. *Sanktpeterburgskiia vedomosti*, Aug. 2, 1856, pp. 1–2.

Obukhov, V. "Deiatel'nost' krest'ianskago banka v Saratovskoi Gubernii" [The Activity of the Peasant Bank in Saratov Province]. In *Materialy k vorposu o nuzhdakh sel'sko-khoziaistvennoi promyshlennosti v Saratovskoi Gubernii*, pp. 1–32.

"Ocherk kolonii inostrannykh poselentsev Saratovskoi i Samarskoi Gubernii v otnoshenii ikh naseleniia" [Sketch of the Colonies of Foreign Settlers of Saratov and Samara Provinces in Regard to Their Population]. *Saratovskiia gubernskiia vedomosti*, no. 26, 1856, pp. 108–10.

"Ocherk sel'skago khoziaistva samarskikh inostrannykh poselentsev v 1855 g." [Sketch of the Agriculture of the Samara Foreign Settlers in 1855]. *Samarskiia gubernskiia vedomosti*, no. 34, 1856, pp. 150–51; no. 35, 1856, pp. 154–55. *Zhurnal ministerstva gosudarstvennykh imushchestv* 61, pt. 1 (1856): 61–65.

"Ocherk statistiki Kamyshinsk. U." [Statistical Survey of Kamyshin District]. *Saratovskiia gubernskiia vedomosti*, no. 11, 1851, pp. 48–51.

"O nemetskikh shkolakh v Kamyshinskom Uezde" [About the German Schools in Kamyshin District]. *Saratovskii dnevnik*, no. 144, 1888, p. 2; no. 153, 1888, p. 2.

"Opisanie kolonii v Saratovskoi Gubernii poselennykh" [Description of the Colonies Settled in Saratov Province]. *Sanktpeterburgskii zhurnal*, no. 7, 1805, pp. 102–29.

"Opisanie selenii Ilovlinskoi volosti, Kamyshinskago Uezda" [Description of the Villages of Ilovlinskaia Township, Kamyshin District]. *Saratovskiia gubernskiia vedomosti*, June 3, 1890, p. 324; June 7, 1890, pp. 332–33; June 17, 1890, pp. 356–58: June 24, 1890, pp. 374–75.

"O poselenii kolonistov v saratovskom krae" [About the Settlement of Colonists in the

Saratov Region]. *Zhurnal ministerstva gosudarstvennykh imushchestv* 70, pt. 3 (1859): 31–40.

"Ot Saratovskago Gubernatora" [From the Saratov Governor]. *Saratovskiia gubernskiia vedomosti*, May 13, 1890, pp. 273–74.

"O zaniatiiakh kommisii [sic] po preobrazovaniiu obshchestvennago upravleniia i pozemel'nago ustroistva inostrannykh kolonistov v Rossii" [About the Proceedings of the Commission for the Reform of Public Administration and Land Organization of the Foreign Colonists in Russia]. *Pravitel'stvennyi vestnik*, Jan. 20, 1870, pp. 1–4; Jan. 21, 1870, pp. 2–4.

Panfilov, E. "Vozmozhnyia izmeneniia v sistemakh polevodstva i sevooborotakh v Novouzenskom Uezde" [Possible Changes in the Systems of Field Crop Cultivation and Crop Rotation in Novouzensk District]. *Sbornik sel'skokhoziaistvennykh svedenii* no. 5, 1909, pp. 32–62.

Pavlov, A. N. "Pochemu nashi nemtsy pereseliaiutsia v Ameriku" [Why Our Germans Are Migrating to America]. *Saratovskii spravochnyi listok*, Dec. 23, 1877, p. 2.

Pearson, Thomas S. "The Origins of Alexander III's Land Captains: A Reinterpretation." *Slavic Review* 40, no. 3 (1981): 384–403.

"Perekhod k otrubnomu khoziaistvu" [The Transition to Individual Farming]. *Sel'skokhoziaistvennyi listok Kamyshinskago Uezdnago Zemstva*, May 1909, p. 14.

"Peter Sinner." Translated by Adam Giesinger. *Journal of the American Historical Society of Germans from Russia* 7 (Spring 1984): 17–20; 7 (Summer 1984): 25–30; and 7 (Fall 1984): 26–32.

P., Ia. V. "O shkol'nom dele v nemetskikh shkolakh" [About Scholastic Matters in German Schools]. *Kamyshinskiia vesti*, Feb. 26, 1910, pp. 1–2.

Pisarevskii, Grigorii G. "Inostrannye kolonisty greko-rossiiskago ispovedaniia v Povolzh'e" [Foreign Colonists of the Greek-Russian Orthodox Faith in the Lower Volga]. *Trudy saratovskoi uchenoi arkhivnoi komissii* 33 (1916): 85–88.

Pisarevskii, Grigorii G. "Nizhnee Povolzh'e v tret'ei chetverti XVIII veka" [The Lower Volga in the Third Quarter of the Eighteenth Century]. *Izvestiia pedagogicheskogo fakul'teta: Obshchestvennye nauki* [Azerbaidzhanskii gosudarstvennyi universitet imeni V. I. Lenina] 14 (1929): 221–29.

Pisarevskii, Grigorii G. "Vnutrennii rasporiadok v koloniiakh Povolzh'ia pri Ekaterine II" [Internal Arrangement of the Volga Colonies during the Reign of Catherine II]. *Varshavskiia universitetskiia izvestiia* 7 (1913): 1–6; 8 (1914): 17–47; 9 (1915): 1–44.

Pisarevskii, Grigorii G. "Vyzov Mennonitov v Rossii (Po neizdannym arkhivnym dokumentam)" [The Call of Mennonites to Russia (Based on Unpublished Archival Documents)]. *Russkaia mysl'*, October 1903, pp. 49–72; November 1903, pp. 85–102.

P. L. "O nemetskoi kolonizatsii v Rossii" [About the German Colonization in Russia]. *Prikhodskii listok* Dec. 31, 1915, pp. 2–3.

"Podrobnyi spisok iarmarok i bazarov Saratovskoi Gubernii" [Detailed List of Fairs and Markets in Saratov

Province]. *Sbornik saratovskago zemstva*, March 1893, pp. 1–97 (appendix).

Pogodin, A. L. "Nemetskiia kolonii v Rossii" [German Colonies in Russia]. *Moskovskii ezhenedel'nik*, no. 16, 1909, pp. 18–22.

Popov, Konstantin I. "Zapiska o Saratove K. I. Popova" [K. I. Popov's Notes about Saratov]. *Saratovskii krai* 1 (1893): 168.

"Po povodu vyseleniia kolonistov" [Apropos of the Eviction of the Colonists]. *Saratovskiia gubernskiia vedomosti*, Feb. 8, 1878, p. 2.

"Presledovanie deputatov posle rospuska Gosudarstvennoi Dumy" [Prosecution of the Deputies after the Dissolution of the State Duma]. *Vestnik partii narodnoi svobody*, Aug. 30, 1906, pp. 1426–27.

"Putevyia zametki ot Saratova do Samary" [Travel Notes from Saratov to Samara]. *Samarskiia gubernskiia vedomosti*, July 5, 1852, pp. 420–22.

Rath, Georg. "Die Russlanddeustchen in den Vereinigten Staaten von Nord-Amerika." *Heimatbuch der Deutschen aus Russland* (1963), pp. 22–55.

Raun, Toivo U. "The Revolution of 1905 in the Baltic Provinces and Finland." *Slavic Review* 43, no. 3 (1984): 451–67.

Rempel, David. "The Expropriation of the German Colonists in South Russia during the Great War." *Journal of Modern History* 4, no. 1 (1932): 49–67.

Robbins, Jr., Richard G. "Russia's System of Food Supply Relief on the Eve of the Famine of 1891–92." *Agricultural History* 45, no. 4 (1971): 259–69.

Rossov, N. "Krest'ianskiia pereseleniia v Saratovskoi Gub." [Peasant Resettlement in Saratov Province]. In *Materialy k voprosu o nuzhdakh sel'sko-khoziaistve-*

nnoi promyshlennosti v Saratovskoi Gubernii, pp. 1–55.

"Rovnoe" [Rovnoe]. *Saratovskii listok*, Sept. 7, 1891, p. 2.

Rozenberg, L. "Nemetskaia koloniia Semenovka, Kubanskoi Oblasti, Kavkazskago Otdela" [The German Colony Semenovka in the Kuban Region, Caucasus Department]. *Sbornik materialov dlia opisaniia mestnostei i plemen Kavkaza* 27, no. 2 (1900): 162–91.

Russkii. "O narodnom obrazovanii v nemetskikh poseleniiakh Povolzh'ia" [About Public Education in the German Settlements of the Lower Volga]. *Russkii vestnik*, August 1897, pp. 43–64; September 1897, pp. 129–46; October 1897, pp. 183–94.

S. "Golos uezda" [The District Voice]. *Privolzhskaia gazeta*, Apr. 9, 1906, p. 3; Apr. 12, 1906, p. 2.

S. "Zemskoe oskudenie" [Impoverishment of the Zemstvo]. *Kamyshinskii ezhenedel'nik*, Jan. 22, 1906, pp. 7–11.

Saar, G. "Saratovskaia promyshlennost' v 90-kh i v nach. 900-kh gg." [Saratov Industry in the 1890s and Early 1900s]. *Nizhne-volzhskoe oblastnoe nauchnoe obshchestvo kraevedeniia* 35, pt. 3 (1928): 1–30.

Saban'shchikov, M. "O vodvorenii kolonistov Saratovskoi Gubernii po Kamyshinskomu Uezdu" [About the Settlement of Saratov Province Colonists in Kamyshin District]. *Zavolzhskii muravei* 3, no. 17 (1832): 944–65.

Saburov, Ia. "Poezdka v Saratov, Astrakhan, i na Kavkaz" [Journey to Saratov, Astrakhan, and the Caucasus]. *Moskovskii nabliudatel'* 2 (1835): 176–229.

"Saratovskaia letopis'" [Saratov Chronicle]. *Saratovskii krai* 1 (1893): 94.

"Saratovskaia sarpinka na kazanskoi vystavke" [Saratov Sarpinka at the Kazan Exhibition]. *Saratovskiia gubernskiia vedomosti*, July 1, 1890, pp. 390–91.

"Saratovskiia kolonii" [Saratov Colonies]. *Severnaia pchela*, Aug. 22, 1838, p. 751.

S. B. "Luga po Volge i neobkhodimost' ikh uluchsheniia" [Volga Meadows and the Need for Their Improvement]. *Sbornik sel'sko-khoziaistvennykh svedenii*, no. 4, 1909, pp. 28–37.

Schach, Paul. "Facts and Fallacies about Russian-German Dialects." *Journal of the American Historical Society of Germans from Russia* 7 (Spring 1984): 21–25.

Schäfer, J. "Eine neu zu errichtende Privatschule für Knaden zu Goloikaramysch." *Saratowsche deutsche Zeitung*, Feb. 26, 1865, p. 273.

Schneider. "Iz Iagodno-Polianskoi Volosti, Saratovskago Uezda" [From Iagodno-Polianskaia Township, Saratov District]. *Saratovskiia gubernskiia vedomosti*, Oct. 29, 1888, p. 1.

Schneider, Obervorsteher C. "Schreiben des Obervorstehers des Ustkulalinschen Kreises Schneider an das Ustkulalinsche Kreisamt und den Landwirthschaftlichen Verein dieses Kreises." *Saratowsche deutsche Zeitung*, Aug. 10, 1865, p. 641.

Schnurr, Joseph. "Die Siedlung, der Hof und das Haus der Russlanddeutschen, eine geographisch-volkskundliche Betrachtung." *Heimatbuch der Deutschen aus Russland* (1967–68), pp. 1–64.

Schwabauer, Constantin. "Die grosse wolgadeutsche Kolonie Balzer." *Heimatbuch der Deutschen aus Russland* (1967–68), pp. 130–33.

Seib, Eduard. "Der Wolgadeutsche im Spiegel seines Brauchtums." *Heimatbuch der Deutschen aus Russland* (1967–68), pp. 145–209.

"Sel. Talovka, Sosnovskoi Vol" [The Village of Talovka, Sosnovskaia Township]. *Privolzhskaia gazeta*, Feb. 23, 1906, p. 3.

Semenov, M. I. "K kharakteristike kustarnoi promyshlennosti v Saratovskoi Gubernii" [Characteristics of Cottage Industry in Saratov Province]. *Saratovskaia zemskaia nedelia*, May 23, 1891, appendix, pp. 1–8; June 6, 1898, appendix, pp. 9–38.

Semenov, M. I. "Krest'ianskie platezhi i nalogi v Saratovskoi Gubernii" [Peasant Payments and Taxes in Saratov Province]. In *Materialy k voprosu o nuzhdakh sel'sko-khoziaistvennoi promyshlennosti v Saratovskoi Gubernii*, pp. 1–68.

Seregny, Scott. "Politics and the Rural Intelligentsia in Russia: A Biographical Sketch of Stepan Anikin, 1869–1919." *Russian History* 7, pts. 1–2 (1980): 169–200.

Shcheglov, S. "Ocherki goroda Kamyshina i ego uezda" [Sketches of the City and District of Kamyshin]. *Saratovskiia gubernskiia vedomosti*, Feb. 18, 1890, pp. 106–8.

Shchetov, G. A. "Vrach P. K. Gallervospitannik Tartuskogo Universiteta" [Doctor P. K. Haller-Alumnus of Tartu University]. *Tartu ulikooli ajaloo kusimusi* 6 (1977): 70–79.

Sheehy, Ann. "The Volga Germans." *AHSGR WorkPaper* 13 (December 1973): 1–9.

Shlegel', P. "Zemskaia agronomiia i naselenie" [Zemstvo Agronomy and the Population]. *Sbornik sel'sko-khoziaistvennykh svedenii*, no. 3, 1909, pp. 7–13.

Shtentsel'. "Stranichka iz proshlago (k istorii nemetskikh kolonii)" [A Page from the Past (Concerning the History of the German Colonies)]. *Vestnik novouzenskago zemstva*, September–December 1913, pp. 182–93.

Shvetsov, V. "Sostoianie sadovodstva i ogorodnichestva v Kamyshinskom Uezde" [The Condition of Gardening and Market Gardening in Kamyshin District]. *Sel'skokhoziaistvennyi listok Kamyshinskago Uezdago Zemstva*, July 1914, pp. 192–98.

Sinel, Allen. "Educating the Russian Peasantry: The Elementary School Reforms of Count Dmitrii Tolstoi." *Slavic Review* 27, no. 1 (1968): 49–70.

Sinel'shchikov, S. "Kak mogut krest'iane obezpechit' urozhai na svoikh poliak i gde mozhno dostat' korm?" [How Can Peasants Secure Harvests on Their Fields and Where Is It Possible to Acquire Feed?] *Sbornik sel'skokhoziaistvennykh svedenii*, no. 2, 1909, pp. 9–15.

S. M. "Chto nemtsy zdorovo, to russkomu smert'" [What Is Healthy for Germans Is Fatal to Russians]. *Otechestvennyia zapiski*, September 1873, pp. 311–74.

Sokolov, S. D. "Saratovtsy pisateli i uchenye" [Saratov Writers and Scholars]. *Trudy saratovskoi uchenoi arkhivnoi komissii* 30 (1913): 257–366; 32 (1915): 221–84; 33 (1916): 135–96.

"Soll man Wälder pflegen, oder nicht?" *Saratowsche deutsche Zeitung*, Aug. 23, 1866, pp. 512–14.

S. R. "Emigratsiia i pereselenie" [Emigration and Migration]. *Vestnik novouzenskago zemstva*, July–August 1913, pp. 8–42.

S. R. "Zur Schulfrage in den deutschen Wolgagemeinden." *Saratower deutsche Zeitung*, Mar. 15, 1906, p. 1.

"Sravnitel'nyi vzgliad na sostoianie saratovskikh kolonii v 1834 i 1835 gg." [Comparative View of the Condition of Saratov Colonies in 1834 and 1835]. *Zhurnal ministerstva vnutrennikh del* 22, no. 10 (1836): 38–43.

Stärkel, Pastor Wilhelm. "A Voice from the Old Country: The Stärkel Letters." Translated by Paul Reitzer. *Journal of the American Historical Society of Germans from Russia* 2 (Spring 1979): 60–65.

"Statisticheskiia svedeniia o kolonistakh vedomstva saratovskoi kontory inostrannykh poselentsev" [Statistical Information about the Colonists from the Saratov Office for the Guardianship of Foreign Settlers]. *Zhurnal ministerstva gosudarstvennykh imushchestv* 51, pt. 2 (1854): 1–8.

"Statisticheskiia svedeniia o Saratovskoi Gub: Iz otcheta g. nachal'nika gubernii o narodn. nravstvennosti" [Statistical Information about Saratov Province: From the Report of the Provincial Governor about People's Morals]. *Saratovskiia gubernskiia vedomosti*, no. 44, 1841, pp. 105–6.

"Statisticheskiia svedeniia ob inostrannykh poseleniiakh v Rossii" [Statistical Information about Foreign Settlements in Russia]. *Zhurnal ministerstva vnutrennikh del* 28, no. 4 (1838): 1–83.

"Statistika pereseleniia poselian vedomstva ministerstva gosudarstvennykh imushchestv" [Statistics of the Migration of Settlers under the Guardianship of the Ministry of State Domains]. *Zhurnal ministerstva gosudarstvennykh imushchestv* 77, pt. 4 (1861): 44–45.

"Svedeniia o sostoianii kolonii v Saratovskoi Gubernii" [Information about the Condition of Colonies in Saratov Province]. *Saratovskiia gubernskiia vedomosti*, no. 81, (April 24, 1871;) no. 83 (April 27); no. 85 (April 29); no. 86 (April 30); and no. 88 (May 2). [No page numbers given.]

"Tabachnaia promyshlenost' [*sic*] i inostrannykh poselentsev Samarskoi i Saratovskoi Gubernii" [The Tobacco Industry and the Foreign Settlers of Samara and Saratov Provinces]. *Zhurnal ministerstva gosudarstvennykh imushchestv* 59, pt. 2 (1856): 27–40.

"Tabakovodstvo u nemetskikh kolonistov v Nikolaevskom Uezde, Samarskoi Gubernii" [Tobacco-Growing among the German Colonists in Nikolaevsk District, Samara Province]. *Saratovskiia gubernskiia vedomosti*, May 20, 1890, pp. 291–93.

Tikheev, I. "Sarepta. Pis'mo 2-e. Istoricheskii ocherk Sarepty" [Sarepta. Second Letter. Historical Sketch of Sarepta]. *Gazeta dlia sel'skikh khoziaev*, no. 59, 1862, pp. 889–95.

Tkach. "Selenie Kliuchi" [The Village of Kliuchi]. *Kamyshinskiia vesti*, Apr. 8, 1909, p. 3.

Tkachenko, N. "Sistemy polevodstva na nadel' noi zemle krest'ian Saratovskoi Gubernii" [Systems of Field Cultivation on the Allotment Lands of the Peasants of Saratov Province]. *Sbornik saratovskago zemstva*, March 1893, pp. 131–83.

Uchitel'. "O sposobakh poddershaniia distsipliny v nemetskikh shkolakh" [About the Methods of Maintaining Discipline in German Schools]. *Vestnik novouzenskago zemstva*, March 1912, pp. 49–52.

Velitsyn, A. A., pseud. [A. A. Paltov]. "Dukhovnaia zhizn' nashikh nemetskikh kolonii" [The Spiritual Life of Our German Colonies]. *Russkii vestnik*, March 1890, pp. 236–60; May 1890, pp. 212–34; September 1890, pp. 47–80.

Velitsyn, A. A., pseud. [A. A. Paltov]. "Nemtsy na Volge" [Germans on the Volga]. *Russkii vestnik*, April 1893, pp. 154–83.

Velitsyn, A. A., pseud. [A. A. Paltov]. "Saratovskie nemtsy" [Saratov Germans]. *Moskovskiia vedomosti*, Oct. 26, 1891, p. 5.

Voeikov, A. "Opisanie Sarepty: Stat'ia A. Voeikova" [Description of Sarepta: Article of A. Voeikov]. *Severnyi arkhiv*, no. 1, 1822, pp. 48–69.

Voeikov, A. "Pis'mo iz Sarepty" [Letter from Sarepta]. *Syn otechestva* 5, no. 18 (1813): 251–60.

Vorotnikov, A. "Khlebnye marshruty" [Grain Routes]. *Pravda*, Aug. 1, 1979, pp. 1–2.

"Vozdelyvanie tabaka v privolzhskikh nemetskikh koloniiakh" [Cultivation of Tobacco in the German Colonies of the Lower Volga]. *Narodnoe bogatstvo*, Nov. 5, 1863, p. 1050.

"Vypiska iz doklada o saratovskikh koloniiakh" [Excerpt from Report about the Saratov Colonies]. *Sanktpeterburgskii zhurnal*, no. 1, 1804, pp. 92–104.

W. "Sarepta" [Sarepta]. *Saratovskii listok*, July 13, 1880, p. 2.

Wagele, Jacob. [No title.] *Saratowsche deutsche Zeitung*, July 16, 1865, p. 581.

White, Colin. "The Impact of Russian Railway Construction on the Market for Grain in the 1860s and 1870s." In Leslie

Symons and Colin White (eds.), *Russian Transport* (London, 1975), pp. 1–43.

Woltner, Margaret. "Wolgadeutsche Schulprobleme." *Osteuropa* 10 (1934–35): 619–32.

-yi. "Zemstvo posledniago vremeni" [The Recent Zemstvo]. *Zemskoe delo*, July 5, 1910, pp. 1029–51.

"Zametki o nemetskikh koloniiakh Saratovskoi Gubernii" [Notes about German Colonies in Saratov Province]. *Russkii listok* 4 (1863): 75.

"Zemleustroistvo i pereselenie" [Organization of Land Use and Migration]. *Sbornik sel'sko-khoziaistvennykh svedenii*, no. 7, 1909, p. 30.

Zhirmunskii, V. M. "Itogi i zadachi dialektologicheskogo i etnograficheskogo izucheniia nemetskikh poselenii SSSR" [Results and Tasks of Dialectal and Ethnographic Investigations of the German Settlements of the USSR]. *Sovetskaia etnografiia*, no. 2, 1933, pp. 84–112.

Zhirmunskii, V. M. "Problemy kolonial'nyi dialektologii" [Problems of Colony Dialectology]. *Iazyk i literatura*, no. 3, 1929, pp. 179–220.

Zienau, Oswald. "Kultureller und wirtschaftlicher Wiederaufbau in der deutschen Wolgarepublik." *Osteuropa* 3 (1927–28): 45–52.

Ziuriukin, V. "Prodazhnye tseny za period s 1870 po 1920 god na rynakh Nemrespubliki" [Selling Prices on the Markets of the German Republic for the 1870–1920 Period]. *Sbornik statei i materialov* [Gosplan ASSR Nemtsev Povolzh'ia] 3 (1928): 139–64.

Ziuriukin, V. "Sarpinotkatskii kustarnyi promysel Nemrespubliki po dannym biudzhatnogo issledovaniia 1925–26 g." [Sarpinka-Weaving Cottage Industry of the German Republic Based on 1925–26 Budget Analyses]. *Sbornik statei i materialov* [Gosplan ASSR Nemtsev Povolzh'ia] 3 (1928): 165–76.

Books

Adres-kalendar nizhegorodskoi iarmarki na 1890 god [1890 Address-Calendar of the Nizhnii Novgorod Fair]. Nizhnii Novgorod: Tip. nizhegorodskago gub. pravleniia, 1890.

Amburger, Erik. *Geschichte des Protestantismus in Russland.* Stuttgart: Evangelisches Verlagswerk, 1961.

Anfimov, A. M. *Rossiiskaia derevnia v gody pervoi mirovoi voiny* [The Russian Village during the First World War]. Moscow: Izd. sotsial'no-ekonomicheskoi literatury, 1962.

Antsiferov, Alexis N., et al. *Russian Agriculture during the War.* New Haven: Yale University Press, 1930.

A. S. *Nemetskii vopros v russkoi publitsistike* [The German Question in Russian Publicism]. Moscow: Tip. akts. o-va moskovskoe izdatel'stvo, 1915.

ASSR Nemtsev Povolzh'ia. Statisticheskoe upravlenie. *Predvaritel'nye vsesoiuznoi perepisi naseleniia 1926 goda po Avton. Sots. Sov. Respublike Nemtsev Povolzh'ia.* [Preliminary 1926 All-Union Census of Population of the Autonomous Socialist Soviet Republic of the Volga Germans]. Pokrovsk: Nemgosizdat, 1927.

Atkinson, Dorothy. *The End of the Russian Land Commune: 1905–1930.* Stanford: Stanford University Press, 1983.

Bartlett, Roger P. *Human Capital: The Settlement of Foreigners in Russia 1762–1804.*

Cambridge: Cambridge University Press, 1979.

Bauer, Gottlieb. *Geschichte der deutschen Ansiedler an der Wolga, seit ihrer Einwanderung nach Russland bis zur Einfuhrung der allgemeinen Wehrpflicht (1762–1874).* Saratov: Buchdruckerei "Energie," 1908.

Bekker, V. *Vospominaniia o Saratovskoi Gubernii.* [Reminiscences about Saratov Province]. Moscow: Tip. Volkov, 1852.

Beratz, Gottlieb. *Die deutschen Kolonien an der unteren Wolga.* Saratov: Druck von H. Schellhorn, 1915.

Blackwell, William L. *The Beginnings of Russian Industrialization 1800–1860.* Princeton: Princeton University Press, 1968.

Blankenburg, Rudolph. *Philadelphia and the Russian Famine of 1891 and 1892.* Philadelphia: The Russian Famine Relief Committee of Philadelphia, 1892.

Bock, Maria. *Vospominaniia o moem ottse P. A. Stolypina* [Reminiscences about My Father P. A. Stolypin]. New York: Izd. im. Chekhova, 1953.

Boiuovich, M. M. *Chleny Gosudarstvennoi Dumy: Pervyi sozyv* [Members of the First State Duma]. Moscow: T-vo I. D. Sytina, 1906.

Boiuovich, M. M. *Chleny Gosudarstvennoi Dumy: Vtoroi sozyv* [Members of the Second State Duma]. Moscow: T-vo I. D. Sytina, 1907.

Bonwetsch, Gerhard. *Geschichte der deutschen Kolonien an der Wolga.* Stuttgart: Verlag J. Engelhorns, 1919.

Brandenburg, Hans. *The Meek and the Mighty.* New York: Oxford University Press, 1977.

Brooks, Jeffrey. *When Russia Learned to Read.* Princeton: Princeton University Press, 1985.

Bruford, W. H. *Germany in the Eighteenth Century: The Social Background of the Literary Revival.* Cambridge: Cambridge University Press, 1952.

Chayanov, A. V. *The Theory of Peasant Economy.* Edited by Daniel Thorner, Basile Kerblay, and R. E. F. Smith. Homewood, Ill.: Dorsey Press, 1966.

Chermenskii, Evgenii D. *IV Gosudarstvennaia duma i sverzhenie tsarisma v Rossii* [The Fourth State Duma and the Overthrow of Tsarism in Russia]. Moscow: "Mysl'," 1976.

Chernyshev, I. V. *Obshchina posle 9 noiabria 1906 g.* [The Commune after November 9, 1906]. 2 vols. Petrograd: Tip. "Ekonomiia," 1917.

Conroy, Mary Schaeffer. *Peter Arkad'evich Stolypin: Practical Politics in Late Tsarist Russia.* Boulder, Colo.: Westview Press, 1976.

Crisp, Olga. *Studies in the Russian Economy before 1914.* London: Macmillan Press, 1976.

Daniels, Robert. *Russia.* Cambridge, Mass.: Harvard University Press, 1985.

Departament okladnykh sborov. *Materialy po statistike dvizheniia zemlevladeniia v Rossii* [Statistical Materials concerning the Movement of Landholding in Russia]. Vol. 23. Petrograd: Tip. P. P. Soikhin, 1914.

Drabkina, Elizaveta Ia. *Natsional'nyi i kolonial'nyi vopros v tsarskoi Rossii* [The Nationality and Colonial Question in Tsarist Russia]. Moscow: Izd. kommunisticheskoi akademii, 1930.

Drotleff, Katharina. *Lasst sie selber sprechen: Berichte russlanddeutscher Aussiedler.* Hannover: Lutherhaus, 1980.

Druzhinin, Nikolai M. *Gosudarstvennye krest'iane i reforma P. D. Kiseleva* [State

Peasants and the Reform of P. D. Kiselev]. 2 vols. Moscow and Leningrad: Izd. Akad. Nauk SSSR, 1946 and 1958.

Dubrovskii, S. M. *Stolypinskaia zemel'naia reforma* [The Stolypin Land Reform]. Moscow: Akad. Nauk SSSR, Institut istorii, 1963.

Dunn, Stephen and Ethel. *The Peasants of Central Russia*. New York: Holt, Rinehart and Winston, 1967.

Dvornikov, P., and S. Sokolov. *Geografiia Rossiiskoi Imperii*. [Geography of the Russian Empire]. 2d ed. Moscow: Izd. magazina sotrudnik shkol, 1913.

Eisenach, George J. *Pietism and the Russian Germans in the United States*. Berne, Ind.: Berne Publishers, 1948.

Eklof, Ben. *Russian Peasant Schools*. Berkeley: University of California Press, 1986.

Emmons, Terence, and Wayne Vucinich (eds.). *The Zemstvo in Russia*. Cambridge: Cambridge University Press, 1982.

Ezioranskii, L. K. *Fabrichno-zavodskiia predpriiatiia Rossiiskoi Imperii* [Factory-Mill Enterprises in the Russian Empire]. St. Petersburg: Tip. min. finansov, 1909.

Fallows, Thomas. "Forging the Zemstvo Movement: Liberalism and Radicalism on the Volga, 1890–1905." Ph.D. dissertation, Harvard University, 1981.

Fitzlyon, Kyril, and Tatiana Browning. *Before the Revolution*. Woodstock, N.Y.: Overlook Press, 1978.

Fleischhauer, Ingeborg. *Die Deutschen im Zarenreich*. Stuttgart: Deutsche Verlags-Anstalt, 1986.

Fleischhauer, Ingeborg, and Benjamin Pinkus. *The Soviet Germans: Past and Present*. New York: St. Martin's Press, 1986.

Fomenko, P. K. *Zakon 2 fevralia 1915 goda o nemetskom zemlevladenii*. [The February 2, 1915, Law on German Landholding]. Odessa: Tip. I. L. Skal'skago, 1915.

Freeze, Gregory L. *The Parish Clergy in Nineteenth-Century Russia*. Princeton: Princeton University Press, 1983.

Fussell, G. E. *Farming Technique from Prehistoric to Modern Times*. London: Pergamon Press, 1965.

Gates, Paul. W. *The Farmer's Age: Agriculture 1815–1860*. New York: Holt, Rinehart and Winston, 1960.

Geraklitov, A. A. *Istoriia saratovskogo kraia v XVI–XVIII vekakh*. [History of the Saratov Region in the 16th and 17th Centuries]. Saratov: Izd. saratov. obshch. istorii, arkheologii i etnografii, 1923.

German, Ivan E. *Istoriia russkago mezhevaniia* [History of Russian Land Surveying]. 2d ed. Moscow: Tipo-litografiia V. Rikhter, 1910.

Giesinger, Adam. *From Catherine to Khrushchev: The Story of Russia's Germans*. Battleford, Sask.: Marion Press, 1974.

Goikhbarg, Aleksandr Grigor'evich. *Zemlevladenie i zemlepol'zovanie podannykh vrazhdebnykh derzhav i nemetskikh vykhodtsev* [Landholding and Land Use of Subjects of Enemy Powers and German Extraction]. Petrograd: Izd. iuridicheskago knizhnago sklada "Pravo," 1915.

Goikhbarg, Aleksandr Grigor'evich. *Zemlevladenie i zemlepol'zovanie poddannykh vrazhdebnykh derzhav i nemetskikh vykhodtsev. Vypusk II: Svodnyi tekst zakonov 2 fevralia i 13 dekabria 1915 g. s vstupitel'nym ocherkom* [Landholding and Land Use of Subjects of Enemy Powers and German Extraction. 2d edition: Summary Text of the February 2 and

December 13, 1915, Laws with an Introductory Essay]. Petrograd: Izd. iuridicheskago knizhnago sklada "Pravo," 1916.

Golovine, Nicholas. *The Russian Army in the World War*. New Haven: Yale University Press, 1931.

Golubev, P. A. *Istoriko-statisticheskiia tablitsy po Saratovskoi Gubernii za period 1862–92 g.* [Historical-Statistical Tables of Saratov Province for the Period 1862–92]. N.p., n. pub., n.d.

Gras, Norman. *A History of Agriculture in Europe and America*. 2d ed. New York: F. S. Crofts, 1946.

Grigor'ev, Vasilii Nikolaevich. *Predmetnyi ukazatel'materialov v zemsko-statisticheskikh trudakh s 1860–kh godov po 1917 g.* [Subject Index of Materials in Zemstvo Statistical Works from the 1860s until 1917]. 2 vols. Moscow: Tsentral'noe statisticheskoe upravlenie SSSR, 1926 and 1927.

Gross, E. *Avt. Sots. Sov. Resp. Nemtsev Povolzh'ia* [The Autonomous Socialist Soviet Republic of the Volga Germans]. Pokrovsk: Nemgosizdat, 1926.

G. U. *Nemetskiia tserkovno-prikhodskiia uchilishcha v Kamyshinskom Uezde* [German Church-Parish Schools in Kamyshin District]. Saratov: Tip. gub. zemstva, n.d.

Gubotdel VOC. *Ukazatel'torgovo-promyshlennykh, kooperativnykh i dr. predpriiatiia po A.S.S.R.N.P. i Saratovskoi Gub. na 1927–28* [Index of Trade, Industrial, Cooperative and Other Enterprises of the Autonomous Socialist Soviet Republic of the Volga Germans]. Saratov: Izd. Gubotdel, 1927.

Habakkuk, H. J., and M. Postan (eds.). *The Cambridge Economic History of Europe*. Vol. 6. Cambridge: Cambridge University Press, 1965.

Haller, Peter. *Vospominaniia P. K. Gallera* [Memoirs of P. K. Haller]. Saratov: n. pub., 1927.

Hans, Nicholas. *History of Russian Educational Policy (1701–1917)*. New York: Russell and Russell, 1964.

Henriksson, Anders. *The Tsar's Loyal Germans*. Boulder, Colo.: East European Monographs, 1983.

Henry, Jerry. "Adam Franzovich Ebel." Unpublished manuscript, Special Collections, Colorado State University Library.

Herskovits, Melville J. *Acculturation*. Gloucester, Mass.: Peter Smith, 1958.

Ianin, V. L. (ed.). *Problemy agrarnoi istorii* [Problems of Agrarian History]. Vol. 2. Minsk: Nauka i tekhnika, 1978.

Ignatiev, Paul N., Dimitry N. Odinetz, and Paul J. Novgorotsev. *Russian Schools and Universities in the World War.* New Haven: Yale University Press, 1929.

Illiustrirovannyi torgovo-promyshlennyi adresnyi i spravochnyi al'bom g. Saratova 1907 g. [The 1907 Illustrated Trade and Industrial Address and Reference Album of the City of Saratov]. Saratov: Tip. A. K. Podzemskago, 1907.

Kabuzan, Vladimir M. *Izmeneniia v razmeshchenii naseleniia Rossii v XVIII–pervoi polovine XIX v. (po materialam revizii).* [Changes in the Distribution of Russia's Population in the Eighteenth and First Half of the Nineteenth Centuries (Based on Census Materials)]. Moscow: "Nauka," 1971.

Kabuzan, Vladimir M. *Narodonaselenie Rossii v XVIII–pervoi polovine XIX v. (po materialam revizii).* [The Population of Russia in the Eighteenth and First Half of the Nineteenth Centuries (Based on Census Materials)]. Moscow: "Nauka," 1963.

Kappeler, Andreas, Boris Meissner, and Gerhard Simon (eds.). *Die Deutschen im Russischen Reich und im Sowjetstaat.* Cologne: Markus Verlag, 1987.

Karavaev, V. F. *Bibliograficheskii obzor zemskoi statisticheskoi i otsenochnoi literatury so veremeni uchrezhdeniia zemstv, 1864–1903 g.* [Bibliographical Review of Zemstvo Statistical and Evaluative Literature from the Time of the Establishment of Zemstvos, 1864–1903]. St. Petersburg: Tipo-litografiia M. P. Frolova i N. L. Nyrkina, 1913.

Kaufman, Aleksandr Arkad'evich. *Pereselenie i kolonizatsiia* [Migration and Colonization]. St. Petersburg: Biblioteka "Obshchestvennoi Pol'zy," 1905.

Kennan, George F. *The Decline of Bismarck's European Order.* Princeton: Princeton University, 1979.

Keussler, Johannes von. *Zur Geschichte und Kritik des bauerlichen Gemeindebesitzes in Russland.* 3 vols. St. Petersburg: Verlag von C. Ricker, 1882, 1883, and 1887.

Khodakov, G. *Ocherki istorii saratovskoi organizatsii KPSS* [Essays on the History of the Saratov Organization of the Communist Party of the Soviet Union]. Vol. 1. Saratov: Knizhnoe izdatel'stvo, 1957.

Kitanina, T. M. *Khlebnaia torgovlia Rossii v 1875–1914 gg.* [The Russian Grain Trade, 1875–1914]. Leningrad: "Nauka," 1978.

Klaus, A. A. *Nashi kolonii* [Our Colonies]. St. Petersburg, 1869. (Reprinted with introduction by R. B. Bartlett. Cambridge: Oriental Research Partners, 1972.)

Kloberdanz, Timothy. "The Volga German Catholic Life Cycle." Master's thesis,

Department of Sociology, Colorado State University, 1974.

Klopov, A. A. *Materialy dlia izucheniia khlebnoi torgovli na Volge.* [Materials for the Study of the Volga Grain Trade]. Moscow: Tip. I. N. Kushnerev, 1886.

Klopov, A. A. *Ocherk mukomol'no-krupchatnoi promyshlennosti v Povolzh'e v 1892–3 g.* [Essay on the Lower Volga Flour Milling Industry in 1892–93]. Tver: Tipo-litografiia i notopechatnia F. S. Murav'eva, 1894.

Klopov, A. A. *Otchet po izsledovaniiu volzhskoi khlebnoi torgovli v 1886* [Report Based on the Study of the Volga Grain Trade in 1886]. St. Petersburg: Tip. V. Kirshbaum, 1887.

Klopov, A. A. *Otchet po izsledovaniiu volzhskoi khlebnoi torgovli v 1887* [Report Based on the Study of the Volga Grain Trade in 1887]. St. Petersburg: Tip. V. Kirshbaum, 1889.

Koch, Fred. *The Volga Germans in Russia and the Americas, from 1763 to the Present.* University Park: Pennsylvania State University Press, 1977.

Kohn, Hans. *The Idea of Nationalism.* New York: Macmillan Company, 1944.

Kolesnikov, G. I. *Kul'turnoe khoziaistvo v nekul'turnom krae* [A Cultivated Economy in a Backward Region]. Saratov: Tip. gub. zemstva, 1908.

König, Lothar. *Die Deutschtuminsel an der Wolga.* Dulmen, Westphalia: Lauman, 1938.

Koval'chenko, I. D., and L. V. Milov. *Vserossiiskii agrarnyi rynok* [The All-Russian Agricultural Market]. Moscow: "Nauka," 1974.

Kovalevskii, Vladimir I. (ed.). *Rossiia v kontse XIX veka* [Russia at the End of the

Nineteenth Century]. St. Petersburg: Tip. akts. obshch. Brokgauz-Efron, 1900.

Kruglikov, P. V. *Ukazatel' fabrik i zavodov Samarskoi Gubernii* [Index of Factories and Mills in Samara Province]. Samara: Gubernskaia tipografiia, 1887.

Kurts, V. A., (ed.). *Sarpino-tkatskaia promyshlennost' s 1921–1922 g.* [The Sarpinka Weaving Industry since 1921–1922]. Pokrovsk: Nemgosizdat, 1922.

Kushner, P. I. (ed.). *Russkie: Istoriko-etnograficheskii atlas iz istorii russkogo narodnogo zhilishcha i kostiuma (ukrashenie krest'ianskikh domov i odezhdy) seredina XIX – nachalo XX v.* [Russians: Historical-Ethnographical Atlas of the History of Russian Popular Dwellings and Dress from the Middle of the Nineteenth to the Beginning of the Twentieth Centuries]. Moscow: "Nauka," 1970.

Langhans, Manfred. *Die Wolgadeutschen: Ihr Staats und Verwaltungsrecht in Vergangenheit und Gegenwart.* Berlin: Ost-Europa Verlag, 1929.

Lehmann, Carl, and Parvus [Alexander Helphand]. *Das hungernde Russland.* Stuttgart: Verlag von I. B. W. Dietz, 1900.

Leikina-Svirskaia, Vera Romanovna. *Intelligentsiia v Rossii vo vtoroi polovine XIX veka* [The Intelligentsia in Russia in the Second Half of the Nineteenth Century]. Moscow: "Mysl'," 1971.

Lenin, V. I. *Sochineniia* [Collected Works]. 4th ed. Vol. 3. Moscow: Gos. izdat. polit. literatury, 1950.

Leopol'dov, Andrei. *Istoricheskii ocherk saratovskago kraia* [Historical Sketch of the Saratov Region]. Moscow: Tip. S. Selivanskago, 1848.

Leopol'dov, Andrei. *Statisticheskoe opisanie Saratovskoi Gubernii* [Statistical Descrip-

tion of Saratov Province]. St. Petersburg: Tip. dept. vneshnei torgovli, 1839.

Lewin, Moshe. *The Making of the Soviet System.* New York: Pantheon Books, 1985.

Liashchenko, P. I. *Mukomol'naia promyshlennost' Rossii i inostrannye potrebitel'nye rynki* [The Russian Flour Milling Industry and Foreign Consumer Markets]. St. Petersburg: Tip. min. finansov, 1909.

Lindeman, Karl Eduardovich. *Prekrashchenie zemlevladeniia i zemlepol'zovaniia poselian' sobstvennikov: Ukazy 2 fevralia i 13 dekabria 1915 goda i 10, 15 iiulia i 19 avgusta 1916 goda i ikh vliianie na ekonomicheskoe sostoianie iuzhnoi Rossii* [The Termination of Settler Proprietors' Landholding and Land Use: The Decrees of February 2 and December 13, 1915, and July 10 and 15, and August 19, 1916, and Their Influence on the Economic Situation in Southern Russia]. Moscow: K. L. Men'shova, 1917.

Lindemann, Karl. *Zakony 2 fevralia i 13 dekabria 1915 g.* [The Laws of February 2 and December 13, 1915]. Moscow: K. L. Men'shova, 1916.

Lingeman, Richard. *Small Town America.* New York: G. P. Putnam's Sons, 1980.

Liprandi, A. P., pseud. [Volynets, A.]. *Germaniia v Rossii* [Germany in Russia]. Kharkov: "Mirnyi trud," 1911.

Liprandi, A. P., pseud. [Volynets, A.]. *Kak ostanovit' mirnoe zavoevanie nashikh okrain? Nemetskii vopros, sushchnost' i znachenie ego v iugo-zapadnoi Rossii* [How to Stop the Peaceful Conquest of Our Borderlands? The German Question, Its Nature and Significance in Southwest Russia]. Kiev: Tip. gen. Bruna, 1890.

Lishin, Ivan. *Ocherk Nikolaevskago Uezda (Samarskoi Gubernii) v statisticheskom i* sel'sko-khoziaistvennom otnosheniiakh [Statistical and Agricultural Sketch of Nikolaevsk District (Samara Province)]. St. Petersburg: Tip. V. S. Balasheva, 1880.

Löbsack, Georg. *Einsam Kampft das Wolgaland.* Leipzig: R. Voigtländer Verlag, 1936.

Long, James. *The German-Russians: A Bibliography.* Santa Barbara: ABC-CLIO Press, 1978.

Loshkarev, S. *Obozrenie Samarskoi Gubernii v khoziaistvennom otnoshenii* [Review of Agricultural Relations in Samara Province]. Moscow: n. pub., 1854.

Luppov, P. *Nemetskiia nachal'nyia shkoly v Rossii* [German Primary Schools in Russia]. Petrograd: Synodal'naia tipografiia, 1916.

Lyashchenko, Peter. *History of the National Economy of Russia.* Translated by L. M. Herman. New York: Macmillan Company, 1949.

Maizul, A. Ia. *Putevoditel' po g. Saratovu* [Guide to the City of Saratov]. Saratov: Tip. t-va sotrudnik shkoly, 1917.

Martov, L., P. Maslov, and A. Potresov (eds.). *Obshchestvennoe dvizhenie v Rossii v nachale XX-go veka* [The Awakening of Social Consciousness in Russia in the Beginning of the Twentieth Century]. 4 vols. St. Petersburg: Tip. "Ob. Pol'za," 1909–11.

Mayhew, Alan. *Rural Settlement and Farming in Germany.* London: Batsford Ltd., 1973.

Medvedev, Roy A., and Zhores A. Medvedev. *Khrushchev: The Years in Power.* Translated by Andrew R. Durkin. New York: W. W. Norton, 1976.

Merk, Frederick. *History of the Westward Movement.* New York: Knopf, 1980.

Miliukov, Paul. *History of Russia.* 3 vols. Translated by Charles Markmann. New York: Funk and Wagnalls, 1969.

Ministerstvo finansov. *Spisok mukomol'nykh mel'nits Rossii v 1908 godu* [List of Flour Mills in Russia in 1908]. St. Petersburg: Tip. min. finansov, 1909.

Ministerstvo gosudarstvennykh imushchestv. *Otchety i izsledovaniia po kustarnoi promyshlennosti v Rossii* [Reports and Studies on Cottage Industry in Russia]. Vol. 1. St. Petersburg: Tip. V. Kirshbaum, 1892.

Ministerstvo gosudarstvennykh imushchestv. *Statisticheskii obzor gosudarstvennykh imushchestv za 1858 god* [The 1858 Statistical Review of State Domains]. St. Petersburg: Tip. min. gosudarstvennykh imushchestv, 1861.

Ministerstvo torgovli i promyshlennosti. *Sbornik svedenii o deistvuiushchikh v Rossii torgovykh domakh* [Collection of Information about Commercial Firms in Russia]. St. Petersburg: Ia. Kravitskii, 1912.

Ministerstvo torgovli i promyshlennosti. *Svod otchetov fabrichnykh inspektorov za 1905 god* [Collection of Factory Inspectors' Reports for 1905]. St. Petersburg: Tip. V. Kirshbaum, 1908.

Ministerstvo vnutrennikh del. *Izvlechenie iz otcheta ministra vnutrennikh del za 1835 god* [Excerpts from the 1835 Report of the Minister of the Interior]. St. Petersburg: Tip. min. vnut. del, 1836.

Ministerstvo vnutrennikh del. *Sbornik pravitel'stvennykh rasporiazhenii po voinskoi povinnosti* [Collection of Government Regulations regarding Military Service Obligations]. Vols. 3–6. St. Petersburg: Tip. min. vnut. del, 1874–77.

Ministerstvo zemledeliia i gosudarstven-nykh imushchestv. *Svod statisticheskikh svedenii po sel'skomu khoziaistvu Rossii k kontsu XIX veka* [Collection of Statistical Information on Russian Agriculture at the End of the Nineteenth Century]. 2 vols. St. Petersburg: Tip. V. Kirshbaum, 1902–3.

Minkh, Aleksandr Nikolaevich. *Istoriko-geograficheskii slovar' Saratovskoi Gubernii* [Historical-Geographical Dictionary of Saratov Province]. 3 vols. Saratov: Tip. gub. zemstva, 1898–1901.

Minkh, Aleksandr Nikolaevich. *Narodnye obychai, sueveriia, predrassudki i obriady krest'ian Saratovskoi Gubernii* [Popular Tales, Superstitions, Prejudices, and Rites of the Peasants of Saratov Province]. St. Petersburg: Tip. Bezobrazov, 1890.

Mitiaev, K. G. (ed.). *Khoziaistvo i byt russkikh krest'ian* [The Rural Economy and Way of Life of Russian Peasants]. Moscow: Sovetskaia Rossiia, 1959.

Mrdjenovic, Aleksander. "The Volga-German *Gemeindeschaft* and Political Autonomy Amidst Domestic Turmoil, 1914–22." Master's thesis, Department of History, University of Kansas, 1976.

Mukomol'noe delo v Rossii [The Flour Milling Business in Russia]. 2d ed. revised. Odessa: Tip. Odesskiia Novost', 1912.

Murav'ev, M. V. (ed.). *"Nemetskoe zlo": Sbornik statei posviashchennykh voprosu o bor'be s nashei "vnutrennei Germaniei"* ["The German Evil": A Collection of Articles Devoted to the Question of The Struggle with Our "Internal Germany"]. Moscow: Tip. A. I. Mamon-tov, 1915.

Mysh, Mikhail Ignat'evich. (ed.). *Ob inostran-ntsakh v Rossii* [Concerning Foreigners in Russia]. 2d ed. revised. St. Petersburg: Tip. A. Benke, 1911.

Nabatov, Grigorii I. *Respublika bez mezhei: Respublika Nemtzev Povolzh'ia* [Republic without Borders: The Republic of Volga Germans]. Moscow: Priboi, 1930.

Nifontov, A. S. *Zernovoe proizvodstvo Rossii vo vtoroi polovine XIX veka* [Russian Grain Production in the Second Half of the Nineteenth Century]. Moscow: "Nauka," 1974.

Nikolaevskoe uezdnoe zemstvo. *Materialy po otsenke zemel' Nikolaevskago Uezda* [Materials for the Land Evaluation of Nikolaevsk District]. Vol. 1. Samara: Zemskaia tipografiia, 1904.

Nolde, Baron Boris. *Russia in the Economic War.* New Haven: Yale University Press, 1928.

Novouzenskoe uezdnoe zemstvo. *Kustarnyia proizvodstva v Novouzenskom Uezde po obsledovaniiu 1904 goda* [Cottage Industry Production in Novouzensk District Based on 1904 Inspections]. N.p., n. pub., n.d.

Novouzenskoe uezdnoe zemstvo. *Novou-zenskii uezd v estestvenno-istoricheskom i khoziaistvennom otnoshenii: Po dannym obsledovaniia 1908 g.* [Novouzensk District in Its Natural, Historical, and Economic Conditions: Based on Figures from 1908 Surveys]. 2 vols. Novouzensk: Tip. obshchestva trudovoi pomoshchi, 1912–13.

Novouzenskoe uezdnoe zemstvo. *Proizvodstvo masterskikh novouzenskago uezdnago zemstva* [Production of the Novouzensk District Zemstvo Workshops]. Saratov: T-vo tip. energiia, 1913.

Oblastnoi sovet narodnogo khoziaistva Oblasti Nemtsev Povolzh'ia. *Sarpino-tkatskaia promyshlennost' v 1921–22 g.* [The Sarpinka Weaving Industry in

1921–22]. Pokrovsk: Tip. obsovnarkhoza Oblasti Nemtsev Povolzh'ia, 1922.

Obolenskii, Valerian V., pseud. [Osinskii]. *Mezhdunarodnye i mezhkontinental'nye migratsii v dovoennoi Rossii i SSSR* [International and Intercontinental Migrations in Prewar Russia and the USSR]. Moscow: Tsentral'noe statisticheskoe upravlenie SSSR, 1928.

Otchet obekonomosoveshcheniia Oblasti Nemtsev Povolzh'ia za vremia s l oktiabria 1921 g. po l ianvaria 1922 goda [Account of the October 1, 1921, to January 1, 1922, Economic Conference of the Volga German Oblast]. N.p., n. pub., n.d.

Otsenochno-statisticheskoe otdelenie samarskago gubernskago zemstva. *Sbornik khoziaistvenno-statisticheskikh svedenii po Samarskoi Gubernii* [Collection of Economic Statistical Information on Samara Province]. Samara: Tip. gub. zemstva, 1912.

Otsenochno-statisticheskoe otdelenie saratovskago gubernskago zemstva. *Materialy dlia otsenki zemel' Saratovskoi Gubernii* [Materials for the Land Evaluation of Saratov Province]. 3 vols. Saratov: T-vo pechatnia S. P. Iakovleva, 1905–10.

Otsenochno-statisticheskoe otdelenie saratovskoi gubernskoi zemskoi upravy. *Sbornik svedenii po Saratovskoi Gubernii za [1899–1907]* [Collection of Information on Saratov Province from 1889 through 1907]. [Years 1899, 1900, 1904, and 1906 each had two volumes. Three volumes appeared in 1905.] Saratov: Tip. gub. zemstva, 1900–08.

Otsenochno-statisticheskoe otdelenie saratovskoi gubernskoi zemskoi upravy. *Spiski naselennykh mest Saratovskoi Gubernii* [Lists of Populated Places in Saratov Province]. Saratov: Zemskaia tipografiia, 1912.

Otzyvy korrespondentov tekushchei statistiki po nekotorym voprosam sel'skoi zhizni Saratovskoi Gubernii [Correspondents' Responses of Current Statistics to a Few Questions regarding Saratov Province Rural Life]. Vol. 1. Saratov: Tip. gub. zemstva, 1902.

Overton, Richard. *Burlington Route*. New York: Knopf, 1965.

Ovsiannikov, N. N. *O torgovle na nizhegorodskoi iarmarke* [Trade at the Nizhnii Novgorod Fair]. Nizhnii Novgorod: Tip. G. A. Pendrin, 1867.

Peretiatkovich, Georgii I. *Povolzh'e v XVII i nachale XVIII veka* [The Lower Volga in the Seventeenth and Early Eighteenth Centuries]. Odessa: P. A. Zelenago, 1882.

Pershin, Pavel Nikolaevich. *Agrarnaia revoliutsiia v Rossii* [Agrarian Revolution in Russia]. Vol. 1. Moscow: "Nauka," 1966.

Pershin, Pavel Nikolaevich. *Uchastkovoe zemlepol'zovanie v Rossii* [Land Tenure in Russia]. Moscow: Izd. narkomzema "Novaia Derevnia," 1922.

Pisarevskii, Grigorii G. *Iz istorii inostrannoi kolonizatsii v Rossii v XVIII v. (Po neizdannym arkhivnym dokumentam)* [From the History of the Foreign Colonization in Russia in the Eighteenth Century (Based on Unpublished Archival Documents)]. Moscow: Pechatnia A. I. Snegirevyi, 1909.

Pisarevskii, Grigorii G. *K istorii iezuitov v Rossii (veroispovednyi vopros v koloniiakh Povolzh'ia sto let tomu nazad)* [Concerning the History of the Jesuits in Russia (the Denomination Question in the Volga Colonies a Century Ago)].

Warsaw: Tipografiia varshavskago uchebnago okruga, 1912.

Pisarevskii, Grigorii G. *Khoziaistvo i forma zemlevladeniia v koloniiakh Povolzh'ia v XVIII–m i v pervoi chetverti XIX–go veka* [Farming and the Form of Landholding in the Volga Colonies in the Eighteenth and First Quarter of the Ninteenth Centuries]. Rostov-on-Don: Tip. A. I. Ter-Abramian, 1916.

Pisarevskii, Grigorii G. *Vnutrennii rasporiadok k koloniiakh Povolzh'ia pri Ekaterina II* [Internal Order in the Volga Colonies during the Reign of Catherine II]. Warsaw: Tipografiia varshavskago uchebnago okruga, 1914.

Podkovyrov, N. G. (ed.). *Spisok naselennykh mest Samarskoi Gubernii, sostavlen v 1910 godu* [List of Populated Places in Samara Province Compiled in 1910]. Samara: Gubernskaia tipografiia, 1910.

Polanyi, Karl. *The Great Transformation.* Boston: Beacon Hill Press, 1957.

Praetorius, Max. *Galka eine deutsche Ansiedlung an der Wolga.* Leipzig: Druck von Thomas & Hubert, 1912.

Priklonskii, S. A. *Ocherki samoupravleniia* [Essays on Self-Government]. St. Petersburg: Tip. "Ob. Pol'za," 1886.

Prilozhenie k vsepoddaneishemu otchetu Samarskago Gubernatora za [1881–87] god [Appendix to the General Report of the Samara Governor for 1881–87]. Samara: Gubernskaia tipografiia, 1882–88.

Radkey, Oliver. *The Agrarian Foes of Bolshevism.* New York: Columbia University Press, 1958.

Radkey, Oliver. *The Election to the Russian Constituent Assembly of 1917.* Cambridge, Mass.: Harvard University Press, 1950.

Raeff, Marc. *Understanding Imperial Russia.* Translated by Arthur Goldhammer. New York: Columbia University Press, 1984.

Raleigh, Donald. *Revolution on the Volga: 1917 in Saratov.* Ithaca: Cornell University Press, 1986.

Redfield, Robert. *The Little Community.* Chicago: University of Chicago Press, 1955.

Reimisch, Fritz Hans. *Die deutschen Wolga-Kolonien von ihrer Gründung bis zu den Tagen ihrer grössten Leidenzeit.* Berlin: Verein der Wolgadeutschen, 1922.

Rennikov, A. M. *Zoloto Reina o Nemtsakh v Rossii* [Gold of the Rhine: About the Germans in Russia]. Petrograd: T-va A. S. Suvorin, 1915.

Roberts, Carl Eric Bechhofer. *Through Starving Russia.* London: Methuen, 1921.

Rudé, George. *Europe in the Eighteenth Century: Aristocracy and the Bourgeois Challenge.* London: Weidenfeld and Nicolson, 1972; New York: Praeger.

Ryndziunskii, P. G. *Krest'ianskaia promyshlennost' v poreformannoi Rossii (60–80-e gody XIX v.)* [Peasant Industry in Reformed Russia (1860–1880)]. Moscow: "Nauka," 1966.

Ryndziunskii, P. G. *Utverzhdenie kapitalizma v Rossii 1850–80 gg.* [The Consolidation of Capitalism in Russia, 1850–80]. Moscow: "Nauka," 1978.

Samarskii gubernskii statisticheskii komitet. *Pamiatnaia knizhka Samarskoi Gubernii za 1863–64 g.* [Memorandum Book of Samara Province for 1863–64]. Samara: Gubernskaia tipografiia, 1864.

Samarskii gubernskii statisticheskii komitet. *Pamiatnaia knizhka Samarskoi Gubernii za 1912 god* [Memorandum Book of Samara Province for 1912]. Samara: Tip. gub. pravleniia, 1913.

Samarskii gubernskii statisticheskii komitet. *Statisticheskiia tablitsy Samarskoi Gubernii* [Statistical Tables of Samara Province]. 2 vols. Samara: Gubernskaia tipografiia, 1870.

Samarskoe gubernskoe zemstvo. *Sbornik statisticheskikh svedenii po Samarskoi Gubernii* [Collection of Statistical Information on Samara Province]. Vols. 6 and 7. Samara: Zemskaia tipografiia, 1889 and 1890.

Samarskoe gubernskoe zemstvo. *Zemsko-statisticheskii spravochnik po Samarskoi Gubernii na 1914 god* [Zemstvo Statistical Reference Book on Samara Province for 1914]. Samara: Zemskaia tipografiia, 1914.

Saratovskaia uchenaia arkhivnaia komissiia. *K piatidesiatiletiiu zemskikh uchrezhdenii* [For the Fiftieth Anniversary of Zemstvo Institutions]. Saratov: Izd. saratov. gub. uchen. arkhiv. kom., 1913.

Saratovskaia uchenaia arkhivnaia komissiia. *Materialy o sostoianii narodnogo obrazovaniia v Saratovskoi Gubernii za 1910–11 god* [Materials concerning the State of Public Education in Saratov Province for 1910–11]. Saratov: Izd. saratov. gub. uchen. arkhiv. kom., 1916.

Saratovskii gubernskii statisticheskii komitet. *Materialy k opisaniiu Saratovskoi Gubernii* [Materials for a Description of Saratov Province]. Saratov: Tip. P. S. Feokritova, 1875.

Saratovskii gubernskii statisticheskii komitet. *Pamiatnaia knizhka Saratovskoi Gubernii na 1872 god* [Memorandum Book of Saratov Province for 1872]. Vol. 2. Saratov: Tip. gub. pravleniia, 1873.

Saratovskii gubernskii statisticheskii komitet. *Pamiatnaia knizhka Saratovskoi Gubernii na 1880.* [Memorandum Book of Saratov Province for 1880]. Saratov: Tip. gub. pravleniia, 1880.

Saratovskii gubernskii statisticheskii komitet. *Statisticheskii obzor Saratovskoi Gubernii za [1895–1911]* [Statistical Survey of Saratov Province for the Years 1895 to 1911]. Saratov: Tip. gub. pravleniia, 1896–1912.

Saratovskii statisticheskii komitet. *Saratovskii sbornik* [Saratov Collection]. 2 vols. Saratov: Tip. gub. pravleniia, 1881 and 1882.

Saratovskoe gubernskoe statisticheskoe biuro. *Tablitsy statisticheskikh svedenii po Saratovskoi Gubernii po dannym vserossiiskoi sel'sko-khoziaistvennoi i gorodskoi perepisei 1917 goda* [Tables of Statistical Information on Saratov Province Based on Figures from the All-Russian Rural and Urban Census of 1917]. Saratov: Tip. no. 7 soveta nar. khoz., 1919.

Saratovskoe gubernskoe zemstvo. *Materialy k voprosu o nuzhdakh sel'sko-khoziaistvennoi promyshlennosti v Saratovskoi Gubernii* [Materials on the Question of the Needs of Agricultural Industry in Saratov Province]. Saratov: Zemskaia tipografiia, 1903.

Saratovskoe gubernskoe zemstvo. *Sbornik statisticheskikh svedenii po Saratovskoi Gubernii* [Collection of Statistical Information on Saratov Province]. Vols. 3, 6, and 11. Saratov: Zemskaia tipografiia, 1884, 1887, and 1891.

Saratovskoe gubernskoe zemstvo. *Sbornik svedenii po Saratovskoi Gubernii za 1899* [Collection of Information on Saratov Province for 1899]. Vol. 2. Saratov: Zemskaia tipografiia, 1901.

Saratovskoe gubernskoe zemstvo. *Sbornik svedenii po Saratovskoi Gubernii za 1902 god* [Collection of Information on Saratov

Province for 1902]. Saratov: Zemskaia tipografiia, 1904.

Sazonov, G. P. *Obzor deiatel'nosti zemstv po narodnomu prodovol'stviiu (1865–1892 gg.)* [Survey of the Activities of the Zemstvos in Provisioning the Population]. Vol. 2. St. Petersburg: Tip. min. vnut. del, 1893.

Schiller, F. P. *Literatura po istorii nemetskikh kolonii v SSSR za vremia 1764–1926 gg.* [Literature on the History of the German Colonies in the USSR for the Period 1764–1926]. Pokrovsk: Nemgosizdat, 1927.

Schleuning, Johannes. *Aus tiefster Not: Schicksale der deutschen Kolonisten in Russland.* Berlin: Fleming und C. T. Wiskott, 1922.

Schmidt, D. *Studien über die Geschichte der Wolgadeutschen.* Pokrovsk: Zentral-Volker-Verlag der Union der Soz. Rate-Rep., 1930.

Schnurr, Joseph. *Die Kirchen und das religiöse Leben der Russlanddeutschen.* Stuttgart: Landsmannschaft der Deutschen aus Russland, 1972.

Schock, Adolph. *In Quest of Free Land.* San Jose: San Jose State College, 1964.

Semenov-Tian-Shanskii, Petr P. (ed.). *Rossiia: Polnoe geograficheskoe opisanie nashego otechestva* [Russia: A Complete Geographical Description of Our Fatherland]. Vol. 6. St. Petersburg: Izd. A. F. Devriena, 1901.

Semenov-Tian-Shanskii, Veniamin Petrovich (ed.). *Povolzh'e priroda, byt, khoziaistvo po Volge, Oke, Kame, Viatke i Beloi* [The Volga Valley: Nature, Life, and Economy along the Volga, Oka, Kama, Viatka, and Belaia]. Leningrad: Tip. transpechati NKPS, 1925.

Serebriakov, F. S. *Nemetskaia kommuna na Volge* [German Commune on the Volga]. Moscow: Tip. M. S. N. Kh., 1922.

Sergeev, Ivan Ivanovich. *Mirnoe zavoevanie Rossii Nemtsami (doklad, prochitannyi v chrezvychainom obshchem sobranii gg. chlenov "Obshchestva 1914 goda" 13 marta 1915 goda)* [The Germans' Peaceful Conquest of Russia (Report Read to the Special General Meeting of the Members of the "Society of 1914")]. Petrograd: Tipo-litografiia N. I. Evstifeev, 1915.

Shalamov, Varlam. *Graphite.* Translated by John Glad. New York: W. W. Norton, 1981.

Shanin, Teodor. *The Awkward Class.* Oxford: Clarendon Press, 1972.

Shelukhin, Sergei. *Nemetskaia kolonizatsiia na iuge Rossii* [German Colonization in the South of Russia]. Odessa: Tip. aktsionernago iuzhno-russkago o-va pechatnago dela, 1915.

Shelukhin, Sergei. *Zakon 14-go iiunia 1910 g. i poseliane-sobstvenniki (kolonisty)* [The Law of June 14, 1910, and the Settler-Proprietors (Colonists)]. Odessa: Tip. Fesenko, 1913.

Shevchenko, M. A. *Nizhnee Povolzh'e* [The Lower Volga Valley]. Moscow and Leningrad: Gosizdat, 1929.

Shtrandt, L. *Kak vedut svoe khoziaistvo nemtsy Povolzh'ia* [How the Volga Germans Operate Their Farms]. Moscow: Gosizdat, 1926.

Sidorov, A. L. (ed.). *Pervaia mirovaia voina* [The First World War]. Moscow: "Nauka," 1968.

Simbirskii, N. *Svoboda na zemle (Druz'ia i vragi russkago zemledel'tsa).* [Freedom on the Land (Friends and Enemies of Russian Farmers)]. St. Petersburg: Tip. "Ulei," 1912.

318

Sinel, Allen. *The Classroom and the Chancellery: State Educational Reform in Russia under Count Dmitry Tolstoi.* Cambridge, Mass.: Harvard University Press, 1973.

Sinner, Peter. *Nemtsy Nizhnego Povolzh'ia* [Germans of the Lower Volga]. Saratov: n. pub., 1925.

Slobodchikov, D. (ed.). *Podvornoe i khutorskoe khoziaistvo v Samarskoi Gubernii* [Household and Separated Homestead Farming in Samara Province]. Vol. 1. Samara: Tip. gub. zemstva, 1909.

Smith, R. E. F. *Peasant Farming in Muscovy.* Cambridge: Cambridge University Press, 1977.

Solov'eva, A. M. *Zheleznodorozhnyi transport Rossii vo vtoroi polovine XIX v.* [Russian Railroad Transport in the Second Half of the 19th Century]. Moscow: "Nauka," 1975.

Speranskii, N. (ed.). *1905 god v Samarskom Krae* [1905 in the Samara Region]. Samara: Izd. samarskogo gubkoma, 1925.

Sputnik po gorodu Saratovu [Guide to the City of Saratov]. Saratov: Tip. P. S. Feokritov, 1898.

Starr, S. Frederick. *Decentralization and Self-Government in Russia, 1830–1870.* Princeton: Princeton University Press, 1972.

Statisticheskii komitet Oblastnago Voiska Donskogo. *Sbornik Oblastnago Voiska Donskogo* [Collection of the Don Forces Oblast]. Vol. 1. Novocherkassk: Obl. voiska donskogo tipografiia, 1901.

Statisticheskii komitet Oblastnogo Voiska Donskogo. *Spisok naselennykh mest Oblasti Voiska Donskogo po pervoi vseobshchei perepisi naseleniia Rossiiskoi Imperii, 1897 goda* [List of Populated Places in the Don Forces Oblast Based on the First General Census of the Population of the Russian Empire]. 2 vols. Novocherkassk: Obl. voiska donskogo tipografiia, 1905.

Statisticheskoe otdelenie pri samarskoi gubernskoi zemskoi uprave. *Sel'sko-khoziaistvennyi obzor Samarskoi Gubernii za 1898–99 god* [Agricultural Survey of Samara Province for 1898–99]. Vol. 2. Samara: Zemskaia tipografiia, 1900.

Statisticheskoe upravlenie A.S.S.R.N.P. *Sbornik statisticheskikh svedenii po Avtonomnoi Sotsialisticheskoi Sovetskoi Respublike Nemtsev Povolzh'ia, 1916–24 gg.* [Collection of Statistical Information on the Autonomous Socialist Soviet Republic of Volga Germans, 1916–24]. Pokrovsk: n. pub., 1924.

Steinberg, Stephen. *The Ethnic Myth.* New York: Atheneum, 1981.

Stepanov, P. N. *Saratovskaia sarpinka* [Saratov Sarpinka]. Marxstadt: Izd. SGSR-KPO, 1920.

Stone, Norman. *The Eastern Front, 1914–17.* New York: Scribner, 1975.

Stumpp, Karl. *Das Schrifttum über das Deutschtum in Russland.* Tübingen: Selbstverlag, 1970.

Stumpp, Karl. *The German-Russians: Two Centuries of Pioneering.* Translated by Joseph Height. New York: Atlantic-Forum Edition, 1971.

Sumner, B. H. *A Short History of Russia.* 2d ed. revised. New York: Harcourt, Brace, and World, 1949.

Svod statisticheskikh dannykh o deistvuiushchikh mel'nitsakh v evropeiskoi Rossii [Collection of Statistical Information about Mills Operating in European Russia]. St. Petersburg: A. Rabinovich, 1895.

Taylor, Philip. *The Distant Magnet: European Emigration to the U.S.A.* London: Eyre and Spottiswoode, 1971.

Tekstil'noe delo v Rossii [The Textile Business in Russia]. Odessa: Tip. "Poriadok," 1910–11.

Teziakov, N. I. *Otkhozhie promysly i rynki naima sel'sko-khoziaistvennykh rabochikh v Saratovskoi Gubernii* [Seasonal Jobs and Markets for Hiring Agricultural Workers in Saratov Province]. Voronezh: n. pub., 1903.

Thaden, Edward. *Russia's Western Borderlands, 1710–1870.* Princeton: Princeton University Press, 1984.

Thaden, Edward (ed.). *Russification in the Baltic Provinces and Finland, 1855–1914.* Princeton: Princeton University Press, 1981.

Tikhmenev, A. G. (ed.). *Sochineniia E. I. Gubera* [Collected Works of E. I. Huber]. 3 vols. St. Petersburg: Izd. A. Smirdina, 1859–60.

Tikhomirov, D. I. *Obshchiia svedeniia o zemskikh shkolakh Saratovskoi Gubernii* [Aggregate Information about the Zemstvo Schools in Saratov Province]. Saratov: Zemskaia tipografiia, 1899.

Timiriazev, D. A., and N. V. Ponomarev (eds.). *Obzor kustarnykh promyslov Rossii* [Survey of Russia's Cottage Industries]. St. Petersburg: Tip. min. zem. i gos. imushch., 1902.

Timoshenko, Vladimir P. *Agricultural Russia and the Wheat Problem.* Stanford: Food Research Institute and the Committee on Russian Research of the Hoover War Library, 1932.

Tsentral'noe statisticheskoe upravlenie, Otdel voennoi statistiki. *Rossiia v mirovoi voine 1914–18 goda* [Russia in the First World War, 1914–18]. Moscow: Tip. tsen. stat. uprav., 1925.

Tsentral'nyi statisticheskii komitet [MVD]. *Pervaia vseobshchaia perepis' naseleniia Rossiiskoi Imperii, 1897 g.* [The First General Census of the Population of the Russian Empire, 1897]. Edited by N. A. Troinitskii. Vols. 36 (Samara Province) and 38 (Saratov Province). St. Petersburg: Izd. tsen. stat. kom. min. vnut. del, 1899 and 1900.

Tsentral'nyi statisticheskii komitet [MVD]. *Spiski naselennykh mest Rossiiskoi Imperii, sostavlennye i izdavaemye tsentral'nym statisticheskim komitetom ministerstva vnutrennikh del (Po svedeniiam 1859).* [Lists of Populated Places of The Russian Empire, Compiled and Published by the Central Statistical Committee of the Ministry of the Interior (Based on 1859 Information]. Vol. 36 (Samara Province) and Vol. 38 (Saratov Province). St. Petersburg: Tip. Karl Vul'f, 1864 and 1862.

Tsentral'nyi statisticheskii komitet [MVD]. *Statistika pozemel'noi sobstvennosti i naselennykh mest evropeiskoi Rossii* [Statistics of Land Ownership and Populated Places in European Russia]. Vol. 4. St. Petersburg: Tip. min. vnut. del, 1884.

Tsentral'nyi statisticheskii komitet [MVD]. *Statistika zemlevladeniia 1905 g.* [1905 Landholding Statistics]. Vols. 2 and 28. St. Petersburg: T-vo N. Ia. Stoikov, 1906.

Tugan-Baranovsky, Mikhail I. *The Russian Factory in the 19th Century.* Translated by Arthur and Claora Levin. Homewood, Ill.: Dorsey Press, 1970.

Val'denberg, D. V. (ed.). *Spravochnaia kniga o pechati vsei Rossii* [Reference Book about the Russian Press]. St. Petersburg: T-vo khudozhestvennoi pechati, 1911.

Vdovin, V. *Krest'ianskii pozemel'nyi bank, 1883–95 gg.* [The Peasant Land Bank, 1883–95]. Moscow: Gosfinizdat, 1959.

Velitsyn, A. A., pseud. [A. A. Paltov]. *Nemetskoe zavoevanie na iuge Rossii* [The German Conquest in Southern Russia]. St. Petersburg: Tip. "Ob. Pol'za," 1890.

Velitsyn, A. A., pseud. [A. A. Paltov]. *Nemtsy v Rossii* [Germans in Russia]. St. Petersburg: Izd. russkago vestnika, 1893.

Verhandlung der Versammlung der Kreisbevollmächtigen der Wolgakolonien in Saratow am 25 bis 27 April 1917. Saratov: Zentralkomitee der deutschen Wolgakolonisten in Saratow, 1917.

Veselovskii, B. B., et al. *Agrarnoe dvizhenie v Rossii 1905–06 gg.* 2 vols. St. Petersburg: Tip. "Ob. Pol'za," 1908.

Veselovskii, Boris. *Istoriia zemstva za sorok let* [History of the Zemstvos during the Last Forty Years]. 4 vols. St. Petersburg: Izd. O. N. Popovoi, 1909–11.

Veselovskii, Boris. *K voprosu o klassovykh interesakh v zemstve* [Concerning the Question of Class Interests in the Zemstvo]. St. Petersburg: Izd. O. N. Popovoi, 1905.

Vigel', Filip Filipovich. *Vospominaniia F. F. Vigelia* [Memoirs of F. F. Vigel]. Vol. 1. Moscow: Universitetskaia tipografiia, 1864.

Vishnevskii, A. G. (ed.). *Brachnost', rozhdaemost', smertnost' v Rossii i v SSSR: Sbornik statei* [Marriage, Birth, and Death Rates in Russia and the USSR: A Collection of Articles]. Moscow: Izd. "Statistika," 1977.

[Departament general'nago shtaba.] *Voenno-statisticheskoe obozrenie Rossiiskoi Imperii* [Military Statistical Survey of the Russian Empire]. Vol. 5: pt. 3 (Samara Province); pt. 4 (Saratov Province). St. Petersburg: Tip. dept. general'nago shtaba, 1852 and 1853.

Vserossiiskii soiuz gorodov. Obzor sostianiia khlebnago rynka za avgust–sentiabr 1916 g. [Survey of the Condition of the Grain Market in August–September 1916]. Petrograd: Amerikanskaia skoropechatnia, 1917.

Warren, Richard. *Education in Rebhausen A German Village*. New York: Holt, Rinehart and Winston, 1967.

Webb, Walter Prescott. *The Great Plains*. Boston: Ginn and Company, 1931.

Wildman, Allan. *The End of the Russian Imperial Army*. Princeton: Princeton University Press, 1980.

Williams, Hattie Plum. *The Czar's Germans: With Particular Reference to the Volga Germans*. Edited by Emma S. Haynes, Phillip B. Legler, and Gerda S. Walker. Denver: American Historical Society of Germans from Russia, 1975.

Wolf, Eric, *Peasants*. Englewood Cliffs, N. J.: Prentice-Hall, 1966.

Yaney, George L. *The Systematization of Russian Government*. Urbana, Ill.: University of Illinois Press, 1973.

Yaney, George L. *The Urge to Mobilize*. Urbana, Ill.: University of Illinois Press, 1982.

Yevreinov, Grigorii A. *Rossiiskie Nemtsy* [Russian Germans]. Petrograd: Tip. glavnago upravleniia udelov, 1915.

Zaionchkovskii, P. A. *Rossiiskoe samoderzhavie v kontse XIX stoletiia* [Russian Autocracy at the End of the Nineteenth Century]. Moscow: "Mysl'," 1970.

Zaionchkovskii, P. A. *Spravochniki po istorii dorevoliutsionnoi Rossii* [Reference Books on the History of Pre-Reform Russia]. Moscow: Kniga, 1971.

Zaionchkovskii, P. A. (ed.). *Istoriia dorevoliutsionnoi Rossii v dnevnikakh i vospominaniiakh* [History of Pre-Reform Russia in Diaries and Memoirs]. 3 vols. Moscow: Kniga, 1976–81.

Zalezskii, K. V. *Sel'sko-khoziaistvennaia statistika Saratovskoi Gubernii* [Agricultural Statistics for Saratov Province]. St. Petersburg: Tip. Leonida Demisa, 1859.

Zhdanov, M. *Putevyia zapiski* [Travel Notes]. St. Petersburg: n. pub., 1843.

Zherebtsov, V. O. *Vospominaniia o saratovskoi pervoi muzhskoi gimnazii* [Reminiscences about Saratov's First Male Gymnasium]. Saratov: Energiia, 1912.

$\mathcal{I}$ndex

238, 242, 243, 244, 250, 251; compared with Russian peasants, 17, 18,
25, 62–64, 75–76, 126, 128–31,
156–57, 249, 264; criticized by Russian press, 57–60, 61, 111, 228–29;
defended by Kerensky, 230; deportation, 252–53; economic levels,
65–70; extended family, 114; family
size, 68, 130, 136, 139; government
policies toward, xiii, 7–8, 10, 16–40,
55–56, 60, 69, 111, 126, 213, 222,
226, 230, 247; history of, 8–15; leadership and administration, 21; misinformation about, xiii-xiv, 56, 128,
146; nationalism, 55–56, 61, 227,
250; oral tradition, 51, 64; patterns of
settlement, 7–15; political activities,
192–95, 199, 203–14, 217–18,
236–45; relations with Russians,
61–65, 69, 146, 161–62, 206; resettlement, 8–11, 111, 116, 253; right to
emigrate, 25; social levels, 65; Soviet
period, 150–53; tax exemptions, 29;
wealth, 68–69; Workers' Commune,
251; World War I, 223–27. *See also
names of individual colonies and
provinces*; Agriculture; Cottage
industries; Education; Emigration;
Government, local; Government,
tsarist; Kontora; Landholding;
Military service; Population trends;
Religion; Russification; Villages
Germany: anti-German feelings in
Russia, 58–59, 222, 227–30; attitude
toward colonists, 60; colonists'
attitude toward, 55; dyes from, 145;
emigration to, 55, 253; Germanization of Poles, 56; nationalism, xiii,
55, 56; pan-Germanism, 206, 213,
236, 243, 250; Soviet efforts to
influence, 251; World War I, 222–23,
226, 227–28
Goebel. *See* Ust' Griaznukha
Gololobovka (Donnhof), 6, 118, 143;
kustar manufacture, 151; medical
services, 179, 180

Golyi Karamysh (Balzer), 6, 13, 20, 181,
234; landholdings, 118; land
redivision, 73; mills, 104, 106; plow
factories, 150; population, 157;
sarpinka industry, 142, 143; school,
158; seasonal workers, 86; tanning
industry, 154; use of Russian
language, 51
Gotovitskii, Mikhail Khristoforovich, 27,
28
Government, local: bureaucracy, 29, 213;
disbandment of Kontora, 21; district
committee, 26; land captains, 26–29;
legislation of 1871, 24–25; mid-1917,
234; petitions for reform of, 194;
townships, 23, 194; village
government, 21. *See also* Assembly,
colony; Assembly, communal;
Assembly, township; Zemstvo
Government, tsarist: aid to famine-
stricken peasants, 65; attack on
teachers, 220; change in attitude to
colonists, 17, 55–56, 60; during
Word War I, 227–28; education
policies, 172–73, 195–96, 222;
electoral tampering, 218–19; grain
reserves, 189; integrationist policies,
69; Kontora, 17–21; land expropriation, 231–32; mail service, 69;
mobilization policies, 224; October
Manifesto, 199, 200; policies toward
colonists, xiii, 7–8, 10, 16–40, 55–56,
60, 69, 111, 126, 213, 222, 226, 230,
247; replacement of Kontora, 21, 26;
suppression of disturbances in
Kamyshin, 216–17. *See also* Kontora;
Landholding; Ministry of State
Domains; Minorities
Grain trade: development of, 94–102;
grain elevators, 104; grain merchants,
78, 94, 98–99, 100; granaries, 20, 78,
100–101; overland transport, 100,
101–2, 107; ports, 97–102; quality of
grain, 97, 98; Samara Province
specialization, 89, 108; Saratov
Province production, 83–84; statistics,